FIAT
124 COUPE/SPIDER &
2000 SPIDER INCLUDES TURBO SPIDER
1971-1984
SHOP MANUAL

ALAN AHLSTRAND
Editor

BROOKLANDS BOOKS LTD.
P.O. BOX 146, COBHAM,
SURREY, KT11 1LG. UK
sales@brooklands-books.com

B-FI71WH   Printed in China   ISBN 1855200791

FIRST EDITION
Published March, 1973

SECOND EDITION
Revised to include 1974-1975 models
Published May, 1976

THIRD EDITION
Revised by Jim Combs to cover 1976-1977 models
Published May, 1977

FOURTH EDITION
Revised by Jim Combs to cover 1978-1979 models
First Printing April, 1979

FIFTH EDITION
Revised by Jim Combs to cover 1980 models
First Printing September, 1980

SIXTH EDITION
Revised by Jim Combs to cover 1981 models
First Printing September, 1981

SEVENTH EDITION
Revised by Alfred Pegal to cover 1982 models
First Printing April, 1983
Second Printing January, 1984
Third Printing November, 1984

EIGHTH EDITION
Updated by Alan Ahlstrand to include all models
First Printing October, 1986
Second Printing December, 1987

NINTH EDITION
Updated by Brooklands Books
First Printing January 1991

COVER: Photographed by Michael Brown Photographic Productions, Los Angeles, California. Automobile courtesy of Donald Young.

Chapter One
General Information   1

Chapter Two
Troubleshooting   2

Chapter Three
Lubrication, Maintenance and Tune-up   3

Chapter Four
Engine   4

Chapter Five
Fuel Exhaust and Emission Control System   5

Chapter Six
Cooling, Heating and Air Conditioning   6

Chapter Seven
Electrical System   7

Chapter Eight
Clutch and Transaxle   8

Chapter Nine
Front Suspension, Wheel Bearings and Steering   9

Chapter Ten
Rear Suspension, Differential and Drive Shaft   10

Chapter Eleven
Brakes   11

Skill Level and Time Estimating Guide   12

Index   13

BROOKLANDS ROAD TEST BOOKS

Brooklands Books

MOTORING

B.B. ROAD TEST SERIES

Abarth Gold Portfolio 1950-1971
AC Ace & Aceca 1953-1983
Alfa Romeo Giulietta Gold Portfolio 1954-1965
Alfa Romeo Giulia Coupés 1963-1976
Alfa Romeo Giulia Coupés Gold Port. 1963-1976
Alfa Romeo Spider 1966-1990
Alfa Romeo Spider Gold Portfolio 1966-1991
Alfa Romeo Alfasud 1972-1984
Alfa Romeo Alfetta Gold Portfolio 1972-1987
Alfa Romeo Alfetta GTV6 1980-1986
Alvis Gold Portfolio 1919-1967
AMX & Javelin Muscle Portfolio 1968-1974
Armstrong Siddeley Gold Portfolio 1945-1960
Aston Martin Gold Portfolio 1948-1971
Aston Martin Gold Portfolio 1972-1985
Aston Martin Gold Portfolio 1985-1995
Audi Quattro Gold Portfolio 1980-1991
Audi Quattro Takes On The Competition
Austin A30 & A35 1951-1962
Austin-Healey 100 & 100/6 Gold Port. 1952-1959
Austin-Healey 3000 Ultimate Portfolio 1959-1967
Austin-Healey Sprite Gold Portfolio 1958-1971
Berkeley Sportscars Limited Edition
BMW 6 & 8 Cyl. Cars Limited Edition 1935-1960
BMW 1600 Collection No. 1 1966-1981
BMW 2002 Gold Portfolio 1968-1976
BMW 6 Cylinder Coupés & Saloons Gold P. 1969-1976
BMW 316, 318, 320 (4 cyl.) Gold Port. 1975-1990
BMW 320, 323, 325 (6 cyl.) Gold Port. 1977-1990
BMW 3 Series Gold Portfolio 1991-1997
BMW 5 Series Gold Portfolio 1981-1987
BMW 5 Series Gold Portfolio 1988-1995
BMW 6 Series Gold Portfolio 1976-1989
BMW 7 Series Performance Portfolio 1977-1986
BMW 8 Series Limited Edition
BMW Alpina Performance Portfolio 1967-1987
BMW Alpina Performance Portfolio 1988-1998
BMW M Series Gold Portfolio 1976-1997
BMW Z3 & Z3M Limited Edition
Borgward Isabella Limited Edition
Bricklin Gold Portfolio 1974-1975
Bristol Cars Portfolio
Buick Performance Portfolio 1947-1962
Buick Muscle Portfolio 1963-1973
Buick Riviera Performance Portfolio 1963-1978
Cadillac Allanté 1986-1993
Cadillac Automobiles 1949-1959
Cadillac Automobiles 1960-1969
Cadillac Eldorado Performance Portfolio 1967-1978
Checker Limited Edition
Chevrolet 1955-1957
Impala & SS Muscle Portfolio 1958-1972
Corvair Performance Portfolio 1959-1969
El Camino & SS Muscle Portfolio 1959-1987
Chevy II & Nova SS Muscle Portfolio 1962-1974
Chevelle & SS Muscle Portfolio 1964-1972
Caprice Limited Edition 1965-1976
Chevrolet Muscle Cars 1966-1971
Chevy Blazer 1969-1981
Camaro Muscle Portfolio 1967-1973
High Performance Camaros 1982-1988
Camaro Performance Portfolio 1993-2000
Chevrolet Corvette Gold Portfolio 1953-1962
Chevrolet Corvette Sting Ray Gold Port. 1963-1967
Chevrolet Corvette Gold Portfolio 1968-1977
High Performance Corvettes 1983-1989
Chrysler 300 Gold Portfolio 1955-1970
Valiant 1960-1962
Citroen Traction Avant Gold Portfolio 1934-1957
Citroen 2CV Ultimate Portfolio 1948-1990
Citroen DS & ID 1955-1975
Citroen DS & ID Gold Portfolio 1955-1975
Shelby Cobra Gold Portfolio 1962-1969
Cobras & Cobra Replicas Gold Portfolio 1962-1989
Crosley & Crosley Specials Limited Edition
Cunningham Automobiles 1951-1955
Datsun Roadsters Performance Portfolio 1960-71
Datsun 240Z & 260Z Gold Portfolio 1970-1978
Datsun 280Z & ZX 1975-1983
DeLorean Gold Portfolio 1977-1995
De Soto Limited Edition 1952-1960
Charger Muscle Portfolio 1966-1974
Dodge Viper Performance Portfolio 1990-1998
ERA Gold Portfolio 1934-1994
Facel Vega 1954-1964
Ferrari Limited Edition 1947-1957
Ferrari Limited Edition 1958-1963
Ferrari Dino 308 & Mondial Gold Portfolio 1974-1985
Ferrari 328 348 Mondial Ultimate Portfolio 1986-94
Fiat 500 Gold Portfolio 1936-1972
Fiat 600 & 850 Gold Portfolio 1955-1972
Fiat Pininfarina 124 & 2000 Spider 1968-1985
Fiat X1/9 Gold Portfolio 1973-1989
Fiat Abarth Performance Portfolio 1972-1987
Ford Consul, Zephyr, Zodiac Mk. I & II 1950-1962
Ford Zephyr, Zodiac, Executive Mk. III & IV 1962-1971
Ford Cortina 1600E & GT 1967-1970
High Performance Capris Gold Portfolio 1969-1987
Capri Muscle Portfolio 1974-1987
High Performance Fiestas 1979-1991
Ford Escort RS & Mexico Limited Edition 1970-1979
High Performance Escorts Mk. I 1968-1974
High Performance Escorts Mk. II 1975-1980
High Performance Escorts 1980-1985
High Performance Escorts 1985-1990
High Perf. Sierras & Merkurs Gold Port. 1983-1990
Ford Thunderbird Performance Portfolio 1955-1957
Ford Thunderbird Performance Portfolio 1958-1963
Ford Thunderbird Performance Portfolio 1964-1976
Ford Automobiles 1949-1959
Ford Fairlane Performance Portfolio 1955-1970
Ford Ranchero Muscle Portfolio 1957-1979
Edsel Limited Edition 1957-1960
Falcon Performance Portfolio 1960-1970
Ford Galaxie & LTD Limited Edition 1960-1973
Ford GT40 Gold Portfolio 1964-1987
Ford Torino Limited Edition 1968-1974
Ford Bronco 4x4 Performance Portfolio 1966-1977
Ford Bronco 1978-1988
Goggomobil Limited Edition
Holden 1948-1962
Honda S500 • S600 • S800 Limited Edition 1962-1970
Honda CRX 1983-1987
International Scout Gold Portfolio 1961-1980
Isetta Gold Portfolio 1953-1964
ISO & Bizzarrini Gold Portfolio 1962-1974
Jaguar and SS Gold Portfolio 1931-1951
Jaguar C-Type & D-Type Gold Portfolio 1951-1960
Jaguar XK120, 140, 150 Gold Portfolio 1948-1960
Jaguar Mk. VII, VIII, IX, X, 420 Gold Port. 1950-1970
Jaguar Mk. 1 & Mk. 2 Gold Portfolio 1959-1969
Jaguar E-Type Gold Portfolio 1961-1971
Jaguar E-Type V-12 1971-1975
Jaguar S-Type & 420 Limited Edition 1963-1968
Jaguar XJ12, XJ5.3, V12 Gold Portfolio 1972-1990
Jaguar XJ6 Series I & II Gold Portfolio 1968-1979
Jaguar XJ6 Series III Perf. Portfolio 1979-1986
Jaguar XJ6 Gold Portfolio 1986-1994
Jaguar XJS Gold Portfolio 1975-1988
Jaguar XJ-S V12 Ultimate Portfolio 1988-1996
Jaguar XK8 Limited Edition
Jeep CJ-5 & CJ-6 1960-1976
Jeep CJ-5 & CJ-7 4x4 Perf. Portfolio 1976-1986
Jeep Wagoneer Performance Portfolio 1963-1991
Jeep J-Series Pickups 1970-1982
Jeepster & Commando Limited Edition 1967-1973
Jeep Cherokee & Comanche Pickups P. P. 1984-91
Jeep Wrangler 4x4 Performance Portfolio 1987-99
Jeep Cherokee & Grand Cherokee 4x4 P. P. 1992-98
Jensen Interceptor Gold Portfolio 1966-1986
Jensen - Healey Limited Edition 1972-1976
Kaiser - Frazer Limited Edition 1946-1955
Lagonda Gold Portfolio 1919-1964
Lancia Aurelia & Flaminia Gold Portfolio 1950-1970
Lancia Fulvia Gold Portfolio 1963-1976
Lancia Beta Gold Portfolio 1972-1984
Lancia Stratos 1972-1985
Lancia Delta & integrale Ultimate Portfolio
Land Rover Series I 1948-1958
Land Rover Series II & IIa 1958-1971
Land Rover Series III 4x4 Perf. Portfolio 1971-1985
Land Rover 90 110 Defender Gold Portfolio 1983-1994
Land Rover Discovery Perf. Port. 1989-2000
Land Rover Story Part One 1948-1971
Fifty Years of Selling Land Rover
Lincoln Gold Portfolio 1949-1960
Lincoln Continental Performance Portfolio 1961-1969
Lincoln Continental 1969-1976
Lotus Sports Racers Portfolio - covering 1951-1965
Lotus Seven Gold Portfolio 1957-1973
Lotus Elite Limited Edition 1957-1964
Lotus Elan Ultimate Portfolio 1962-1974
Lotus Elan & SE 1989-1992
Lotus Europa Gold Portfolio 1966-1975
Lotus Elite & Eclat 1974-1982
Lotus Elise Limited Edition
Marcos Coupés & Spyders Gold Portfolio 1960-1997
Matra Limited Edition 1965-1983
Mazda Miata MX-5 Performance Portfolio 1989-1997
Mazda Miata MX-5 Takes On The Competition
Mazda RX-7 Gold Portfolio 1978-1991
McLaren F1 Sportscar Limited Edition
Mercedes 190 & 300 SL 1954-1963
Mercedes G-Wagen 1981-1994
Mercedes S & 600 1965-1972
Mercedes S Class 1972-1979
Mercedes 230 • 250 • 280SL Gold Portfolio 1963-1971
Mercedes SLs & SLCs Gold Portfolio 1971-1989
Mercedes SLs Performance Portfolio 1989-1994
Mercedes 190 Limited Edition Extra 1983-1993
Mercedes CLK & SLK Limited Edition
Mercury Limited Edition 1947-1959
Mercury Comet & Cyclone Limited Edition 1960-1970
Cougar Limited Edition 1967-1973
Messerschmitt Gold Portfolio 1954-1964
MG Gold Portfolio 1929-1939
MG TA & TC Gold Portfolio 1936-1949
MG TD & TF Gold Portfolio 1949-1955
MGA & Twin Cam Gold Portfolio 1955-1962
MG Midget Gold Portfolio 1961-1979
MGB Roadsters 1962-1980
MGB MGC & V8 Gold Portfolio 1962-1980
MGB GT 1965-1980
MGC & MGB GT V8 Limited Edition
MG Y-Type & Magnette ZA/ZB Limited Edition
MGF Limited Edition
Mini Gold Portfolio 1959-1969
Mini Gold Portfolio 1969-1980
Mini Gold Portfolio 1981-1997
High Performance Minis Gold Portfolio 1960-1973
Mini Cooper Gold Portfolio 1961-1971
Mini Moke Gold Portfolio 1964-1994
Morgan Three-Wheeler Gold Portfolio 1910-1952
Morgan Plus 4 & Four 4 Gold Portfolio 1936-1967
Morris Minor Collection No. 1 1948-1980
Shelby Mustang Muscle Portfolio 1965-1970
Mustang Muscle Portfolio 1967-1973
High Performance Mustang IIs 1974-1978
Mustang 5.0L Muscle Portfolio 1982-1993
Mustang 5.0L Takes On The Competition
Nash & Nash-Healey Limited Edition 1949-1957
Nash-Austin Metropolitan Gold Portfolio 1954-1962
NSU Ro80 Limited Edition
NSX Performance Portfolio 1989-1999
Oldsmobile Automobiles 1955-1963
Oldsmobile Muscle Portfolio 1964-1971
Cutlass & 4-4-2 Muscle Portfolio 1964-1974
Oldsmobile Toronado 1966-1978
Opel GT Gold Portfolio 1968-1973
Opel Manta Limited Edition 1970-1975
Packard Gold Portfolio 1946-1958
Pantera Gold Portfolio 1970-1989
Panther Gold Portfolio 1972-1990
Barracuda Muscle Portfolio 1964-1974
Pontiac Limited Edition 1949-1960
Pontiac Tempest & GTO 1961-1965
GTO Muscle Portfolio 1964-1974
Firebird & Trans-Am Muscle Portfolio 1967-1972
Firebird & Trans-Am Muscle Portfolio 1973-1981
High Performance Firebirds 1982-1988
Firebird & Trans Am Performance Portfolio 1993-2000
Pontiac Fiero Performance Portfolio 1984-1988
Porsche 356 Gold Portfolio 1953-1965
Porsche 912 Limited Edition
Porsche 911 1965-1969
Porsche 911 1970-1972
Porsche 911 1973-1977
Porsche 911 SC & Turbo Gold Portfolio 1978-1983
Porsche 911 Carrera & Turbo Gold Port. 1984-1989
Porsche 911 Gold Portfolio 1990-1997
Porsche 911 Takes On The Competition 1990-1997
Porsche 914 Ultimate Portfolio
Porsche 924 Gold Portfolio 1975-1988
Porsche 928 Performance Portfolio 1977-1994
Porsche 928 Takes On The Competition
Porsche 944 Ultimate Portfolio
Porsche 968 Limited Edition
Porsche Boxster Limited Edition
Railton & Brough Superior Gold Portfolio 1933-1950
Range Rover Gold Portfolio 1970-1985
Range Rover Gold Portfolio 1985-1995
Range Rover Takes on the Competition
Reliant Scimitar 1964-1986
Renault Alpine Gold Portfolio 1958-1994
Riley Gold Portfolio 1924-1939
R. R. Silver Cloud & Bentley 'S' Series Gold P. 1955-65
Rolls Royce Silver Shadow Ultimate Portfolio 1965-80
Rolls Royce & Bentley Gold Portfolio 1980-1989
Rolls Royce & Bentley Limited Edition 1990-1997
Rover P4 1949-1959
Rover 3 & 3.5 Litre Gold Portfolio 1958-1973
Rover 2000 & 2200 1963-1977
Rover 3500 & Vitesse 1976-1986
Saab Sonett Collection No.1 1966-1974
Saab Turbo 1976-1983
Studebaker Gold Portfolio 1947-1966
Studebaker Hawks & Larks 1956-1963
Avanti 1962-1990
Starion & Conquest Performance Portfolio 1982-90
Suzuki SJ Gold Portfolio 1971-1997
Vitara, Sidekick & Geo Tracker Perf. Port. 1988-1997
Sunbeam Tiger & Alpine Gold Portfolio 1959-1967
Toyota Land Cruiser Gold Portfolio 1956-1987
Toyota Land Cruiser 1988-1997
Toyota MR2 Gold Portfolio 1984-1997
Toyota MR2 Takes On The Competition
Triumph TR2 & TR3 Gold Portfolio 1952-1961
Triumph TR4, TR5, TR250 1961-1968
Triumph TR6 Gold Portfolio 1969-1976
Triumph Herald 1959-1971
Triumph Vitesse 1962-1971
Triumph Spitfire Gold Portfolio 1962-1980
Triumph 2000, 2.5, 2500 1963-1977
Triumph GT6 Gold Portfolio 1966-1974
Triumph Stag Gold Portfolio 1970-1977
Triumph Dolomite Sprint Limited Edition
TVR Gold Portfolio 1959-1986
TVR Performance Portfolio 1986-1994
TVR Performance Portfolio 1995- 2000
VW Beetle Gold Portfolio 1935-1967
VW Beetle Gold Portfolio 1968-1991
VW Beetle Collection No.1 1970-1982
VW Karmann Ghia 1955-1982
VW Bus, Camper, Van 1954-1967
VW Bus, Camper, Van Perf. Portfolio 1968-1979
VW Bus, Camper, Van 1979-1989
VW Scirocco 1974-1981
Volvo PV444 & PV544 1945-1965
Volvo 120 Amazon Ultimate Portfolio
Volvo 1800 Gold Portfolio 1960-1973
Volvo 140 & 160 Series Gold Portfolio 1966-1975
Forty Years of Selling Volvo
Westfield Limited Edition

B.B. ROAD & TRACK SERIES

Road & Track on Alfa Romeo 1964-1970
Road & Track on Alfa Romeo 1971-1976
Road & Track on Aston Martin 1962-1990
Road & Track on Audi & Auto Union 1952-1980
Road & Track on Audi & Auto Union 1980-1986
Road & Track on Austin Healey 1953-1970
Road & Track on BMW Cars 1966-1974
Road & Track on BMW Cars 1975-1978
Road & Track on BMW Cars 1979-1983
R & T on Cobra, Shelby & Ford GT40 1962-1992
Road & Track on Corvette 1953-1967
Road & Track on Corvette 1968-1982
Road & Track on Corvette 1982-1986
Road & Track on Corvette 1986-1990
Road & Track on Ferrari 1975-1981
Road & Track on Ferrari 1981-1984
Road & Track on Ferrari 1984-1988
Road & Track on Fiat Sports Cars 1968-1987
Road & Track on Jaguar 1950-1960
Road & Track on Jaguar 1961-1968
Road & Track on Jaguar 1968-1974
Road & Track on Jaguar 1974-1982
Road & Track on Jaguar 1983-1989
Road & Track on Lamborghini 1964-1985
Road & Track on Lotus 1972-1983
R & T on Mazda RX-7 & MX-5 Miata 1986-1991
Road & Track on Mercedes 1952-1962
Road & Track on Mercedes 1963-1970
Road & Track on Mercedes 1971-1979
Road & Track on Mercedes 1980-1987
Road & Track on MG Sports Cars 1949-1961
Road & Track on MG Sports Cars 1962-1980
R & T on Nissan 300-ZX & Turbo 1984-1989
Road & Track on Pontiac 1960-1983
Road & Track on Porsche 1951-1967
Road & Track on Porsche 1968-1971
Road & Track on Porsche 1972-1975
Road & Track on Porsche 1975-1978
Road & Track on Porsche 1979-1982
Road & Track on Porsche 1985-1988
R & T on Rolls Royce & Bentley 1950-1965
R & T on Rolls Royce & Bentley 1966-1984
Road & Track on Saab 1972-1992
R & T on Toyota Sports & GT Cars 1966-1984
R & T on Triumph Sports Cars 1953-1967
R & T on Triumph Sports Cars 1967-1974
R & T on Triumph Sports Cars 1974-1982
Road & Track on Volkswagen 1951-1968
Road & Track on Volkswagen 1968-1978
Road & Track on Volkswagen 1978-1985
Road & Track on Volvo 1957-1974
Road & Track on Volvo 1977-1994
Road & Track - Henry Manney at Large & Abroad
Road & Track - Best of PS
Road & Track - Peter Egan "At Large"
Road & Track - Peter Egan Side Glances 1983-92
Road & Track - Peter Egan Side Glances 1992-97

B.B. CAR AND DRIVER SERIES

Car and Driver on BMW 1955-1977
Car and Driver on Corvette 1978-1982
Car and Driver on Corvette 1983-1988
C and D on Datsun Z 1600 & 2000 1966-1984
Car and Driver on Ferrari 1955-1962
Car and Driver on Ferrari 1963-1975
Car and Driver on Ferrari 1976-1983
Car and Driver on Mopar 1956-1967
Car and Driver on Mustang 1964-1972
Car and Driver on Pontiac 1961-1975
Car and Driver on Porsche 1955-1962
Car and Driver on Porsche 1963-1970
Car and Driver on Porsche 1970-1976
Car and Driver on Porsche 1977-1981
Car and Driver on Porsche 1982-1986
Car and Driver on Volvo 1955-1986

RACING & THE LAND SPEED RECORD

The Land Speed Record 1898-1919
The Land Speed Record 1920-1929
The Land Speed Record 1930-1939
The Land Speed Record 1940-1962
The Land Speed Record 1963-1999
The Land Speed Record 1898-1999 - Hard Bound
Can-Am Racing 1966-1969
Can-Am Racing 1970-1974
Can-Am Racing Cars 1966-1974
The Carrera Panamericana Mexico - 1950-1954
Le Mans - The Bentley & Alfa Years - 1923-1939
Le Mans - The Jaguar Years - 1949-1957
Le Mans - The Ferrari Years - 1958-1965
Le Mans - The Ford & Matra Years - 1966-1974
Le Mans - The Porsche Years - 1975-1982
Le Mans - The Porsche & Jaguar Years - 1983-91
Le Mans - The Porsche & Peugeot Years - 1992-99
Le Mans - 1923-1999 - Hard Bound
Mille Miglia - The Alfa & Ferrari Years - 1927-1951
Mille Miglia - The Ferrari & Mercedes Years - 1952-57
Targa Florio - The Post War Years - 1948-1973 - H.B.
Targa Florio - The Porsche & Ferrari Years - 1955-1964
Targa Florio - The Porsche Years - 1965-1973

B.B. PRACTICAL CLASSICS SERIES

PC on Austin A40 Restoration
PC on Land Rover Restoration
PC on Midget/Sprite Restoration
PC on MGB Restoration
PC on Sunbeam Rapier Restoration
PC on Triumph Herald/Vitesse

B.B. HOT ROD 'ENGINE' SERIES

Chevy 265 & 283
Chevy 302 & 327
Chevy 348 & 409
Chevy 350 & 400
Chevy 396 & 427
Chevy 454 thru 512
Chrysler Hemi
Chrysler 273, 318, 340 & 360
Chrysler 361, 383, 400, 413, 426 & 440
Ford 289, 302, Boss 302 & 351W
Ford 351C & Boss 351
Ford Big Block

B.B. RESTORATION & GUIDE SERIES

BMW 2002 - A Comprehensive Guide
BMW '02 Restoration Guide
Classic Camaro Restoration
Chevrolet High Performance Tips & Techniques
Chevy Engine Swapping Tips & Techniques
Chevy-GMC Pickup Repair
Engine Swapping Tips & Techniques
Land Rover Restoration Portfolio
MG 'T' Series Restoration Guide
MGA Restoration Guide
Mustang Restoration Tips & Techniques
The Great Classic Muscle Cars Compared

MOTORCYCLING

B.B. ROAD TEST SERIES

AJS & Matchless Gold Portfolio 1945-1966
BMW Motorcycles Gold Portfolio 1950-1971
BMW Motorcycles Gold Portfolio 1971-1976
BSA Singles Gold Portfolio 1945-1963
BSA Singles Gold Portfolio 1964-1974
BSA Twins A7 & A10 Gold Portfolio 1946-1962
BSA Twins A50 & A65 Gold Portfolio 1962-1973
BSA & Triumph Triples Gold Portfolio 1968-1976
Ducati Gold Portfolio 1974-1978
Ducati Gold Portfolio 1978-1982
Harley-Davidson Sportsters Pref. Port. 1965-1976
Harley-Davidson Super Glide Perf. Port. 1971-1981
Harley-Davidson FXR Series Perf. Port. 1982-1992
Honda CB750 Gold Portfolio 1969-1978
Honda CB500 & 550 Fours Perf. Port. 1971-1977
Honda CB350 & 400 Fours Perf. Port. 1972-1978
Honda Gold Wing Gold Portfolio 1975-1995
Honda CBX 1000 Gold Portfolio 1978-1982
Honda RC30 Performance Portfolio 1988-1992
Kawasaki Z1 900 Performance Portfolio 1972-1977
Kawasaki 500 & 750 Triples Perf. Port. 1969-1976
Kawasaki GPZ 900R Ninja Perf. Port. 1984-1996
Laverda Gold Portfolio 1967-1977
Laverda Performance Portfolio 1978-1988
Laverda Jota Performance Portfolio 1976-1985
Moto Guzzi Gold Portfolio 1949-1973
Moto Guzzi Le Mans Performance Portfoio 1976-89
Moto Morini 3½ & 500 Performance Port. 1974-84
Norton Dominators Performance Portfolio 1949-68
Norton Commando Ultimate Portfolio 1968-1977
Norton Rotarys Performance Portfolio 1984-1992
Suzuki GT750 Performance Portfolio 1971-1977
Suzuki GS1000 Performance Portfolio 1978-1981
Triumph Bonneville Gold Portfolio 1959-1983
Vincent Gold Portfolio 1945-1980
Yamaha RD350/400 Performance Portfolio 1972-79
Yamaha XS650 Performance Portfolio 1969-1985

B.B. CYCLE WORLD SERIES

Cycle World on BMW 1974-1980
Cycle World on BMW 1981-1986
Cycle World on Ducati 1982-1991
Cycle World on Harley-Davidson 1978-1983
Cycle World on Harley-Davidson 1983-1987
Cycle World on Harley-Davidson 1987-1990
Cycle World on Harley-Davidson 1990-1992
Cycle World on Honda 1962-1967
Cycle World on Honda 1968-1971
Cycle World on Honda 1971-1974
Cycle World on Husqvarna 1966-1976
Cycle World on Husqvarna 1977-1984
Cycle World on Kawasaki 1966-1971
Cycle World on Kawasaki Off-Road Bikes 1972-1979
Cycle World on Kawasaki Street Bikes 1972-1976
Cycle World on Norton 1962-1971
Cycle World on Suzuki 1962-1970
Cycle World on Suzuki Off-Road Bikes 1971-1976
Cycle World on Suzuki Street Bikes 1971-1976
Cycle World on Triumph 1967-1972
Cycle World on Yamaha 1962-1969
Cycle World on Yamaha Off-Road Bikes 1970-1974
Cycle World on Yamaha Street Bikes 1970-1974

MILITARY

VEHICLES & AEROPLANES

Complete WW2 Military Jeep Manual
Dodge WW2 Military Portfolio 1940-1945
German Military Equipment WW2
Hail To The Jeep
Land Rover Military Portfolio
Military & Civilian Amphibians 1940-1990
Off Road Jeeps Civilian & Military 1944-1971
Silhouette Handbook of US Army Air Forces Aeroplanes
US Military Vehicles 1941-1945
US Army Military Vehicles WW2-TM9-2800
VW Kubelwagen Military Portfolio 1940-1990
WW2 Allied Vehicles Military Portfolio 1939-1945
WW2 Jeep Military Portfolio 1941-1945

30/3Z1

CONTENTS

QUICK REFERENCE DATA IX

CHAPTER ONE
GENERAL INFORMATION 1

Manual organization
Service hints
Safety first
Expendable supplies

Shop tools
Emergency tool kit
Troubleshooting and
    tune-up equipment

CHAPTER TWO
TROUBLESHOOTING 12

Starting system
Charging system
Engine performance
Engine oil pressure light
Fuel system
Fuel pump test
    (mechanical, electric)
Emission control system
Engine noise

Electrical accessories
Cooling system
Clutch
Manual transmission/transaxle
Automatic transmission
Brakes
Steering and suspension
Tire wear analysis
Wheel balancing

CHAPTER THREE
LUBRICATION, MAINTENANCE AND TUNE-UP 33

Fuel stop checks
Scheduled maintenance
Tune-up
Compression test
Valve adjustment
Spark plugs

Distributor cap, wires and rotor
Breaker points
Ignition timing
Carburetor adjustments
Fuel injection
    system adjustment

CHAPTER FOUR
ENGINE **57**

Engine removal
Engine installation
Disassembly checklists
Timing belt
Intake and
  exhaust manifolds
Camshafts
Cylinder head
Valves and valve seats
Oil pan and oil pump

Auxiliary shaft
Flywheel
Torque converter
  drive plate
Oil seals
Piston/connecting
  rod assemblies
Crankshaft
Cylinder block inspection

CHAPTER FIVE
FUEL, EXHAUST AND EMISSION CONTROL SYSTEMS **112**

Air cleaner
Carburetor
Fuel injection
Turbocharger
Crankcase emission
  control system
Evaporative emission
  control system

Exhaust emission control
  system (carburetted models)
Exhaust emission control system
  (fuel injected models)
Throttle linkage
Exhaust system
Fuel pump

CHAPTER SIX
COOLING, HEATING AND AIR CONDITIONING **150**

Cooling system flushing
Thermostat
Water pump
Electric fan

Radiator
Heater
Air conditioning

CHAPTER SEVEN
ELECTRICAL SYSTEM **163**

Battery
Charging system
Starter

Lighting system
Windshield wipers and washers
Fuses

CHAPTER EIGHT
CLUTCH AND TRANSAXLE **185**

Clutch   Automatic tranmission
Manual transaxle

CHAPTER NINE
FRONT SUSPENSION, WHEEL BEARINGS AND STEERING **239**

Front suspension   Steering
Wheel bearings   Wheel alignment

CHAPTER TEN
REAR SUSPENSION, DIFFERENTIAL AND DRIVE SHAFT **252**

Rear suspension   Drive shaft
Rear axle

CHAPTER ELEVEN
BRAKES **266**

Front brakes   Handbrake
Rear brakes   Brake lines and hoses
Master cylinder   Brake bleeding
Brake booster

SKILL LEVEL AND TIME ESTIMATING GUIDE **280**

INDEX **288**

QUICK REFERENCE DATA

TUNE-UP SPECIFICATIONS

Valve clearance (cold engine)	
Intake	0.43-0.48 mm (0.017-0.019 in.)
Exhaust	0.48-0.53 mm (0.019-0.021 in.)
Spark plug type	
Through 1973	
Champion	N6Y
AC Delco	41-2 XLS
Marelli	CW 8 LP
1974-1977	
Champion	N7Y
AC Delco	41-42 XLS
Marelli	CW 78 LP
1978-1980	
Champion	N9Y, RN9Y*
AC Delco	42 XLS, R42 XLS*
Marelli	CW 7 LP, CW 7 LPR*
Bosch	W175 T30, W175 TR30*
1981-on	
Champion	N9Y, RN9Y*
AC	42 XLS, R42 XLS*, R43 XLS*
Bosch	W7D, WR7D*, WR7D2*
Marelli	CW 7 LP, CW 7 LPR*, CW 67 LPR*
Fiat	1L4J, 1L4JR*
Spark plug thread size	14×1.25 mm
Spark plug gap	
Through 1977	0.5-0.7 mm (0.020-0.027 in.)
1978-on (non-resistor)	0.6-0.7 mm (0.023-0.027 in.)
1978-on (resistor)	0.7-0.8 mm (0.027-0.031 in.)
Firing order	1-3-4-2 clockwise
Points gap	
Through 1974	0.37-0.43 mm (0.015-0.017 in.)
1975-1978	
Primary points	0.37-0.43 mm (0.015-0.017 in.)
Secondary points	0.31-0.49 mm (0.012-0.019 in.)
Dwell angle (through 1978)	55°
Ignition timing (at idle speed)	
Through 1978	0° (TDC)
1979-on	10° BTDC
Idle speed	
Through 1978	850 rpm
1979-on	
Manual transmission	700-800 rpm
Automatic transmission (in DRIVE)	700-750 rpm

* Resistor-type plug

FRONT SUSPENSION SPECIFICATIONS

Caster*	
1971-1972	3° 30', −10', +30'
1973-on	3° 30' ±30'
Camber*	0° 30' ±30'
Toe-in*	3 ±2 mm (0.120 ±0.039 in.)
Steering axis inclination	6°
Steering lock angles	
Inner wheel	35° 50' ±1° 30'
Outer wheel	28° 30'
Load factor	
1971-1972 Coupe	3 persons plus 66 lb. luggage
1973-1974 Coupe	2 persons plus 44 lb. luggage
1975 Coupe	4 persons plus 90 lb. luggage
1971-1974 Spider	2 persons plus 44 lb. luggage
1975-on Spider	2 persons plus 130 lb. luggage

* These angles are measured @ the indicated load factor.

TIGHTENING TORQUES

Fastener	Thread size	mkg	ft.-lb.
Wheel bearing nut	See text		
Crossmember-to-side member bolts	M12×1.25	9.5	69
Crossmember to side member lower nuts	M10×1.25	5.5	40
Lower control arm to crossmember nut	M12×1.25	6	43
Lower control arm pin to crossmember nut	M14×1.5	10	72
Upper control arm nut	M14×1.5	9	65
Shock absorber upper nut	M8	1.5	11
Shock absorber lower nut	M10×1.25	6	43
Caliper carrier plate bolt	M10×1.25	5	36
Steering wheel nut	M16×1.5	5	36
Steering gear to body			
1971-1974	M10×1.25	4	29
1975-on*	M10×1.25	3	22
Hydraulic damper (idler arm) to body			
1971-1974	M10×1.25	4	29
1975-on	M10×1.25	3	22
Tie rod end nuts			
1971-1974	M10×1.25	3	22
1975-on*	M10×1.25	3.5	25

* Self-locking nut.

TORQUE SPECIFICATIONS (MANUAL TRANSMISSION)

Fastener	Thread size	mkg	ft.-lb.
Detent spring cover bolt	M8	2.5	18
Transmission-to-engine bolts	M12×1.25	8.3	61
Clutch housing to transmission bolts/nuts			
Large	M10×1.25	4.9	36
Small	M8	2.5	18
Rear cover nut	M8	2.5	18
Rear cover bolt	M8	2.0	14
Countershaft rear bearing nut	M18×1.5	11.8	87
Countershaft front bearing bolt	M12×1.25	9.3	69
Shift fork bolts	M6	2.0	14
Main shaft nut	M20×1	14.7	108

SCHEDULED MAINTENANCE (1971-1978)

Every 3,000 miles	• Battery
Every 6,000 miles	• Engine oil and filter
Every 12,500 miles	• Fuel filter • Clutch pedal • Air cleaner filter element • Brakes • Vacuum hoses • Steering linkage • Emission controls • Hinges, latches, locks • Cooling system hoses and connections • Tune-up • Drive belts
Every 25,000 miles	• Timing belt • Automatic transmission fluid • Carbon canister • Differential oil • Manual transmission oil • Wheel bearings

SCHEDULED MAINTENANCE (1979-ON)

Every 3,000 miles	• Battery • Automatic transmission fluid
Every 3,750 miles (Turbo)	• Engine oil and filter
Every 7,500 miles (non-Turbo)	• Engine oil and filter
Every 15,000 miles	• Fuel filter (carburetted cars only) • Clutch pedal • Air cleaner filter element • Brakes • Vacuum hoses • Steering linkage • Emission controls • Hinges, latches, locks • Turbocharger • Tune-up • Drive belts
Every 30,000 miles	• Timing belt • Wheel bearings • Manual transmission oil • Lambda sensor replacement • Automatic transmission fluid (fuel injected cars only) • Differential oil
Every 45,000 miles	• Cooling system

TRANSMISSION REAR RATIOS

1971-1978	
First	3.667:1
Second	2.100:1
Third	1.361:1
Fourth	1.0:1
Fifth	0.881:1
Reverse	3.526:1
1979-1980	
First	3.612:1
Second	2.045:1
Third	1.357:1
Fourth	1.0:1
Fifth	0.830:1
Reverse	3.244:1
1981-on	
First	3.667:1
Second	2.100:1
Third	1.361:1
Fourth	1.0:1
Fifth	0.881:1
Reverse	3.244:1

VALVE SHIM THICKNESS

mm	in.	mm	in.
3.25	0.128	4.00	0.157
3.30	0.130	4.05	0.159
3.35	0.132	4.10	0.161
3.40	0.134	4.15	0.163
3.45	0.136	4.20	0.165
3.50	0.138	4.25	0.167
3.55	0.140	4.30	0.169
3.60	0.142	4.35	0.171
3.65	0.144	4.40	0.173
3.70	0.146	4.45	0.175
3.75	0.148	4.50	0.177
3.80	0.150	4.55	0.179
3.85	0.152	4.60	0.181
3.90	0.154	4.65	0.183
3.95	0.156	4.70	0.185

RECOMMENDED LUBRICANTS AND FLUIDS

Engine oil	API service SE-CC
Manual transmission and differential oil	SAE 90 (not EP)
Automatic transmission fluid	DEXRON
Steering gear	SAE 90 (EP)
Constant velocity joints	Lithium-based grease, NLGI No. 2, containing molybdenum disulfide
Antifreeze	Ethylene glycol type
Brake and clutch fluid	DOT 3
Fuel tank	
Without catalytic converter	Leaded or unleaded gasoline, Research octane number 91 or higher*
With catalytic converter	Unleaded gasoline, Research octane number 91 or higher*

* Gasoline pumps usually display an average of Research and Motor octane numbers. In this case, the minimum octane number is 87.

APPROXIMATE REFILL CAPACITIES

Fluid	Liters	Quarts
Engine oil		
Through 1974	3.75	4
1975-on	4.125	4 1/4
Cooling system		
Through 1974	7.5	8
1975-on	8	8 1/2
Manual transmission	1.65	1 3/4
Automatic transmission		
Drain and fill	2.8	3
New or rebuilt transmission	5.6	6
Steering gear	0.215	3/8 pt.
Fuel tank	43	11.4

FIAT
124 COUPE/SPIDER &
2000 SPIDER INCLUDES TURBO SPIDER
1971-1984
SHOP MANUAL

INTRODUCTION

This detailed comprehensive manual covers the 1971-1982 Fiat 124 and 2000 Coupe and Spider, and the 1984 Pininfarina Azzura. The expert text gives complete information on maintenance, repair and overhaul. Hundreds of photos and drawings guide you through every step. The book includes all you need to know to keep your Fiat running right.

Where repairs are practical for the owner/mechanic, complete procedures are given. Equally important, difficult jobs are pointed out. Such operations are usually more economically performed by a dealer or independent garage.

Where special tools are required or recommended, the tool numbers are provided. These tools can sometimes be rented from rental dealers, but they can always be purchased from Fiat parts and service centers or Kent-Moore Tool Division, 28635 Mound Road, Warren, MI. 48092

A shop manual is a reference. You want to be able to find information fast. As inall Clymer books, this one is designed with such use in mind. All chapters are thumb tabbed. Important items are indexed at the rear of the book. All the most frequently used specifications and capacities are summarized on the *Quick Reference Data* pages at the front of the book.

Keep the book handy. Carry it in your glove box. It will help you to better understand your car, lower repair and maintenance costs and generally improve your satisfaction with your vehicle.

CHAPTER ONE

GENERAL INFORMATION

The troubleshooting, tune-up, maintenance, and step-by-step repair procedures in this book are written for the owner and home mechanic. The text is accompanied by useful photos and diagrams to make the job as clear and correct as possible.

Troubleshooting, tune-up, maintenance, and repair are not difficult if you know what tools and equipment to use and what to do. Anyone not afraid to get their hands dirty, of average intelligence, and with some mechanical ability can perform most of the procedures in this book.

In some cases, a repair job may require tools or skills not reasonably expected of the home mechanic. These procedures are noted in each chapter and it is recommended that you take the job to your dealer, a competent mechanic, or machine shop.

MANUAL ORGANIZATION

This chapter provides general information and safety and service hints. Also included are lists of recommended shop and emergency tools as well as a brief description of troubleshooting and tune-up equipment.

Chapter Two provides methods and suggestions for quick and accurate diagnosis and repair of problems. Troubleshooting procedures discuss typical symptoms and logical methods to pinpoint the trouble.

Chapter Three explains all periodic lubrication and routine maintenance necessary to keep your vehicle running well. Chapter Three also includes recommended tune-up procedures, eliminating the need to constantly consult chapters on the various subassemblies.

Subsequent chapters cover specific systems such as the engine, transmission, and electrical systems. Each of these chapters provides disassembly, repair, and assembly procedures in a simple step-by-step format. If a repair requires special skills or tools, or is otherwise impractical for the home mechanic, it is so indicated. In these cases it is usually faster and less expensive to have the repairs made by a dealer or competent repair shop. Necessary specifications concerning a particular system are included at the end of the appropriate chapter.

When special tools are required to perform a procedure included in this manual, the tool is illustrated either in actual use or alone. It may be possible to rent or borrow these tools. The inventive mechanic may also be able to find a suitable substitute in his tool box, or to fabricate one.

The terms NOTE, CAUTION, and WARNING have specific meanings in this manual. A NOTE provides additional or explanatory information. A CAUTION is used to emphasize areas where equipment damage could result if proper precautions are not taken. A WARNING is used to stress those areas where personal injury or death could result from negligence, in addition to possible mechanical damage.

SERVICE HINTS

Observing the following practices will save time, effort, and frustration, as well as prevent possible injury.

Throughout this manual keep in mind two conventions. ''Front'' refers to the front of the vehicle. The front of any component, such as the transmission, is that end which faces toward the front of the vehicle. The ''left'' and ''right'' sides of the vehicle refer to the orientation of a person sitting in the vehicle facing forward. For example, the steering wheel is on the left side. These rules are simple, but even experienced mechanics occasionally become disoriented.

Most of the service procedures covered are straightforward and can be performed by anyone reasonably handy with tools. It is suggested, however, that you consider your own capabilities carefully before attempting any operation involving major disassembly of the engine.

Some operations, for example, require the use of a press. It would be wiser to have these performed by a shop equipped for such work, rather than to try to do the job yourself with makeshift equipment. Other procedures require precision measurements. Unless you have the skills and equipment required, it would be better to have a qualified repair shop make the measurements for you.

Repairs go much faster and easier if the parts that will be worked on are clean before you begin. There are special cleaners for washing the engine and related parts. Brush or spray on the cleaning solution, let it stand, then rinse it away with a garden hose. Clean all oily or greasy parts with cleaning solvent as you remove them.

WARNING
Never use gasoline as a cleaning agent. It presents an extreme fire hazard. Be sure to work in a well-ventilated area when using cleaning solvent. Keep a fire extinguisher, rated for gasoline fires, handy in any case.

Much of the labor charge for repairs made by dealers is for the removal and disassembly of other parts to reach the defective unit. It is frequently possible to perform the preliminary operations yourself and then take the defective unit in to the dealer for repair, at considerable savings.

Once you have decided to tackle the job yourself, make sure you locate the appropriate section in this manual, and read it entirely. Study the illustrations and text until you have a good idea of what is involved in completing the job satisfactorily. If special tools are required, make arrangements to get them before you start. Also, purchase any known defective parts prior to starting on the procedure. It is frustrating and time-consuming to get partially into a job and then be unable to complete it.

Simple wiring checks can be easily made at home, but knowledge of electronics is almost a necessity for performing tests with complicated electronic testing gear.

During disassembly of parts keep a few general cautions in mind. Force is rarely needed to get things apart. If parts are a tight fit, like a bearing in a case, there is usually a tool designed to separate them. Never use a screwdriver to pry apart parts with machined surfaces such as cylinder head and valve cover. You will mar the surfaces and end up with leaks.

Make diagrams wherever similar-appearing parts are found. You may think you can remember where everything came from — but mistakes are costly. There is also the possibility you may get sidetracked and not return to work for days or even weeks — in which interval, carefully laid out parts may have become disturbed.

Tag all similar internal parts for location, and mark all mating parts for position. Record number and thickness of any shims as they are removed. Small parts such as bolts can be identified by placing them in plastic sandwich bags that are sealed and labeled with masking tape.

Wiring should be tagged with masking tape and marked as each wire is removed. Again, do not rely on memory alone.

When working under the vehicle, do not trust a hydraulic or mechanical jack to hold the vehicle up by itself. Always use jackstands. See **Figure 1**.

Disconnect battery ground cable before working near electrical connections and before disconnecting wires. Never run the engine with the battery disconnected; the alternator could be seriously damaged.

Protect finished surfaces from physical damage or corrosion. Keep gasoline and brake fluid off painted surfaces.

Frozen or very tight bolts and screws can often be loosened by soaking with penetrating oil like Liquid Wrench or WD-40, then sharply striking the bolt head a few times with a hammer and punch (or screwdriver for screws). Avoid heat unless absolutely necessary, since it may melt, warp, or remove the temper from many parts.

Avoid flames or sparks when working near a charging battery or flammable liquids, such as brake fluid or gasoline.

No parts, except those assembled with a press fit, require unusual force during assembly. If a part is hard to remove or install, find out why before proceeding.

Cover all openings after removing parts to keep dirt, small tools, etc., from falling in.

When assembling two parts, start all fasteners, then tighten evenly.

The clutch plate, wiring connections, brake shoes, drums, pads, and discs should be kept clean and free of grease and oil.

When assembling parts, be sure all shims and washers are replaced exactly as they came out.

Whenever a rotating part butts against a stationary part, look for a shim or washer. Use new gaskets if there is any doubt about the condition of old ones. Generally, you should apply gasket cement to one mating surface only, so the parts may be easily disassembled in the future. A thin coat of oil on gaskets helps them seal effectively.

Heavy grease can be used to hold small parts in place if they tend to fall out during assembly. However, keep grease and oil away from electrical, clutch, and brake components.

High spots may be sanded off a piston with sandpaper, but emery cloth and oil do a much more professional job.

Carburetors are best cleaned by disassembling them and soaking the parts in a commercial carburetor cleaner. Never soak gaskets and rubber parts in these cleaners. Never use wire to clean out jets and air passages; they are easily damaged. Use compressed air to blow out the carburetor, but only if the float has been removed first.

Take your time and do the job right. Do not forget that a newly rebuilt engine must be broken in the same as a new one. Refer to your owner's manual for the proper break-in procedures.

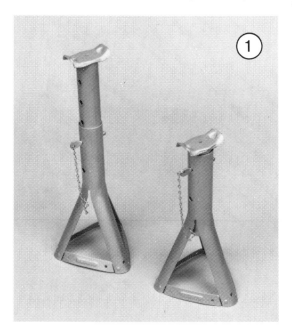

SAFETY FIRST

Professional mechanics can work for years and never sustain a serious injury. If you observe a few rules of common sense and safety, you can enjoy many safe hours servicing your vehicle. You could hurt yourself or damage the vehicle if you ignore these rules.

1. Never use gasoline as a cleaning solvent.

2. Never smoke or use a torch in the vicinity of flammable liquids such as cleaning solvent in open containers.

3. Never smoke or use a torch in an area where batteries are being charged. Highly explosive hydrogen gas is formed during the charging process.

4. Use the proper sized wrenches to avoid damage to nuts and injury to yourself.

5. When loosening a tight or stuck nut, be guided by what would happen if the wrench should slip. Protect yourself accordingly.

6. Keep your work area clean and uncluttered.

7. Wear safety goggles during all operations involving drilling, grinding, or use of a cold chisel.

8. Never use worn tools.

9. Keep a fire extinguisher handy and be sure it is rated for gasoline (Class B) and electrical (Class C) fires.

EXPENDABLE SUPPLIES

Certain expendable supplies are necessary. These include grease, oil, gasket cement, wiping rags, cleaning solvent, and distilled water.

Also, special locking compounds, silicone lubricants, and engine cleaners may be useful. Cleaning solvent is available at most service stations and distilled water for the battery is available at most supermarkets.

SHOP TOOLS

For proper servicing, you will need an assortment of ordinary hand tools (**Figure 2**).

As a minimum, these include:

a. Combination wrenches
b. Sockets
c. Plastic mallet
d. Small hammer
e. Snap ring pliers
f. Gas pliers
g. Phillips screwdrivers
h. Slot (common) screwdrivers
i. Feeler gauges
j. Spark plug gauge
k. Spark plug wrench

Special tools necessary are shown in the chapters covering the particular repair in which they are used.

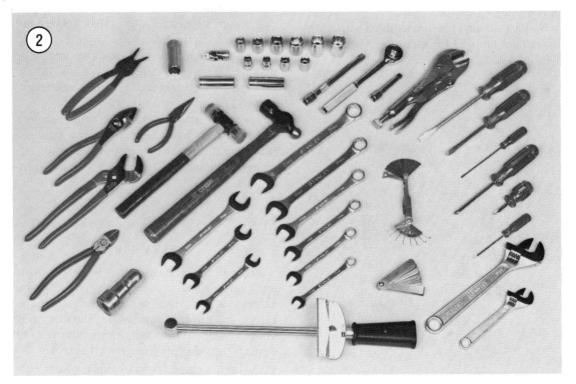

Engine tune-up and troubleshooting procedures require other special tools and equipment. These are described in detail in the following sections.

EMERGENCY TOOL KIT

A small emergency tool kit kept in the trunk is handy for road emergencies which otherwise could leave you stranded. The tools listed below and shown in **Figure 3** will let you handle most roadside repairs.

    a. Combination wrenches

    b. Crescent (adjustable) wrench

    c. Screwdrivers — common and Phillips

    d. Pliers — conventional (gas) and needle nose

    e. Vise Grips

    f. Hammer — plastic and metal

    g. Small container of waterless hand cleaner

    h. Rags for clean up

    i. Silver waterproof sealing tape (duct tape)

    j. Flashlight

    k. Emergency road flares — at least four

    l. Spare drive belts (water pump, alternator, etc.)

TROUBLESHOOTING AND TUNE-UP EQUIPMENT

Voltmeter, Ohmmeter, and Ammeter

For testing the ignition or electrical system, a good voltmeter is required. For automotive use, an instrument covering 0-20 volts is satisfac-

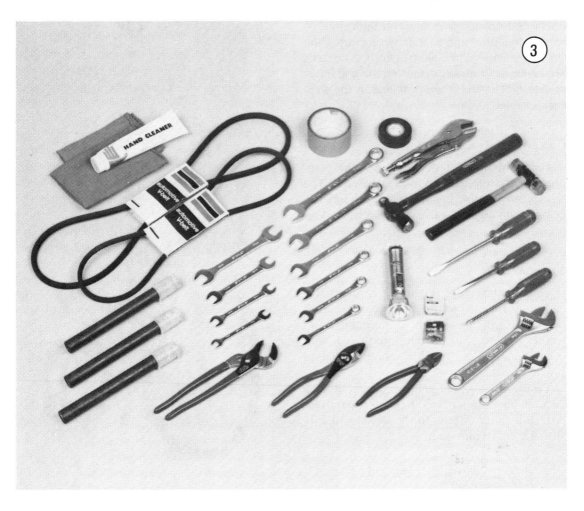

(3)

tory. One which also has a 0-2 volt scale is necessary for testing relays, points, or individual contacts where voltage drops are much smaller. Accuracy should be ± ½ volt.

An ohmmeter measures electrical resistance. This instrument is useful for checking continuity (open and short circuits), and testing fuses and lights.

The ammeter measures electrical current. Ammeters for automotive use should cover 0-50 amperes and 0-250 amperes. These are useful for checking battery charging and starting current.

Several inexpensive vom's (volt-ohm-milliammeter) combine all three instruments into one which fits easily in any tool box. See **Figure 4**. However, the ammeter ranges are usually too small for automotive work.

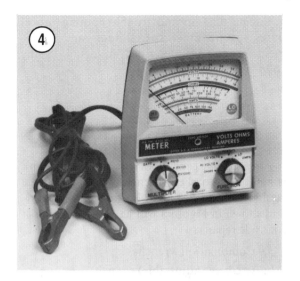

Hydrometer

The hydrometer gives a useful indication of battery condition and charge by measuring the specific gravity of the electrolyte in each cell. See **Figure 5**. Complete details on use and interpretation of readings are provided in the electrical chapter.

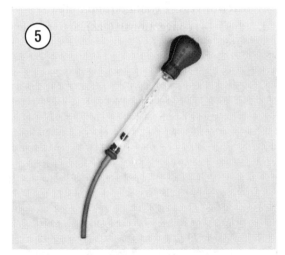

Compression Tester

The compression tester measures the compression pressure built up in each cylinder. The results, when properly interpreted, can indicate general cylinder and valve condition. See **Figure 6**.

Vacuum Gauge

The vacuum gauge (**Figure 7**) is one of the easiest instruments to use, but one of the most difficult for the inexperienced mechanic to interpret. The results, when interpreted with other findings, can provide valuable clues to possible trouble.

To use the vacuum gauge, connect it to a vacuum hose that goes to the intake manifold. Attach it either directly to the hose or to a T-fitting installed into the hose.

NOTE: *Subtract one inch from the reading for every 1,000 ft. elevation.*

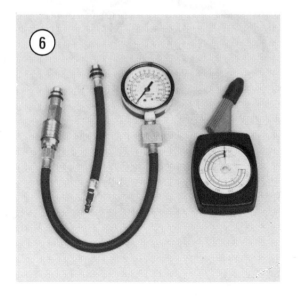

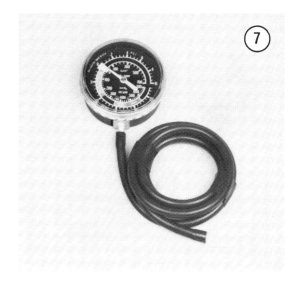

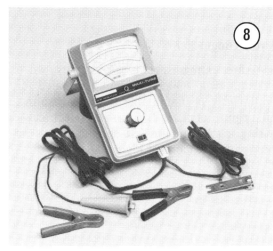

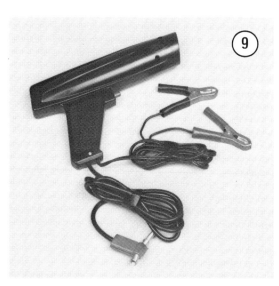

Fuel Pressure Gauge

This instrument is invaluable for evaluating fuel pump performance. Fuel system troubleshooting procedures in this manual use a fuel pressure gauge. Usually a vacuum gauge and fuel pressure gauge are combined.

Dwell Meter (Contact Breaker Point Ignition Only)

A dwell meter measures the distance in degrees of cam rotation that the breaker points remain closed while the engine is running. Since this angle is determined by breaker point gap, dwell angle is an accurate indication of breaker point gap.

Many tachometers intended for tuning and testing incorporate a dwell meter as well. See **Figure 8**. Follow the manufacturer's instructions to measure dwell.

Tachometer

A tachometer is necessary for tuning. See **Figure 8**. Ignition timing and carburetor adjustments must be performed at the specified idle speed. The best instrument for this purpose is one with a low range of 0-1,000 or 0-2,000 rpm for setting idle, and a high range of 0-4,000 or more for setting ignition timing at 3,000 rpm. Extended range (0-6,000 or 0-8,000 rpm) instruments lack accuracy at lower speeds. The instrument should be capable of detecting changes of 25 rpm on the low range.

Strobe Timing Light

This instrument is necessary for tuning, as it permits very accurate ignition timing. The light flashes at precisely the same instant that No. 1 cylinder fires, at which time the timing marks on the engine should align. Refer to Chapter Three for exact location of the timing marks for your engine.

Suitable lights range from inexpensive neon bulb types ($2-3) to powerful xenon strobe lights ($20-40). See **Figure 9**. Neon timing lights are difficult to see and must be used in dimly lit areas. Xenon strobe timing lights can be used outside in bright sunlight. Both types work on this vehicle; use according to the manufacturer's instructions.

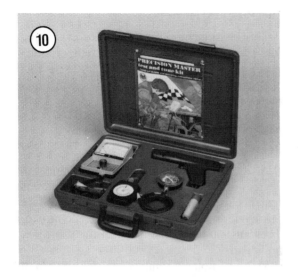

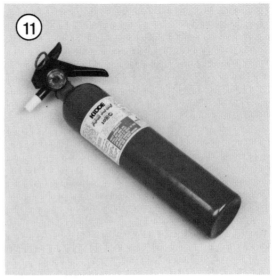

Tune-up Kits

Many manufacturer's offer kits that combine several useful instruments. Some come in a convenient carry case and are usally less expensive than purchasing one instrument at a time. **Figure 10** shows one of the kits that is available. The prices vary with the number of instruments included in the kit.

Fire Extinguisher

A fire extinguisher is a necessity when working on a vehicle. It should be rated for both *Class B* (flammable liquids—gasoline, oil, paint, etc.) and *Class C* (electrical—wiring, etc.) type fires. It should always be kept within reach. See **Figure 11**.

TROUBLESHOOTING

Troubleshooting can be a relatively simple matter if it is done logically. The first step in any troubleshooting procedure must be defining the symptoms as closely as possible. Subsequent steps involve testing and analyzing areas which could cause the symptoms. A haphazard approach may eventually find the trouble, but in terms of wasted time and unnecessary parts replacement, it can be very costly.

The troubleshooting procedures in this chapter analyze typical symptoms and show logical methods of isolation. These are not the only methods. There may be several approaches to a problem, but all methods must have one thing in common — a logical, systematic approach.

STARTING SYSTEM

The starting system consists of the starter motor and the starter solenoid. The ignition key controls the starter solenoid, which mechanically engages the starter with the engine flywheel, and supplies electrical current to turn the starter motor.

Starting system troubles are relatively easy to find. In most cases, the trouble is a loose or dirty electrical connection. **Figures 1 and 2** provide routines for finding the trouble.

CHARGING SYSTEM

The charging system consists of the alternator (or generator on older vehicles), voltage regulator, and battery. A drive belt driven by the engine crankshaft turns the alternator which produces electrical energy to charge the battery. As engine speed varies, the voltage from the alternator varies. A voltage regulator controls the charging current to the battery and maintains the voltage to the vehicle's electrical system at safe levels. A warning light or gauge on the instrument panel signals the driver when charging is not taking place. Refer to **Figure 3** for a typical charging system.

Complete troubleshooting of the charging system requires test equipment and skills which the average home mechanic does not possess. However, there are a few tests which can be done to pinpoint most troubles.

Charging system trouble may stem from a defective alternator (or generator), voltage regulator, battery, or drive belt. It may also be caused by something as simple as incorrect drive belt tension. The following are symptoms of typical problems you may encounter.

1. *Battery dies frequently, even though the warning lamp indicates no discharge* — This can be caused by a drive belt that is slightly too

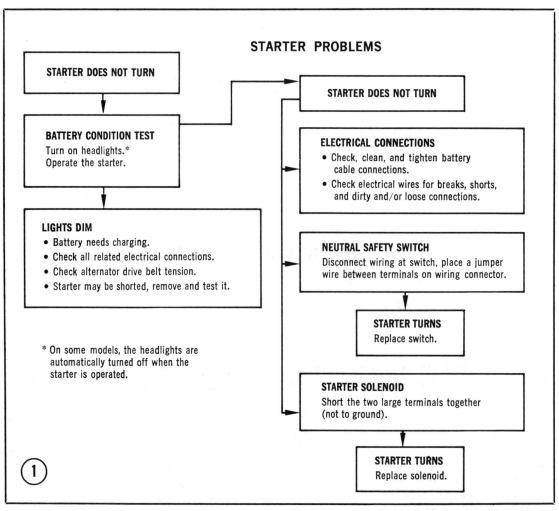

STARTER PROBLEMS

STARTER DOES NOT TURN

BATTERY CONDITION TEST
Turn on headlights.*
Operate the starter.

LIGHTS DIM
- Battery needs charging.
- Check all related electrical connections.
- Check alternator drive belt tension.
- Starter may be shorted, remove and test it.

* On some models, the headlights are
automatically turned off when the
starter is operated.

STARTER DOES NOT TURN

ELECTRICAL CONNECTIONS
- Check, clean, and tighten battery
  cable connections.
- Check electrical wires for breaks, shorts,
  and dirty and/or loose connections.

NEUTRAL SAFETY SWITCH
Disconnect wiring at switch, place a jumper
wire between terminals on wiring connector.

STARTER TURNS
Replace switch.

STARTER SOLENOID
Short the two large terminals together
(not to ground).

STARTER TURNS
Replace solenoid.

①

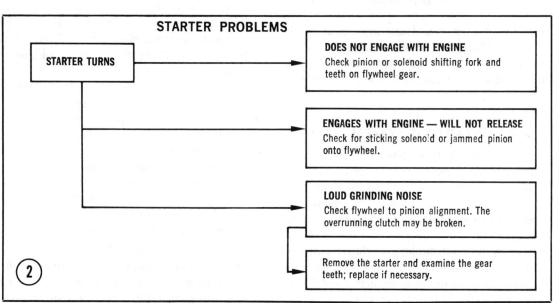

STARTER PROBLEMS

STARTER TURNS

DOES NOT ENGAGE WITH ENGINE
Check pinion or solenoid shifting fork and
teeth on flywheel gear.

ENGAGES WITH ENGINE — WILL NOT RELEASE
Check for sticking solenoid or jammed pinion
onto flywheel.

LOUD GRINDING NOISE
Check flywheel to pinion alignment. The
overrunning clutch may be broken.

Remove the starter and examine the gear
teeth; replace if necessary.

②

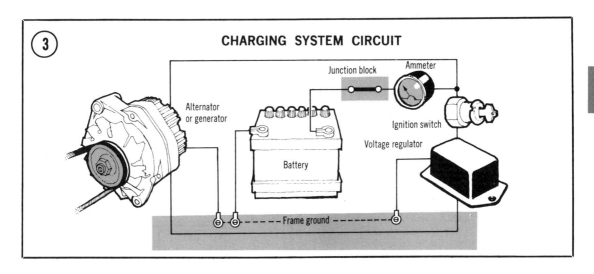

CHARGING SYSTEM CIRCUIT

③

Alternator or generator

Junction block

Ammeter

Ignition switch

Voltage regulator

Battery

Frame ground

2

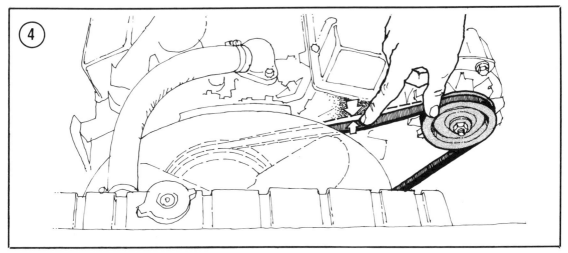

④

loose. Grasp the alternator (or generator) pulley and try to turn it. If the pulley can be turned without moving the belt, the drive belt is too loose. As a rule, keep the belt tight enough that it can be deflected about ½ in. under moderate thumb pressure between the pulleys **(Figure 4)**. The battery may also be at fault; test the battery condition.

2. *Charging system warning lamp does not come on when ignition switch is turned on* — This may indicate a defective ignition switch, battery, voltage regulator, or lamp. First try to start the vehicle. If it doesn't start, check the ignition switch and battery. If the car starts, remove the warning lamp; test it for continuity with an ohmmeter or substitute a new lamp. If the lamp is good, locate the voltage regulator

and make sure it is properly grounded (try tightening the mounting screws). Also the alternator (or generator) brushes may not be making contact. Test the alternator (or generator) and voltage regulator.

3. *Alternator (or generator) warning lamp comes on and stays on* — This usually indicates that no charging is taking place. First check drive belt tension **(Figure 4)**. Then check battery condition, and check all wiring connections in the charging system. If this does not locate the trouble, check the alternator (or generator) and voltage regulator.

4. *Charging system warning lamp flashes on and off intermittently* — This usually indicates the charging system is working intermittently.

Check the drive belt tension (**Figure 4**), and check all electrical connections in the charging system. Check the alternator (or generator). *On generators only*, check the condition of the commutator.

5. *Battery requires frequent additions of water, or lamps require frequent replacement* — The alternator (or generator) is probably overcharging the battery. The voltage regulator is probably at fault.

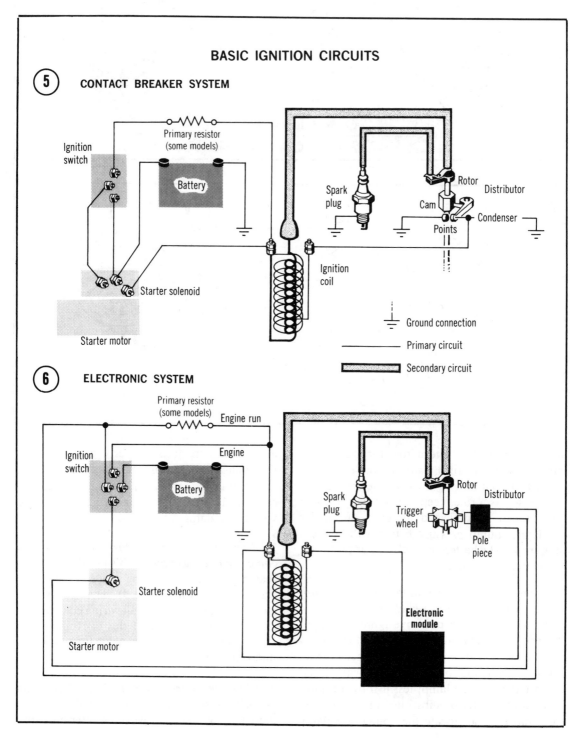

2

6. *Excessive noise from the alternator (or generator)* — Check for loose mounting brackets and bolts. The problem may also be worn bearings or the need of lubrication in some cases. If an alternator whines, a shorted diode may be indicated.

IGNITION SYSTEM

The ignition system may be either a conventional contact breaker type or an electronic ignition. See electrical chapter to determine which type you have. **Figures 5 and 6** show simplified diagrams of each type.

Most problems involving failure to start, poor performance, or rough running stem from trouble in the ignition system, particularly in contact breaker systems. Many novice troubleshooters get into trouble when they assume that these symptoms point to the fuel system instead of the ignition system.

Ignition system troubles may be roughly divided between those affecting only one cylinder and those affecting all cylinders. If the trouble affects only one cylinder, it can only be in the spark plug, spark plug wire, or portion of the distributor associated with that cylinder. If the trouble affects all cylinders (weak spark or no spark), then the trouble is in the ignition coil, rotor, distributor, or associated wiring.

The troubleshooting procedures outlined in **Figure 7** (breaker point ignition) or **Figure 8**

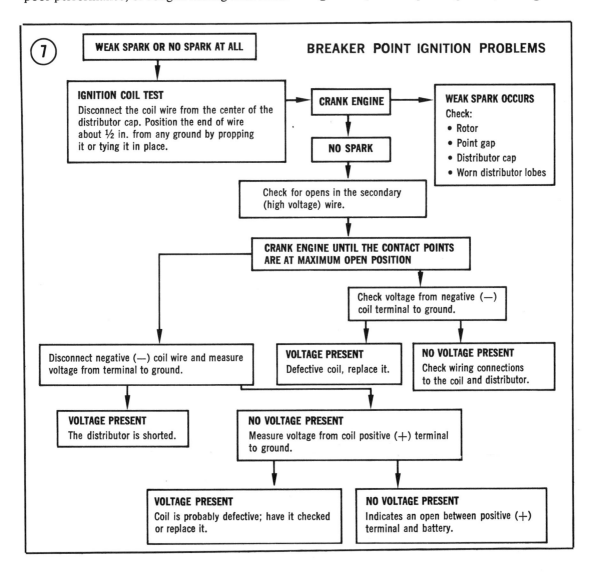

(electronic ignition) will help you isolate ignition problems fast. Of course, they assume that the battery is in good enough condition to crank the engine over at its normal rate.

ENGINE PERFORMANCE

A number of factors can make the engine difficult or impossible to start, or cause rough running, poor performance and so on. The majority of novice troubleshooters immediately suspect the carburetor or fuel injection system. In the majority of cases, though, the trouble exists in the ignition system.

The troubleshooting procedures outlined in **Figures 9 through 14** will help you solve the majority of engine starting troubles in a systematic manner.

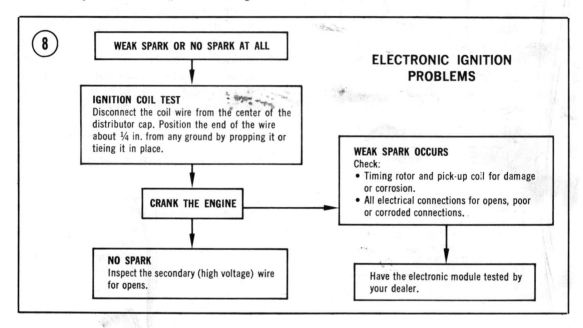

8

WEAK SPARK OR NO SPARK AT ALL

ELECTRONIC IGNITION PROBLEMS

IGNITION COIL TEST
Disconnect the coil wire from the center of the distributor cap. Position the end of the wire about ¼ in. from any ground by propping it or tieing it in place.

WEAK SPARK OCCURS
Check:
• Timing rotor and pick-up coil for damage or corrosion.
• All electrical connections for opens, poor or corroded connections.

CRANK THE ENGINE

NO SPARK
Inspect the secondary (high voltage) wire for opens.

Have the electronic module tested by your dealer.

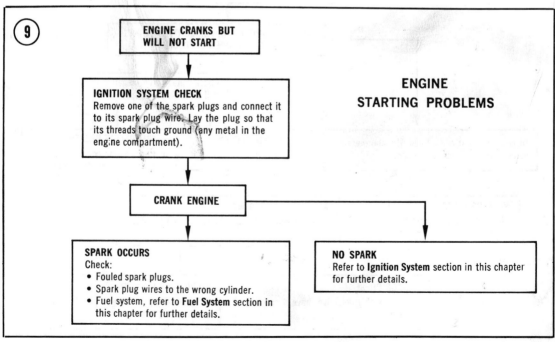

9

ENGINE CRANKS BUT WILL NOT START

ENGINE STARTING PROBLEMS

IGNITION SYSTEM CHECK
Remove one of the spark plugs and connect it to its spark plug wire. Lay the plug so that its threads touch ground (any metal in the engine compartment).

CRANK ENGINE

SPARK OCCURS
Check:
• Fouled spark plugs.
• Spark plug wires to the wrong cylinder.
• Fuel system, refer to **Fuel System** section in this chapter for further details.

NO SPARK
Refer to **Ignition System** section in this chapter for further details.

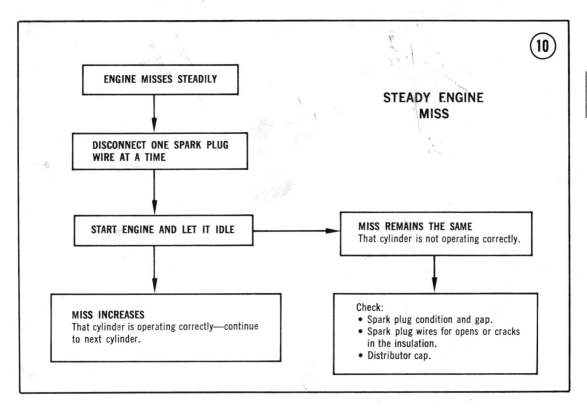

⑩

ENGINE MISSES STEADILY

STEADY ENGINE MISS

DISCONNECT ONE SPARK PLUG WIRE AT A TIME

START ENGINE AND LET IT IDLE

MISS REMAINS THE SAME
That cylinder is not operating correctly.

MISS INCREASES
That cylinder is operating correctly—continue to next cylinder.

Check:
• Spark plug condition and gap.
• Spark plug wires for opens or cracks in the insulation.
• Distributor cap.

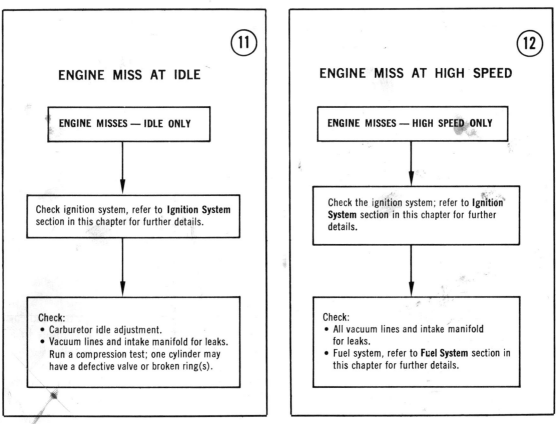

⑪

ENGINE MISS AT IDLE

ENGINE MISSES — IDLE ONLY

Check ignition system, refer to **Ignition System** section in this chapter for further details.

Check:
• Carburetor idle adjustment.
• Vacuum lines and intake manifold for leaks. Run a compression test; one cylinder may have a defective valve or broken ring(s).

⑫

ENGINE MISS AT HIGH SPEED

ENGINE MISSES — HIGH SPEED ONLY

Check the ignition system; refer to **Ignition System** section in this chapter for further details.

Check:
• All vacuum lines and intake manifold for leaks.
• Fuel system, refer to **Fuel System** section in this chapter for further details.

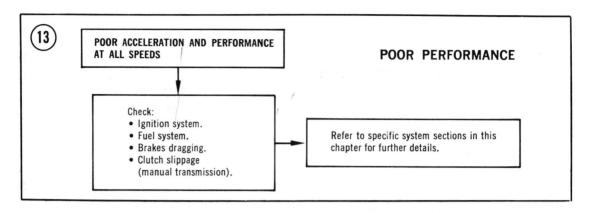

⑬

POOR ACCELERATION AND PERFORMANCE
AT ALL SPEEDS

POOR PERFORMANCE

Check:
• Ignition system.
• Fuel system.
• Brakes dragging.
• Clutch slippage
  (manual transmission).

Refer to specific system sections in this
chapter for further details.

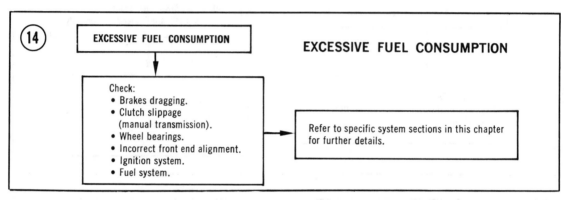

⑭

EXCESSIVE FUEL CONSUMPTION

EXCESSIVE FUEL CONSUMPTION

Check:
• Brakes dragging.
• Clutch slippage
  (manual transmission).
• Wheel bearings.
• Incorrect front end alignment.
• Ignition system.
• Fuel system.

Refer to specific system sections in this chapter
for further details.

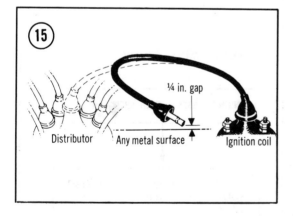

⑮ Distributor   ¼ in. gap   Any metal surface   Ignition coil

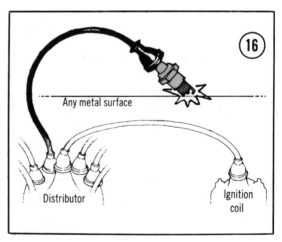

⑯ Any metal surface   Distributor   Ignition coil

Some tests of the ignition system require running the engine with a spark plug or ignition coil wire disconnected. The safest way to do this is to disconnect the wire with the engine stopped, then prop the end of the wire next to a metal surface as shown in **Figures 15 and 16**.

WARNING
Never disconnect a spark plug or ignition coil wire while the engine is running. The high voltage in an ignition system, particularly the newer high-

energy electronic ignition systems could cause serious injury or even death.

Spark plug condition is an important indication of engine performance. Spark plugs in a properly operating engine will have slightly pitted electrodes, and a light tan insulator tip. **Figure 17** shows a normal plug, and a number of others which indicate trouble in their respective cylinders.

2

NORMAL
- Appearance — Firing tip has deposits of light gray to light tan.
- Can be cleaned, regapped and reused.

CARBON FOULED
- Appearance — Dull, dry black with fluffy carbon deposits on the insulator tip, electrode and exposed shell.
- Caused by — Fuel/air mixture too rich, plug heat range too cold, weak ignition system, dirty air cleaner, faulty automatic choke or excessive idling.
- Can be cleaned, regapped and reused.

OIL FOULED
- Appearance — Wet black deposits on insulator and exposed shell.
- Caused by — Excessive oil entering the combustion chamber through worn rings, pistons, valve guides or bearings.
- Replace with new plugs (use a hotter plug if engine is not repaired).

LEAD FOULED
- Appearance — Yellow insulator deposits (may sometimes be dark gray, black or tan in color) on the insulation tip.
- Caused by — Highly leaded gasoline.
- Replace with new plugs.

LEAD FOULED
- Appearance — Yellow glazed deposits indicating melted lead deposits due to hard acceleration.
- Caused by — Highly leaded gasoline.
- Replace with new plugs.

OIL AND LEAD FOULED
- Appearance — Glazed yellow deposits with a slight brownish tint on the insulator tip and ground electrode.
- Replace with new plugs.

FUEL ADDITIVE RESIDUE
- Appearance — Brown colored hardened ash deposits on the insulator tip and ground electrode.
- Caused by — Fuel and/or oil additives.
- Replace with new plugs.

WORN
- Appearance — Severly worn or eroded electrodes.
- Caused by — Normal wear or unusual oil and/or fuel additives.
- Replace with new plugs.

PREIGNITION
- Appearance — Melted ground electrode.
- Caused by — Overadvanced ignition timing, inoperative ignition advance mechanism, too low of a fuel octane rating, lean fuel/air mixture or carbon deposits in combustion chamber.

PREIGNITION
- Appearance — Melted center electrode.
- Caused by — Abnormal combustion due to overadvanced ignition timing or incorrect advance, too low of a fuel octane rating, lean fuel/air mixture, or carbon deposits in combustion chamber.

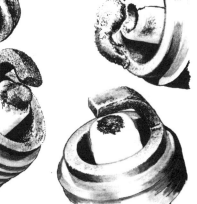

INCORRECT HEAT RANGE
- Appearance — Melted center electrode and white blistered insulator tip.
- Caused by — Incorrect plug heat range selection.
- Replace with new plugs.

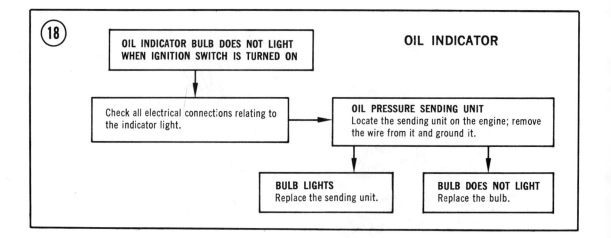

ENGINE OIL PRESSURE LIGHT

Proper oil pressure to the engine is vital. If oil pressure is insufficient, the engine can destroy itself in a comparatively short time.

The oil pressure warning circuit monitors oil pressure constantly. If pressure drops below a predetermined level, the light comes on.

Obviously, it is vital for the warning circuit to be working to signal low oil pressure. Each time you turn on the ignition, but before you start the car, the warning light should come on. If it doesn't, there is trouble in the warning circuit, not the oil pressure system. See **Figure 18** to troubleshoot the warning circuit.

Once the engine is running, the warning light should stay off. If the warning light comes on or acts erratically while the engine is running there is trouble with the engine oil pressure system. *Stop the engine immediately*. Refer to **Figure 19** for possible causes of the problem.

FUEL SYSTEM (CARBURETTED)

Fuel system problems must be isolated to the fuel pump (mechanical or electric), fuel lines, fuel filter, or carburetor. These procedures assume the ignition system is working properly and is correctly adjusted.

1. *Engine will not start* — First make sure that fuel is being delivered to the carburetor. Remove the air cleaner, look into the carburetor throat, and operate the accelerator

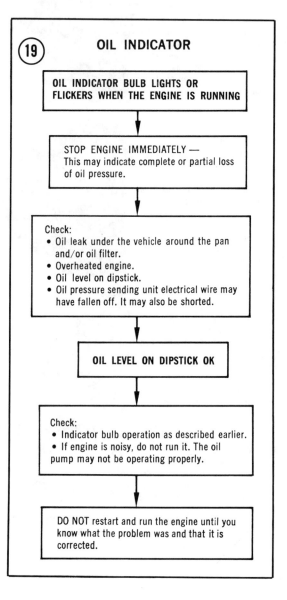

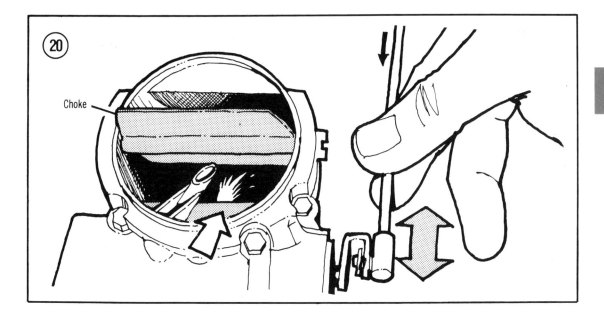

Choke

linkage several times. There should be a stream of fuel from the accelerator pump discharge tube each time the accelerator linkage is depressed (**Figure 20**). If not, check fuel pump delivery (described later), float valve, and float adjustment. If the engine will not start, check the automatic choke parts for sticking or damage. If necessary, rebuild or replace the carburetor.

2. *Engine runs at fast idle* — Check the choke setting. Check the idle speed, idle mixture, and decel valve (if equipped) adjustment.

3. *Rough idle or engine miss with frequent stalling* — Check idle mixture and idle speed adjustments.

4. *Engine "diesels" (continues to run) when ignition is switched off* — Check idle mixture (probably too rich), ignition timing, and idle speed (probably too fast). Check the throttle solenoid (if equipped) for proper operation. Check for overheated engine.

5. *Stumbling when accelerating from idle* — Check the idle speed and mixture adjustments. Check the accelerator pump.

6. *Engine misses at high speed or lacks power* — This indicates possible fuel starvation. Check fuel pump pressure and capacity as described in this chapter. Check float needle valves. Check for a clogged fuel filter or air cleaner.

7. *Black exhaust smoke* — This indicates a badly overrich mixture. Check idle mixture and idle speed adjustment. Check choke setting. Check for excessive fuel pump pressure, leaky floats, or worn needle valves.

8. *Excessive fuel consumption* — Check for overrich mixture. Make sure choke mechanism works properly. Check idle mixture and idle speed. Check for excessive fuel pump pressure, leaky floats, or worn float needle valves.

FUEL SYSTEM (FUEL INJECTED)

Troubleshooting a fuel injection system requires more thought, experience, and know-how than any other part of the vehicle. A logical approach and proper test equipment are essential in order to successfully find and fix these troubles.

It is best to leave fuel injection troubles to your dealer. In order to isolate a problem to the injection system make sure that the fuel pump is operating properly. Check its performance as described later in this section. Also make sure that fuel filter and air cleaner are not clogged.

FUEL PUMP TEST (MECHANICAL AND ELECTRIC)

1. Disconnect the fuel inlet line where it enters the carburetor or fuel injection system.

2. Fit a rubber hose over the fuel line so fuel can be directed into a graduated container with about one quart capacity. See **Figure 21**.

3. To avoid accidental starting of the engine, disconnect the secondary coil wire from the coil or disconnect and insulate the coil primary wire.

4. Crank the engine for about 30 seconds.

5. If the fuel pump supplies the specified amount (refer to the fuel chapter later in this book), the trouble may be in the carburetor or fuel injection system. The fuel injection system should be tested by your dealer.

6. If there is no fuel present or the pump cannot supply the specified amount, either the fuel pump is defective or there is an obstruction in the fuel line. Replace the fuel pump and/or inspect the fuel lines for air leaks or obstructions.

7. Also pressure test the fuel pump by installing a T-fitting in the fuel line between the fuel pump and the carburetor. Connect a fuel pressure gauge to the fitting with a short tube (**Figure 22**).

8. Reconnect the coil wire, start the engine, and record the pressure. Refer to the fuel chapter later in this book for the correct pressure. If the pressure varies from that specified, the pump should be replaced.

9. Stop the engine. The pressure should drop off very slowly. If it drops off rapidly, the outlet valve in the pump is leaking and the pump should be replaced.

EMISSION CONTROL SYSTEMS

Major emission control systems used on nearly all U.S. models include the following:

a. Positive crankcase ventilation (PCV)
b. Thermostatic air cleaner
c. Air injection reaction (AIR)
d. Fuel evaporation control
e. Exhaust gas recirculation (EGR)

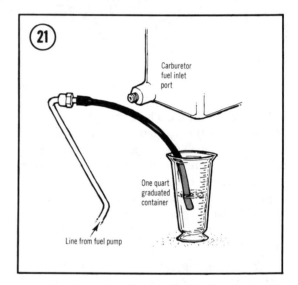

Carburetor fuel inlet port
One quart graduated container
Line from fuel pump

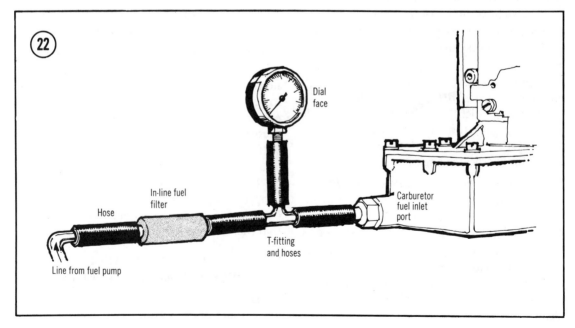

Dial face
In-line fuel filter
Hose
Carburetor fuel inlet port
T-fitting and hoses
Line from fuel pump

Emission control systems vary considerably from model to model. Individual models contain variations of the four systems described here. In addition, they may include other special systems. Use the index to find specific emission control components in other chapters.

Many of the systems and components are factory set and sealed. Without special expensive test equipment, it is impossible to adjust the systems to meet state and federal requirements.

Troubleshooting can also be difficult without special equipment. The procedures described below will help you find emission control parts which have failed, but repairs may have to be entrusted to a dealer or other properly equipped repair shop.

With the proper equipment, you can test the carbon monoxide and hydrocarbon levels.

Figure 23 provides some sources of trouble if the readings are not correct.

Positive Crankcase Ventilation

Fresh air drawn from the air cleaner housing scavenges emissions (e.g., piston blow-by) from the crankcase, then the intake manifold vacuum draws emissions into the intake manifold. They can then be reburned in the normal combustion process. **Figure 24** shows a typical system. **Figure 25** provides a testing procedure.

Thermostatic Air Cleaner

The thermostatically controlled air cleaner maintains incoming air to the engine at a predetermined level, usually about 100°F or higher. It mixes cold air with heated air from the exhaust manifold region. The air cleaner in-

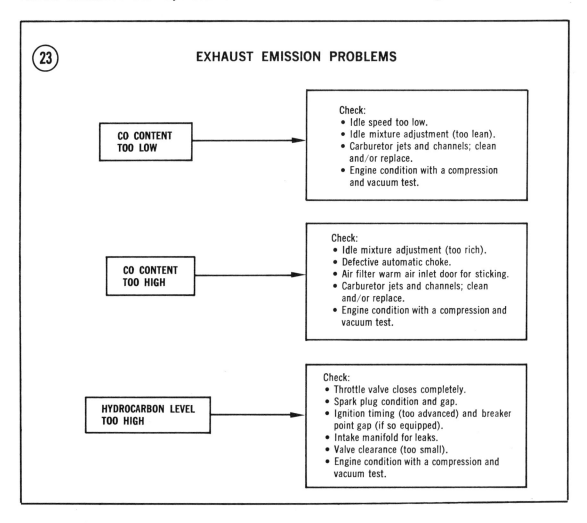

(23) **EXHAUST EMISSION PROBLEMS**

CO CONTENT TOO LOW →
Check:
- Idle speed too low.
- Idle mixture adjustment (too lean).
- Carburetor jets and channels; clean and/or replace.
- Engine condition with a compression and vacuum test.

CO CONTENT TOO HIGH →
Check:
- Idle mixture adjustment (too rich).
- Defective automatic choke.
- Air filter warm air inlet door for sticking.
- Carburetor jets and channels; clean and/or replace.
- Engine condition with a compression and vacuum test.

HYDROCARBON LEVEL TOO HIGH →
Check:
- Throttle valve closes completely.
- Spark plug condition and gap.
- Ignition timing (too advanced) and breaker point gap (if so equipped).
- Intake manifold for leaks.
- Valve clearance (too small).
- Engine condition with a compression and vacuum test.

cludes a temperature sensor, vacuum motor, and a hinged door. See **Figure 26**.

The system is comparatively easy to test. See **Figure 27** for the procedure.

Air Injection Reaction System

The air injection reaction system reduces air pollution by oxidizing hydrocarbons and carbon monoxide as they leave the combustion chamber. See **Figure 28**.

The air injection pump, driven by the engine, compresses filtered air and injects it at the exhaust port of each cylinder. The fresh air mixes with the unburned gases in the exhaust and promotes further burning. A check valve prevents exhaust gases from entering and damaging the air pump if the pump becomes inoperative, e.g., from a fan belt failure.

Figure 29 explains the testing procedure for this system.

Fuel Evaporation Control

Fuel vapor from the fuel tank passes through the liquid/vapor separator to the carbon canister. See **Figure 30**. The carbon absorbs and

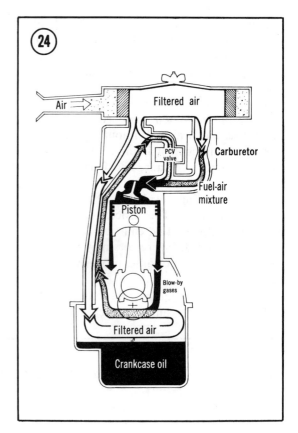

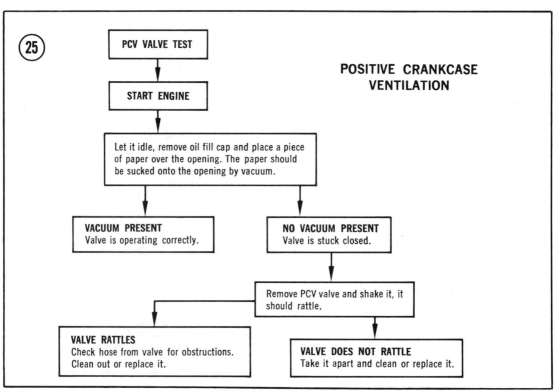

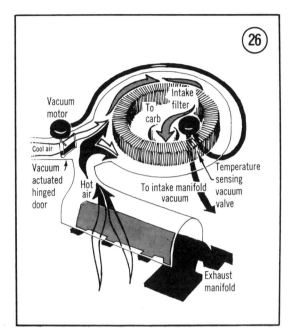

(26)

Vacuum motor

Intake filter

To carb

Cool air

Vacuum actuated hinged door

Hot air

To intake manifold vacuum

Temperature sensing vacuum valve

Exhaust manifold

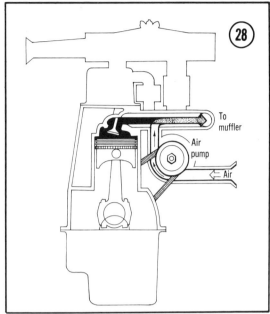

(28)

To muffler

Air pump

Air

2

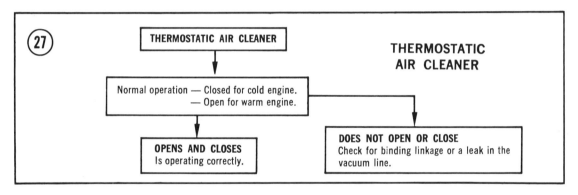

(27)

THERMOSTATIC AIR CLEANER

Normal operation — Closed for cold engine.
— Open for warm engine.

OPENS AND CLOSES
Is operating correctly.

DOES NOT OPEN OR CLOSE
Check for binding linkage or a leak in the vacuum line.

THERMOSTATIC AIR CLEANER

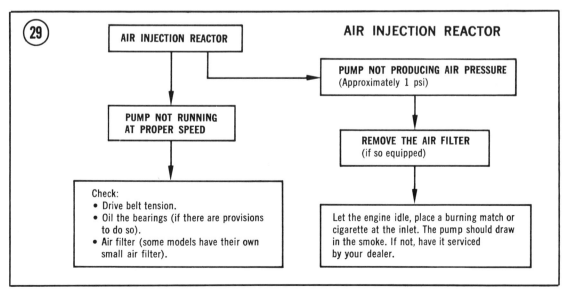

(29)

AIR INJECTION REACTOR

AIR INJECTION REACTOR

PUMP NOT PRODUCING AIR PRESSURE
(Approximately 1 psi)

PUMP NOT RUNNING AT PROPER SPEED

REMOVE THE AIR FILTER
(if so equipped)

Check:
• Drive belt tension.
• Oil the bearings (if there are provisions to do so).
• Air filter (some models have their own small air filter).

Let the engine idle, place a burning match or cigarette at the inlet. The pump should draw in the smoke. If not, have it serviced by your dealer.

stores the vapor when the engine is stopped. When the engine runs, manifold vacuum draws the vapor from the canister. Instead of being released into the atmosphere, the fuel vapor takes part in the normal combustion process.

Exhaust Gas Recirculation

The exhaust gas recirculation (EGR) system is used to reduce the emission of nitrogen oxides (NOx). Relatively inert exhaust gases are introduced into the combustion process to slightly reduce peak temperatures. This reduction in temperature reduces the formation of NOx.

Figure 31 provides a simple test of this system.

ENGINE NOISES

Often the first evidence of an internal engine trouble is a strange noise. That knocking, clicking, or tapping which you never heard before may be warning you of impending trouble.

While engine noises can indicate problems, they are sometimes difficult to interpret correctly; inexperienced mechanics can be seriously misled by them.

Professional mechanics often use a special stethoscope which looks similar to a doctor's stethoscope for isolating engine noises. You can do nearly as well with a "sounding stick" which can be an ordinary piece of doweling or a section of small hose. By placing one end in contact with the area to which you want to listen and the other end near your ear, you can hear

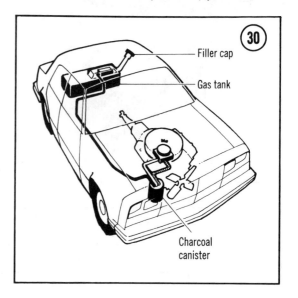

30

— Filler cap

— Gas tank

Charcoal canister

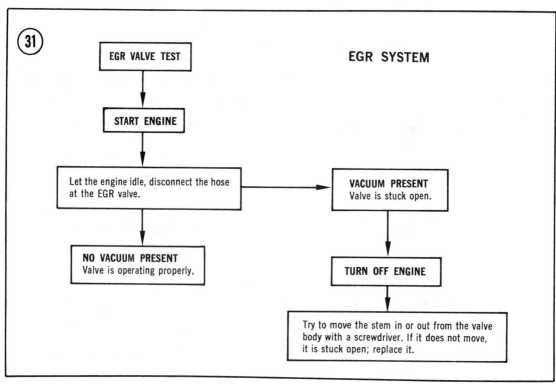

31

EGR VALVE TEST

EGR SYSTEM

START ENGINE

Let the engine idle, disconnect the hose at the EGR valve.

VACUUM PRESENT
Valve is stuck open.

NO VACUUM PRESENT
Valve is operating properly.

TURN OFF ENGINE

Try to move the stem in or out from the valve body with a screwdriver. If it does not move, it is stuck open; replace it.

sounds emanating from that area. The first time you do this, you may be horrified at the strange noises coming from even a normal engine. If you can, have an experienced friend or mechanic help you sort the noises out.

Clicking or Tapping Noises

Clicking or tapping noises usually come from the valve train, and indicate excessive valve clearance.

If your vehicle has adjustable valves, the procedure for adjusting the valve clearance is explained in Chapter Three. If your vehicle has hydraulic lifters, the clearance may not be adjustable. The noise may be coming from a collapsed lifter. These may be cleaned or replaced as described in the engine chapter.

A sticking valve may also sound like a valve with excessive clearance. In addition, excessive wear in valve train components can cause similar engine noises.

Knocking Noises

A heavy, dull knocking is usually caused by a worn main bearing. The noise is loudest when the engine is working hard, i.e., accelerating hard at low speed. You may be able to isolate the trouble to a single bearing by disconnecting

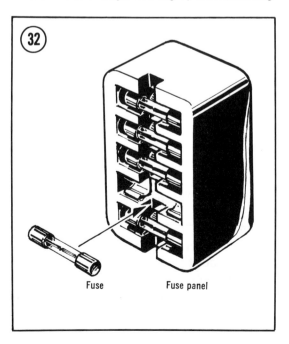

③②

Fuse   Fuse panel

the spark plugs one at a time. When you reach the spark plug nearest the bearing, the knock will be reduced or disappear.

Worn connecting rod bearings may also produce a knock, but the sound is usually more "metallic." As with a main bearing, the noise is worse when accelerating. It may even increase further just as you go from accelerating to coasting. Disconnecting spark plugs will help isolate this knock as well.

A double knock or clicking usually indicates a worn piston pin. Disconnecting spark plugs will isolate this to a particular piston, however, the noise will *increase* when you reach the affected piston.

A loose flywheel and excessive crankshaft end play also produce knocking noises. While similar to main bearing noises, these are usually intermittent, not constant, and they do not change when spark plugs are disconnected.

Some mechanics confuse piston pin noise with piston slap. The double knock will distinguish the piston pin noise. Piston slap is identified by the fact that it is always louder when the engine is cold.

ELECTRICAL ACCESSORIES

Lights and Switches (Interior and Exterior)

1. *Bulb does not light* — Remove the bulb and check for a broken element. Also check the inside of the socket; make sure the contacts are clean and free of corrosion. If the bulb and socket are OK, check to see if a fuse has blown or a circuit breaker has tripped. The fuse panel (**Figure 32**) is usually located under the instrument panel. Replace the blown fuse or reset the circuit breaker. If the fuse blows or the breaker trips again, there is a short in that circuit. Check that circuit all the way to the battery. Look for worn wire insulation or burned wires.

If all the above are all right, check the switch controlling the bulb for continuity with an ohmmeter at the switch terminals. Check the switch contact terminals for loose or dirty electrical connections.

2. *Headlights work but will not switch from either high or low beam* — Check the beam selector switch for continuity with an ohmmeter

at the switch terminals. Check the switch contact terminals for loose or dirty electrical connections.

3. *Brake light switch inoperative* — On mechanically operated switches, usually mounted near the brake pedal arm, adjust the switch to achieve correct mechanical operation. Check the switch for continuity with an ohmmeter at the switch terminals. Check the switch contact terminals for loose or dirty electrical connections.

4. *Back-up lights do not operate* — Check light bulb as described earlier. Locate the switch, normally located near the shift lever. Adjust switch to achieve correct mechanical operation. Check the switch for continuity with an ohmmeter at the switch terminals. Bypass the switch with a jumper wire; if the lights work, replace the switch.

Directional Signals

1. *Directional signals do not operate* — If the indicator light on the instrument panel burns steadily instead of flashing, this usually indicates that one of the exterior lights is burned out. Check all lamps that normally flash. If all are all right, the flasher unit may be defective. Replace it with a good one.

2. *Directional signal indicator light on instrument panel does not light up* — Check the light bulbs as described earlier. Check all electrical connections and check the flasher unit.

3. *Directional signals will not self-cancel* — Check the self-cancelling mechanism located inside the steering column.

4. *Directional signals flash slowly* — Check the condition of the battery and the alternator (or generator) drive belt tension (**Figure 4**). Check the flasher unit and all related electrical connections.

Windshield Wipers

1. *Wipers do not operate* — Check for a blown fuse or circuit breaker that has tripped; replace or reset. Check all related terminals for loose or dirty electrical connections. Check continuity of the control switch with an ohmmeter at the switch terminals. Check the linkage and arms

for loose, broken, or binding parts. Straighten out or replace where necessary.

2. *Wiper motor hums but will not operate* — The motor may be shorted out internally; check and/or replace the motor. Also check for broken or binding linkage and arms.

3. *Wiper arms will not return to the stowed position when turned off* — The motor has a special internal switch for this purpose. Have it inspected by your dealer. Do not attempt this yourself.

Interior Heater

1. *Heater fan does not operate* — Check for a blown fuse or circuit breaker that has tripped. Check the switch for continuity with an ohmmeter at the switch terminals. Check the switch contact terminals for loose or dirty electrical connections.

2. *Heat output is insufficient* — Check the heater hose/engine coolant control valve usually located in the engine compartment; make sure it is in the open position. Ensure that the heater door(s) and cable(s) are operating correctly and are in the open position. Inspect the heat ducts; make sure that they are not crimped or blocked.

COOLING SYSTEM

The temperature gauge or warning light usually signals cooling system troubles before there is any damage. As long as you stop the vehicle at the first indication of trouble, serious damage is unlikely.

In most cases, the trouble will be obvious as soon as you open the hood. If there is coolant or steam leaking, look for a defective radiator, radiator hose, or heater hose. If there is no evidence of leakage, make sure that the fan belt is in good condition. If the trouble is not obvious, refer to **Figures 33 and 34** to help isolate the trouble.

Automotive cooling systems operate under pressure to permit higher operating temperatures without boil-over. The system should be checked periodically to make sure it can withstand normal pressure. **Figure 35** shows the equipment which nearly any service station has for testing the system pressure.

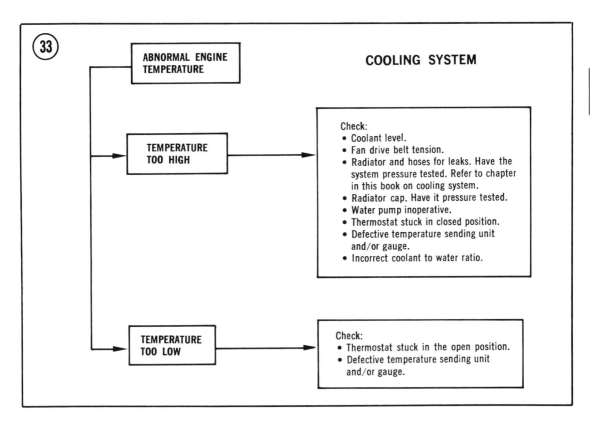

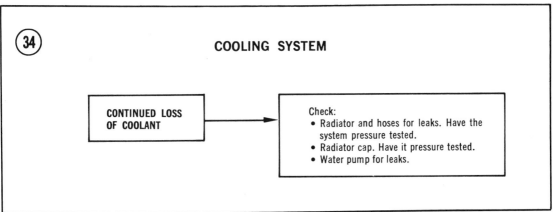

CLUTCH

All clutch troubles except adjustments require transmission removal to identify and cure the problem.

1. *Slippage* — This is most noticeable when accelerating in a high gear at relatively low speed. To check slippage, park the vehicle on a level surface with the handbrake set. Shift to 2nd gear and release the clutch as if driving off. If the clutch is good, the engine will slow and stall. If the clutch slips, continued engine speed will give it away.

Slippage results from insufficient clutch pedal free play, oil or grease on the clutch disc, worn pressure plate, or weak springs.

2. *Drag or failure to release* — This trouble usually causes difficult shifting and gear clash, especially when downshifting. The cause may be excessive clutch pedal free play, warped or bent pressure plate or clutch disc, broken or

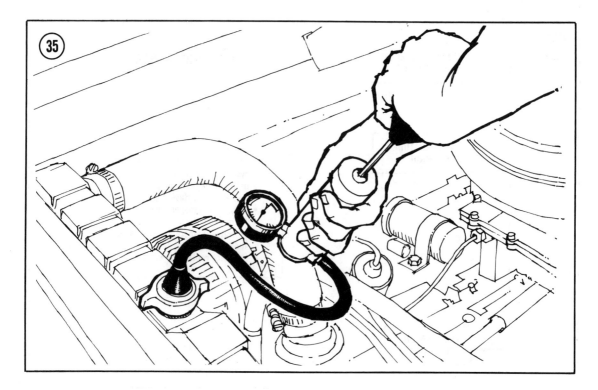

(35)

loose linings, or lack of lubrication in pilot bearing. Also check condition of transmission main shaft splines.

3. *Chatter or grabbing* — A number of things can cause this trouble. Check tightness of engine mounts and engine-to-transmission mounting bolts. Check for worn or misaligned pressure plate and misaligned release plate.

4. *Other noises* — Noise usually indicates a dry or defective release or pilot bearing. Check the bearings and replace if necessary. Also check all parts for misalignment and uneven wear.

MANUAL TRANSMISSION/TRANSAXLE

Transmission and transaxle troubles are evident when one or more of the following symptoms appear:

   a. Difficulty changing gears

   b. Gears clash when downshifting

   c. Slipping out of gear

   d. Excessive noise in NEUTRAL

   e. Excessive noise in gear

   f. Oil leaks

Transmission and transaxle repairs are not recommended unless the many special tools required are available.

Transmission and transaxle troubles are sometimes difficult to distinguish from clutch troubles. Eliminate the clutch as a source of trouble before installing a new or rebuilt transmission or transaxle.

AUTOMATIC TRANSMISSION

Most automatic transmission repairs require considerable specialized knowledge and tools. It is impractical for the home mechanic to invest in the tools, since they cost more than a properly rebuilt transmission.

Check fluid level and condition frequently to help prevent future problems. If the fluid is orange or black in color or smells like varnish, it is an indication of some type of damage or failure within the transmission. Have the transmission serviced by your dealer or competent automatic transmission service facility.

BRAKES

Good brakes are vital to the safe operation of the vehicle. Performing the maintenance speci-

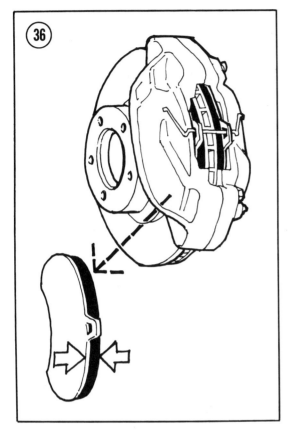

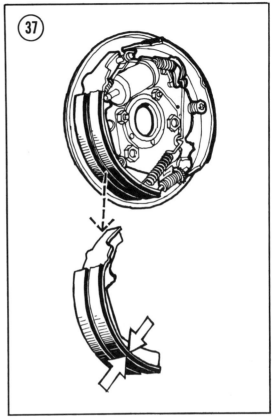

fied in Chapter Three will minimize problems with the brakes. Most importantly, check and maintain the level of fluid in the master cylinder, and check the thickness of the linings on the disc brake pads **(Figure 36)** or drum brake shoes **(Figure 37)**.

If trouble develops, **Figures 38 through 40** will help you locate the problem. Refer to the brake chapter for actual repair procedures.

STEERING AND SUSPENSION

Trouble in the suspension or steering is evident when the following occur:

a. Steering is hard
b. Car pulls to one side
c. Car wanders or front wheels wobble
d. Steering has excessive play
e. Tire wear is abnormal

Unusual steering, pulling, or wandering is usually caused by bent or otherwise misaligned suspension parts. This is difficult to check without proper alignment equipment. Refer to the suspension chapter in this book for repairs that you can perform and those that must be left to a dealer or suspension specialist.

If your trouble seems to be excessive play, check wheel bearing adjustment first. This is the most frequent cause. Then check ball-joints (refer to Suspension chapter). Finally, check tie rod end ball-joints by shaking each tie rod. Also check steering gear, or rack-and-pinion assembly to see that it is securely bolted down.

TIRE WEAR ANALYSIS

Abnormal tire wear should be analyzed to determine its causes. The most common causes are the following:

a. Incorrect tire pressure
b. Improper driving
c. Overloading
d. Bad road surfaces
e. Incorrect wheel alignment

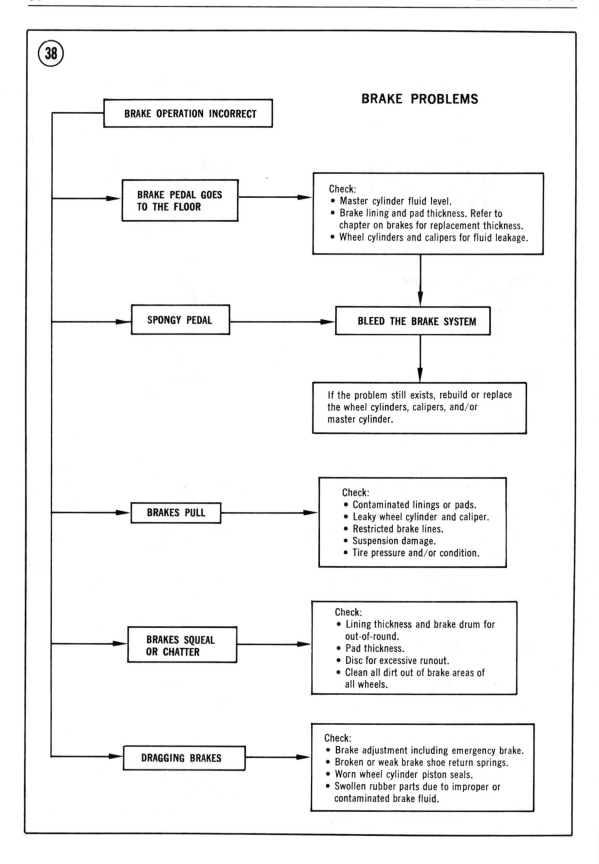

BRAKE PROBLEMS

(38)

- **BRAKE OPERATION INCORRECT**

- **BRAKE PEDAL GOES TO THE FLOOR** →

  Check:
  - Master cylinder fluid level.
  - Brake lining and pad thickness. Refer to chapter on brakes for replacement thickness.
  - Wheel cylinders and calipers for fluid leakage.

- **SPONGY PEDAL** → **BLEED THE BRAKE SYSTEM**

  If the problem still exists, rebuild or replace the wheel cylinders, calipers, and/or master cylinder.

- **BRAKES PULL** →

  Check:
  - Contaminated linings or pads.
  - Leaky wheel cylinder and caliper.
  - Restricted brake lines.
  - Suspension damage.
  - Tire pressure and/or condition.

- **BRAKES SQUEAL OR CHATTER** →

  Check:
  - Lining thickness and brake drum for out-of-round.
  - Pad thickness.
  - Disc for excessive runout.
  - Clean all dirt out of brake areas of all wheels.

- **DRAGGING BRAKES** →

  Check:
  - Brake adjustment including emergency brake.
  - Broken or weak brake shoe return springs.
  - Worn wheel cylinder piston seals.
  - Swollen rubber parts due to improper or contaminated brake fluid.

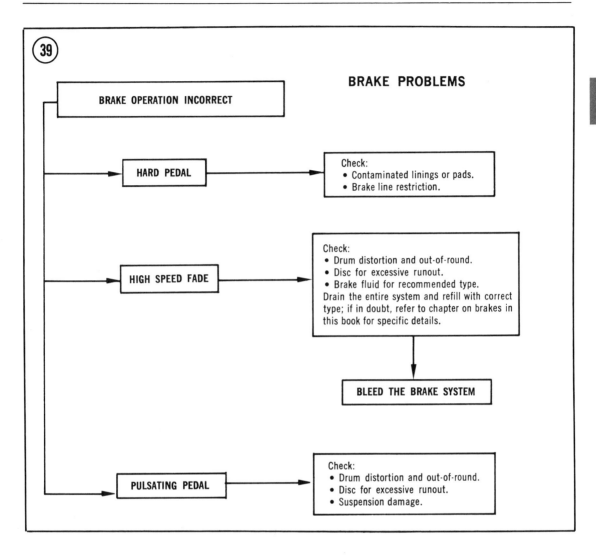

39

BRAKE PROBLEMS

2

BRAKE OPERATION INCORRECT

HARD PEDAL

Check:
• Contaminated linings or pads.
• Brake line restriction.

HIGH SPEED FADE

Check:
• Drum distortion and out-of-round.
• Disc for excessive runout.
• Brake fluid for recommended type.
Drain the entire system and refill with correct type; if in doubt, refer to chapter on brakes in this book for specific details.

BLEED THE BRAKE SYSTEM

PULSATING PEDAL

Check:
• Drum distortion and out-of-round.
• Disc for excessive runout.
• Suspension damage.

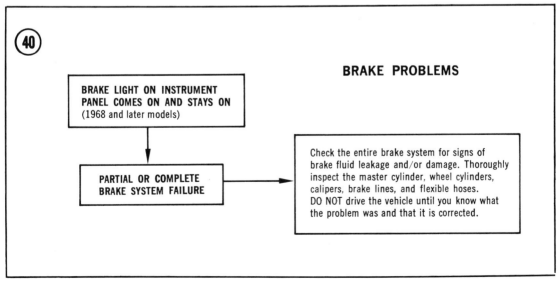

40

BRAKE PROBLEMS

BRAKE LIGHT ON INSTRUMENT PANEL COMES ON AND STAYS ON
(1968 and later models)

PARTIAL OR COMPLETE BRAKE SYSTEM FAILURE

Check the entire brake system for signs of brake fluid leakage and/or damage. Thoroughly inspect the master cylinder, wheel cylinders, calipers, brake lines, and flexible hoses.
DO NOT drive the vehicle until you know what the problem was and that it is corrected.

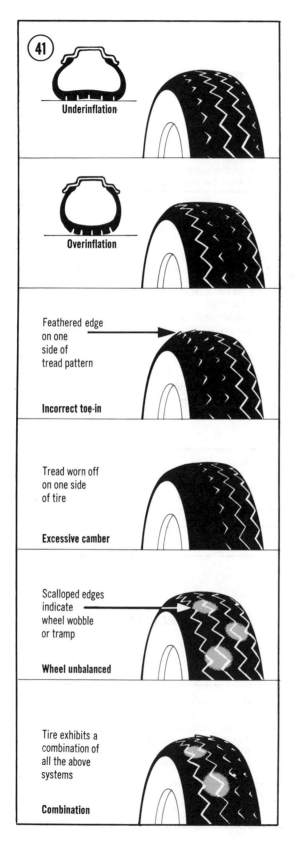

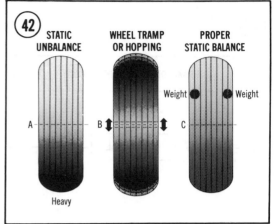

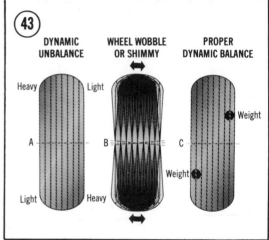

Figure 41 identifies wear patterns and indicates the most probable causes.

WHEEL BALANCING

All four wheels and tires must be in balance along two axes. To be in static balance (**Figure 42**), weight must be evenly distributed around the axis of rotation. (A) shows a statically unbalanced wheel; (B) shows the result — wheel tramp or hopping; (C) shows proper static balance.

To be in dynamic balance (**Figure 43**), the centerline of the weight must coincide with the centerline of the wheel. (A) shows a dynamically unbalanced wheel; (B) shows the result — wheel wobble or shimmy; (C) shows proper dynamic balance.

CHAPTER THREE

3

LUBRICATION, MAINTENANCE AND TUNE-UP

This chapter deals with the maintenance necessary to keep your car running properly. **Table 1** and **Table 2** list maintenance intervals for cars given normal use. Some procedures are done at fuel stops, while others are done at specified intervals of miles or time.

More frequent service is required under the following conditions:

   a. Stop-and-go driving.
   b. Constant high-speed driving.
   c. Severe dust.
   d. Rough or salted roads.
   e. Very hot, very cold or rainy weather.

Some maintenance procedures are included under *Tune-up* at the end of the chapter and detailed instructions will be found there. Other steps are described in various chapters. Chapter references are included with these steps.

FUEL STOP CHECKS

1. With the engine off, pull out the engine oil dipstick. See **Figure 1** (with carburetor) or **Figure 2** (with fuel injection). Wipe the dipstick with a clean rag, insert it and pull it out again. Check oil level. Top up to the "MAX" mark on the dipstick if necessary, using an oil recommended in **Table 3** and **Table 4**. Add oil through the hole in the rocker arm cover (**Figure 1** or **Figure 2**).
2. Check coolant level in the expansion tank (**Figure 3**). It should be about 70 mm (2 3/4 in.) above the "MIN" mark. Top up as needed.

WARNING
The engine should be cold for the next step. The radiator cap should not be

*removed when the engine is warm or hot. If this is unavoidable, cover the cap with a thick rag. Turn it slowly counterclockwise against the first stop (about 1/4 turn). Let **all** pressure (hot water and steam) escape. Then press the cap down and turn counterclockwise to remove. If the cap is removed too soon, a fountain of scalding coolant may shoot out of the radiator and spray all over you.*

3. If the expansion tank is empty, remove the radiator cap. Fill the radiator to the top as shown in **Figure 4**. Since the lack of coolant in the expansion tank may indicate a leak, check the cooling system for leaks. If none are apparent and the cooling system continues to lose coolant, have it pressure tested by a dealer or service station.
4. Check fluid in the windshield washer tank or bag. **Figure 5** shows the tank used on late models. Early models used a fluid bag mounted on the right-hand side of the engine compartment. The tank or bag should be kept full. Use windshield washer solvent, following the manufacturer's instructions.

CAUTION
Do not use radiator antifreeze in the washer container. The runoff may damage the car's paint.

5. Check fluid level in the brake master cylinder (**Figure 6**). Since the reservoir is translucent, this can be done at a glance. Fluid should be up to the

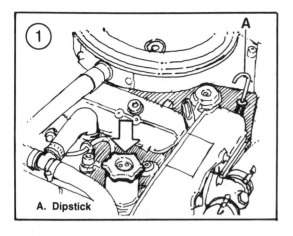

A. Dipstick

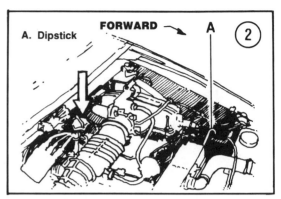

A. Dipstick   FORWARD   A

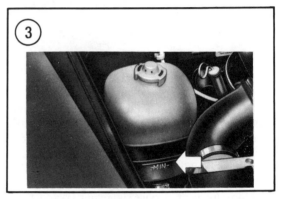

"MAX" line. If low, top up with brake fluid marked DOT 3 or DOT 4.

> *CAUTION*
> *Do not remove the reservoir cap unless topping up fluid. Clean the area around the cap before removal.*

6. Check tire pressures (**Table 5**). This should be done when the tires are cold (after driving less than one mile). When the tires heat up from driving, the air in them expands and gives false high-pressure readings.

SCHEDULED MAINTENANCE

Battery Electrolyte

The battery on 1971-1973 models is located in the engine compartment. On 1974 and later cars the battery is in the trunk.

> *WARNING*
> *During the next step, keep all heat sources (such as lighted cigarettes) away from the battery. Batteries give off explosive hydrogen gas. If the gas ignites, the battery may explode and spray acid.*

1. On 1974 and later models, open the trunk and remove the battery cover.
2. Check the battery terminals (**Figure 7**) for looseness or corrosion. Tighten or clean as needed.
3. Remove the battery filler caps and check electrolyte level. See **Figure 8**. It should be 10-20 mm (1/2-3/4 in.) above the plates inside the battery. Top up with distilled water if necessary. Do not overfill.

Automatic Transmission
Fluid Check

1. Drive the car approximately 6 miles to warm the fluid.

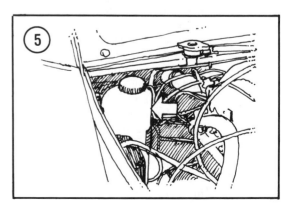

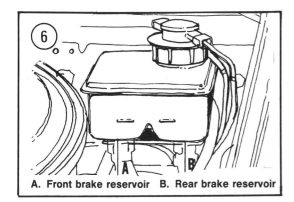

A. Front brake reservoir   B. Rear brake reservoir

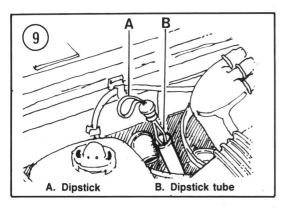

A. Dipstick   B. Dipstick tube

3

2. Park the car on a level surface. With the engine idling, move the lever through the gear positions to PARK.

3. Pull out the dipstick (**Figure 9**). Wipe it clean with a lint-free cloth, reinsert it and pull it out.

4. If fluid level is below the "MAX" mark on the dipstick, add fluid through the dipstick tube. Use DEXRON type automatic transmission fluid. Do not use any other type.

CAUTION
Do not overfill the transmission. Overfilling can cause the fluid to foam, resulting in wear or damage.

Engine Oil and Filter

If the car is given normal use, change the oil when recommended in **Table 1** or **Table 2**. If it is used for stop-and-go driving, in dusty areas, left idling for long periods or used extensively in cold weather, change the oil more often.

Use an oil recommended in **Table 3** and **Table 4**. The rating is printed on top of the can (**Figure 10**).

CAUTION
The oil rating is critical for Turbos. Be sure to use exactly the right type. Do not mix oils of different ratings or brands. Do not use oil additives of any kind in Turbos.

CAUTION
Fully synthetic oils may be used in Turbos. However, the extended oil change intervals recommended by synthetic oil manufacturers must be ignored. The oil and filter must be changed every 3,750 miles or excessive engine and turbocharger wear will result. Also, your warranty may be voided.

To drain the oil and change the filter, you will need:

    a. Drain pan.
    b. Oil can spout or can opener and funnel.
    c. Filter wrench.
    d. Drain plug wrench.
    e. 5 quarts of oil.
    f. Oil filter.

There are several ways to discard the old oil safely. The easiest is to pour it from the drain pan into a gallon bleach or milk bottle. The discarded oil can be taken to a service station for recycling.

1. Warm the engine to operating temperature, then shut it off.

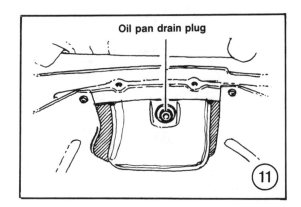

Oil pan drain plug

WARNING
During the next step, move your hand away quickly once the drain plug is loose. Otherwise, hot oil may run down your arm.

2. Put the drain pan under the drain plug (**Figure 11**). Remove the plug and let the oil drain for at least 10 minutes.

3. Unscrew the oil filter (**Figure 12**) counterclockwise. Use a filter wrench (**Figure 13**) if the filter is too tight to remove by hand.

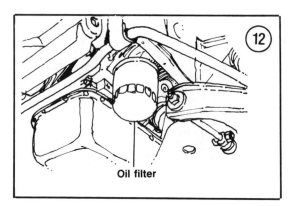

Oil filter

NOTE
The oil filter is larger in diameter than most oil filters. A larger than normal flter wrench may be necessary to remove it.

4. Wipe the gasket surface on the engine block clean with a lint-free cloth.

5. Coat the neoprene gasket on the new filter with clean engine oil. See **Figure 14**.

6. Screw the filter onto the engine *by hand* until the gasket just touches the engine block. At this point, there will be a very slight resistance when turning the filter.

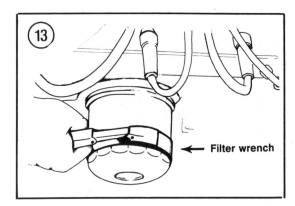

Filter wrench

7. Tighten the filter 1/2 turn more *by hand*. If the filter wrench is used, the filter will probably be overtightened. This will cause an oil leak. In addition, tightening with the filter wrench will make the filter extremely difficult to remove at the next oil change.

8. Install the oil pan drain plug. Tighten it securely.

9. Remove the oil filler cap (**Figure 1** or **Figure 2**).

10. Pour oil into the engine. Capacity is listed in **Table 6**.

11. Start the engine and let it idle. The instrument panel oil pressure light will remain on for 15-30

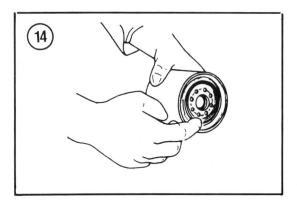

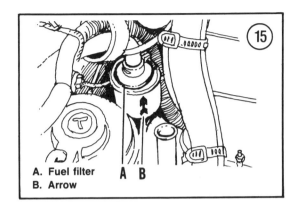

A. Fuel filter
B. Arrow

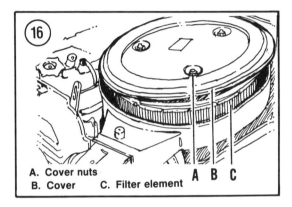

A. Cover nuts
B. Cover   C. Filter element

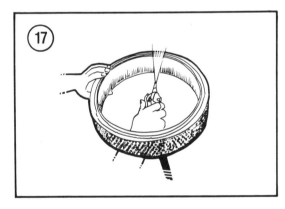

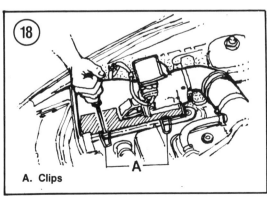

A. Clips

seconds, then go out (or the gauge will indicate zero, then give a reading).

CAUTION
Do not rev the engine to make the oil pressure light go out. It takes time for the oil to reach all areas of the engine and revving it could damage dry parts.

12. While the engine is running, check the drain plug and oil filter for leaks.
13. Turn the engine off. Let the oil settle for several minutes, then check level on the dipstick. Add oil if necessary to bring the level up to the "MAX" mark, but *do not* overfill.

Fuel Filter

This procedure applies to carburetted cars only. Routine fuel filter replacement is not required on fuel injected cars.
1. To replace the fuel filter, disconnect its lines and take it out. See **Figure 15**.
2. Check the fuel filter hoses and clamps for damage or deterioration. Replace as needed.
3. Connect a new filter to the hoses.

NOTE
Fiat filters have an arrow indicating the direction of fuel flow. The arrow must point toward the carburetor. If you buy an aftermarket filter, make sure it has a similar arrow.

**Air Cleaner Filter Element
(Carburetted Cars)**

On 1971-1978 models, replace the element every 12,500 miles. On 1979 and later models, clean and inspect the element every 15,000 miles and replace it every 30,000 miles.
1. Remove the cover nuts and lift off the cover. See **Figure 16**.
2. Lift out the filter element (**Figure 16**).
3. To clean, tap the element on a workbench. If compressed air is available, blow the element out as shown in **Figure 17**.
4. Installation is the reverse of removal.

**Air Cleaner Filter Element
(Fuel Injected Cars)**

The element should be replaced every 30,000 miles under normal conditions. If the car is driven in heavy traffic or in sandy or dusty areas, replace the element every 15,000 miles.
1. Pry back the cover clips. See **Figure 18**.
2. Lift off the air cleaner cover. See **Figure 19**. Take out the filter element and install a new one.
3. Install the cover. Secure the clips by pressing on the curved sections. See **Figure 20**.

Vacuum Hoses

Check all emission control system vacuum hoses for loose connections, cracks or deterioration. Tighten or replace as needed. Refer to Chapter Five for details.

Emission Controls

Inspect the crankcase emission control system, evaporative emission control system and exhaust emission contol system as described in Chapter Five.

Cooling System Hoses and Connections

Check all hoses and their connections as described in Chapter Six.

Turbocharger

Every 15,000 miles, check the exhaust manifold, turbocharger and exhaust pipe fasteners. See **Figure 21**.

Drive Belts

1. Check drive belts for wear or fraying. Replace as needed.
2. Press on each drive belt halfway between pulleys. See **Figures 22-25**. The belts should deflect about 13 mm (1/2 in.) under moderate finger pressure.
3. To adjust the alternator belt, loosen its mounting and adjusting bolts (**Figure 26**). Pull the alternator away from the engine to tighten the belt or push it toward the engine to loosen. Once tension is set correctly, tighten the mounting and adjusting bolts.
4A. *Air pump (with V-belt):* To adjust the air pump belt, loosen its mounting and adjusting bolts. Pull the air pump away from the engine to tighten the belt or push it toward the engine to loosen. Once

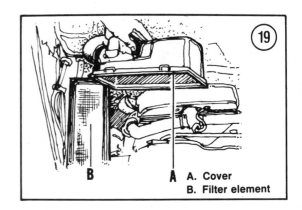

A. Cover
B. Filter element

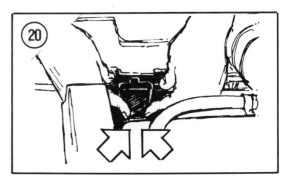

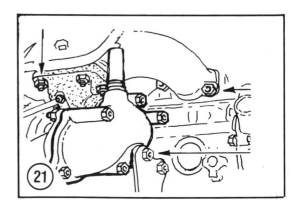

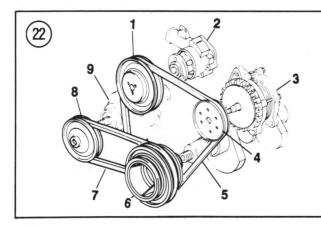

1. Water pump pulley
2. Water pump
3. Alternator
4. Alternator pulley
5. Water pump/alternator belt
6. Crankshaft pulley
7. Air pump belt
8. Air pump pulley
9. Air pump

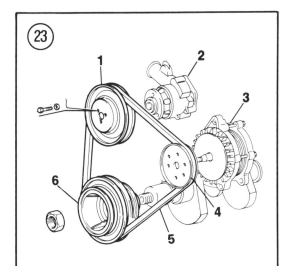

1. Water pump pulley
2. Water pump
3. Alternator
4. Alternator pulley
5. Water pump/alternator belt
6. Crankshaft pulley

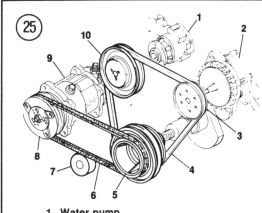

1. Water pump
2. Alternator
3. Alternator pulley
4. Water pump/alternator belt
5. Crankshaft pulley
6. Air conditioning compressor belt
7. Eccentric idler pulley
8. Air conditioning compressor clutch
9. Air conditioning compressor
10. Water pump pulley

3

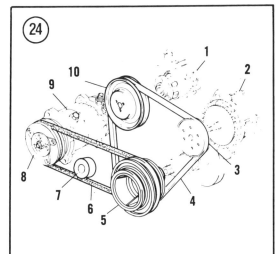

1. Water pump
2. Alternator
3. Alternator pulley
4. Water pump/alternator belt
5. Crankshaft pulley
6. Air conditioning compressor belt
7. Eccentric idler pulley
8. Air conditioning compressor clutch
9. Air conditioning compressor
10. Water pump pulley

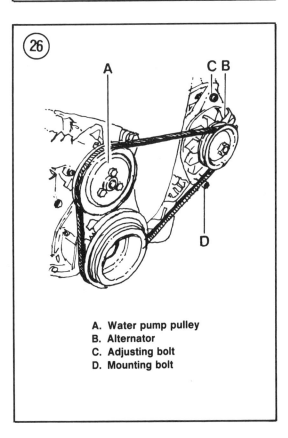

A. Water pump pulley
B. Alternator
C. Adjusting bolt
D. Mounting bolt

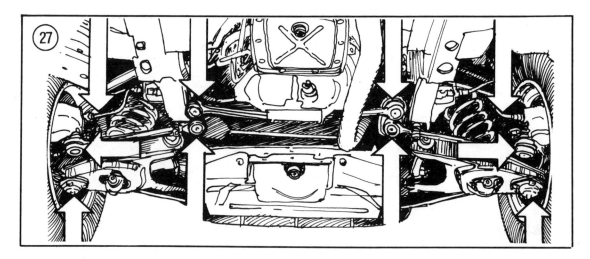

tension is set correctly, tighten the mounting and adjusting bolts.

4B. *Air pump (with cogged belt):* Some early models use a cogged air pump belt driven by the right camshaft, rather than a V-belt. To replace this type of belt, remove the timing belt cover as described in Chapter Four. Loosen the air pump mounting bolts if necessary to provide slack in the belt, slide the belt off and slide the new one on. Tighten the air pump bolts (if loosened), then install the timing belt cover. The belt is not adjustable.

5. To adjust the air conditioner belt on cars without turbochargers, loosen the idler pulley. See **Figure 24**. Rotate the idler pulley down to tighten the bolt, then tighten the idler pulley eccentric bolt.

6. To adjust the air conditioner belt on Turbos, loosen the idler pulley bolt. See **Figure 25**. Rotate the idler pulley upward against the belt to set tension, then tighten the idler pulley bolt.

Clutch Pedal

Check pedal height and adjust if necessary as described in Chapter Eight.

Brakes

1. Referring to Chapter Eleven, check front and rear brake pads for wear.
2. Check for fluid leaks at the calipers and at all brake line connections.
3. Check brake lines for condition.
4. Check handbrake operation and adjust if necessary.

Steering Linkage

At specified intervals, inspect the steering linkage and suspension ball-joints (**Figure 27**). Check for looseness and damaged dust boots.

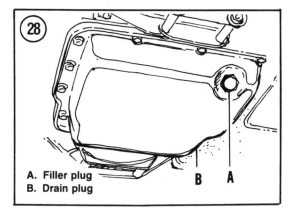

A. Filler plug
B. Drain plug

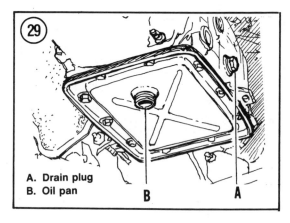

A. Drain plug
B. Oil pan

Replace parts that show these conditions. Replacement procedures are described in Chapter Nine.

Hinges, Latches and Locks

Lightly grease the hood latch and trunk lock with molybdenum disulfide grease. Apply 1-2 drops of oil to hinges on doors, hood and trunk. Lubricate

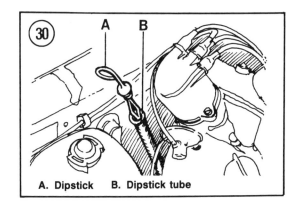

A. Dipstick   B. Dipstick tube

striker plates with a non-staining stick lube such as Door Ease. Lubricate lock tumblers by applying a thin coat of Lubriplate, lock oil or graphite to the key. Insert and work the lock several times. Wipe the key clean.

Timing Belt

Inspect the timing belt at intervals specified in **Table 1** or **Table 2**. Replace as needed. Inspection and replacement are described in Chapter Four.

Carbon Canister

Replace the carbon canister at intervals specified in **Table 1** or **Table 2**. Label the hoses as you disconnect them from the old canister so that they can be properly installed on the new canister.

Manual Transmission Oil Change

1. Drive the car until the engine warms to normal operating temperature. This warms the transmission oil.
2. Park the car on a level surface.
3. Working beneath the car, remove the transmission filler plug (**Figure 28**).

> *WARNING*
> *During the next step, move your hand away quickly once the drain plug is loose. Otherwise hot oil may run down your arm.*

4. Place a pan beneath the transmission drain plug (**Figure 28**), then remove the drain plug.
5. Allow the oil to drain for at least 10 minutes.
6. Reinstall the drain plug.
7. Fill the transmission through the filler plug hole. Use an oil recommended in **Table 3** and **Table 4**. Capacity is approximately 1.6 liters (1 3/4 qt.). Fill to the bottom of the filler plug hole, then install the filler plug.

Automatic Transmission Fluid Change

> *CAUTION*
> *Work in a clean, dust-free area. If you must remove the transmission pan in Step 4, don't let dirt or contamination enter the transmission.*

1. Drive the car until the engine warms to normal operating temperature. This warms the transmission fluid.
2. Park the car on a level surface. Set the handbrake and make sure the car can't roll.

> *WARNING*
> *During the next step, hot fluid may shoot out of the transmission. Move your hand away quickly once the drain plug is removed so hot fluid doesn't run down your arm.*

3. Remove the drain plug (**Figure 29**). Let the fluid drain for at least 10 minutes.
4. Inspect the fluid in the drain pan. If it is dirty, remove the transmission pan and gasket. Detach the filter from the bottom of the transmission and install a new one.
5. Install the pan and gasket (if removed). Install the drain plug and tighten securely.
6. Remove the transmission fluid dipstick (**Figure 30**). Add 2.8 liters (3 qt.) of DEXRON type automatic transmission fluid through the dipstick tube.
7. Check transmission fluid level as described in this chapter. Add or remove fluid to bring the level within the marks on the dipstick.

> *CAUTION*
> *Do not overfill. Overfilling can cause the fluid to foam, resulting in wear or damage.*

Differential Oil Change

1. Drive the car until the engine warms to normal operating temperature. This warms the differential oil so it can drain freely.
2. Place a pan beneath the differential. See **Figure 31** (through early 1978) or **Figure 32** (mid-1978 and later). Remove the filler plug.

> *WARNING*
> *During the next step, hot oil may shoot out of the drain plug hole. Move your hand out of the way quickly once the plug is removed so hot oil doesn't run down your arm.*

3. Remove the drain plug (**Figure 31** or **Figure 32**). Let the oil drain for at least 10 minutes.
4. Install the drain plug and tighten securely.

3

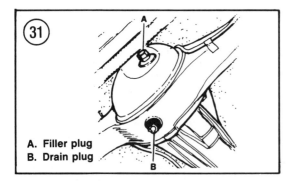

A. Filler plug
B. Drain plug

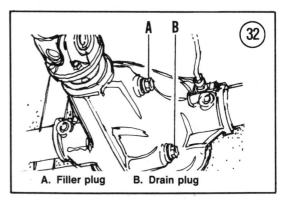

A. Filler plug   B. Drain plug

5. Fill the differential to the bottom of the filler hole with an oil recommended in **Table 3** and **Table 4**. Approximate capacity is 1.3 liters (1 2/5 qt.).

Wheel Bearings

Clean, repack and adjust front wheel bearings as described in Chapter Nine.

Lambda Sensor Replacement

This procedure applies to fuel injected cars only.

WARNING
Allow the exhaust system time to cool before starting this procedure.

1. Unplug the Lambda sensor wiring connector. See **Figure 33**.
2. Unscrew the Lambda sensor from the exhaust manifold. See **Figure 34**.

CAUTION
*During the next step, do not allow anti-seize compound to touch the area shown in **Figure 35**. This would ruin the sensor.*

3. Coat the threads of a new sensor with electrically conductive anti-seize compound in the area shown in **Figure 35**.
4. Install the sensor in the exhaust manifold and tighten to 4.2-5.0 mkg (30-36 ft.-lb.).

Cooling System

Drain, flush and refill the cooling system as described in Chapter Six.

TUNE-UP

Under normal conditions, a tune-up should be done at the intervals specified in **Table 1** or **Table 2**. More frequent tune-ups may be needed if the car is used primarily for stop-and-go driving or left idling for long periods.

Since different engine systems interact, a tune-up should be done in the following order:

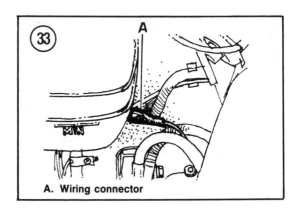

A. Wiring connector

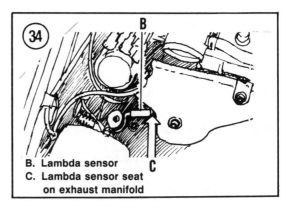

B. Lambda sensor
C. Lambda sensor seat on exhaust manifold

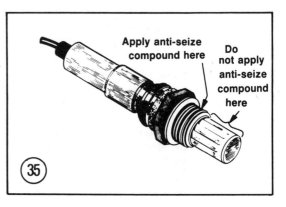

Apply anti-seize compound here

Do not apply anti-seize compound here

a. Compression check.
b. Valve adjustment.
c. Ignition system inspection and adjustment.
d. Fuel system adjustment.

COMPRESSION TEST

Periodic compression testing is not required. Compression should be tested if any of the following conditions exist:.
a. The engine performs poorly.
b. Smoke appears at the tailpipe.

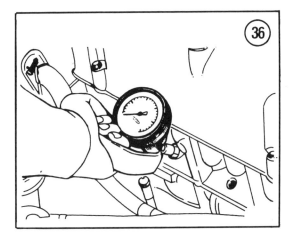

c. Engine oil requires frequent topping up and there is no visible leak.
d. Coolant requires frequent topping up and there is no visible leak.

There are 2 types of compression test; "wet" and "dry." These tests are intepreted together to isolate problems in cylinders and valves. The dry compression test is done first. Test as follows.
1. Warm the engine to normal operating temperature.
2. Remove the spark plugs.
3. Connect the compression tester to one cylinder following manufacturer's instructions. **Figure 36** shows a hand-held compression tester in use. You can also use the screw-in type described in Chapter One.

NOTE
Hand-held compression testers require 2 people, one to hold the compression tester and one to crank the engine. Screw-in compression testers require only one person.

4. Crank the engine over until there is no further increase in compression reading.
5. Remove the tester and write down the reading.
6. Repeat Steps 3-5 for each cylinder. Compare results with **Table 7** in this chapter.

When interpreting the results, actual readings are not as important as the differences in readings. Low readings, although they may be even, are a sign of wear. Low readings in 2 adjacent cylinders may indicate a defective head gasket. If the dry compression test indicates a problem, isolate the cause with a wet compression test. This is done in the same way as the dry compression test, except that about one tablespoon of oil is poured down the spark plug holes before performing Steps 3-6. If the wet compression readings are much geater than the dry readings, the trouble is probably due to worn or broken rings. If there is little difference between wet and dry readings, the trouble is probably due to leaky or sticking valves. If 2 adjacent cylinders are low and the wet and dry readings are close, the head gasket may be damaged.

VALVE ADJUSTMENT

Valve clearances should be checked at each tune-up or when the valves become noisy. Valves are adjusted with the engine cold.

Preparation (Carburetted Engines)

1. Remove the air cleaner.
2. Referring to **Figure 37**, detach the accelerator rod from the carburetor.

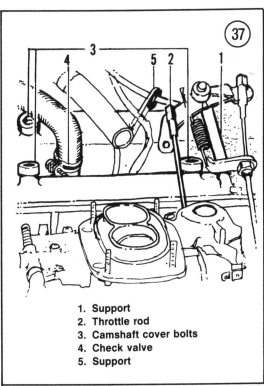

1. Support
2. Throttle rod
3. Camshaft cover bolts
4. Check valve
5. Support

3. If equipped with an air pump, disconnect the hose from the check valve (**Figure 37**).

4. Remove the camshaft cover bolts (**Figure 38**) and take the covers off.

Preparation (Fuel Injected and Turbocharged Engines)

1A. On non-Turbos, loosen the clamps (1, **Figure 39**) and remove the air intake line.

1B. On Turbos, remove the air plenum.

2. Disconnect the line from the auxiliary air regulator, then remove the auxiliary air regulator from the cylinder head.

3. Disconnect the coolant line from the throttle plate heater.

4. Detach the upper half of the intake manifold (9, **Figure 39**). Lift the upper half of the manifold up and back to clear the cam cover.

5. Detach the spark plug wires (11, **Figure 39**) from the bracket.

6. Remove the cam cover bolts and take the covers off.

Adjustment (All Models)

1. Find valve clearance specifications in **Table 7**.

2. Remove the spark plugs. This makes it easier to turn the engine.

CAUTION
*See **Spark Plugs** in this chapter for correct removal procedures.*

3. Turn the engine so that the cam lobe for the valve being checked points upward, at right angles to the valve. See **Figure 40**.

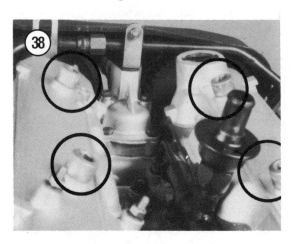

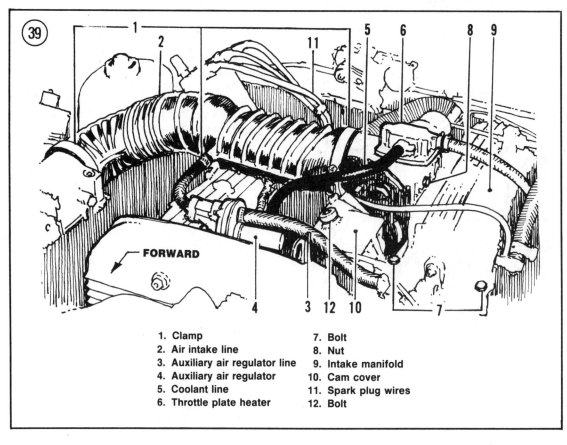

1. Clamp	7. Bolt
2. Air intake line	8. Nut
3. Auxiliary air regulator line	9. Intake manifold
4. Auxiliary air regulator	10. Cam cover
5. Coolant line	11. Spark plug wires
6. Throttle plate heater	12. Bolt

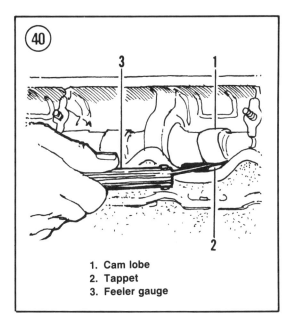

1. Cam lobe
2. Tappet
3. Feeler gauge

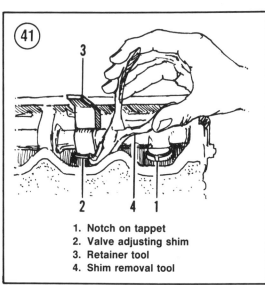

1. Notch on tappet
2. Valve adjusting shim
3. Retainer tool
4. Shim removal tool

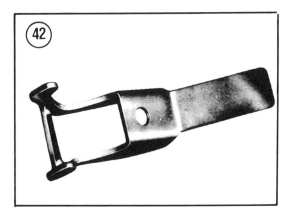

4. Slip a feeler gauge of the specified clearance between cam lobe and tappet. See **Figure 40**. It should fit with a very slight drag:

    a. If the feeler gauge fits as described, the valve clearance is correct. Check clearance on the remaining valves.

    b. If the feeler gauge is too loose or too tight, the valve will need to be adjusted. Perform the following steps.

5. Measure actual clearance between tappet and cam lobe with a feeler gauge. Calculate the difference between this measurement and specified clearance. Write this figure down and call it "A."

6. Compress the valve being adjusted and remove the shim. To do this, turn the engine so the cam lobe compresses the valve. Place a retainer tool (Fiat part No. A.60594; part Kent-Moore No. J28229) between the cam lobe and tappet. **Figure 41** shows the tool in use; **Figure 42** shows it alone. The tool is available at dealers.

7. Turn the engine so the cam lobe is points up. The tappet will be held down by the retainer tool so the shim can be removed.

8. Remove the shim from the top of the tappet. This can be done with a pointed tool and magnet.

9. Measure shim thickness with a micrometer. Write this down and call it "B."

10. Determine the thickness of the new valve adjusting shim as follows:

    a. If valve clearance was too small in Step 5, subtract "A" from "B" to determine the thickness of the new shim.

    b. If valve clearance was too large in Step 5, add "A" to "B" to determine the thickness of the new shim.

11. Select a new shim (**Table 8**). Install the new shim, remove the retainer tool and recheck valve clearance.

12. Once the clearance of all valves is within specifications, reverse the preparation steps.

SPARK PLUGS

Removal

> *CAUTION*
> *When spark plugs are removed, dirt from around the plugs can fall into the spark plug holes. This can cause expensive engine damage.*

1. Blow out any foreign matter from around spark plugs with compressed air. Use a compressor if you have one. Another method is to use a can of compressed inert gas, available from photo stores. If the area around the spark plugs is greasy, clean

the engine with engine cleaner. Let all rinse water evaporate from the engine if engine cleaner is used.
2. Mark spark plug wires with the cylinder numbers so you can reconnect them properly. Wires are numbered 1 through 4, counting from the front of the car.

NOTE
To make labels, wrap a small strip of masking tape around each wire.

3. Disconnect spark plug wires. Pull off by grasping the connector, *not* the wire. See **Figure 43**. Pulling on the wire may break it.

CAUTION
If the boots seem to be stuck, twist them 1/2 turn to break the seal. Do not pull on boots with pliers. The pliers could cut the insulation, causing an electrical short.

4. Remove the plugs with a 13/16 in. spark plug socket. Keep the plugs in order so you know which cylinder they came from.

NOTE
The rear plug (No. 4) may be difficult to remove because it is angled toward the firewall. Use a 3/8-in. drive universal adapter between the spark plug socket and ratchet.

5. Examine each spark plug. Compare its condition with the illustrations in Chapter Two. Spark plug condition indicates engine condition and can warn of developing trouble.
6. Discard the plugs. Although they could be cleaned, regapped and reused if in good condition, they seldom last very long; new plugs are inexpensive and far more reliable.

Gapping and Installaton

New plugs should be carefully gapped to ensure a reliable, consistent spark. Use a special spark plug tool with a wire gauge. See **Figure 44** or **Figure 45**.

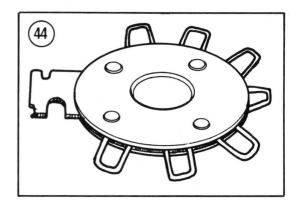

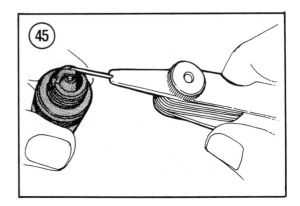

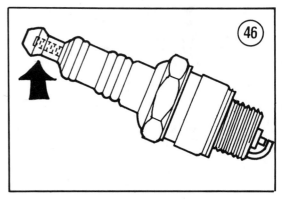

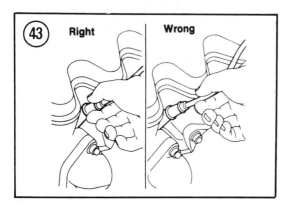

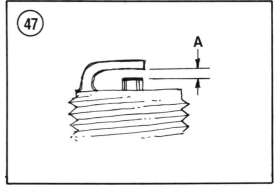

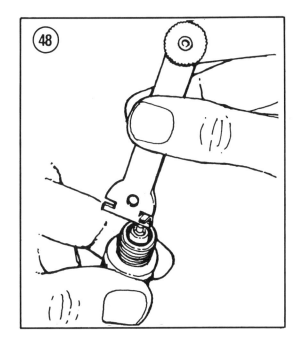

1. Remove the plugs from the boxes. If the plugs have removable end pieces (**Figure 46**), make sure they are screwed on. If not, install them.

2. Find the correct spark plug gap for your car in **Table 7**. Insert the correct diameter wire gauge between the spark plug electrodes. See **Figure 47** and **Figure 45**. If the gap is correct, there will be a slight drag as the wire is pulled through. If there is no drag, or if the wire won't pull through, bend the side electrode with the gapping tool (**Figure 48**) to change the gap.

3. Put a small amount of aluminum anti-seize compound on the first few threads of each spark plug.

4. Crank the starter for about 5 seconds to blow away any dirt around the spark plug holes.

5. Screw each plug in by hand until it seats. Very little effort is required. If force is necessary, the plug is cross-threaded. Unscrew it and try again.

6. Tighten the spark plugs. If you have a torque wrench, tighten to 1.5-2.0 mkg (11-14 ft.-lb.). If not, tighten the plug with fingers, then tighten an additional 1/4-1/2 turn with the plug wrench.

> *CAUTION*
> *Do not overtighten. This prevents the plugs from seating.*

DISTRIBUTOR CAP, WIRES AND ROTOR

> *NOTE*
> *If either the cap or rotor must be replaced, replace them together as a set for peak ignition performance.*

1. Loosen the distributor cap screws and remove the cap.

2. Check the distributor cap terminals for dirt or corrosion. See **Figure 49**. Clean or replace as needed.

3. Replace the wires if the insulation is melted, brittle or cracked.

4. Check the rotor for burns, cracks or wear. Replace it if these conditions can be seen.

5. Install the rotor. Install the distributor cap and reconnect the wires. Be sure they are connected to the right terminals. Spark plugs are numbered from 1 through 4, counting from the front of the car. Distributor cap terminal numbers are molded into the cap.

BREAKER POINTS

The 1971-1974 models use a single set of breaker points. The 1975-1978 cars use 2 sets of points. The main set, or running points, operates when engine temperature is above approximately 15° C (60° F). The secondary set, or starting points, operates when engine temperature is below this figure. The starting points provide an additional 10° of ignition timing advance to improve cold-engine performance.

The 1979 and later cars use a breakerless electronic ignition system. See Chapter Seven for electronic ignition test procedures.

Replacement and Adjustment

1. Remove the distributor cap and rotor.

2. Loosen the points wire screws and remove the points retaining screws. See **Figure 50** (single points) or **Figure 51** (dual points). Lift the points off.

3. Install new points and connect the wires.

4. Loosen the distributor locknut. Turn the distributor body until a cam lobe opens the points to the maximum gap. See **Figure 52**.

5. Measure the gap with a flat feeler gauge and compare with **Table 7**:

   a. If the gap is correct, install the rotor and distributor cap.

   b. If the gap is incorrect, perform the following steps to adjust it.

6. Loosen the points securing screws. Insert a screwdriver in the adjusting slot and twist it to change the gap. When the gap is correct, tighten the points securing screws.

7. Recheck the gap to make sure it didn't change when the securing screws were tightened. Readjust the gap if it did change.

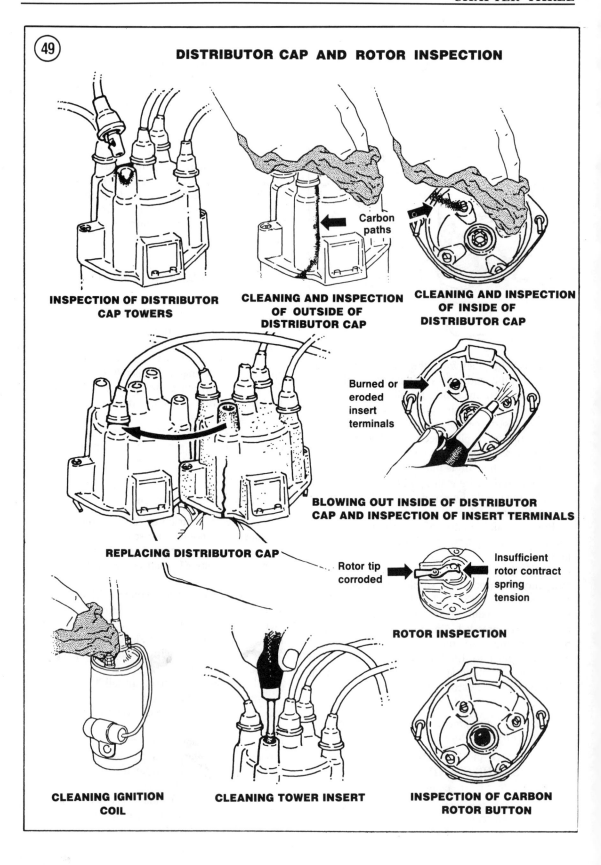

49 DISTRIBUTOR CAP AND ROTOR INSPECTION

INSPECTION OF DISTRIBUTOR
CAP TOWERS

Carbon paths

CLEANING AND INSPECTION
OF OUTSIDE OF
DISTRIBUTOR CAP

CLEANING AND INSPECTION
OF INSIDE OF
DISTRIBUTOR CAP

Burned or
eroded
insert
terminals

BLOWING OUT INSIDE OF DISTRIBUTOR
CAP AND INSPECTION OF INSERT TERMINALS

REPLACING DISTRIBUTOR CAP

Rotor tip
corroded

Insufficient
rotor contract
spring
tension

ROTOR INSPECTION

CLEANING IGNITION
COIL

CLEANING TOWER INSERT

INSPECTION OF CARBON
ROTOR BUTTON

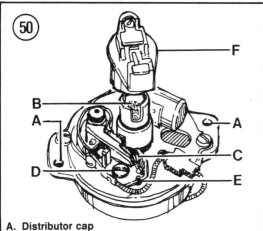

A. Distributor cap
   securing screw holes   D. Points securing screw
B. Distributor oiling wick   E. Points adjusting slot
C. Breaker points   F. Rotor

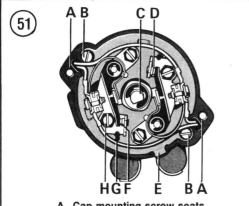

A. Cap mounting screw seats
B. Breaker plate mounting screws
C. Distributor shaft
D. Main breaker points
E. Alignment key
F. Secondary points
G. Screwdriver adjustment slot
H. Adjustment screw

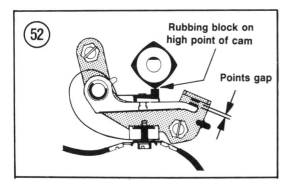

Rubbing block on
high point of cam

Points gap

8. If equipped with dual points, adjust the remaining set as described in Steps 4-7. Note that starting points gap differs from running points gap.

9. Once points gap is set correctly, install the rotor and distributor cap. Ignition timing *must* be checked after the points have been replaced or adjusted.

IGNITION TIMING

Adjustment (1971-1974)

1. Warm the engine to normal operating temperature, then shut it off.

2. Connect a timing light, dwell meter and tune-up tachometer to the engine. Follow the instrument manufacturer's instructions.

3. Start the engine and let it idle. Compare idle speed with **Table 7**. Adjust if necessary as described in this chapter:

4. Check dwell angle and compare with **Table 7**. Since the dwell angle affects ignition timing, the dwell angle must be set correctly. If dwell is incorrect, shut off the engine. Set dwell angle by changing the points gap as described in this chapter.

   a. To increase dwell angle, decrease the points gap.
   b. To decrease dwell angle, increase the points gap.

> *WARNING*
> *During the next step, keep your hands and hair away from all belts and pulleys. Under the timing light, they may appear to be standing still. They are actually spinning at more than 10 times every second and can cause serious injury.*

5. Restart the engine. Point the timing light at the timing marks (**Figure 53**). The notch in the

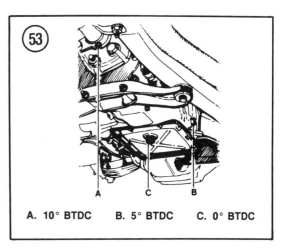

A. 10° BTDC   B. 5° BTDC   C. 0° BTDC

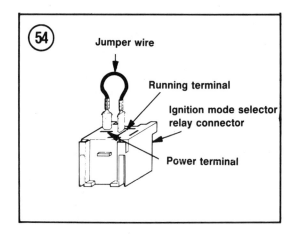

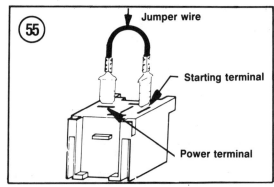

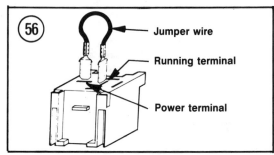

crankshaft pulley should align with the 0 degree (TDC) mark.

> *WARNING*
> *During the next step, do not touch the thick wires running to the distributor cap. This can cause a painful shock, even if the insulation is in perfect condition.*

6. If timing is incorrect, loosen the distributor locknut. Turn the distributor to change timing, then tighten the locknut.

Adjustment (1975-1978)

1. Warm the engine to normal operating temperature, then shut it off.
2. Connect a timing light and tune-up tachometer to the engine. Connect a dwell meter to the running points (green distributor wire). Follow the instrument manufacturer's instructions.
3. Start the engine and let it idle. Compare idle speed with **Table 7**. Adjust if necessary as described in this chapter.
4. Shut off the engine.
5. Locate the ignition mode selector relay on the panel below the glove compartment.
6. Connect a short length of wire between the POWER terminal and RUNNING terminal on the plastic socket. See **Figure 54**.
7. Crank the engine with the starter. Check dwell angle of the running points and compare with **Table 7**. Since the dwell angle affects ignition timing, the dwell angle must be set correctly. If dwell is incorrect, shut off the engine. Set dwell angle by changing the points gap as described in this chapter.
   a. To increase dwell angle, decrease the points gap.
   b. To decrease dwell angle, increase the points gap.

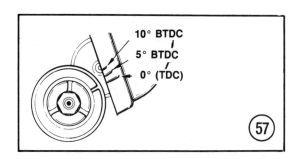

8. Connect the short length of wire between the POWER terminal and STARTING terminal as shown in **Figure 55**.
9. Connect the dwell meter to the starting points (green-black wire). Crank the engine and check dwell. If not within specifications, adjust the starting points gap to change it:
   a. To increase dwell angle, decrease the points gap.
   b. To decrease dwell angle, increase the points gap.
10. Connect the short length of wire between the POWER terminal and RUNNING terminal as shown in **Figure 56**.

> *WARNING*
> *During the next step, keep your hands and hair away from all belts and pulleys. Under the timing light, they may appear to be standing still. They*

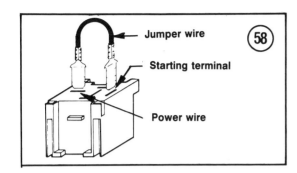

Jumper wire (58)

Starting terminal

Power wire

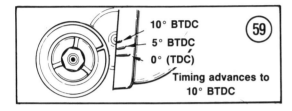

10° BTDC (59)
5° BTDC
0° (TDC)
Timing advances to 10° BTDC

are actually spinning at more than 10 times every second and can cause serious injury.

11. Start the engine. Point the timing light at the timing marks (**Figure 57**). The notch in the crankshaft pulley should align with the 0 degree (TDC) mark.

WARNING
During the next step, do not touch the thick wires running to the distributor cap. This can cause a painful shock, even if the insulation is in perfect condition.

12. If timing is incorrect, loosen the distributor locknut. Turn the distributor to change timing, then tighten the locknut. Shut the engine off.
13. Connect the short length of wire between the POWER terminal and STARTING terminal. See **Figure 58**.

WARNING
During the next step, keep your hands and hair away from all belts and pulleys. Under the timing light, they may appear to be standing still. They are actually spinning at more than 10 times every second and can cause serious injury.

14. Restart the engine. Point the timing light at the timing marks (**Figure 59**). The notch in the crankshaft pulley should align with the 10° BTDC mark.
15. If timing is incorrect in Step 14, adjust it by changing the points gap of the starting points. Do *not* adjust it by turning the distributor.

a. If timing is less than 10° BTDC, increase the starting points gap to decrease dwell.
b. If timing is more than 10° BTDC, decrease the starting points gap to increase dwell.
16. After setting the dwell angle, recheck timing of the starting points. Continue adjusting the starting points' dwell angle until timing is correct.

Adjustment (1979-On)

Under normal conditions, ignition timing should be adjusted every 15,000 miles. If the car is used primarily in stop-and-go traffic or in dusty areas, check timing every 7,500 miles.
1. Warm the engine to normal operating temperature, then shut it off.
2. Connect a timing light and tune-up tachometer to the engine. Follow the instrument manufacturer's instructions.
3. Start the engine and let it idle. Compare idle speed with **Table 7**. Adjust if necessary as described in this chapter.

WARNING
During the next step, keep your hands and hair away from all belts and pulleys. Under the timing light, they may appear to be standing still. They are actually spinning at more than 10 times every second and can cause serious injury.

4. Point the timing light at the timing marks (**Figure 57**). The notch in the crankshaft pulley should align with the 0 degree (TDC) mark.

WARNING
During the next step, do not touch the thick wires running to the distributor cap. This can cause a painful shock, even if the insulation is in perfect condition.

5. If timing is incorrect, loosen the distributor locknut. Turn the distributor to change timing, then tighten the locknut.

CARBURETOR ADJUSTMENTS

Idle speed adjustment on all carburetted models requires only a tachometer and screwdriver. Idle mixture adjustment, however, requires a CO (carbon monoxide) meter on all except 1979-1980 cars. If you don't have a CO meter, have idle mixture adjusted by a dealer or mechanic familiar with Fiat emission controls.

1971-1974

1. Warm the engine to normal operating temperature.

3

2. Connect a tune-up tachometer to the engine, following manufacturer's instructions.

3. Compare idle speed with **Table 7**. Adjust if necessary by turning the idle speed screw (B, **Figure 60**).

4. If a CO meter is available, adjust idle mixture to specifications by turning the mixture screw (A, **Figure 60**).

5. Press the button (**Figure 61**) to energize the fast idle electrovalve. Raise engine speed to about 2,500 rpm, then release the throttle while holding the button down. Engine speed should increase to 1,550-1,650 rpm. If it runs at a different speed, adjust (with the button held down) by turning the fast idle screw (**Figure 60**).

1975-1978

1. Warm the engine to normal operating temperature. Connect a tune-up tachometer to the engine, following manufacturer's instructions.

2A. If equipped with air injection, pinch off the hose between the check valve and T-fitting with locking pliers.

2B. If equipped with air induction, remove the air cleaner cover. Block the air inlet to the reed valves, then reinstall the cover.

3. Let the engine idle. Check idle speed on the tachometer and compare with **Table 7**. Adjust if necessary by turning the idle speed screw (**Figure 62**).

4. If a CO meter is available, check CO percentage in the exhaust gas and compare with **Table 7**. Adjust if necessary by turning the idle mixture screw (**Figure 62**). If a CO meter is not available, have CO percentage checked by a dealer or mechanic familiar with Fiat emission controls.

5. Once idle speed and mixture are set, remove the pliers or plug the reed valve air intake. If equipped with air injection, idle speed will increase by 50 rpm. Do not readjust idle speed.

6. Move the throttle linkage by hand to raise engine speed to 2,500 rpm. Holding the engine at this speed, hold down the button on the fender well (**Figure 63**) and release the throttle linkage. Idle speed should drop to the "fast idle speed" listed in **Table 7**:

    a. If fast idle speed is correct, release the button.

    b. If fast idle speed is incorrect, hold the button down and turn the fast idle screw (**Figure 62**) to adjust fast idle. Once fast idle is set, release the button.

1979-1980 (With CO Meter)

1. Warm the engine to normal operating temperature. Connect a tune-up tachometer to the engine, following manufacturer's instructions.

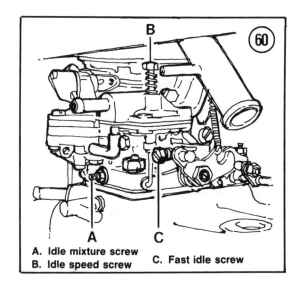

A. Idle mixture screw
B. Idle speed screw
C. Fast idle screw

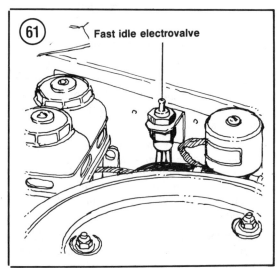

Fast idle electrovalve

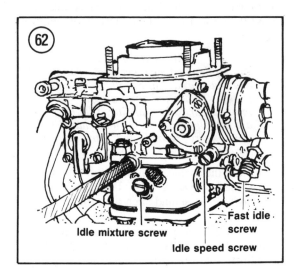

Idle mixture screw
Idle speed screw
Fast idle screw

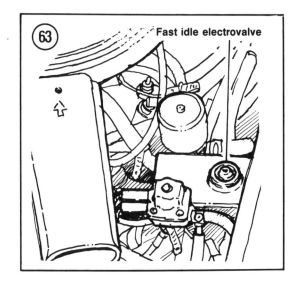

Fast idle electrovalve

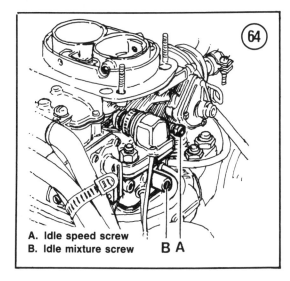

A. Idle speed screw
B. Idle mixture screw   **B A**

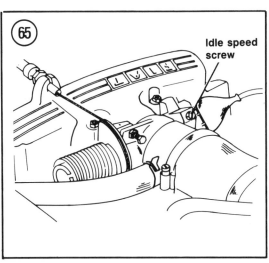

Idle speed
screw

2. Pinch off the air injection hose upstream of the check valve with locking pliers.

3. Let the engine idle. Check idle speed on the tachometer and compare with **Table 7**. Adjust if necessary by turning the idle speed screw (A, **Figure 64**).

4. Check CO percentage in the exhaust gas and compare with **Table 7**. Adjust if necessary by turning the idle mixture screw (B, **Figure 64**).

5. Once idle speed and mixture are set, remove the locking pliers.

3

1979-1980 (Without CO Meter)

1. Warm the engine to normal operating temperature. Connect a tune-up tachometer to the engine, following manufacturer's instructions.

2. Pinch off the air injection hose upstream of the check valve with locking pliers.

3. Let the engine idle. Check idle speed on the tachometer and compare with **Table 7**. Adjust if necessary by turning the idle speed screw (A, **Figure 64**).

4. Turn the idle mixture screw (B, **Figure 64**) to obtain maximum engine speed.

5. Turn the idle speed screw to reduce idle speed to specifications.

6. Turn the idle mixture screw (B, **Figure 64**) to reduce idle by the following amounts:

    a. Manual transmission—45-55 rpm.

    b. Automatic transmission—20-25 rpm.

7. Raise idle speed back to specifications by turning the idle speed screw (A, **Figure 64**).

8. Once idle speed and mixture are set, remove the locking pliers.

FUEL INJECTION
SYSTEM ADJUSTMENT

The only periodic fuel injection system adjustment is idle speed. The idle mixture screw is sealed to prevent routine adjustment.

1. Warm the engine to normal operating temperature. This occurs when the cooling fan has turned on, then turned back off, twice.

2. Connect a tune-up tachometer, following manufacturer's instructions.

3. Make sure the cooling fan is off. If it is on, wait for it to stop.

4. Check idle speed on the tachometer and compare with **Table 7**. Adjust if necessary by turning the idle speed screw (**Figure 65**).

Table 1 SCHEDULED MAINTENANCE (1971-1978)

Every 3,000 miles	• Battery	
Every 6,000 miles	• Engine oil and filter	
Every 12,500 miles	• Fuel filter • Air cleaner filter element • Vacuum hoses • Emission controls • Cooling system hoses and connections • Drive belts	• Clutch pedal • Brakes • Steering linkage • Hinges, latches, locks • Tune-up
Every 25,000 miles	• Timing belt • Carbon canister • Manual transmission oil	• Automatic transmission fluid • Differential oil • Wheel bearings

Table 2 SCHEDULED MAINTENANCE (1979-ON)

Every 3,000 miles	• Battery • Automatic transmission fluid	
Every 3,750 miles (Turbo)	• Engine oil and filter	
Every 7,500 miles (non-Turbo)	• Engine oil and filter	
Every 15,000 miles	• Fuel filter (carburetted cars only) • Air cleaner filter element • Vacuum hoses • Emission controls • Turbocharger • Drive belts	• Clutch pedal • Brakes • Steering linkage • Hinges, latches, locks • Tune-up
Every 30,000 miles	• Timing belt • Manual transmission oil • Automatic transmission fluid • Differential oil	• Wheel bearings • Lambda sensor replacement (fuel injected cars only)
Every 45,000 miles	• Cooling system	

Table 3 RECOMMENDED LUBRICANTS AND FLUIDS

Engine oil	API service SE-CC
Manual transmission and differential oil	SAE 90 (not EP)
Automatic transmission fluid	DEXRON
Steering gear	SAE 90 (EP)
Constant velocity joints	Lithium-based grease, NLGI No. 2, containing molybdenum disulfide
Antifreeze	Ethylene glycol type
Brake and clutch fluid	DOT 3
Fuel tank	
Without catalytic converter	Leaded or unleaded gasoline, Research octane number 91 or higher*
With catalytic converter	Unleaded gasoline, Research octane number 91 or higher*

* Gasoline pumps usually display an average of Research and Motor octane numbers. In this case, the minimum octane number is 87.

Table 4 OIL AND WINDSHIELD WASHER FLUID TEMPERATURE RECOMMENDATIONS

Engine oil	
Outdoor temperature	
Below −15° C (5° F)	SAE 10W
−15 to 0° C (5-32° F)	SAE 20W, 15W/40
0-35° C (32-95° F)	SAE 30, 15W/40
0 to above 35° C (0 to above 95° F)	SAE 40, 15W/40
Windshield washer solvent (percentage in tank)	
Outdoor temperature	
Below −10° C (14° F)	50 %
Down to −10° C (14° F)	30 %
Above 0° C (32° F)	3 %

Table 5 TIRE PRESSURES

Coupe	28 psi front and rear
Spider	
Through 1979	26 psi front and rear
1980-on	28 psi front and rear

Table 6 APPROXIMATE REFILL CAPACITIES

Fluid	Liters	Quarts
Engine oil		
Through 1974	3.75	4
1975-on	4.125	4 1/4
Cooling system		
Through 1974	7.5	8
1975-on	8	8 1/2
Manual transmission	1.65	1 3/4
Automatic transmission		
Drain and fill	2.8	3
New or rebuilt transmission	5.6	6
Steering gear	0.215	3/8 pt.
Fuel tank	43	11.4

Table 7 TUNE-UP SPECIFICATIONS

Valve clearance (cold engine)	
Intake	0.43-0.48 mm (0.017-0.019 in.)
Exhaust	0.48-0.53 mm (0.019-0.021 in.)
Spark plug type	
Through 1973	
Champion	N6Y
AC Delco	41-2 XLS
Marelli	CW 8 LP
1974-1977	
Champion	N7Y
AC Delco	41-42 XLS
Marelli	CW 78 LP
1978-1980	
Champion	N9Y, RN9Y*
AC Delco	42 XLS, R42 XLS*
Marelli	CW 7 LP, CW 7 LPR*
Bosch	W175 T30, W175 TR30*

(continued)

Table 7 TUNE-UP SPECIFICATIONS (continued)

1981-on	
Champion	N9Y, RN9Y*
AC	42 XLS, R42 XLS*, R43 XLS*
Bosch	W7D, WR7D*, WR7D2*
Marelli	CW 7 LP, CW 7 LPR*, CW 67 LPR*
Fiat	1L4J, 1L4JR*
Spark plug thread size	14×1.25 mm
Spark plug gap	
Through 1977	0.5-0.7 mm (0.020-0.027 in.)
1978-on (non-resistor)	0.6-0.7 mm (0.023-0.027 in.)
1978-on (resistor)	0.7-0.8 mm (0.027-0.031 in.)
Firing order	1-3-4-2 clockwise
Points gap	
Through 1974	0.37-0.43 mm (0.015-0.017 in.)
1975-1978	
Primary points	0.37-0.43 mm (0.015-0.017 in.)
Secondary points	0.31-0.49 mm (0.012-0.019 in.)
Dwell angle (through 1978)	55°
Ignition timing (at idle speed)	
Through 1978	0° (TDC)
1979-on	10° BTDC
Idle speed	
Through 1978	850 rpm
1979-on	
Manual transmission	700-800 rpm
Automatic transmission (in DRIVE)	700-750 rpm

* Resistor-type plug

Table 8 VALVE SHIM THICKNESSES

mm	in.	mm	in.
3.25	0.128	4.00	0.157
3.30	0.130	4.05	0.159
3.35	0.132	4.10	0.161
3.40	0.134	4.15	0.163
3.45	0.136	4.20	0.165
3.50	0.138	4.25	0.167
3.55	0.140	4.30	0.169
3.60	0.142	4.35	0.171
3.65	0.144	4.40	0.173
3.70	0.146	4.45	0.175
3.75	0.148	4.50	0.177
3.80	0.150	4.55	0.179
3.85	0.152	4.60	0.181
3.90	0.154	4.65	0.183
3.95	0.156	4.70	0.185

4

ENGINE

All models use a 4-cylinder overhead cam engine. The left-hand camshaft operates the intake valves. The right-hand camshaft operates the exhaust valves. The valves are opened by bucket tappets. The crankshaft rides on 5 main bearings. The crankshaft turns the camshafts through a toothed rubber belt. An auxiliary shaft, turned by the same belt, drives the fuel pump (models equipped with mechanical fuel pump) and oil pump. The gear-type oil pump is mounted inside the oil pan.

Tables 1-3 are at the end of the chapter.

ENGINE REMOVAL

WARNING
The engine is heavy, awkward to handle and has sharp edges. It may shift or drop suddenly during removal. To prevent serious injury, always observe the following precautions.
1. Never place any part of your body where a moving or falling engine may trap, cut or crush you.
2. If you must push the engine during removal, use a board or similar tool to keep your hands out of danger.
3. Be sure the hoist is designed to lift engines and has enough load capacity for your engine.
4. Be sure the hoist is securely attached to safe lifting points on the engine.
5. The engine should not be difficult to lift with a proper hoist. If it is, stop lifting, lower the engine back onto its mounts and make sure the engine has been completely separated from the vehicle.

1. Disconnect the battery negative cable. **Figure 1** shows the trunk-mounted battery used on 1973

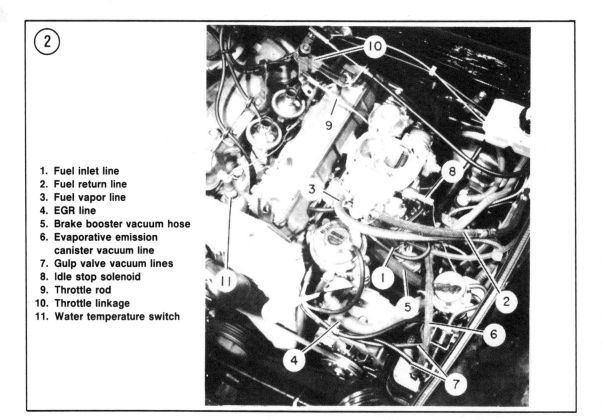

1. Fuel inlet line
2. Fuel return line
3. Fuel vapor line
4. EGR line
5. Brake booster vacuum hose
6. Evaporative emission
   canister vacuum line
7. Gulp valve vacuum lines
8. Idle stop solenoid
9. Throttle rod
10. Throttle linkage
11. Water temperature switch

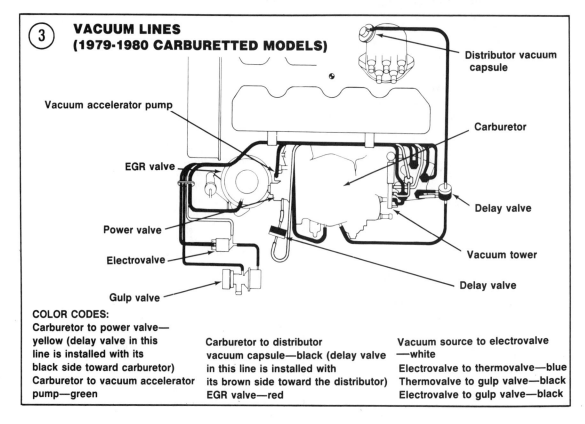

**VACUUM LINES
(1979-1980 CARBURETTED MODELS)**

Distributor vacuum capsule

Vacuum accelerator pump

Carburetor

EGR valve

Delay valve

Power valve

Electrovalve

Vacuum tower

Gulp valve

Delay valve

COLOR CODES:
Carburetor to power valve—
yellow (delay valve in this
line is installed with its
black side toward carburetor)
Carburetor to vacuum accelerator
pump—green

Carburetor to distributor
vacuum capsule—black (delay valve
in this line is installed with
its brown side toward the distributor)
EGR valve—red

Vacuum source to electrovalve
—white
Electrovalve to thermovalve—blue
Thermovalve to gulp valve—black
Electrovalve to gulp valve—black

and later models. On earlier models, the battery is mounted in the engine compartment.

2. Loosen the fuel filler cap.

3. Remove the hood as described in Chapter Twelve.

4. Drain the cooling system as described under *Cooling System Flushing*, Chapter Six.

NOTE
Steps 5-12 apply to carburetted models.

5. Remove the air cleaner as described in Chapter Five.

6. Referring to **Figure 2**, label and disconnect the following:

   a. Fuel inlet and return lines.

   b. Fuel vapor line and vapor canister vacuum line (cars with evaporative emission control system).

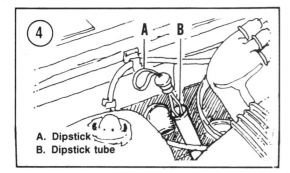

A. Dipstick
B. Dipstick tube

   c. EGR line (cars equipped with exhaust gas recirculation system).

   d. Gulp valve vacuum lines (cars with air injection system).

   e. Carburetor electrical wiring.

   f. Choke heater hoses.

NOTE
*The vacuum lines on 1979-1980 carburetted models are color coded for easy reconnection. **Figure 3** identifies color codes.*

7. Detach the throttle rod from the linkage. Detach the linkage from the cam cover and lay it aside. See Chapter Five for details.

8. Label and disconnect the water temperature sender wires from the top of the cylinder head.

9. If equipped with automatic transmission, disconnect the transmission vacuum line from the intake manifold. Remove the dipstick (**Figure 4**) and detach the transmission dipstick tube bracket from the engine. See **Figure 5**.

10. Disconnect the wires from the alternator and oil pressure sender.

11 Disconnect the primary wire(s) (thin wires) and coil wire (thick wire). See **Figure 6**.

12. Loosen the clamps and disconnect the heater hoses at the firewall. See **Figure 7**.

NOTE
Steps 13-29 apply to fuel injected models.

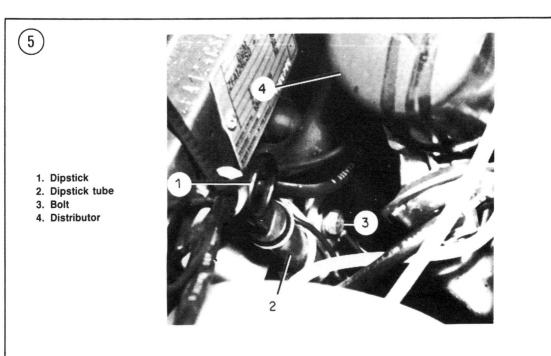

1. Dipstick
2. Dipstick tube
3. Bolt
4. Distributor

13. Remove the air cleaner as described in Chapter Five.

14. Referring to **Figure 8**, disconnect the brake booster vacuum line and carbon canister vacuum line from the intake manifold.

15. If equipped with automatic transmission, disconnect the transmission vacuum line from the intake manifold.

16. Remove the bolts and clamps (**Figure 8**) that attach the wiring harness to the intake manifold. Pull the wiring connectors straight out to detach them from the intake manifold.

17. Turn the throttle lever (**Figure 9**) and detach the throttle cable.

> *WARNING*
> *Because of the high pressure in fuel injection system lines, Steps 18-20 must be followed carefully.*

18. Remove the fuel tank filler cap.

19. Disconnect the vacuum hose from the pressure regulator (**Figure 10**).

20. Attach a hand vacuum pump to the pressure regulator as shown in **Figure 10**. Apply 25 in. Hg vacuum to the pressure regulator. This will release fuel line pressure into the tank.

> *CAUTION*
> *The fuel injection system can easily be damaged by dirt contamination. Take care not to let dirt enter any openings durings the following steps.*

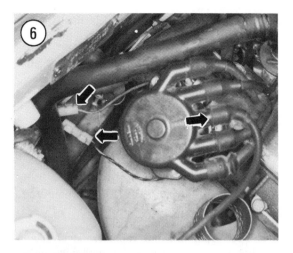

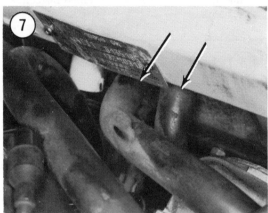

1. Brake booster vacuum hose
2. Evaporative emission canister vacuum line
3. Clamp
4. Wiring harness

21. Disconnect the fuel return hose from the regulator. See **Figure 11**. Disconnect the flexible hose from the metal line near the left wheel well.

22. Disconnect the crankcase breather hose (**Figure 12**). Disconnect the wires from alternator, starter and oil pressure sender.

23. Label and disconnect the water temperature sender wires on top of the cylinder head.

24. Loosen the hose clamps and disconnect the heater hoses at the right rear corner of the engine compartment.

25. If equipped with an automatic transmission, detach the dipstick tube from the cam housing.

26. Referring to **Figure 13**, remove the plastic nut and clamp that secure the Lambda sensor wiring harness. Unplug the Lambda sensor connector and electronic control module wire.

27. Disconnect the coil wire from the distributor.

28. Disconnect the engine ground wire from the rear of the right cam housing.

29. On Turbos, disconnect the vacuum lines from the turbocharger pressure switches (**Figure 14**).

NOTE
Steps 30-39 apply to all models.

30. Remove the radiator as described in Chapter Six.

31. Remove the thermostat and its hoses. See **Figure 15**.

32. Remove the windshield washer container from the left wheel well (if so equipped).

33. Set the handbrake. Place the transmission in FIRST (manual) or PARK (automatic).

34. Securely block both rear wheels so the car will not roll in either direction.

35. Jack up the front of the car and place it on jackstands.

36. On non-Turbos, detach the exhaust pipe from the manifold. Detach and remove the exhaust pipe bracket (**Figure 16**), then pull the exhaust pipe down to separate it from the manifold.

37. On Turbos, remove the nuts and Allen bolts attaching the exhaust pipe to the exhaust elbow. See **Figure 17**. Detach the bracket from the exhaust

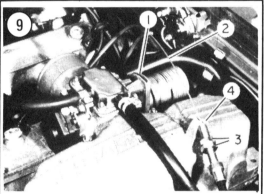

1. Throttle lever
2. Throttle cable
3. Adjusting nuts
4. Throttle cable bracket

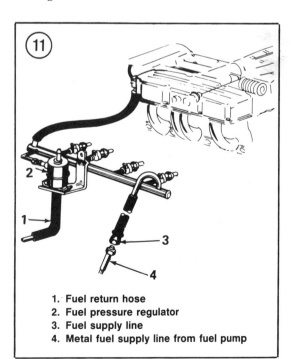

1. Fuel return hose
2. Fuel pressure regulator
3. Fuel supply line
4. Metal fuel supply line from fuel pump

1. Vacuum hose
2. Fuel pressure regulator
3. Hand vacuum pump

1. Crankcase breather hose
2. Starter
3. Alternator
4. Fuel supply line
5. Fuel pressure regulator

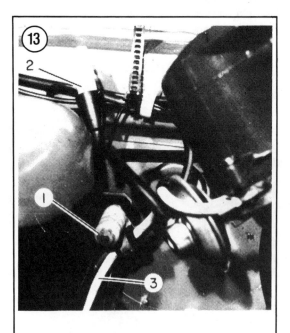

1. Plastic nut
2. Lambda sensor connector
3. Distributor

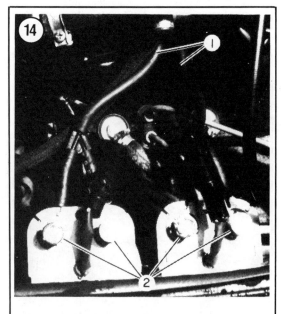

1. Vacuum line
2. Turbocharger pressure switches

pipe and transmission, then pull the exhaust pipe away from the exhaust elbow.

38. Remove the starter as described in Chapter Seven.

39. Remove the lower inspection cover from the clutch housing (manual) or torque converter housing (automatic). See **Figure 18**.

NOTE
Step 40 and Step 41 apply to automatic transmission models.

40. Remove the 3 bolts that secure the torque converter to the drive plate (**Figure 19**). Turn the crankshaft with a wrench on the crankshaft pulley bolt to provide access to each of the 3 bolts.

41. Push the torque converter as far back as it will go, away from the drive plate.

NOTE
The following steps apply to all models.

4

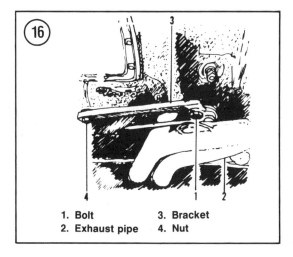

1. Bolt
2. Exhaust pipe
3. Bracket
4. Nut

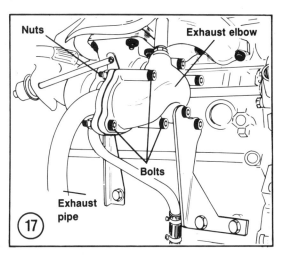

Nuts
Exhaust elbow
Bolts
Exhaust pipe

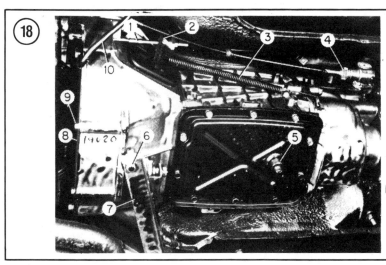

1. Clutch cable
2. Throw-out arm
3. Clutch return spring
4. Speedometer cable connector
5. Drain plug
6. Bolt
7. Bracket
8. Bolt
9. Lower inspection cover
10. Engine ground cable

42. Remove the transmission-to-engine bolts with a socket, universal adapter and long extension.

43. Remove the engine mount nuts through the access holes in the crossmember (**Figure 20**).

44. Remove the jackstands and lower the front of the car to the ground.

45. Place a jack beneath the transmission to support it. Use a block of wood between jack and transmission oil pan so the oil pan won't collapse.

46. Attach a hoist to the engine. Portable hydraulic crane type hoists, available from rental dealers, are effective and easy to use.

CAUTION
At this point, there should not be any hoses, linkages, fasteners or wires attaching the engine to the car. Recheck this to make sure nothing can hamper engine removal.

WARNING
The engine is heavy and may shift suddenly during removal. Never place your hands where a sudden shift of the engine may trap them and cause injury. Never place your hands beneath the engine or transmission. If you must push on the engine to move it, use a board or similar tool.

47. Lift the engine, tilting as shown in **Figure 21**, until the mount bolts clear the crossmember. Move the engine up and forward as necessary to separate it from the transmission.

CAUTION
If equipped with a manual transmission, pull the engine far enough forward so the clutch clears the transmission input shaft. Raising the transmission slightly with the jack will make this easier.

48. Lift the engine until it clears the body, then take it out of the engine compartment. As soon as the engine is clear of the car, lower it to the ground or attach it to a suitable engine stand.

ENGINE INSTALLATION

Engine installation is the reverse of removal, plus the following.

1. Fasten the engine and transmission securely to their mounts before tightening anything else.

2. Adjust the clutch as described in Chapter Eight.

3. Fill the engine and transmission with oils recommended in Chapter Three.

4. Fill the cooling system as described in Chapter Six.

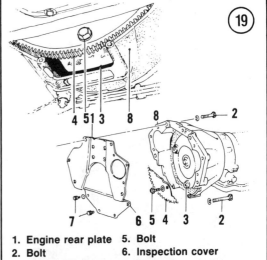

1. Engine rear plate   5. Bolt
2. Bolt   6. Inspection cover
3. Torque converter   7. Bolt
4. Drive plate   8. Torque converter housing

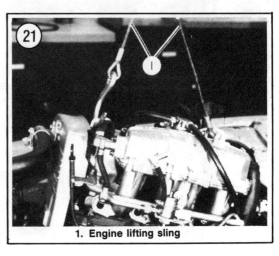

1. Engine lifting sling

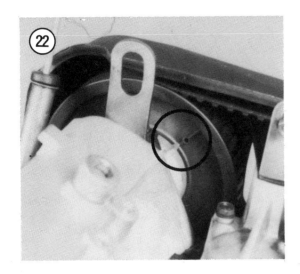

DISASSEMBLY CHECKLISTS

The following checklists tell how much of the engine to remove and disassemble to do a specific type of service, such as a valve job.

To use these checklists, remove and inspect each part mentioned. Then go through the sequences backwards, installing the parts. Each major part is covered in this chapter, unless otherwise noted.

Decarbonizing or Valve Service

1. Remove the camshafts and lifters.
2. Remove the exhaust and intake manifolds.
3. Remove the cylinder head.
4. Remove and inspect valves. Inspect valve guides and seats, repairing or replacing as necessary.
5. Assemble by reversing Steps 1-4.

Valve and Ring Service

1. Perform Steps 1-4 for *Decarbonizing or Valve Service.*
2. Remove the oil pan.
3. Remove the pistons together with the connecting rods.
4. Remove the piston rings. It is not necessary to separate the pistons from the connecting rods unless a piston, piston pin or connecting rod needs repair or replacement.
5. Assemble by reversing Steps 1-4.

General Overhaul

NOTE
During an overhaul, the following parts should be taken to a machine shop for inspection and service: cylinder block and head, crankshaft, piston/ connecting rod assemblies, manifolds

and flywheel (torque converter drive plate on automatic transmissions).

1. Remove the engine from the car.
2. Remove the clutch as described in Chapter Eight.
3. Remove the flywheel and timing belt as described in this chapter.
4. Remove the end covers and oil seals as described in this chapter.
5. If available, place the engine on a stand. Stands can be rented from tool rental dealers.
6. Remove the dipstick, oil filter and oil pressure sender.
7. Remove the motor mounts.
8. If equipped with a carburetor, remove the carburetor and fuel pump as described in Chapter Five.
9. If equipped with fuel injection, remove the system components as described in Chapter Five.
10. If equipped with a turbocharger, remove the system components as described in Chapter Five.
11. If equipped with an air injection system, remove the air pump and air injection manifold.
12. Remove the crankcase ventilation system as described in Chapter Five.
13. Remove the water pump and thermostat as described in Chapter Six.
14. Remove the alternator as described in Chapter Seven.
15. Remove the distributor as described in Chapter Seven.
16. Remove the camshaft and lifters.
17. Remove the cylinder head.
18. Remove the auxiliary shaft.
19. Remove the oil pan, oil pickup tube and oil pump.
20. Remove the piston and connecting rod assemblies.
21. Remove the crankshaft.
22. Inspect the cylinder block.
23. Assemble by reversing Steps 1-21.

TIMING BELT

Inspection (On-car)

1. Disconnect the negative cable from the battery.
2. Remove the spark plugs as described in the *Tune-up* section of Chapter Three. This makes it easier to turn the engine.
3. Turn the engine by hand (or by pushing the car in high gear on manual transmission models) until the camshaft timing marks align with the marks on the camshaft housings. See **Figure 22** (intake) and **Figure 23** (exhaust).

4. With the camshaft marks aligned, note whether the timing pointer on the front of the engine aligns with the crankshaft pulley notch. See **Figure 24** (1971-1978) or **Figure 25** (1979-on). If it doesn't, the belt is stretched and must be replaced.

5. Check the belt for wear or damage. Replace it if its condition is in any doubt. If the belt breaks while the engine is running, severe and expensive engine damage will result.

Replacement

> *CAUTION*
> *Timing belts must not be reused and they must not be loosened after initial adjustment. Once a timing belt has been loosened, it must be replaced with a new one. Otherwise it may slip on the pulleys, with results ranging from poor performance to engine damage.*

1. Disconnect the negative cable from the battery.

2. Remove the spark plugs as described in Chapter Three. This makes it easier to turn the engine.

3. Turn the engine by hand until No. 4 cylinder is at top dead center on its compression stroke. When this occurs, the zero degree mark on the crankshaft pulley will align with the pointer on the front cover. See **Figure 24** (1971-1978) or **Figure 25** (1979-on). In addition, the camshaft timing marks will align with the marks on the camshaft housings. See **Figure 26** (intake) and **Figure 27** (exhaust).

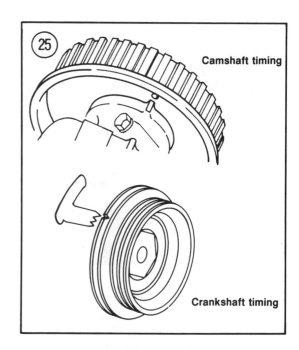

Camshaft timing

Crankshaft timing

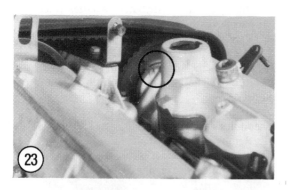

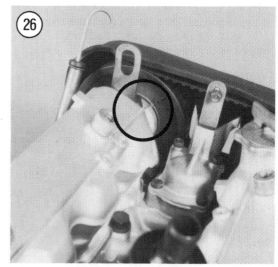

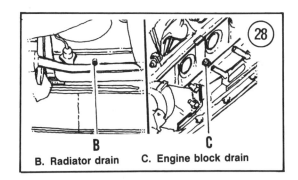

B. Radiator drain   C. Engine block drain

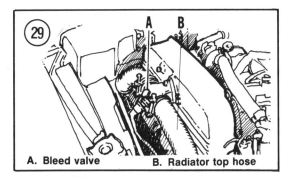

A. Bleed valve   B. Radiator top hose

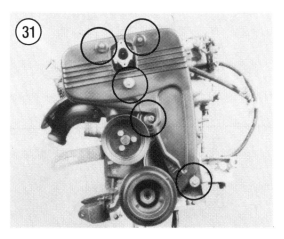

NOTE
Be sure to check each camshaft mark as well as the crankshaft marks. The crankshaft marks also line up when No. 4 piston is at TDC on its exhaust stroke.

4. Set the handbrake. If equipped with a manual transmission, place the transmission in high gear. If equipped with an automatic, place the transmission in PARK.
5. Remove the hot air hose (if so equipped) from in front of the timing belt cover.
6. Place a pan beneath the radiator drain tap (**Figure 28**) and drain about one gallon of coolant.

WARNING
Coolant is poisonous and may attract animals. Do not leave the drained coolant where it is accessible to children or pets.

7. Detach the radiator top hose from the union on the front of the cylinder head (**Figure 29**).
8. Detach the union (and distributor vacuum line if so equipped) from the head. See **Figure 30**.
9. Remove all drive belts as described in Chapter Three.
10. Remove the timing cover securing bolts and washers. See **Figure 31**. Take the cover off.
11. Remove the water pump pulley (**Figure 32**). The pulley can be held from turning by placing its drive belt in the groove and squeezing the belt. If this doesn't work, use a chain wrench as shown in **Figure 33**.
12. On 2000 cc engines, remove the inner timing belt cover (**Figure 34**).
13. If the camshaft or auxiliary shaft pulleys are to be removed (to remove the camshafts or auxiliary shaft, for example), loosen their bolts now. See **Figure 35**. Hold the crankshaft pulley from turning with a chain wrench as shown in **Figure 36**.
14. Remove the crankshaft pulley nut (**Figure 37**).

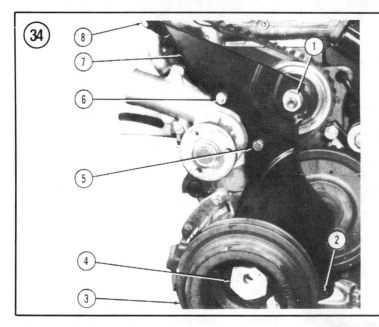

1. Nut
2. Bolt
3. Crankshaft pulley
4. Nut
5. Bolt
6. Nut
7. Cover
8. Bolt

If the engine is in the car (manual transmission models only), the crankshaft can be held from turning by placing the transmission in FIRST and setting the handbrake. Another method is to hold the crankshaft pulley with a chain wrench as shown in **Figure 36**.

NOTE
The crankshaft pulley is secured by a 38 mm nut. If a 38 mm socket is not available, a 1 1/2 in. socket will work. Large sockets are available from some tool rental dealers.

15. Loosen the tensioner bracket bolt and idler pulley (**Figure 38**). Pry the pulley as shown in **Figure 39** to release belt tension, then tighten the tensioner bracket bolt.

CAUTION
Do not turn the engine after the next step. If the engine is turned while the belt is off, the valves will be forced against the piston tops and may be damaged.

16. Slip the timing belt off the camshaft pulleys (**Figure 40**) and remove it from the engine.
17. Make sure the pointers on the front of the engine line up with the camshaft sprocket marks (**Figure 41**).
16. Install the new belt on the crankshaft pulley (**Figure 42**).

18. Make sure the auxiliary shaft sprocket is positioned as shown in **Figure 43**, then position the belt teeth in the sprocket (on both sides).

19. Make sure there is no slack in the belt and slip it over the intake camshaft pulley, then the exhaust camshaft pulley. See **Figure 44**. Finally, slide the belt over the tensioner pulley (**Figure 45**).

> *CAUTION*
> *Do not pry the belt over the tensioner pulley. If it is difficult to install, make sure the belt is installed correctly.*

20. Loosen the tensioner bracket bolt and tensioner pulley (**Figure 46**). Let the tensioner pulley move to tighten the timing belt.

21. Turn the crankshaft clockwise exactly 2 full turns. Make sure the camshaft and auxiliary shaft

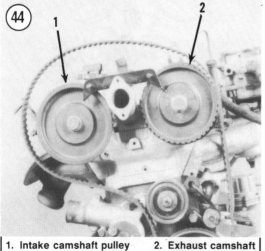

| 1. Intake camshaft pulley | 2. Exhaust camshaft pulley |

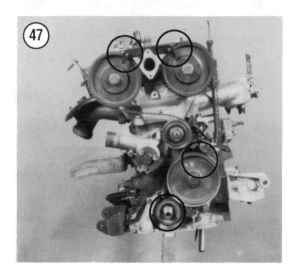

timing marks line up correctly. See **Figure 47**. Make sure the Woodruff key in the crankshaft is positioned as shown.

CAUTION
If the marks do not line up as shown, the belt is incorrectly installed. Install it correctly before proceeding further.

22. Tighten the tensioner bracket bolt (**Figure 48**) to 4.5 mkg (31 ft.-lb.).

CAUTION
Never push the car backward in gear, never turn the engine backwards with a wrench and never let the engine run backwards (this sometimes happens when an engine diesels). This will create slack in the timing belt so it jumps to the wrong cogs. If this happens, the results will range from poor performance to engine damage.

23. On 2000 cc engines, install the inner timing belt cover.
24. Install the crankshaft and water pump pulleys (**Figure 49**).
25. Install the timing belt cover (**Figure 50**).
26. Attach the union to the cylinder head (**Figure 51**). Use a new gasket, coated on both sides with gasket sealer. Connect the radiator top hose to the union. See **Figure 52**.

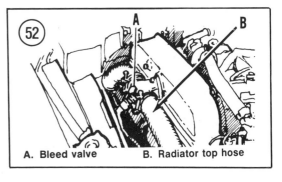

A. Bleed valve   B. Radiator top hose

27. Fill the cooling system as described in Chapter Six.

28. Install the drive belts as described in Chapter Three.

29. Install the hot air hose (if so equipped).

CAUTION
After installation, turn the engine in its normal direction of rotation (clockwise, viewed from the front of the car) with a wrench on the crankshaft pulley bolt. The engine should turn easily. If you can feel mechanical resistance, the timing belt is installed incorrectly and the valves are striking the piston tops. Severe damage will result if the engine is run in this condition. Repeat the timing belt installation procedure and the check described in this paragraph until the engine can be turned without the valves striking the piston tops.

INTAKE AND EXHAUST MANIFOLDS

Intake Manifold Removal/ Installation (With Carburetor)

1. Perform Steps 1-7 of *Carburetor Removal/Installation,* Chapter Five.

2. On 1979 and later models, drain about one gallon of coolant from the radiator.

WARNING
Antifreeze is poisonous and may attract animals. Do not leave the drained coolant where it is accessible to children or pets.

3. Remove the dipstick tube. See **Figure 53** and **Figure 54**.

4. On cars equipped with exhaust gas recirculation, disconnect the EGR tube at the point shown in **Figure 55**. Remove the EGR tube plug

(Figure 56) with a 10 mm Allen wrench. Loosen the inner fitting **(Figure 57)** with the same tool, then pivot the tube upward far enough to clear the engine lifting bracket on the left front corner of the cylinder head.

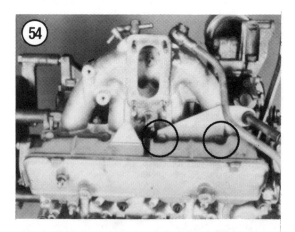

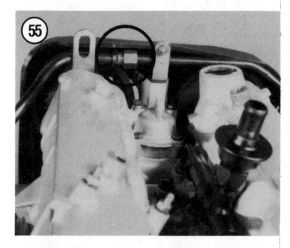

5. Disconnect the brake booster and EGR vacuum lines (if so equipped). See **Figure 58**.

6. Remove the liquid-vapor separator (**Figure 59**).

> *CAUTION*
> *The manifold should come off easily during the next step. If not, make sure all fasteners have been removed. Do not force the manifold off.*

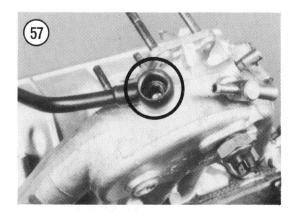

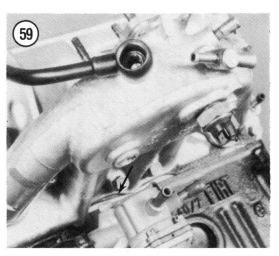

7. Remove the manifold nuts and bolts and take the manifold off the engine. See **Figure 60**.

8. Installation is the reverse of removal. Use a new gasket. Tighten manifold fasteners evenly, starting at the center and working outward.

**Intake Manifold Removal/
Installation (With Fuel Injection)**

> *WARNING*
> *Because of the high pressure in fuel system lines, the next step must be followed exactly.*

1. Disconnect the vacuum hose from the fuel pressure regulator (**Figure 61**). Connect a hand vacuum pump to the regulator and pump vacuum to 25 in. Hg. This releases fuel pressure into the fuel tank through the return hose.

2. Disconnect all fuel injection wires and hoses from the air intake and intake manifold. See Chapter Five for details.

3. Disconnect the throttle cable from the linkage. If equipped with automatic transmission, disconnect the kickdown cable as well. See Chapter Five.

4. Remove the nuts and washers securing the air intake to the manifolds, then lift the air intake off. See **Figure 62**.

> *CAUTION*
> *The intake manifold should come off easily during the next step. If not, make sure all fasteners have been removed. Do not force the manifold off.*

5. Remove the manifold nuts and bolts, then take the manifold off the engine. See **Figure 62**.

6. Installation is the reverse of removal. Use new gaskets. Tighten the manifold nuts and bolts to specifications (**Table 2**).

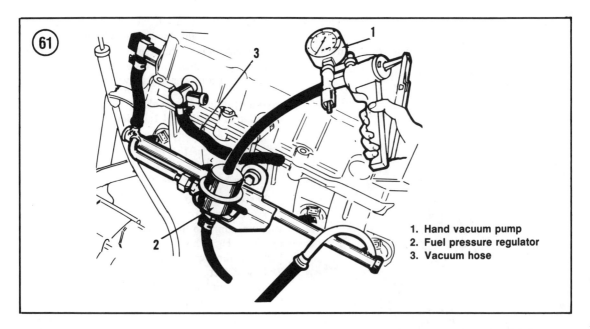

1. Hand vacuum pump
2. Fuel pressure regulator
3. Vacuum hose

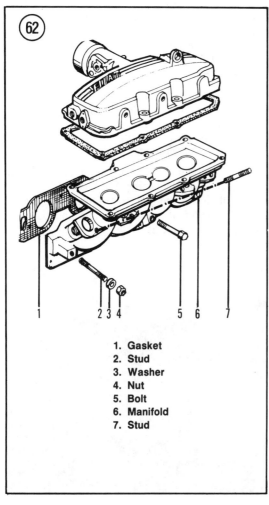

1. Gasket
2. Stud
3. Washer
4. Nut
5. Bolt
6. Manifold
7. Stud

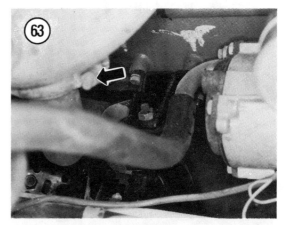

1. Cover
2. Nuts
3. Air cleaner
4. Hot air hose
5. Reed valve hose

Exhaust Manifold
Removal/Installation

1. On Turbos, remove the turbocharger as described in Chapter Five.

2. Detach the exhaust pipe from the manifold. See **Figure 63**.

3. Disconnect the hot air hose from the heat shroud. **Figure 64** shows a typical hot air hose used with carburetted engines. The shroud used with fuel injected engines is basically the same.

4. If equipped with exhaust gas recirculation, detach the EGR tube at the points shown in **Figure 65** and **Figure 66**.

5. If the heat shroud is to be removed, do it now. See **Figure 67** and **Figure 68**.

> *CAUTION*
> *The manifold should be easy to remove during the next step. If not, make sure all fasteners have been removed. Do not force the manifold off.*

6. Remove the manifold nuts (**Figure 69**). Take the manifold off.

7. Installation is the reverse of removal. Tighten the manifold nuts evenly, starting with the center

and working outward. Tighten all fasteners to specifications (end of chapter).

CAMSHAFTS

Removal/Installation

1. Remove the timing belt cover as described under *Timing Belt* in this chapter.

2. Hold the crankshaft from turning. If the engine is installed in the car (manual transmission models only), this can be done by placing the transmission in FIRST and setting the handbrake. Another method is to place a chain wrench on the drive belt pulley as shown in **Figure 70**.

3. Loosen the camshaft pulley bolts (**Figure 71**).

4. Remove the timing belt as described in this chapter.

5. On carburetted cars, remove the air cleaner as described in Chapter Five.

6. On fuel injected cars, remove the air intake hose and auxiliary air regulator. See Chapter Five.

7. On fuel injected cars, remove the air intake from the intake manifold. See *Intake and Exhaust Manifolds* in this chapter.

8. On Turbos, remove the compressor discharge plenum as described under *Turbocharger* in Chapter Five.

9. Unscrew the fitting at the bottom of the dipstick tube (**Figure 72**).

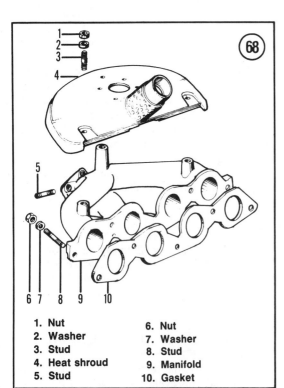

1. Nut
2. Washer
3. Stud
4. Heat shroud
5. Stud
6. Nut
7. Washer
8. Stud
9. Manifold
10. Gasket

10. On cars equipped with a carburetor and exhaust gas recirculation, disconnect the EGR tube at the point shown in **Figure 73**. Loosen the tube at its connection to the intake manifold (**Figure 74**), then pivot it out of the way.

11. Remove the camshaft covers (**Figure 75**).

NOTE
*If the covers are difficult to remove, tap gently on the protrusions shown in **Figure 76** with a wooden hammer handle.*

CAUTION
During the next step, undo the nuts and bolts in 2 or 3 stages, working from the center outward. Otherwise the camshaft housings could be warped.

12. Remove the nuts and bolts that secure the camshaft housings to the cylinder head. See **Figure 77** and **Figure 78**.

CAUTION
During the next step, push down on the tappets so they stay on the valve stems. See **Figure 79**. *Otherwise the tappets may be lifted away with the camshaft housing and fall on the floor.*

13. Take the camshaft housings off the engine. Remove the tappets from the valve stems. See **Figure 80**.

NOTE
Make a holder to keep the tappets in order so they can be returned to their original locations during assembly. Keep the tappets and valve adjusting washers together.

14. Remove the camshaft housing end cover and gasket (**Figure 81**).
15. Carefully remove the camshaft from the rear end of the housing. See **Figure 82**.
16. Remove the oil seal from the front end of the camshaft housing. If available, use a puller as shown in **Figure 83**. If not, pry out the oil seal as shown in **Figure 84**.

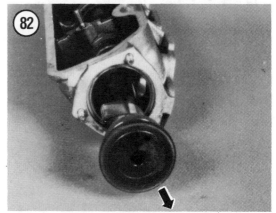

85

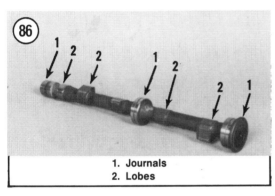

86

1. Journals
2. Lobes

87

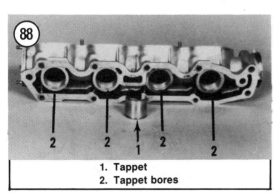

88

1. Tappet
2. Tappet bores

17. Tap a new seal into the camshaft housing. Use a block of wood to spread the hammer's force so the seal won't tip sideways and jam. See **Figure 85**. The seal lip faces into the camshaft housing.

18. Installation is the reverse of removal. Use new gaskets, coated with a thin, even layer of gasket sealer. Tighten the camshaft housing bolts and nuts evenly to 2 mkg (14 ft.-lb.).

Inspection

If you don't have the necessary precision measuring equipment, the next steps can be done inexpensively by a machine shop.

1. Measure outer diameter of the camshaft journals (**Figure 86**) with a micrometer. Compare with specifications in **Table 1**. Measure in 2 directions to check for uneven wear. If wear is excessive or uneven, replace the camshaft.

2. Check the journal and lobe surfaces (**Figure 86**) for scoring, pits or signs of seizure. Minor imperfections may be removed with an extra-fine oilstone. If defects are serious, replace the camshaft.

3. Place the camshaft between accurate centers, such as V-blocks or a lathe. Rotate the camshaft one full turn and measure bend with a dial indicator. Maximum bend (total indicator reading) is 0.03 mm (0.001 in.). If excessive, replace the camshaft.

4. Check the camshaft bearing bores for smoothness. Replace the camshaft housing if the bearing surfaces are not perfectly smooth.

5. Measure the camshaft bearing bores with a bore gauge. This can be done inexpensively by a machine shop if you don't have a bore gauge. If the diameter exceeds specifications, replace the camshaft housing.

6. Check the valve adjusting shim surfaces (**Figure 87**) for smoothness. Replace the adjusting shims as described in the *Valve Adjustment* section of Chapter Three if the surfaces are not perfectly smooth.

7. Check the lifter bores in the camshaft housings and the outer surfaces of the lifters for visible wear, taper and out-of-roundness. See **Figure 88**. Replace parts that show these conditions.

8. Measure lifter outer diameter and lifter bore inner diameter. Compare with **Table 2** at the end of the chapter. Replace parts that don't meet specifications.

Camshaft Installation

1. Liberally coat the camshaft bearing bores with clean engine oil. Install the camshafts in the

housings, taking care not to nick the bearing bores. Rotate the camshafts to ease installation.

NOTE
*Be sure to install the intake and exhaust camshafts in the proper housings. On 1967-1970 models, install the camshafts according to the labels made during removal. On 1971 and later cars, the exhaust camshaft has a distributor drive gear (**Figure 89**) and the intake camshaft does not.*

2. Install the end cover and its gasket (**Figure 90**). Coat both sides of the gasket with a thin, even layer of gasket sealer.
3. Install the tappets and their adjusting shims in the camshaft housing. See **Figure 91**. If installing the old tappets, be sure to return them to the bores from which they were removed.
4. Turn the camshafts so their dowels are positioned as shown in **Figure 92** (exhaust) or **Figure 93** (intake).
5. Place a new camshaft housing gasket on the cylinder head. See **Figure 94**.
6. Carefully install the camshaft housing on the engine. Hold the tappets so they don't fall out. Guide the tappets over the valve stems (**Figure 95**).
7. Thread the dipstick tube fitting into the block partway. See **Figure 96**. Install the dipstick tube bracket bolts (**Figure 97**) and tighten them slightly.
8. Install the camshaft housing nuts and bolts. See **Figure 97** (intake) or **Figure 98** (exhaust). Tighten in 2 or 3 stages, working outward from the center, to prevent warping the camshaft housings.

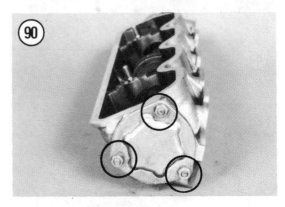

CAUTION
Do not turn the camshaft during the next step. This will force the valves against the piston tops and bend the valves.

9. Install the camshaft pulleys. Wrap the old timing belt around each pulley to hold it and tighten the pulley bolt as much as possible. See **Figure 99**.
10. Install a new timing belt as described in this chapter.
11. Adjust the valves as described in the *Tune-up* section of Chapter Three.
12. Install the camshaft housing covers (**Figure 100**). Use new gaskets, coated on both sides with gasket sealer.

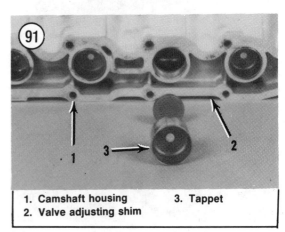

1. Camshaft housing   3. Tappet
2. Valve adjusting shim

CYLINDER HEAD

Removal

1. Drain the cooling system as described in the *Cooling System Flushing* section of Chapter Six.

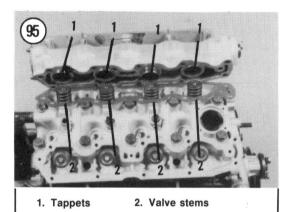

1. Tappets 2. Valve stems

2. Remove the intake and exhaust manifolds as described in this chapter.

3. Remove the camshafts and housings as described in this chapter.

4. Remove the cylinder head bolts. Loosen the bolts in several stages, in the order shown in **Figure 101**. This is necessary to prevent warping the head.

5. Lift the head off. If it is difficult to remove, try tapping gently with a rubber mallet. Do not pry the head off.

Inspection

1. Check the cylinder head for water leaks before cleaning.

2. Clean the cylinder head thoroughly in solvent. While cleaning, check for cracks or other visible damage. Look for corrosion or foreign material in oil or water passages. Clean the passages with a stiff spiral wire brush, then blow them out with compressed air.

1. **Temperature switches**
2. **Air manifold**

NOTE
*If the head is hard to clean, have it bead blasted by a machine shop. If so equipped, remove the temperature sensors and air manifold (**Figure 102**) before taking the head to the machine shop.*

3. Check the cylinder head bottom (block mating) surface for flatness. Place an accurate straightedge along its surface (**Figure 103**). If there is any gap, measure it with a feeler gauge. Measure along the diagonal lines shown in **Figure 104** as well as along the length of the head. If the gap exceeds specifications, have the head resurfaced by a machine shop.

4. Check the manifold surfaces (**Figure 105** and **Figure 106**) for warping in the same manner as the block mating surface.

5. Check studs in the cylinder head for damage. Replace damaged studs.

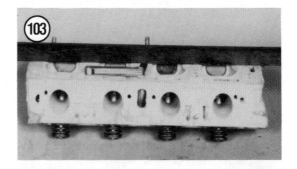

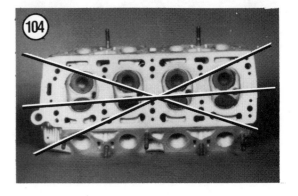

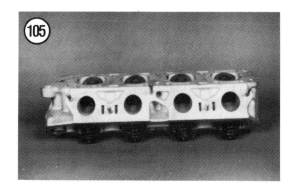

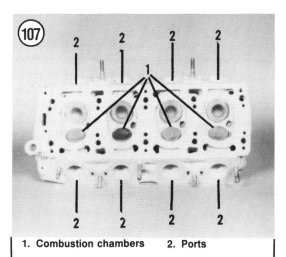

1. Combustion chambers   2. Ports

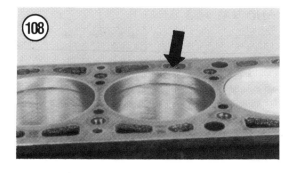

5. Check threaded holes in the head for wear or damage. If worn or damaged, have a thread insert installed in the hole by a machine shop.

6. Check threaded holes in the head for wear or damage. If worn or damaged, have a thread insert installed in the hole by a machine shop.

7. Inspect valves and valve seats as described in the *Valves and Valve Seats* section of this chapter.

Decarbonizing

1. Without removing valves, remove all deposits from the combustion chambers, intake ports and exhaust ports. See **Figure 107**. Use a plastic or hardwood scraper. Be careful not to scratch or gouge the combustion chambers.

2. After all carbon is removed from the combustion chambers and ports, clean the entire head in solvent.

3. Clean away all carbon on the piston tops. Do not remove the carbon ridge at the top of the cylinder bore (**Figure 108**).

Cylinder Head Installation

1. Be sure the cylinder head, block and cylinder bores are clean. Check all visible oil passages for cleanliness.

2. Install a new cylinder head gasket. Never reuse an old head gasket. Do *not* use gasket sealer on the head gasket. Position the gasket on the block so the word "ALTO" is up. See **Figure 109**.

3. Install the cylinder head bolts. Tighten in 2 stages, first to 29 ft.-lb., then to 61.5 ft.-lb. Tighten in the sequence shown in **Figure 110** to prevent warping the cylinder head.

VALVES AND VALVE SEATS

Some of the following procedures must be done by a dealer or machine shop, since they require special knowledge and expensive machine tools. Others, while possible for the home mechanic, are difficult or time-consuming. A general practice among those who do their own service is to remove the cylinder head, perform all disassembly except valve removal and take the head to a machine shop for inspection and service. Since the cost is low in relation to the required effort and equipment, this is usually the best approach, even for experienced mechanics.

Valve Removal

1. Remove the cylinder head as described in this chapter.
2. Compress each valve spring with a compressor. Valve spring compressors are available from tool rental dealers. Remove the valve keepers and release the spring tension. Remove the spring washer, oil seal, inner and outer valve springs, lower cup and spring seat. See **Figure 111**.

CAUTION
Remove any burrs from valve stem grooves before removing the valves. Otherwise the valve guides will be damaged.

Valve and Valve Guide Inspection

1. Clean the valves with a wire brush and solvent. Discard cracked, warped or burned valves.
2. Measure valve stems at top, center and bottom for wear. See **Figure 112**. A machine shop can do this when the valves are ground. Also measure the length of each valve and the diameter of each valve head.
3. The valve faces and stem ends should be resurfaced when the valves are ground. No more than 0.5 mm (0.020 in.) may be removed from

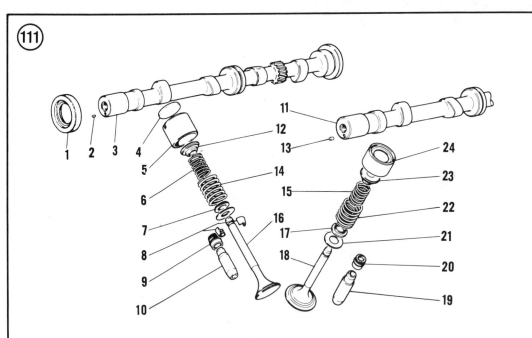

CAMSHAFTS AND VALVES

1. Camshaft oil seal
2. Exhaust camshaft dowel
3. Exhaust camshaft
4. Valve adjusting shim
5. Exhaust valve tappet
6. Exhaust valve inner spring
7. Lower spring seat
8. Valve keepers
9. Exhaust valve oil seal
10. Exhaust valve guide
11. Intake camshaft
12. Upper spring seat
13. Dowel
14. Exhaust valve outer spring
15. Intake valve inner spring
16. Exhaust valve
17. Lower spring seat
18. Intake valve
19. Intake valve guide
20. Oil seal
21. Washer
22. Intake valve outer spring
23. Upper spring seat
24. Intake valve tappet

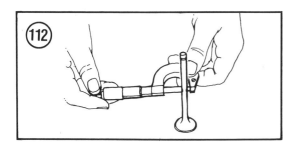

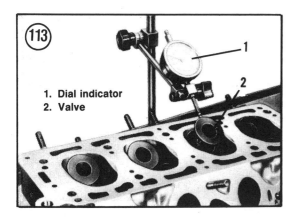

1. Dial indicator
2. Valve

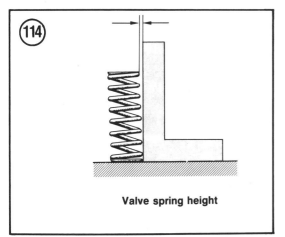

Valve spring height

valve stem ends. Valve faces may not be ground thinner than 0.5 mm (0.020 in.).

4. Remove all carbon and varnish from valve guides with a stiff spiral wire brush.

NOTE
The next step assumes that all valve stems have been measured and are within specifications. Replace worn valves before performing this step.

5. Set up a dial indicator as shown in **Figure 113**. Insert each valve into the guide from which it was removed. Hold the valve face approximately 1/8 in. off its seat and rock the valve sideways. If play exceeds 0.03 mm (0.0012 in.), replace the valve guide. This is a job for a dealer or mechine shop, although the procedure is described in this chapter.

6. Measure valve spring free length and compare with specifications. Replace springs that are too long or too short. Measure spring bend with a square (**Figure 114**). Replace springs bent beyond specifications.

7. Test the valve springs under load on a spring tester. See **Figure 115**. Replace weak springs.

8. Inspect valve seats (**Figure 116**). If worn or burned, they must be reconditioned. This is a job

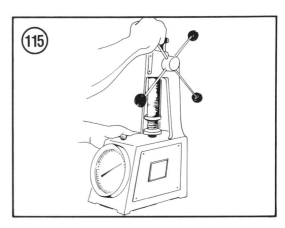

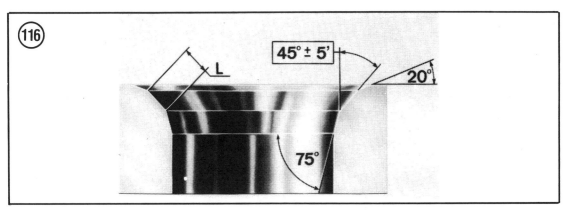

for a dealer or machine shop, although the procedure is described in this chapter.

Valve Guide Replacement

This procedure requires special tools. If you do not have the necessary equipment, take the job to a dealer or machine shop.

1. Tap out guides from the combustion chamber side with a drift such as Fiat tool part No. A.60395 (**Figure 117**).
2. Drive the new guides in with Fiat tool part No. A.60642 (**Figure 118**).
3. Replacement guides are prefinished, but if installation causes minor distortions, ream the new guides with Fiat tool part No. A.90310 (**Figure 119**).
4. Position a pilot tool such as Fiat tool part No. A.60313 over the valve guide. See **Figure 120**.
5. Tap a new stem seal onto the guide with a drift such as Fiat tool part No. A.60313/2. See **Figure 121**.

Valve Seat Reconditioning

1. Cut the valve seats to specifed dimensions, using a 45° cutter or special stone. See **Figure 116**. After cutting the seats, reduce seat width to specifications using 20° and 75° cutters.
cutters.
2. Grind valve faces to 45° 30' ± 5'.
3. Coat the corresponding valve face with Prussian blue dye.
4. Insert the valve into the valve guide.
5. Rotate the valve under light pressure approximately 1/4 turn.
6. Lift the valve out. If it seats properly, the dye will transfer evenly to the valve face.

Valve Installation

1. Coat the valves with oil and install them in the cylinder head.

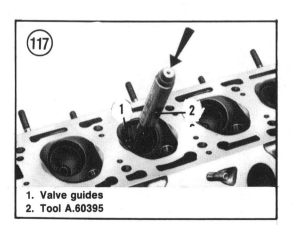

1. Valve guides
2. Tool A.60395

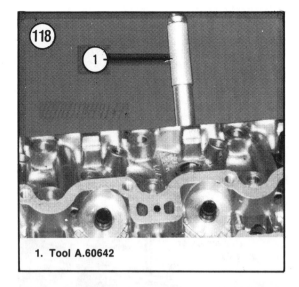

1. Tool A.60642

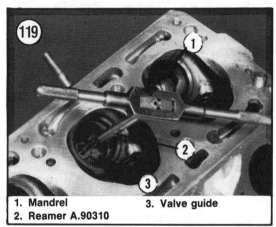

1. Mandrel   3. Valve guide
2. Reamer A.90310

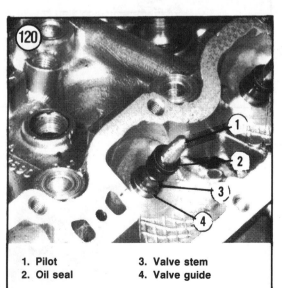

1. Pilot   3. Valve stem
2. Oil seal   4. Valve guide

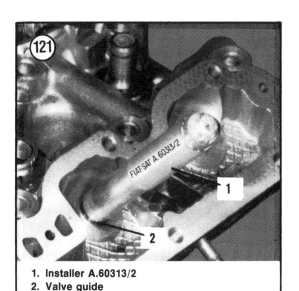

1. Installer A.60313/2
2. Valve guide

2. Install the valve spring flat washers, lower cups, inner and outer springs and upper cups. See **Figure 111**. Compress the valve springs and install the keepers.

OIL PAN AND
OIL PUMP

Figure 122 and **Figure 123** show the lubrication system.

Oil Pan Removal/Installation

1. Drain the engine oil (Chapter 3).
2. Remove the splash shield from under the front of the car.
3. On Turbos, loosen the clamp on the oil return hose (**Figure 124**). Push the hose upward, off of the fitting on the oil pan.
4. Remove the engine mount nuts through the crossmember access holes. See **Figure 125**.

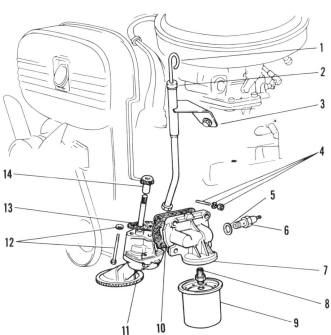

**LUBRICATION SYSTEM
(PART ONE)**

1. Dipstick
2. Dipstick seal
3. Dipstick bracket
4. Stud, lockwasher and nut
5. Gasket
6. Oil pressure switch
7. Oil filter adapter
8. Oil filter mounting fitting
9. Oil filter
10. Oil filter adapter gasket
11. Oil pump
12. Bolt and spring washer
13. Oil pump gasket
14. Oil pump drive gear

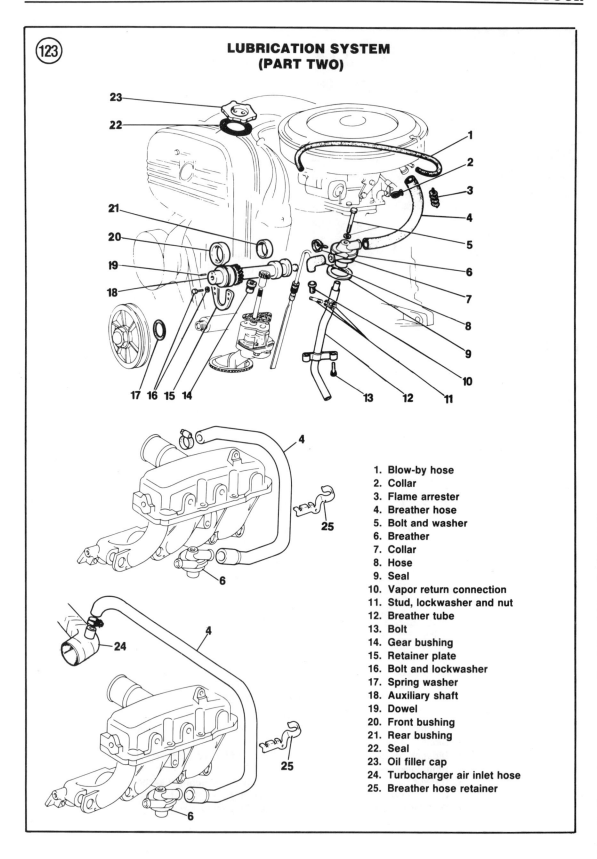

(123)

LUBRICATION SYSTEM
(PART TWO)

1. Blow-by hose
2. Collar
3. Flame arrester
4. Breather hose
5. Bolt and washer
6. Breather
7. Collar
8. Hose
9. Seal
10. Vapor return connection
11. Stud, lockwasher and nut
12. Breather tube
13. Bolt
14. Gear bushing
15. Retainer plate
16. Bolt and lockwasher
17. Spring washer
18. Auxiliary shaft
19. Dowel
20. Front bushing
21. Rear bushing
22. Seal
23. Oil filler cap
24. Turbocharger air inlet hose
25. Breather hose retainer

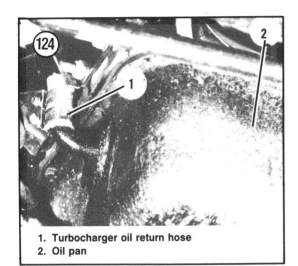

1. Turbocharger oil return hose
2. Oil pan

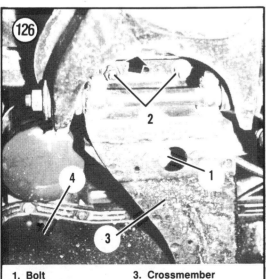

1. Bolt   3. Crossmember
2. Nuts   4. Oil pan

5. Remove the upper bolts that secure the crossmember to the body. See **Figure 126**.

6. Loosen the crossmember nuts (**Figure 126**) until about 2 threads are visible on the bottom of the stud (above the nut).

7. Repeat Step 5 and Step 6 on the other side of the car.

8. Lower the crossmember.

NOTE
The next step requires a hoist that can support the engine for the time the oil pan is off. Hydraulic crane type hoists, available from rental dealers, work well for this.

9. Attach a hoist to the engine and raise it just enough to provide removal clearance for the oil pan.

CAUTION
Check to make sure no hoses, wires or linkages are strained when the engine is hoisted. Disconnect parts as needed.

10. Remove the oil pan bolts, then take off the pan and gasket. See **Figure 127**.

11. Check the oil pan for cracks or dents. Replace the pan if cracked or dented. Clean the pan thoroughly in solvent. If it is difficult to clean, a machine shop can boil it out for a small fee. A thorough boiling will remove all deposits from inside the pan as well as stripping the paint from the outside.

12. Installation is the reverse of removal. Clean all traces of old gasket and sealer from the oil pan and engine. Tighten the pan bolts evenly to prevent warping the pan.

Oil Pump Removal/Installation

1. Remove the oil pan as described in this chapter.

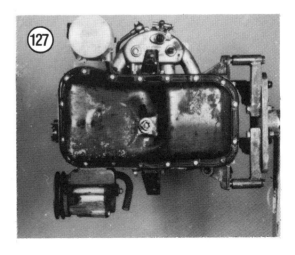

2. Remove the oil pump mounting bolts (**Figure 128**). Take the pump and its gasket off the engine.

3. Installation is the reverse of removal. Use a new pump gasket. Make sure the pump is seated properly on the engine before tightening the bolts.

Oil Pump Inspection

1. Place the oil pump in a vise and remove the pickup (**Figure 129**).

2. Remove the spring, relief valve and cover (**Figure 130**).

3. Take the drive shaft and gears out of the housing. See **Figure 131**.

4. Thoroughly clean all parts in solvent. While cleaning, check for obvious wear or damage. Replace worn or damaged parts.

5. Place the drive shaft and gears in the housing. Measure gear-to-housing clearance as shown in **Figure 132**. If it exceeds specifications, replace the gears or housing, whichever is worn.

6. Insert the feeler gauge blade between the gear teeth and measure backlash. See **Figure 133**. Replace the gears if backlash exceeds specifications.

7. Place a straightedge across the housing and gears as shown in **Figure 134**. Measure clearance with a feeler gauge. If it exceeds specifications, replace the gears or housing, whichever is worn.

8. Make sure there is no looseness at all between the drive shaft and drive gear. If the gear is loose on the shaft, replace the shaft and gear.

NOTE
The next 2 steps require a micrometer and bore gauge. A machine shop can do the steps inexpensively if you don't have the necessary equipment.

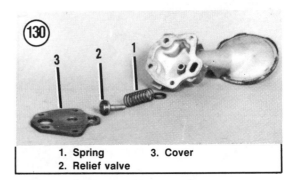

1. Spring   3. Cover
2. Relief valve

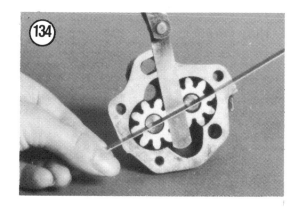

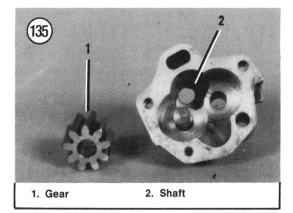

1. Gear   2. Shaft

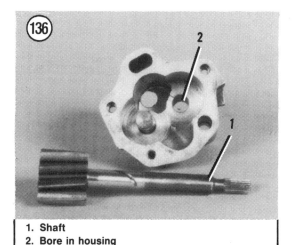

1. Shaft
2. Bore in housing

9. Check for excessive clearance between the driven gear and its shaft. See **Figure 135**. If it exceeds specifications, replace the gear or shaft, whichever is worn.

10. Check for excessive clearance between the pump drive shaft and housing. See **Figure 136**. If it exceeds specifications, replace the shaft or housing, whichever is worn.

11. Check the relief valve (**Figure 137**) for wear and replace it if wear can be seen.

12. Have the relief valve spring tested under load. Replace the spring if it is not within specifications.

13. Assemble by reversing Steps 1-3. During assembly, coat the oil pump gears and shaft with clean engine oil.

AUXILIARY SHAFT

The auxiliary shaft is mounted in the cylinder block. It drives the distributor (1967-1970 only), fuel pump (carburetted models only) and oil pump.

Removal/Installation

1. On 1967-1970 models, remove the distributor as described in Chapter Seven.

2. If equipped with a carburetor, remove the fuel pump as described in Chapter Five.

3. Remove the oil pan and pump as described in this chapter.

4. Remove the timing belt cover as described with *Timing Belt* in of this chapter.

5. Insert a wooden hammer handle between the crankshaft and cylinder block to keep the crankshaft from turning (**Figure 138**). Loosen the auxiliary shaft sprocket bolt (**Figure 139**).

6. Remove the timing belt as described in this chapter.

7. Remove the auxiliary shaft sprocket (**Figure 140**). If the sprocket is difficult to remove, carefully pry it off with 2 screwdrivers or small pry bars.

8. Thread the sprocket bolt back into the auxiliary shaft to provide a handle for removal. Remove the auxiliary shaft seal housing and gasket (**Figure 141**), then remove the lockplate (**Figure 142**).

9. Carefully pull out the auxiliary shaft. Rotate the shaft while pulling to ease removal.

10. Replace the auxiliary shaft seal as described under *Oil Seals* in this chapter.

11. Installation is the reverse of removal. Liberally coat the auxiliary shaft with clean engine oil before installation. Use a new seal housing gasket. Tighten all nuts and bolts to specifications.

> *NOTE*
> *Position the auxiliary shaft sprocket on the auxiliary shaft and turn it by hand while evenly tightening the oil pump bolts. If the sprocket becomes difficult to turn while tightening the bolts, loosen them and start over.*

12. After installation, turn the auxiliary shaft sprocket so its alignment mark is positioned as shown in **Figure 143**.

Inspection

1. Check the auxiliary shaft bearing surfaces (**Figure 144**) for wear or damage. If their condition is in doubt, have the surfaces checked by a machine shop. If worn beyond specifications, replace the auxiliary shaft.

2. Inspect the oil pump drive gear (**Figure 144**). On cars so equipped, inspect the fuel pump lobe. Replace the auxiliary shaft if either is worn or damaged.

3. Check the auxiliary shaft bearings (**Figure 145**) for wear or damage. If their condition is in doubt, have the bearings inspected and replaced if necessary by a machine shop.

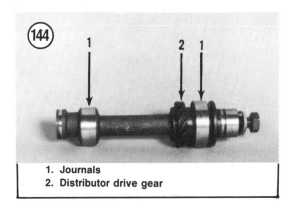

1. Journals
2. Distributor drive gear

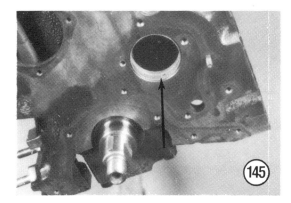

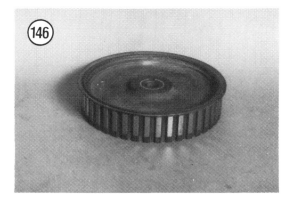

4. Check the auxiliary shaft sprocket (**Figure 146**) for wear or damage to the teeth or timing belt flange. Replace as needed.

FLYWHEEL

Removal/Inspection/Installation

1. To gain access to the flywheel, either remove the engine as described in this chapter or remove the transmission as described in Chapter Nine. If flywheel work or main oil seal replacement are the only procedures you plan to do, it will be easier to remove just the transmission.

2. Remove the clutch from the flywheel as described in Chapter Eight.

3. Hold the flywheel from turning. One way to do this is to reinstall a transmission-to-engine bolt, place the tip of a large screwdriver or pry bar in the ring gear teeth and place the side of the screwdriver or pry bar against the engine-to-transmission bolt. See **Figure 147**. A chain wrench (**Figure 148**) can also be used to hold the crankshaft pulley from turning.

NOTE
*If the tool or a substitute isn't available, remove the oil pan as described in this chapter. Insert a wooden hammer handle between the crankshaft and cylinder block (**Figure 149**) to hold the flywheel from turning.*

4. Check the flywheel friction surface (**Figure 150**) for scoring and wear. If the surface is glazed or slightly scratched, have it resurfaced by a machine shop. Replace the flywheel if damage is serious.

5. Measure flywheel runout with a dial indicator as shown in **Figure 151**. If runout is excessive, remove the flywheel and check for foreign material on the mating surfaces of flywheel and crankshaft. Clean the surfaces, reinstall the flywheel and check runout again. If it is still excessive, replace the flywheel or have it resurfaced.

6. Inspect the flywheel ring gear teeth (**Figure 150**). If the teeth are chipped, broken or excessively worn, have a new ring gear shrunk onto the flywheel by a machine shop.

7. Remove the flywheel bolts (**Figure 152**). Take the flywheel off the crankshaft.

8. Installation is the reverse of removal. Tighten flywheel bolts to specifications (end of chapter). Tighten gradually in a diagonal pattern.

TORQUE CONVERTER DRIVE PLATE

The torque converter drive plate is used with automatic transmissions. It is inspected, removed and installed in the same manner as the flywheel used with manual transmissions. However, the entire drive plate must be replaced if the ring gear teeth are defective.

OIL SEALS

This section provides replacement procedures for the auxiliary shaft oil seal, crankshaft front seal and rear main oil seal.

Auxiliary Shaft Seal Replacement

1. Remove the timing belt and auxiliary shaft sprocket as described in this chapter.

2. Place the seal housing on blocks (**Figure 153**). Tap the seal out with a hammer and blunt punch, using the hole shown in **Figure 154**.

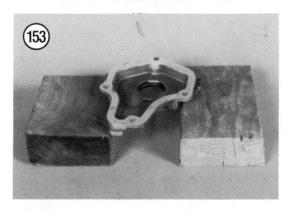

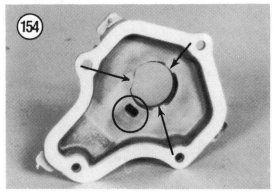

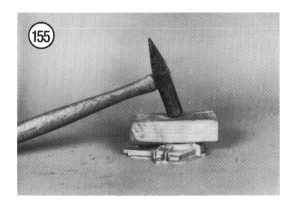

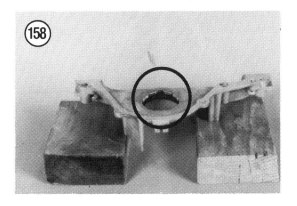

3. Tap a new seal in so its lip will face into the engine when installed. Use a block of wood to spread the hammer's force so the seal won't tilt sideways and jam. See **Figure 155**.

> *NOTE*
> *Make sure the seal is centered on the seal housing's 3 protrusions. See **Figure 154**.*

4. Coat the seal lip with multipurpose grease.

5. Install the seal housing on the engine as described under *Auxiliary Shaft* in this chapter.

Crankshaft Front Oil Seal Replacement

1. Remove the timing belt and auxiliary shaft sprocket as described in this chapter.

2. Remove the crankshaft sprocket (**Figure 156**). If the sprocket is difficult to remove, pry it off with 2 screwdrivers or small pry bars.

3. Remove the seal housing (**Figure 157**).

4. Place the seal housing on blocks (**Figure 158**). Tap the seal out with a blunt punch, using the notch shown.

5. Tap a new seal into the housing. Position the seal so its lip will face into the engine when the housing is installed. Use a block of wood to spread the hammer's force so the seal won't tilt sideways and jam. See **Figure 159**.

> *NOTE*
> *Make sure the seal is centered on the seal housing's 3 protrusions (**Figure 160**).*

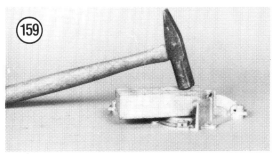

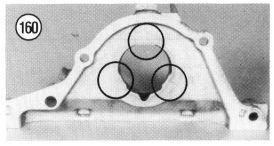

6. Clean all traces of old gasket and sealer from the housing and the front of the cylinder block. If the oil pan is on the engine, cut off the front portion of the pan gasket and scrape it off the pan. See **Figure 161**. Cut the front part off a new oil pan gasket, coat it with gasket sealer and install it on the oil pan.

7. Install the oil seal housing on the engine. Use a new gasket, coated on both sides with a thin layer of gasket sealer. Tighten all nuts and bolts to specifications.

8. Install the crankshaft sprocket.

9. Install the auxiliary shaft sprocket and timing belt as described in this chapter.

Rear Main Oil Seal Replacement

1. Remove the flywheel (manual transmission) or torque converter drive plate (automatic transmission) as described in this chapter.

2. Remove the seal housing and gasket from the cylinder block.

3. Place the seal housing on blocks (**Figure 162**). Tap the seal out with a hammer and blunt punch, using the notch shown.

4. Tap a new seal into the housing. Position the seal so its lip will face into the engine when the housing is installed. Use a block of wood to spread the hammer's force so the seal won't tilt sideways and jam. See **Figure 163**.

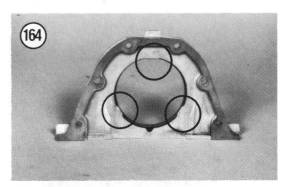

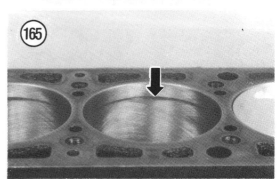

1. Connecting rod cap
2. Connecting rod cap nuts

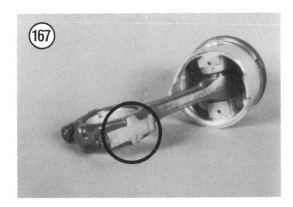

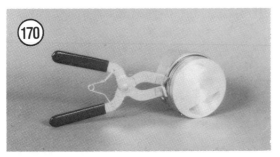

NOTE
*Make sure the seal is centered on the housing's 3 protrusions. See **Figure 164**.*

5. Install the seal housing on the engine. Use a new gasket, coated on both sides with a thin layer of gasket sealer.

PISTON/CONNECTING ROD ASSEMBLIES

Removal

1. Remove the cylinder head, oil pan and oil pump as described in this chapter.
2. Remove the carbon ridge at the top of the cylinder bore with a ridge reamer. See **Figure 165**. These are available from rental dealers.
3. Rotate the crankshaft so the piston is at the bottom of its travel and the connecting rod is centered in the bore. See **Figure 166**.

NOTE
*Check for identifying marks stamped on connecting rod and cap (**Figure 167**). The marks should be on the side of the connecting rod farthest from the auxiliary shaft. If the rods are not marked with cylinder numbers, make your own number marks.*

4. Remove the nuts securing the connecting rod cap (**Figure 166**). Lift off the cap, together with the lower bearing half. See **Figure 168**.

NOTE
*This is a convenient time to measure bearing clearance as described in this chapter. To do so, push the connecting rod partway out of the bore with a wooden hammer handle or taped screwdriver as shown in **Figure 169**. Wipe all oil off the crankpin, upper bearing half and lower bearing half. See **Connecting Rod Bearing Clearance Measurement** in this chapter for further details.*

5. Push the piston and connecting rod out of the bore with a wooden hammer handle or taped screwdriver. See **Figure 169**.
6. Remove the piston rings with a ring expander (**Figure 170**).

Inspection

1. To check for wear, place each piston/connecting rod assembly in a vise and twist the piston. Any rocking motion (not sliding) indicates a worn piston, pin or connecting rod bushing. Perform the following steps to find the problem.

2. The piston pins are a light slip fit in the connecting rods and pistons. To remove a piston pin, take out the lockrings (**Figure 171**). Push the piston pin out and take the piston off the connecting rod. See **Figure 172**.

3. Clean the piston pin and its bore in the piston. Lightly oil the pin and push it into the piston. It should be possible to push the pin in with light thumb pressure (**Figure 173**). However, the pin should be a tight enough fit that when held vertically as shown in **Figure 174**, the pin should not fall out of the piston under its own weight. If the pin does not fit properly, replace the pin and piston as a set.

4. If the pin fits correctly in the piston but had a rocking motion in Step 1, have pin diameter and connecting rod bushing bore diameter checked by a machine shop. If not within specifications, replace the pin or bushing, whichever is worn.

> *NOTE*
> *If the pin is worn, it must be replaced as a set with the piston. If the bushing is worn, have it replaced and reamed as necessary by the machine shop.*

> *NOTE*
> *When buying new pistons, note the piston class and piston pin class stamped on the base of the piston. See* **Figure 175**. *Also be sure to compare valve notch depths. The shallow-notched pistons used on some models have been superseded by pistons with deeper notches. See* **Figure 176**. *If*

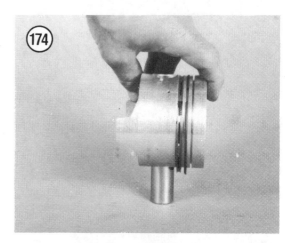

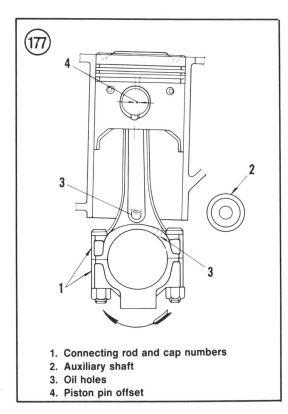

1. Connecting rod and cap numbers
2. Auxiliary shaft
3. Oil holes
4. Piston pin offset

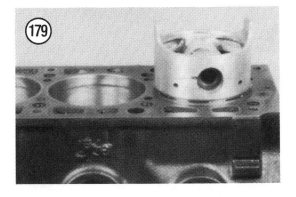

deep-notched pistons are the only replacements available, all 4 pistons should be replaced as a set.

5. If the piston was removed from the connecting rod, install it. Note that the piston pin bore in the piston is slightly offset away from the auxiliary shaft side of the engine. See **Figure 177**. The large valve notch in the piston top goes toward the intake side of the engine (left side when installed in the car). The small valve notch goes toward the exhaust side of the engine (right side when installed in the car).

Piston Clearance Check

1. Place the piston upright in its bore as shown in **Figure 178**. Measure clearance with a feeler gauge as shown.

NOTE
Position the feeler gauge at a point 27.5 mm (1.08 in.) from the bottom edge of the piston skirt and at right angles to the piston pin.

2. If clearance exceeds specifications, measure piston diameter with a micrometer at the same point on the piston where clearance was measured. If the piston is worn beyond specifications, it must be replaced. Check cylinder bore diameter as described under *Cylinder Block Inspection* in this chapter. If cylinder bore is within specifications, the pistons can be replaced with pistons of the same diameter. If the cylinder bores are worn excessively, the cylinders must be rebored and oversized pistons installed.

3. Repeat the procedure for all 4 cylinders and pistons.

Piston Ring Fit/Installation

1. Check the ring gap of each piston ring. To do this, position the ring at the top or bottom of the ring travel area and square it by tapping gently with an inverted piston. See **Figure 179**.

NOTE
If the cylinders have not been rebored, check the gap at the bottom of the ring travel, where the cylinder is least worn.

2. Measure ring gap with a feeler gauge as shown in **Figure 180**. Compare with specifications at the end of the chapter.

3. Check side clearance of the rings as shown in **Figure 181**. Place the feeler gauge alongside the ring all the way into the groove. Specifications are listed in **Table 1**.

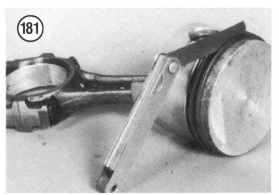

4. Using a ring expander tool (**Figure 170**), carefully install the oil control ring, then the compression rings. See **Figure 182**.

5. Position the ring gaps 120° apart. Make sure the gaps are not in line with the front-to-rear or side-to-side directions of an installed piston.

Connecting Rod Inspection

Have connecting rod straightness checked by a dealer or machine shop. Compare with specifications for bend and twist (**Table 1**).

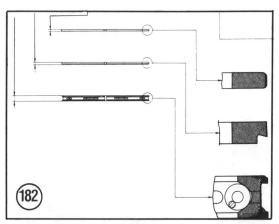

Connecting Rod Bearing Clearance Measurement

> *CAUTION*
> *If the connecting rods have been removed from the cylinder block, carefully follow the installation procedures in this chapter during bearing clearance measurement.*

1. Place connecting rods and upper bearing halves on the proper crankpins (connecting rod journals). See **Figure 183**.

2. Cut a piece of Plastigage (**Figure 184**) the width of the bearing. Place the Plastigage on the crankpin, then install the lower bearing half and cap.

> *NOTE*
> *Do not place Plastigage over the crankpin oil hole.*

3. Install the connecting rod cap and lower bearing half. Make sure the identifying marks are on the same side (**Figure 185**). Tighten the connecting rod cap to specifications. Do not rotate the crankshaft while the Plastigage is in place.

4. Remove the connecting rod cap. Bearing clearance is determined by comparing the width of the flattened Plastigage to the markings on the

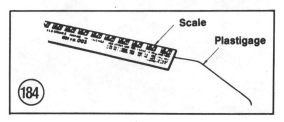

Scale

Plastigage

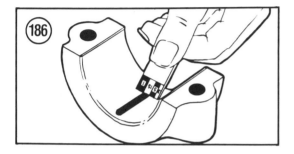

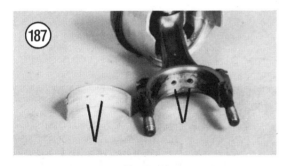

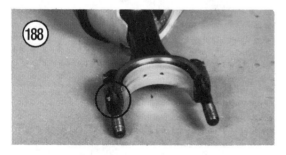

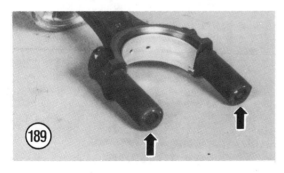

envelope (**Figure 186**). If clearance is excessive, the crankshaft must be reground and undersize bearings installed.

Installation

1. Make sure the pistons are correctly installed on the connecting rods. Note that the piston pin bore in the piston is slightly offset away from the auxiliary shaft side of the engine. See **Figure 177**. The large valve notch in the piston top goes toward the intake side of the engine (left side when installed in the car). The small valve notch goes toward the exhaust side of the engine (right side when installed in the car). The number marks on connecting rod and cap are on the side away from the auxiliary shaft.

2. Be sure the ring gaps are positioned correctly.

> *CAUTION*
> *During the next step, be sure the oil holes in the bearing align with the oil holes in the connecting rod. See **Figure 187**. If they don't, the cylinder walls will be damaged by lack of lubrication.*

3. Thoroughly clean the bearings, including the back sides. Install the upper bearing halves in the connecting rods. Be sure the small formed tangs in the bearing halves align with the machined notches in the connecting rods. See **Figure 188**.

4. Slide short pieces of hose over the connecting rod studs to protect the crankshaft. See **Figure 189**.

5. Immerse the entire piston in clean engine oil. Coat the cylinder wall and connecting rod upper bearing half with oil.

6. Slide a ring compressor over the rings. Compress the rings into the grooves. See **Figure 190**. Ring compressors are available from tool rental dealers.

> *NOTE*
> *The type of ring compressor shown in **Figure 190** has small protrusions on one edge. These go toward the bottom as shown.*

7. Install the piston/connecting rod assembly in its cylinder as shown in **Figure 191**. Tap lightly with a wooden hammer handle to insert the piston. Be sure the connecting rod number corresponds to the cylinder number (counting from the front of the engine).

> *CAUTION*
> *Use extreme care not to let the connecting rod nick the crankpin.*

8. Remove the hose from the connecting rod studs.

9. Place the lower bearing half in the connecting rod cap. Be sure the small formed tang in the bearing half aligns with the machined groove in the cap. See **Figure 192**. Coat the crankpins and bearings with clean engine oil.

10. Install the connecting rod cap (**Figure 193**). Make sure the identifying marks on the rod and cap are on the same side (away from the auxiliary shaft). Tighten the cap nuts (**Figure 194**) to specifications.

CRANKSHAFT

Removal

1. Remove the engine as described in this chapter.
2. Remove the transmission from the engine as described in Chapter Eight.
3. Remove the flywheel or torque converter drive plate as described in this chapter.
4. Remove the drive belts. See Chapter Three.
5. Remove the timing belt as described in this chapter.
6. Remove the oil pan.

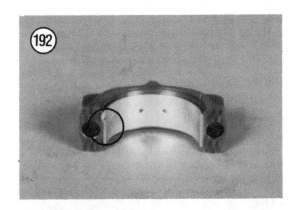

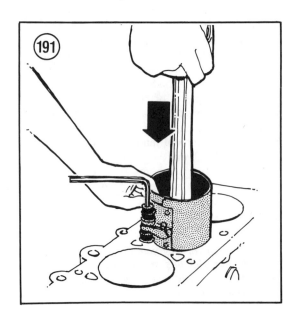

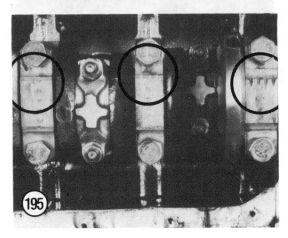

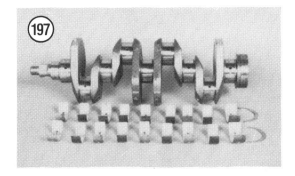

7. Remove the connecting rod caps.

8. Remove the crankshaft front and rear oil seals as described under *Oil Seals* in this chapter.

9. Set up a dial indicator with its pointer contacting the front end of the crankshaft. Pry the crankshaft to the front and rear with 2 screwdrivers and note the reading (crankshaft end play). If it exceeds specifications (end of chapter), replace the thrust rings.

10. Check the main bearing caps for the notches that indicate cap number. The front cap has no notches, the second cap has one notch, the center cap has 2 notches, No. 4 cap has 3 notches and the rear cap has 4 notches. See **Figure 195**. If the notches are not visible, clean the main bearing caps with a wire brush. If the notches are still not visible, make your own number marks with a sharp punch.

11. Unbolt the main bearing caps (**Figure 196**). Loosen the caps in 2 or 3 stages, starting with the center cap and working outward.

12. Place the caps in order on a clean workbench.

13. Lift the crankshaft out of the engine. Lay the crankshaft, main bearings and bearing caps in order on a clean workbench. See **Figure 197**.

Inspection

1. Clean the crankshaft thoroughly with solvent. Flush the oil passages with solvent, then blow them dry with compressed air.

NOTE
If you do not have precision measuring equipment, have a machine shop perform Steps 2 and 3.

2. Check crankpins and main bearing journals for wear, scoring and cracks. Check all journals against specifications for out-of-roundness, taper and wear. See **Figure 198**. Have the crankshaft reground if necessary.

3. Check the crankshaft for bending. Mount the crankshaft between accurate centers (such as V-blocks or a lathe) and rotate it one full turn with a dial indicator contacting the center journal. If bent beyond specifications, the crankshaft may be straightened with a hyraulic press. However, it may be more practical to replace the crankshaft with a new one. Check with local machine shops before choosing a course of action.

Pilot Bearing Inspection

The pilot bearing (**Figure 199**) supports the input shaft on manual transmission. Cars with automatic transmissions do not have pilot bearings.

1. Turn the bearing with a finger and check for looseness or rough movement. If either of these

conditions is found, remove the bearing with a puller like the one shown in **Figure 200**. These are available from rental dealers.

2. Tap a new bearing in with a drift that bears against the bearing outer race. If you do not have the proper drift, tap the bearing in with a hammer and block of wood as shown in **Figure 201**.

Main Bearing Clearance Measurement

Main bearing clearance is measured in the same manner as connecting rod bearing clearance, described in this chapter. Excessive clearance requires that the bearings be replaced, the crankshaft be reground or both.

Installation

1. Thoroughly clean bearings, including the back sides.

> *CAUTION*
> *During the next step, be sure the bearing oil holes align with the block oil holes (**Figure 202**). Otherwise the crankshaft will run without lubrication and be ruined.*

2. Install the bearings in the cylinder block and bearing caps. Make sure the bearing locating tangs are correctly positioned in the cylinder block and bearing cap grooves. See **Figure 203**.

3. Coat the bearings freely with clean engine oil. Lay the crankshaft in the block. See **Figure 204**. Coat the crankshaft journals with engine oil.

4. Coat the thrust bearings with clean engine oil, then install them in the block and cap at the rear end of the engine. See **Figure 205**. The oil grooves (**Figure 206**) face the crankshaft (away from the cylinder block).

5. Install bearing halves in the bearing caps. Be sure the small formed tangs fit in the machined notches. See **Figure 207**.

6. Install the bearing caps and tighten the cap bolts slightly. See **Figure 208**. Make sure the identification numbers on the caps are upright when viewed from the flywheel end of the engine. Make sure the number marks (**Figure 209**) are in order, starting from the front end of the engine.

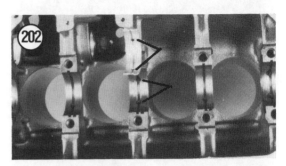

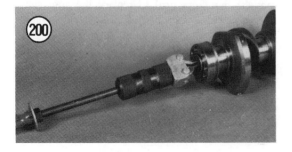

7. Gently push the crankshaft toward front and rear of the engine to verify that the bearings and caps are properly aligned and seated.

8. Tighten the cap bolts to specifications. Tighten gradually in 2 or 3 stages, starting with the end caps and working toward the center. Rotate the crankshaft during tightening to make sure it isn't binding. If the crankshaft becomes hard to turn, stop and find out why before continuing. Check for foreign material on bearings and journals. Make absolutely certain the bearings are the correct size, especially if the crankshaft has been reground. Never use undersize bearings if the crankshaft has not been reground.

9. Recheck crankshaft end play, as described during removal.

10. Install new crankshaft front and rear oil seals as described under *Oil Seals* in this chapter.

11. Install the connecting rod caps.

12. Install the oil pan.

13. Install the timing belt.

14. Install the drive belts (Chapter Three).

15. Install the flywheel or torque converter drive plate.

16. Install the transmission (Chapter Eight).

17. Install the engine in the car.

CYLINDER BLOCK INSPECTION

1. Clean the block thoroughly with solvent and check all core plugs (**Figure 210**) for leaks. Replace any core plugs that are suspect. It is a good idea to replace all of them. While cleaning, check oil and water passages for sludge, dirt and corrosion. If the passages are very dirty, the block should be boiled out by a machine shop.

NOTE
Block boiling necessitates replacement of all core plugs and auxiliary shaft bushings. However, a block dirty enough to need boiling almost certainly needs these parts replaced anyway.

2. Examine the block for cracks.

3. Check flatness of the cylinder block's top surface. Use an accurate straightedge as shown in **Figure 211**. Measure in the directions shown in **Figure 212**. Have the block resurfaced if it is warped at all.

4. Measure the cylinder bores for out-of-roundness or excessive wear with a bore gauge (**Figure 213**). Measure the bores at top, center and bottom, in front-to-rear and side-to-side directions. Compare measurements to specifications at the end of the chapter. If the cylinders exceed maximum tolerances, they must

be rebored. Reboring is also necessary if the cylinder walls are badly scuffed or scored.

NOTE
If the bores can be cleaned up by removing less than 0.015 mm (0.006 in.), honing is acceptable.

NOTE
*Bore grades are stamped in the cylinder block next to each bore. See **Figure 214**.*

5. Check auxiliary shaft bushings (**Figure 215**) for wear or damage. Have worn or damaged bushings replaced by a machine shop.

6. Check the oil pump drive shaft bushing (**Figure 216**) for visible wear or damage. If wear or damage can be seen or if the bushing is loose in its bore, have it replaced by a machine shop.

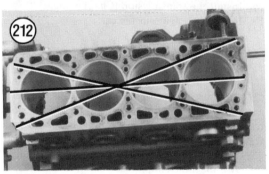

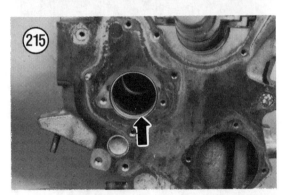

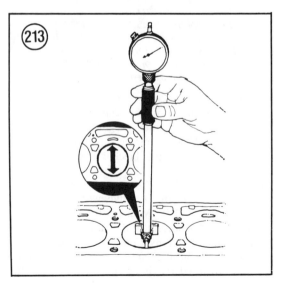

Table 1 ENGINE SPECIFICATIONS

	mm	in.
Camshaft housings		
Bearing bore diameters		
Front	30.009-30.034	1.1814-1.1824
Center	45.800-45.825	1.8031-1.8042
Rear	46.200-46.225	1.8189-1.8198
Journal diameter		
Front	29.944-29.960	1.1787-1.1795
Center	45.755-45.771	1.8031-1.8042
Rear	46.155-46.171	1.8171-1.8178
Camshaft bearing clearance		
Front	0.049-0.090	0.0019-0.0035
Center and rear	0.029-0.070	0.0011-0.0027
Lifters		
Lifter bore diameter	37.000-37.025	1.4567-1.4576
Lifter diameter	36.975-36.995	1.4557-1.4565
Lifter clearance in bore	0.005-0.050	0.0002-0.0020
Cylinder head and valves		
Maximum head warp	0.05	0.002
Valve guide bore		
Through 1978	14.950-14.977	0.5886-0.5896
1979-on	13.950-13.977	0.5492-0.5502
Valve guide outside diameter		
Through 1978	14.998-15.016	0.5905-0.5912
1979-on	14.040-14.058	0.5527-0.5534
Available guide oversize		
Through 1978	0.2	0.008
1979-on	0.05, 0.10, 0.25, 0.45	0.0019, 0.0039, 0.0098, 0.0177
Guide inside diameter	8.022-8.040	0.3158-0.3165
Guide interference fit in head		
Through 1978	0.021-0.066	0.0008-0.0026
1979-on	0.063-0.1CC	0.0025-0.0042
Valve stem diameter	7.974-9.992	0.3139-0.3146
Valve stem-to-guide clearance	0.030-0.066	0.0012-0.0026
Valve seat angle in head	45° ±5'	
Valve face angle	45° 30' ±5'	
Valve head diameter		
1608 cc engine (type 125BC)[1]		
Intake	41.4	1.6299
Exhaust	36	1.4173
1592 cc engine (type 132AC)[1]		
Intake	41.20-41.60	1.6220-1.6378
Exhaust	35.85-36.45	1.4115-1.4350
1756 cc engine (type 132A1, 1974-1978)		
Intake	42.20-42.60	1.6614-1.6772
Exhaust	35.85-36.45	1.4115-1.4350
1995 cc engine (1979-on)		
Intake	41.60-42.00	1.6377-1.6535
Exhaust	35.85-36.45	1.4115-1.4350
Valve seat width	2	0.0787
Valve head runout, maximum	0.03	0.0012
Valve spring installed height		
Outer spring @ 38.9 kg		
(85.5 lb.)	36	1.417
Inner spring @ 14.9 kg		
(832.8 lb.)	31	1.220
	(continued)	

Table 1 ENGINE SPECIFICATIONS (continued)

	mm	in.
Minimum spring tension @ installed height		
Outer spring	36 kg	79 lb.
Inner spring		
1971-1972	13.5 kg	29.7 lb.
1973-on	14.5 kg	32.5 lb.
Oil pump		
Gear-to-cover clearance		
Through 1974	0.031-0.116	0.0012-0.0045
1975-on	0.026-0.131	0.0010-0.0051
Gear-to-pump body clearance	0.11-0.18	0.0043-0.0071
Auxiliary shaft		
Bushing bores in block		
Front	51.120-51.150	2.0126-2.0138
Rear	42.030-42.060	1.6547-1.6559
Bushing inside diameter		
Front	48.084-48.104	1.8930-1.8938
Rear	39.000-39.020	1.5354-1.5362
Journal diameter		
Front	48.013-48.038	1.8903-1.8913
Rear	38.929-38.954	1.5326-1.5336
Journal-to-bushing clearance	0.046-0.091	0.0018-0.0036
Pistons and piston rings		
Piston diameter, standard		
1608 cc engine (type 125BC)[1]		
Class A	79.925-79.935	3.1466-3.1470
Class C	79.945-79.955	3.1474-3.1478
Class E	79.965-79.975	3.1482-3.1486
1592 cc engine (type 132AC)[1]		
Class A	79.950-79.960	3.1476-3.1479
Class C	79.970-79.980	3.1483-3.1487
Class E	79.990-80.000	3.1491-3.1496
Available oversizes	0.2, 0.4, 0.6	0.008, 0.016, 0.024
1756 cc and 1995 cc engines (1974-on)		
Class A	83.950-83.960	3.3051-3.3055
Class C	83.970-83.980	3.3058-3.3063
Class E	83.990-84.000	3.3066-3.3070
Piston-to-bore clearance		
1608 cc engine (type 125BC)[1]	0.065-0.085	0.0025-0.0033
1592 cc engine (type 132AC)[1]	0.040-0.060	0.0016-0.0024
1756 and 1995 cc engines (1974-on)	0.040-0.060	0.0016-0.0024
Piston pin bore diameter		
Class 1	21.996-21.999	0.8660-0.8661
Class 2	21.999-22.002	0.8661-0.8662
Piston pin diameter		
Class 1	21.991-21.994	0.8658-0.8659
Class 2	21.994-21.997	0.8659-0.8660
Piston pin-to-piston clearance	0.002-0.008	0.0001-0.0003
Available oversize piston pins	0.2	0.008
Piston ring gap		
1608 and 1592 cc engines		
Top compression ring	0.30-0.45	0.012-0.018
Second compression ring	0.20-0.35	0.008-0.014
Oil ring	0.20-0.35	0.008-0.014
1756 cc and 1995 cc engines		
Compression rings	0.30-0.45	0.012-0.018
Oil ring	0.25-0.40	0.010-0.016
	(continued)	

Table 1 ENGINE SPECIFICATIONS (continued)

	mm	in.
Piston ring side clearance		
Top compression ring	0.045-0.077	0.0018-0.0030
Second compression ring	0.040-0.072	0.0016-0.0028
Oil ring	0.030-0.062	0.0011-0.0024
Connecting rods		
Bearing clearance		
1608 cc engine (type 125BC)[1]		
Class A (color coded red)	0.046-0.080	0.0018-0.0031
Class B (color coded blue)	1.520-1.524	0.0598-0.0599
1592 cc engine (type 132AC)[1]		
Class A (color coded red)	1.521-1.525	0.0599-0.0600
Class B (color coded blue)	1.525-1.529	0.0600-0.0602
1756 cc engine		
Class A (color coded red)	0.045-0.079	0.0018-0.0031
Class B (color coded blue)	0.047-0.081	0.0019-0.0032
1995 cc engine	0.021-0.065	0.0008-0.0025
Bearing thickness		
1608 cc engine (type 125BC)[1]		
Class A (color coded red)	1.516-1.520	0.0597-0.0598
Class B (color coded blue)	1.520-1.524	0.0598-0.0600
1592 cc engine (type 132AC)[1]		
Class A (color coded red)	1.521-1.525	0.0599-0.0600
Class B (color coded blue)	1.525-1.529	0.0600-0.0602
1756 cc engine		
Class A (color coded red)	1.521-1.525	0.0599-0.0600
Class B (color coded blue)	1.525-1.529	0.0600-0.0602
1995 cc engine	1.5338-1.5370	0.0603-0.0605
Big end bore diameter		
1608 cc engine	51.330-51.346	2.0208-2.0214
All except 1608 cc engine	53.897-53.913	2.1219-2.1225
Small end bore diameter	23.939-23.972	0.9424-0.9438
Small end bushing outside diameter	24.016-24.041	0.9455-0.9465
Small end bushing inside diameter (after finish reaming)		
Grade 1	22.004-22.007	0.8663-0.8664
Grade 2	22.007-22.010	0.8664-0.8665
Maximum misalignment between centerlines of small end and big end, measured @ 125 mm (4.92 in. from the shank)	±0.10	±0.0039
Crankshaft		
Main bearing clearance		
All except 1995 cc engine	0.050-0.095	0.0020-0.0037
1995 cc engine	0.032-0.077	0.0012-0.0030
Journal diameter		
1608 cc engine	50.775-50.985	1.9994-2.0002
All except 1608 cc engine	52.985-53.005	2.0860-2.0868
Crankpin diameter		
1608 cc engine		
Class A (color coded red)	48.234-48.244	1.8990-1.8994
Class B (color coded blue)	48.224-48.234	1.8986-1.8990
All except 1608 cc engine		
Class A (color coded red)	50.792-50.802	1.9997-2.0001
Class B (color coded blue)	50.782-50.792	1.9993-1.9997
Maximum out-of-round and taper, journals and crankpins	0.005	0.0002

(continued)

Table 1 ENGINE SPECIFICATIONS (continued)

	mm	in.
Maximum misalignment of main bearing journals[2]	0.03	0.0012
Maximum misalignment of crankpins to main bearing journals	±0.35	±0.014
Crankshaft end play		
1971-1972	0.055-0.265	0.0021-0.0104
1973-on	0.055-0.305	0.0021-0.0020
Cylinder block[3]		
Bore diameter		
1608 and 1592 cc engines	80.000-80.050	3.1496-3.1516
1756 cc and 1995 cc engines	84.000-84.050	3.3070-3.3090
Flywheel		
Maximum variation between flywheel friction surface and flywheel mounting surface on crankshaft	0.10	0.004
Maximum runout of friction surface	0.10	0.004

1. The 1608 cc engine (type 125BC) was used on 1971 through early 1973 models. The 1592 cc engine (type 132AC) was used on late 1973 models only. To tell which engine a 1973 model has, refer to the vehicle identification plate in the engine compartment.
2. Total indicator reading.
3. Cylinder bores are graded into classes with 0.01 mm (0.0004 in.) increments.

Table 2 TIGHTENING TORQUES

Fastener	Thread size	mkg	ft.-lb.
Air pump support stud nut	M10×1.25	5	36
Air pump support nut	M8	2.8	20
Air pump bracket bolt			
Without green coating	M10×1.25	5.3	38
With green coating	M10×1.25	7.2	52
Alternator lower bracket to engine (self-locking nut)*	M12×1.25	5.5	40
Alternator upper bracket to engine			
Screw (1608 and 1592 cc)	M10×1.25	5.5	40
Nut (1765 and 1995 cc)	M12×1.25	7	50
Alternator to upper bracket nut	M10×1.25	4.5	33
Alternator to lower bracket nut	M12×1.25	7	50
Camshaft housings to engine			
Nuts (1608 and 1592 cc)	M8	2.5	18
Bolts (1756 and 1995 cc)	M8	2	14
Camshaft sprocket bolts	M12×1.25	12	87
Connecting rod nuts			
1608 and 1592 cc	M9×1	5.5	40
1756 and 1995 cc	M10×1	7.5	54
Crankshaft pulley nut			
1971-1972	M20×1.5	12	87
1973-on	M20×1.5	25	181
Cylinder head bolts			
1971-1972	M10×1.25	8	58
1973 (1608 cc)	M10×1.25	8.5	61.5
1973 (1592 cc)	M10×1.25	7.5	54
1974-on	M10×1.25	8.5	61.5
Liquid-vapor separator bolt	M8	2.3	17

(continued)

Table 2 TIGHTENING TORQUES (continued)

Fastener	Thread size	mkg	ft.-lb.
Main bearing cap bolts			
1971-1973 (1608 cc)	M10×1.25	8	58
1973 (1592 cc)			
One small bolt (front cap)	M10×1.25	8	58
Nine large bolts	M12×1.25	11.5	83
1974-on			
One small bolt (front cap)	M10×1.25	8.2	59
Nine large bolts	M12×1.25	11.5	83
Manifold bolts/nuts*	M8	2.5	18
Flywheel bolts			
	M10×1.25 bolts	8.5	61
	M12×1.25 bolts	14.5	105
Timing belt tensioner nut	M10×1.25	4.5	33
Turbocharged engine			
Turbocharger to exhaust manifold		22	
Exhaust manifold nuts		22	
Outlet elbow to turbocharger bolts		22	
Outlet elbow to exhaust pipe nuts		22	
Turbocharger support bracket to cylinder block bolts		22	
Outlet elbow support bracket to cylinder block nuts		30	
Plenum support bracket to plenum bolt		12	
Spark plugs		14	
Oxygen sensor		30	
Exhaust manifold heat shield		22	

* 22 ft.-lb. on Turbo exhaust manifold nuts.

4

Table 3 ENGINE APPLICATIONS

1971-1972	1608 cc (98.13 cu. in.)
1973	
Spider, chassis numbers beginning with 124 BS.1	1608 cc (98.13 cu. in.)
Coupe, chassis numbers beginning with 124 BC.1	1608 cc (98.13 cu. in.)
Spider, chassis numbers beginning with 124 CS	1592 cc (97.17 cu. in.)
Coupe, chassis numbers beginning with 124 CC	1592 cc (97.17 cu. in.)
1974-1978	1756 cc (107.13 cu. in.)
1979-on	1995 cc (121.74 cu. in.)

CHAPTER FIVE

FUEL, EXHAUST AND EMISSION CONTROL SYSTEMS

This chapter provides service procedures for the air cleaner, carburetor, fuel injection system, turbocharger, emission control systems, throttle linkage, exhaust system and fuel pump.

Table 1 is at the end of the chapter.

AIR CLEANER

Removal/Installation
(With Carburetor)

1. On 1975 and later models, disconnect the hot air duct from the air cleaner.
2. Disconnect the air injection hose(s) from the side of the air cleaner (if so equipped).
3. Remove the air cleaner cover nuts and lift off the cover. See **Figure 1**.
4. Remove 4 nuts securing the air cleaner spacer to the carburetor.
5. Lift the air cleaner up, disconnect the hoses from the bottom and take the air cleaner out.
6. Installation is the reverse of removal, plus the following:
   a. Make sure the metal bushings are installed in the air cleaner spacer.
   b. On 1971-1974 models, position the intake nozzle according to outside temperature. For warm climates, position the nozzle pointing forward (**Figure 2**). For cold climates, position the nozzle pointing downward so it will draw in hot air from around the exhaust manifold.
   c. On 1975-1978 models, position the cover baffle according to outside temperature. If temperatures are above 15° C (60° F), align the

letter "E" on the cover with the intake nozzle arrow. See **Figure 1**. If temperatures are below 15° C (60° F), align the letter "I" on the cover with the intake nozzle arrow.

Removal/Installation
(With Fuel Injection)

1. Loosen the air supply hose clamps and remove the hose. See **Figure 3**.
2. Remove the wing nut, lift the top off the air cleaner and remove the filter element.
3. Remove the air cleaner mounting nuts and take the air cleaner out.
4. Installation is the reverse of removal.

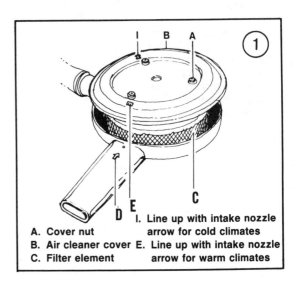

A. Cover nut
B. Air cleaner cover
C. Filter element
I. Line up with intake nozzle arrow for cold climates
E. Line up with intake nozzle arrow for warm climates

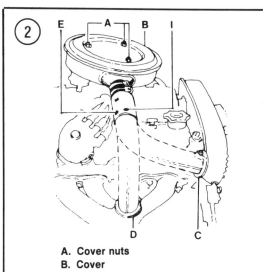

②

A. Cover nuts
B. Cover
C. Intake nozzle in
   warm-weather position
D. Intake nozzle in
   cold-weather position
E. Turn this mark upward
   for cold-weather position
I. Turn this mark upward
   for warm-weather position

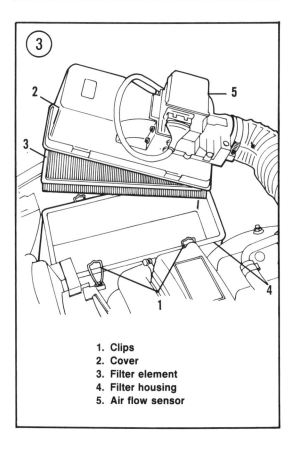

③

1. Clips
2. Cover
3. Filter element
4. Filter housing
5. Air flow sensor

CARBURETOR

All carburetted models use a 2-barrel downdraft carburetor. The 1971-1974 cars are equipped with a manual choke. The 1975 and later models use a water-heated automatic choke.

Removal/Installation

1. Remove the air cleaner as described in this chapter.
2. Disconnect the fuel inlet and return lines.
3. Unplug the wiring connectors (if so equipped).
4. Label and disconnect all vacuum lines.
5. On 1971-1974 carburetors, disconnect the choke cable.
6. On 1975 and later carburetors, disconnect the choke water hoses.
7. Disconnect the throttle linkage from the carburetor.
8. Remove the carburetor mounting nuts. Lift off the carburetor and gasket.
9. Installation is the reverse of removal. Use a new gasket.

Disassembly

This section gives step-by-step overhaul procedures for the carburetor used on 1975-1978 models. All other carburetor designs are basically the same, but differ in some construction details. For points that differ from 1975-1978 models, refer to the following illustrations:

    a. 1971-1974—**Figure 4** and **Figure 5**.
    b. 1979-on—**Figures 6-8**.

Repair kits are available which include all necessary parts for overhaul. **Figure 9** shows a factory repair kit. Kits are also available from aftermarket suppliers.

NOTE
Aftermarket repair kits may contain parts for several carburetor models.

1. Remove the choke water jacket bolt, water jacket and gasket. See **Figure 10**.
2. Remove 3 choke spring housing retainer screws and the choke spring housing. See **Figure 11**.
3. Remove the nylon plate from the choke housing (**Figure 12**).

CAUTION
The E-ring mentioned in the next step is delicate and the repair kit does not contain a replacement. Do not damage it.

4. Remove the E-ring that secures the choke plate lever to the connecting link. See **Figure 13**.
5. Inspect the choke mechanism (fast idle cam, lever and spring shown in **Figure 14**). Replace

5

WEBER DFH CARBURETOR

1. Screw
2. Washer
3. Pin
4. Lever
5. Lockwasher
6. Nut
7. Filter
8. Plate
9. Link
10. Spring
11. Diaphragm
12. Cover
13. Screw
14. Valve
15. Screw
16. Stud
17. Cover
18. Shaft
19. Float
20. Plug
21. Jet
22. Jet
23. Screw
24. Link
25. Plug
26. Choke plate
27. Gasket
28. Gasket
29. Valve
30. Pin
31. Gasket
32. Valve
33. Screw
34. Pipe

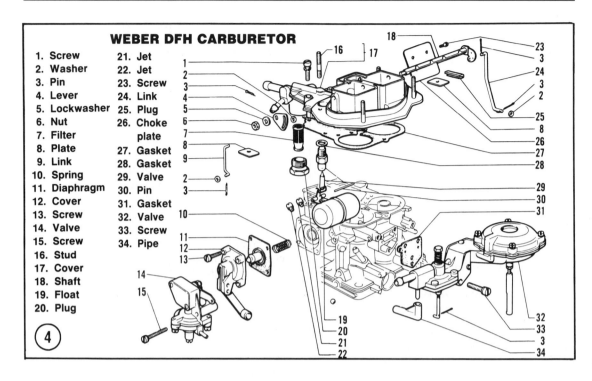

CARBURETOR AIR HORN (1979-ON)

1. Choke water jacket
2. Gasket and choke coil
3. Plate
4. Bolt
5. O-ring
6. Screw
7. Screw
8. Washer
9. Choke housing
10. O-ring
11. Screw
12. Fuel inlet assembly
13. Washer
14. Needle valve, needle valve seat, float and pivot pin

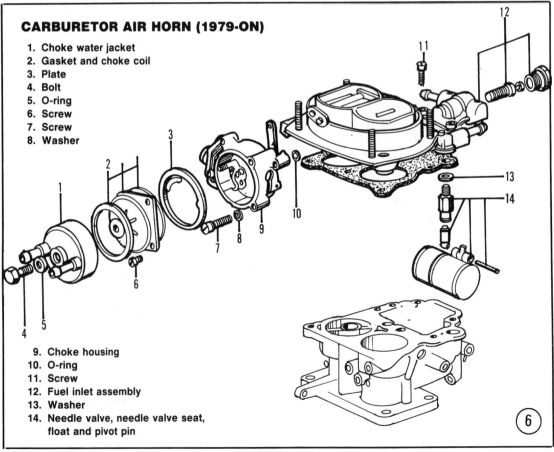

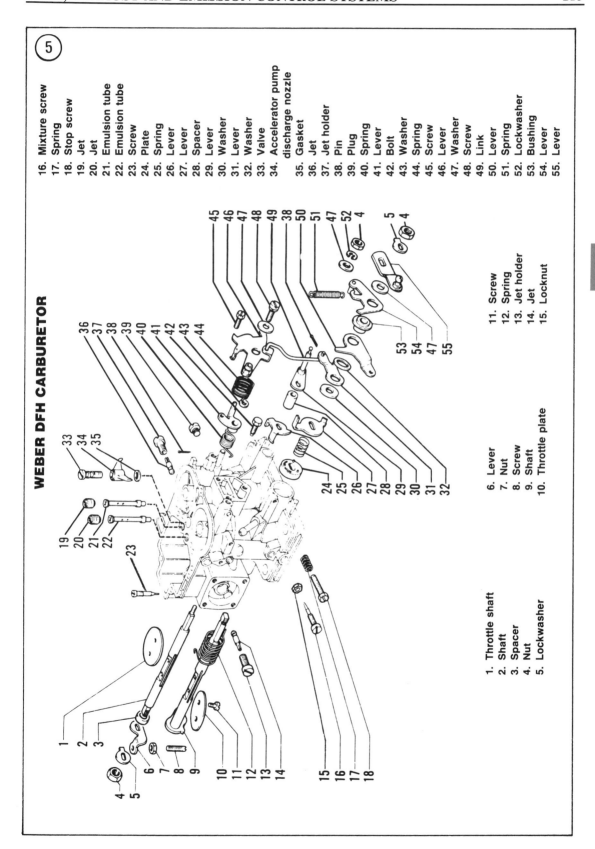

WEBER DFH CARBURETOR

1. Throttle shaft
2. Shaft
3. Spacer
4. Nut
5. Lockwasher
6. Lever
7. Nut
8. Screw
9. Shaft
10. Throttle plate
11. Screw
12. Spring
13. Jet holder
14. Jet
15. Locknut
16. Mixture screw
17. Spring
18. Stop screw
19. Jet
20. Jet
21. Emulsion tube
22. Emulsion tube
23. Screw
24. Plate
25. Spring
26. Lever
27. Lever
28. Spacer
29. Lever
30. Washer
31. Lever
32. Washer
33. Valve
34. Accelerator pump discharge nozzle
35. Gasket
36. Jet
37. Jet holder
38. Pin
39. Plug
40. Spring
41. Lever
42. Bolt
43. Washer
44. Spring
45. Screw
46. Lever
47. Washer
48. Screw
49. Link
50. Lever
51. Spring
52. Lockwasher
53. Bushing
54. Lever
55. Lever

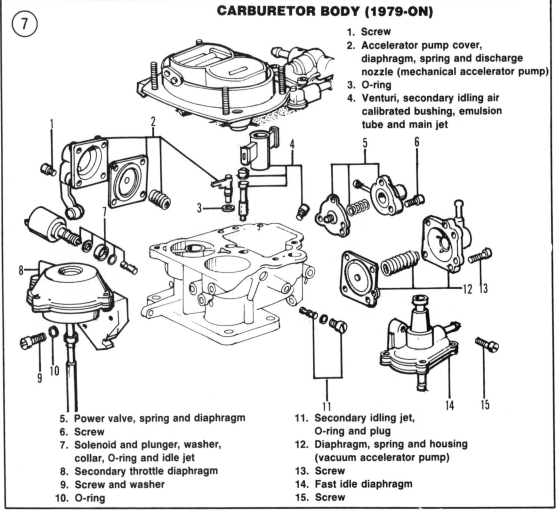

CARBURETOR BODY (1979-ON)

1. Screw
2. Accelerator pump cover, diaphragm, spring and discharge nozzle (mechanical accelerator pump)
3. O-ring
4. Venturi, secondary idling air calibrated bushing, emulsion tube and main jet
5. Power valve, spring and diaphragm
6. Screw
7. Solenoid and plunger, washer, collar, O-ring and idle jet
8. Secondary throttle diaphragm
9. Screw and washer
10. O-ring
11. Secondary idling jet, O-ring and plug
12. Diaphragm, spring and housing (vacuum accelerator pump)
13. Screw
14. Fast idle diaphragm
15. Screw

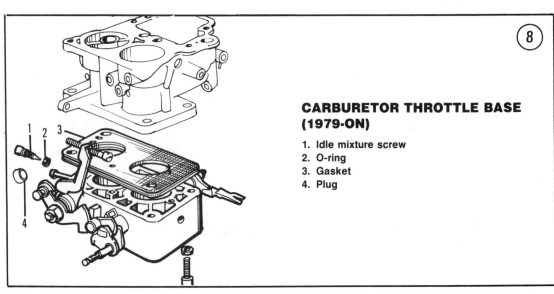

CARBURETOR THROTTLE BASE (1979-ON)

1. Idle mixture screw
2. O-ring
3. Gasket
4. Plug

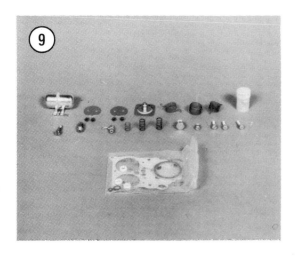

1. Bolt 2. Choke water jacket

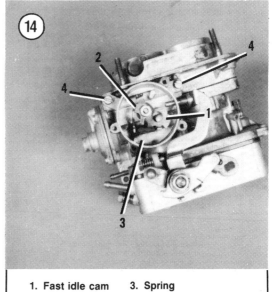

1. Fast idle cam   3. Spring
2. Lever   4. Choke housing screws

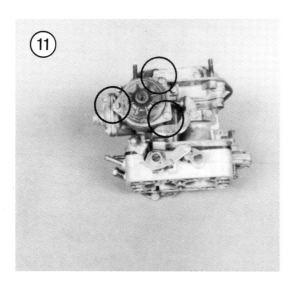

5

worn or damaged parts. If parts are serviceable, leave them in place and do not remove the nut.

6. Remove the choke housing screws, lockwashers and plain washers (**Figure 14**). Pull the fast idle cam screw out of the way and take the choke housing off.

7. Remove the plastic rod guide retainer and rubber O-ring (**Figure 15**).

8. Remove the plastic rod guide (**Figure 16**) through the retainer hole.

9. Remove 2 screws and take off the fast idle electrovalve. See **Figure 17**.

NOTE
The electrovalve O-ring may come off with the electrovalve or remain on the carburetor body.

10. Remove the accelerator pump cover and lever assembly (**Figure 18**).

11. Remove the accelerator pump diaphragm (**Figure 19**).

12. Remove the diaphragm spring (**Figure 20**).

13. Remove the inlet passage plug (**Figure 21**).

14. Pull the strainer out of the inlet passage (**Figure 22**).

15. Remove the top cover screws (**Figure 23**).

16. Remove the float pivot pin (**Figure 24**). Unhook the float from the needle valve, then remove the float and air horn gasket.

17. Lift out the needle valve (**Figure 25**). Unscrew the needle valve seat and remove the valve seat's aluminum washer.

18. Remove 2 screws with lockwashers and plain washers (**Figure 26**), then separate the throttle chamber and spacer from the carburetor body.

19. Remove the brass plug (**Figure 27**) from the carburetor body.

20. Remove the secondary idling jet and its O-ring from the brass plug and the hole in the carburetor body. See **Figure 28** and **Figure 29**.

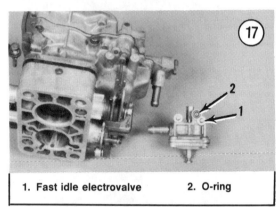

1. Fast idle electrovalve   2. O-ring

1. Plastic rod guide retainer   2. Rubber O-ring

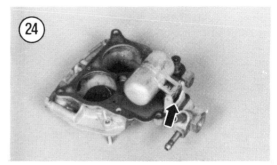

5

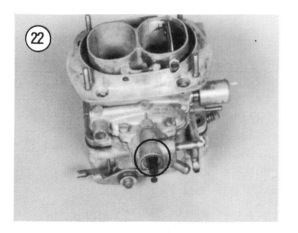

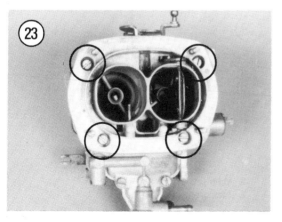

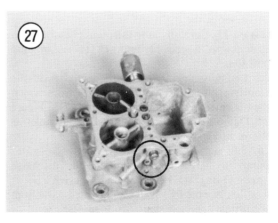

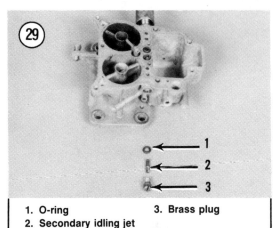

1. O-ring   3. Brass plug
2. Secondary idling jet

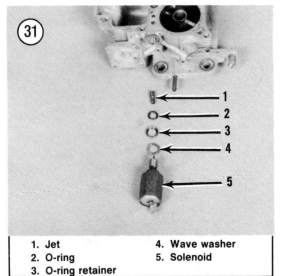

1. Jet   4. Wave washer
2. O-ring   5. Solenoid
3. O-ring retainer

21. Unscrew the solenoid (**Figure 30**) from the carburetor body.

22. Separate the jet, O-ring, O-ring retainer and wave washer from the solenoid. See **Figure 31**.

23. Clean all traces of gasoline from the solenoid and jet, then slip the solenoid onto the jet. Connect the positive terminal of a 12-volt battery to the solenoid terminal with a jumper wire as shown in **Figure 32**. Touch the solenoid body to the negative terminal. The solenoid should click each time it is touched to the negative terminal. If not, replace it.

24. Remove the main jets and air correction jets (**Figure 33**). Carefully note the number stamped in each jet so it can be returned to its original position.

25. Carefully note the different hole sizes in the emulsion tubes (located in the holes from which the air correction jets were removed). See **Figure 34**. Dump the emulsion tubes out of the holes as shown in **Figure 35**.

26. Pull out the small venturis and accelerator pump discharge nozzle. Remove the discharge nozzle O-ring. See **Figure 36** and **Figure 37**.

27. Remove the PCV valve and related parts from the primary throttle shaft. See **Figure 38**.

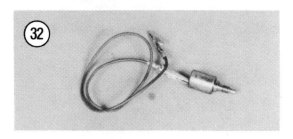

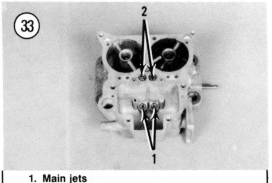

1. Main jets
2. Air correction jets

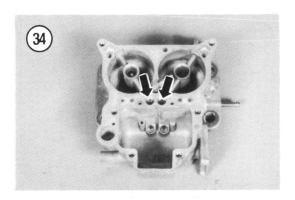

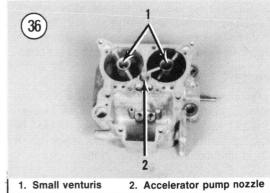

1. Small venturis   2. Accelerator pump nozzle

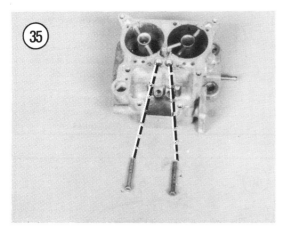

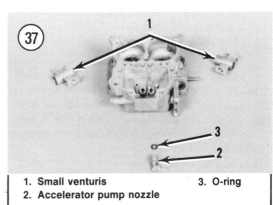

1. Small venturis   3. O-ring
2. Accelerator pump nozzle

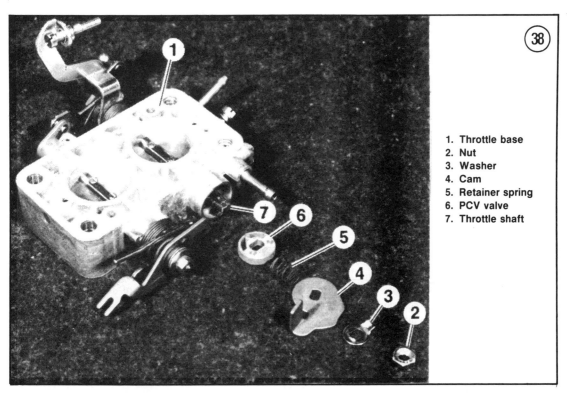

1. Throttle base
2. Nut
3. Washer
4. Cam
5. Retainer spring
6. PCV valve
7. Throttle shaft

28. Note the number of turns required to unscrew the idle mixture screw from the throttle chamber. Write down the number of turns to the nearest 1/8 turn. Remove the idle mixture screw and spring.

Inspection

1. Thoroughly clean all metal parts (except the solenoid) in solvent or dip-type carburetor cleaner. O-rings, gaskets and diaphragms should be replaced if they are included in the repair kit. If not, clean them with a lint-free cloth.

> *CAUTION*
> *Do not insert objects such as drill bits or pieces of wire into jets and passages while cleaning them. These openings are carefully calibrated and scratching them may seriously affect carburetor performance.*

2. If jets and passages are difficult to clean, blow them out with compressed air. If a compressor is not available, use an aerosol carburetor cleaner. These usually come with plastic tubes that fit into the can's nozzle, making it easy to spray the cleaner through jets and passages.

3. Check the needle valve and seat for wear. Replace as needed. If a new needle valve and seat are included in the repair kit, install the new parts no matter what the apparent condition of the old parts.

4. Check all castings for cracks. Replace cracked castings.

5. Check the idle mixture screw for wear at the tip. Replace it if wear can be seen.

6. Check diaphragms for cracks, brittleness or holes. Replace diaphragms if their condition is in any doubt.

Float Level Adjustment

1. If you haven't already done so, remove the top cover from the carburetor. Install a new gasket on the top cover.

2. Hold the top cover so the float hangs vertically as shown in **Figure 39**.

3. Measure distance A (from float to top cover gasket). It should be 6 mm (0.236 in.) on 1971-1974 models and 6.75-7.25 mm (0.266-0.285 in.) on 1975 and later carburetors.

4. If distance A is incorrect, carefully bend the float tang (7, **Figure 39**) to adjust it.

5. Hold the float up and measure the amount it travels from the vertical position. This should be 9 mm (0.354 in.) on all models. If not, carefully bend the float lug (3, **Figure 39**).

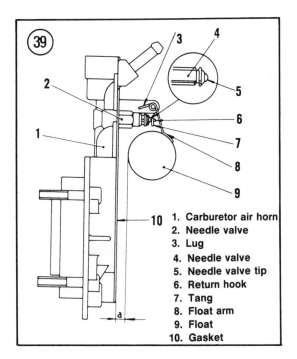

1. Carburetor air horn
2. Needle valve
3. Lug
4. Needle valve
5. Needle valve tip
6. Return hook
7. Tang
8. Float arm
9. Float
10. Gasket

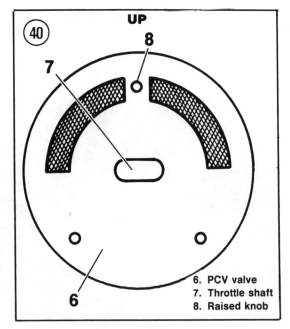

6. PCV valve
7. Throttle shaft
8. Raised knob

Assembly

Assembly is the reverse of disassembly, plus the following:

   a. The PCV valve should fit onto its shaft easily if installed correctly. It can be forced on the wrong way, but this will cause pressure in the crankcase and high oil consumption. The 3 raised knobs on the PCV valve should face

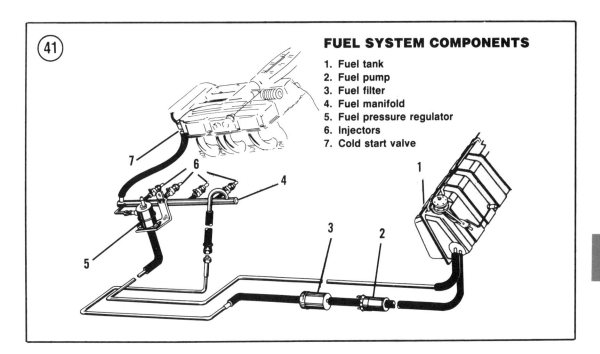

FUEL SYSTEM COMPONENTS

1. Fuel tank
2. Fuel pump
3. Fuel filter
4. Fuel manifold
5. Fuel pressure regulator
6. Injectors
7. Cold start valve

outward when installed and a single knob should be upward as shown in **Figure 40**.

b. When installing the idle mixture screw and spring, turn the mixture screw in the same number of turns required to remove it.

FUEL INJECTION

The 1980 California models and all 1981 and later cars use Bosch L-Jetronic fuel injection. The L stands for the German word "Luft" (air). Air flow into the engine is the key factor in the fuel injection system's operation. Unlike carburetors, which use engine vacuum to mix fuel and air, the fuel injection system forces fuel under pressure into the intake ports.

The fuel injection system is very complicated. Component removal and installation procedures are provided here, but diagnosis and repair should be left to a Fiat dealer or other mechanic familiar with the system. The following explanation should enable you to discuss the system intelligently with your mechanic. Refer to the following illustrations.

a. Fuel system—**Figure 41**.
b. Air intake system—**Figure 42**.
c. Electrical system—**Figure 43**.

The injectors are solenoid valves. They open to admit fuel to the engine or close to cut it off. Injector open time—and thus the amount of fuel delivered to the intake ports—is regulated by the control unit.

The control unit receives signals from several sources. The air flow meter indicates the quantity of intake air. The throttle plate switch indicates whether the throttle is at idle, wide open or at a point in between. The air temperature sensor indicates intake air temperature. The coolant temperature sensor indicates engine coolant temperature.

The control unit uses the input signals to determine injector open time. It then sends an electric current to each injector.

The Lambda sensor, located in the exhaust manifold, measures the percentage of oxygen in the exhaust gas. This signal, sent to the control unit, tells the control unit whether the air-fuel mixture entering the engine has been burned completely. The control unit uses this input in combination with the other inputs to make corrections to the air-fuel mixture as needed.

The electric current to open the injectors comes from the battery. It passes through the ignition switch and one part of the fuel injection relay set. The other part of the relay set carries current for the fuel pump and the auxiliary air regulator.

When the engine is cold, the cold start valve supplies extra fuel to the intake manifold. To prevent engine flooding from repeated starter operation, the cold start valve is regulated by the thermotime switch. The switch sends an operating signal to the cold start valve during cold-engine starting. It discontinues the signal after a specified time, regardless of coolant temperature.

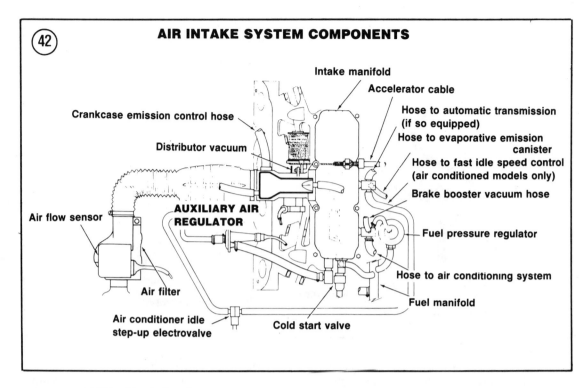

42

AIR INTAKE SYSTEM COMPONENTS

Intake manifold

Accelerator cable

Crankcase emission control hose

Hose to automatic transmission (if so equipped)

Distributor vacuum

Hose to evaporative emission canister

Hose to fast idle speed control (air conditioned models only)

Brake booster vacuum hose

Air flow sensor

AUXILIARY AIR REGULATOR

Fuel pressure regulator

Air filter

Hose to air conditioning system

Air conditioner idle step-up electrovalve

Cold start valve

Fuel manifold

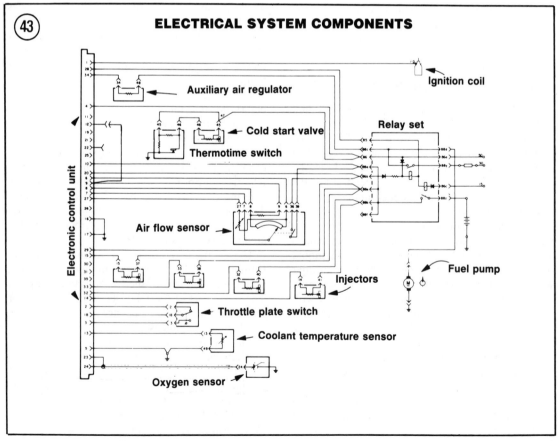

43

ELECTRICAL SYSTEM COMPONENTS

Ignition coil

Auxiliary air regulator

Relay set

Cold start valve

Thermotime switch

Electronic control unit

Air flow sensor

Fuel pump

Injectors

Throttle plate switch

Coolant temperature sensor

Oxygen sensor

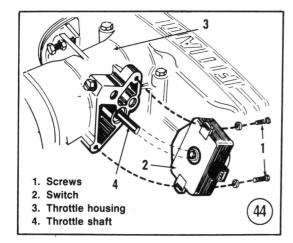

1. Screws
2. Switch
3. Throttle housing
4. Throttle shaft

(44)

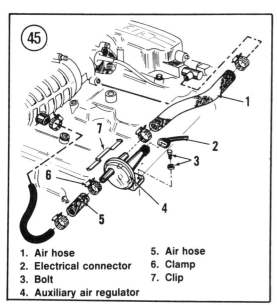

(45)

1. Air hose
2. Electrical connector
3. Bolt
4. Auxiliary air regulator
5. Air hose
6. Clamp
7. Clip

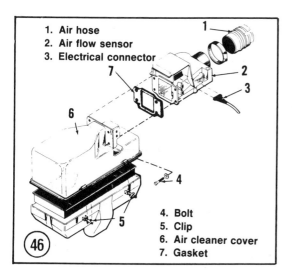

1. Air hose
2. Air flow sensor
3. Electrical connector
4. Bolt
5. Clip
6. Air cleaner cover
7. Gasket

(46)

The auxiliary air regulator admits extra air to increase idle speed during cold-engine running.

The air conditioner electrovalve admits extra air to increase idle speed when the air conditioner is operating.

The fuel pump is a high-pressure vane type. It has an internal relief valve which opens if fuel pressure becomes excessive. Be sure to relieve fuel system pressure before opening any fuel system connections.

Throttle Plate Switch
Removal/Installation

1. Unplug the throttle plate switch wiring connector. See **Figure 44**.
2. Remove the screws and washers (1, **Figure 44**). Slowly remove the throttle plate switch.
3. Installation is the reverse of removal. Make sure the flat in the switch hole is aligned with the flat on the shaft.

Auxiliary Air Regulator
Removal/Installation

1. Disconnect the regulator air hoses (**Figure 45**).
2. Unplug the regulator wiring connector.
3. Remove the regulator mounting bolts and washers. Take the regulator off of the cylinder head.
4. Installation is the reverse of removal. Make sure the clip (7, **Figure 45**) is installed under the clamps on the regulator.

Air Flow Sensor
Removal/Installation

1. Disconnect the air hose from the air flow sensor. See **Figure 46**.
2. Unplug the sensor wiring connectors.
3. Undo the air cleaner cover clips and lift off the air cleaner cover.
4. Remove the bolts and washers that secure the air flow sensor to the air cleaner cover. Separate the air flow sensor and gasket from the air cleaner cover.
5. Installation is the reverse of removal. Make sure the air hose is securely connected to the air flow sensor.

Fuel Pressure Regulator
Removal/Installation

WARNING
Because of the high pressure in fuel injection system lines, Steps 1-3 must be followed carefully.

1. Disconnect the vacuum hose from the fuel pressure regulator. See **Figure 47**.

2. Connect a hand vacuum pump to the regulator as shown. Pump vacuum to 20 in. Hg.

3. Release the vacuum and disconnect the vacuum pump.

4. Place a container beneath the fuel pressure regulator to catch dripping fuel.

5. Disconnect the fuel return hose from the pressure regulator. See **Figure 48**.

6. Disconnect the fuel manifold fitting from the pressure regulator.

7. Remove the nut (4, **Figure 48**) that secures the pressure regulator to the fuel manifold. Take the pressure regulator off.

8. Installation is the reverse of removal. After installation, run the engine and check for fuel leaks.

Cold Start Valve
Removal/Installation

> *WARNING*
> *Because of the high pressure in fuel injection system lines, Steps 1-3 must be followed carefully.*

1. Disconnect the vacuum hose from the fuel pressure regulator. See **Figure 47**.

2. Connect a hand vacuum pump to the regulator as shown. Pump vacuum to 20 in. Hg.

3. Release the vacuum, disconnect the vacuum pump and reconnect the fuel pressure regulator hose.

> *CAUTION*
> *Do not pull too hard on the hose during the next step. The valve body is plastic.*

4. Loosen the fuel hose clamp and pull the fuel hose off the valve. See **Figure 49**.

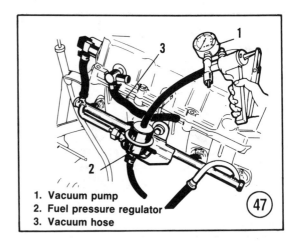

1. Vacuum pump
2. Fuel pressure regulator
3. Vacuum hose

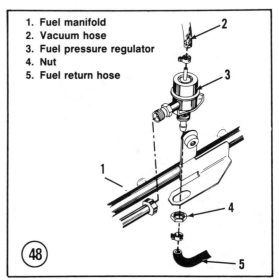

1. Fuel manifold
2. Vacuum hose
3. Fuel pressure regulator
4. Nut
5. Fuel return hose

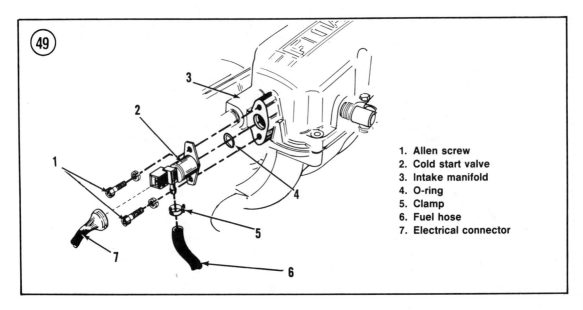

1. Allen screw
2. Cold start valve
3. Intake manifold
4. O-ring
5. Clamp
6. Fuel hose
7. Electrical connector

CAUTION
During the next steps, take care to keep dirt out of the fuel injection system.

5. Remove the cold start valve mounting screws with a 5 mm Allen wrench. Take off the valve and its O-ring.

6. Installation is the reverse of removal. Make sure the fuel hose is pushed all the way onto the cold start valve. After installation, run the engine and check for fuel leaks.

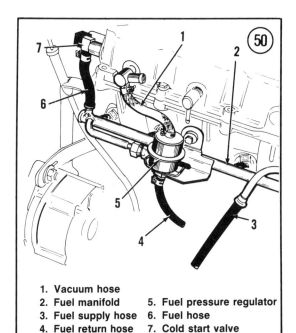

1. Vacuum hose
2. Fuel manifold
3. Fuel supply hose
4. Fuel return hose
5. Fuel pressure regulator
6. Fuel hose
7. Cold start valve

Fuel Injector Removal

WARNING
Because of the high pressure in fuel injection system lines, Steps 1-3 must be followed carefully.

1. Disconnect the vacuum hose from the fuel pressure regulator. See **Figure 47**.

2. Connect a hand vacuum pump to the regulator as shown. Pump vacuum to 20 in. Hg.

3. Release the vacuum, disconnect the vacuum pump and reconnect the fuel pressure regulator hose.

4. Unplug the fuel injector wiring connectors.

5. Keep a pan handy to catch dripping fuel. Place rags under disconnected fuel hoses to catch leaks.

6. Refer to **Figure 50** and disconnect the following:
   a. Fuel supply hose (3). Use one wrench to hold the fuel supply tube and another wrench to turn the hose connection.
   b. Fuel return hose from pressure regulator.
   c. Vacuum hose from pressure regulator.
   d. Fuel hose from cold start valve.

CAUTION
The cold start valve body is plastic. Use care when pulling the hose off.

7. Remove the bolt (2, **Figure 51**) that secures the fuel manifold to the intake manifold.

8. Remove the nuts and washers that secure the injector retainers to the intake manifold.

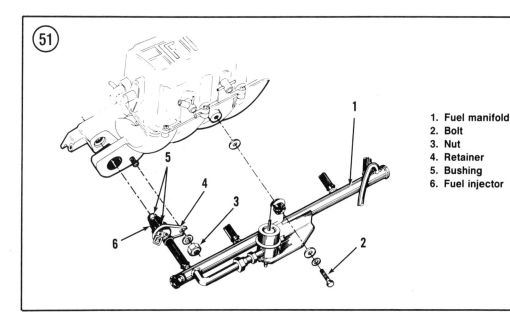

1. Fuel manifold
2. Bolt
3. Nut
4. Retainer
5. Bushing
6. Fuel injector

CAUTION
During the next step, be careful not to let the rubber bushings fall off of the fuel injectors (or out of the intake manifold) as the injectors are pulled out of the intake manifold.

9. Remove the fuel manifold together with the injectors and regulator.
10. Remove the rubber bushings and retainers from the injectors. See **Figure 51**.
11. Check the bushings for cracks or deterioration. Replace them if there is any doubt about their condition.
12. If an injector is to be replaced with a new one, replace its hose as well. Pull the hose off the fuel manifold with a twisting, rocking motion. See **Figure 52**.
13. If the injector is good and only the hose is to be replaced, slit both ends of the hose and pull it off the injector and fuel manifold.
14. Installation is the reverse of removal. If a new hose is being installed, place the collars on the injector and fuel manifold as shown in **Figure 52**. Push the hose all the way onto the injector and fuel manifold until the hose ends fit inside the collars and the collars fit tightly against the shoulders.

Throttle Plate Assembly Removal

1. Label all lines, wires and hoses so they can be reconnected.

WARNING
Because of the high pressure in fuel injection system lines, Steps 2-4 must be followed carefully.

1. Disconnect the vacuum hose from the fuel pressure regulator. See **Figure 47**.

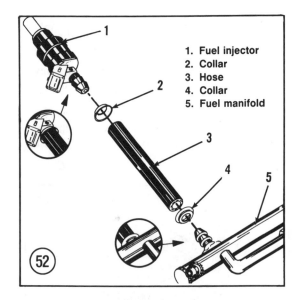

1. Fuel injector
2. Collar
3. Hose
4. Collar
5. Fuel manifold

1. Fuel pressure regulator hose
2. Brake booster hose
3. Evaporative emission hose

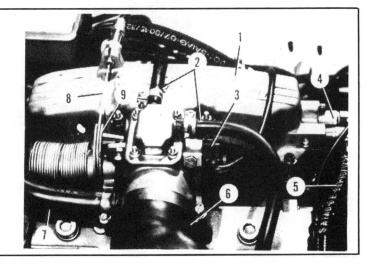

1. Intake manifold
2. Water hose
3. Throttle plate switch
4. Cold start valve
5. Auxiliary air regulator hose
6. Main air hose
7. Crankcase emission hose
8. Accelerator cable
9. Throttle lever

2. Connect a hand vacuum pump to the regulator as shown. Pump vacuum to 20 in. Hg.

3. Release the vacuum and disconnect the vacuum pump.

4. Place a container beneath the fuel pressure regulator to catch dripping fuel.

5. Disconnect the following vacuum hoses from the intake manifold:

  a. Automatic transmission (if so equipped).
  b. Fuel pressure regulator (**Figure 53**).
  c. Brake booster (**Figure 53**).
  d. Charcoal canister (**Figure 53**).
  e. Boost switches (Turbos only).

6. Refer to **Figure 54** and disconnect the following:

  a. Electrical connectors from cold start valve and throttle plate switch.

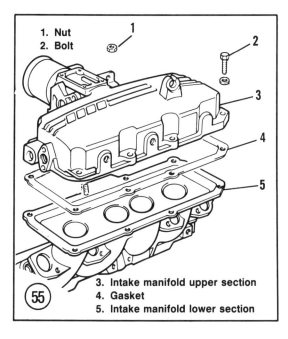

1. Nut
2. Bolt
3. Intake manifold upper section
4. Gasket
5. Intake manifold lower section

(55)

b. Auxiliary air regulator hose from intake manifold.

c. Air hose from throttle housing.

d. Crankcase emission hose from throttle housing (non-Turbos only).

e. Distributor vacuum line from throttle housing.

f. Accelerator cable from throttle lever and support bracket on intake manifold.

g. Fuel hose from cold start valve. Use care when disconnecting the hose. The valve body is plastic.

h. Water hoses from throttle plate heater.

CAUTION
The upper section of the intake manifold should come off easily during the next step. If not, make sure all fasteners have been removed. Do not force the upper section off.

7. Detach the upper section of the intake manifold from the lower section. See **Figure 55**. Lift the upper section off.

8. If necessary, disassemble the throttle plate assembly, referring to **Figure 56**. Assembly is the reverse of disassembly.

9. Installation is the reverse of removal, plus the following:

  a. Make sure all air hose connections are airtight.
  b. Run the engine and check for fuel leaks.
  c. Have the throttle plate adjusted by a dealer or a mechanic familiar with Bosch fuel injection.

TURBOCHARGER

A turbocharger is optional on 1981-1982 models. **Figure 57** is a cutaway view of the

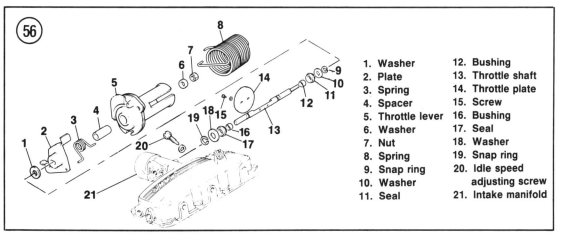

(56)

1. Washer	12. Bushing
2. Plate	13. Throttle shaft
3. Spring	14. Throttle plate
4. Spacer	15. Screw
5. Throttle lever	16. Bushing
6. Washer	17. Seal
7. Nut	18. Washer
8. Spring	19. Snap ring
9. Snap ring	20. Idle speed
10. Washer	adjusting screw
11. Seal	21. Intake manifold

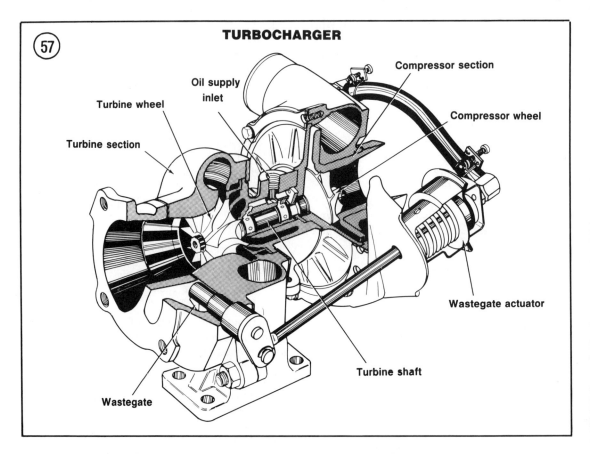

TURBOCHARGER

57

- Oil supply inlet
- Turbine wheel
- Turbine section
- Compressor section
- Compressor wheel
- Wastegate actuator
- Turbine shaft
- Wastegate

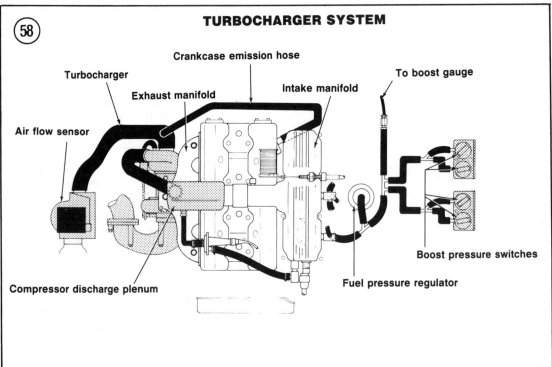

TURBOCHARGER SYSTEM

58

- Crankcase emission hose
- Turbocharger
- Exhaust manifold
- Intake manifold
- To boost gauge
- Air flow sensor
- Boost pressure switches
- Compressor discharge plenum
- Fuel pressure regulator

turbocharger; **Figure 58** shows the turbocharger system.

The turbocharger is a Warner-ISHI unit. The light weight and resulting low inertia provide quick throttle response. The turbine wheel is made of heat resistant material (Inconel-713C) and the turbine housing is made of aircraft quality high-temperature NI-Resist. The exhaust manifold is made of annealed nodular iron rather than conventional cast iron. The compressor discharge plenum is made of aluminum for efficient heat dissipation (and also for pleasing appearance).

The turbocharger is a vane pump driven by exhaust gases from the engine. Exhaust gas flowing from the exhaust manifold turns the turbine wheel at speeds up to 100,000 rpm. The turbine wheel spins the compressor wheel, which is mounted on the same shaft. The compressor wheel pulls air through the air flow sensor, compresses it and feeds it into the discharge plenum and intake manifold. More fuel and air are forced into the engine than it would normally draw in (this is termed "boost pressure"). This increases horsepower and torque.

The turbocharger uses a wastegate to prevent excessive boost pressure. See **Figure 57**. Boost pressure in the turbocharger outlet is applied to the wastegate actuator diaphragm. When the pressure reaches 6 psi, it begins to overcome the wastegate return spring. The wastegate opens, allowing part of the exhaust gas to bypass the turbocharger's compressor wheel. Additional exhaust gas pressure causes the wastegate to open farther so boost pressure is maintained at a maximum of 6 psi.

Switches

The turbocharger system includes 4 boost pressure switches, mounted on the left fender well. See **Figure 59**. Switch colors are:
a. Load enrichment—blue.
b. Overboost protection—black.
c. 1 psi enrichment—yellow.
d. 5 psi enrichment—green.
The check valve (**Figure 59**) prevents boost pressure from pressurizing the charcoal canister.

The 2 boost enrichment switches and the load enrichment switch signal the fuel injection system's electronic control unit to enrich the fuel mixture when the turbocharger is providing boost pressure.

The overboost protection switch prevents engine damage from excessive boost if the wastegate should fail. If boost pressure reaches 9 psi, the overboost protection switch signals the electronic control unit to close the fuel injectors. This reduces engine speed, which in turn reduces boost pressure.

Troubleshooting

A list of turbocharger problems and common causes is described in **Table 1**.

Removal/Installation

Refer to **Figure 60** for this procedure.

> *CAUTION*
> *The turbocharger and exhaust manifold must be removed and installed together. Do not try to separate the turbocharger from the exhaust manifold when the exhaust manifold is on the engine.*

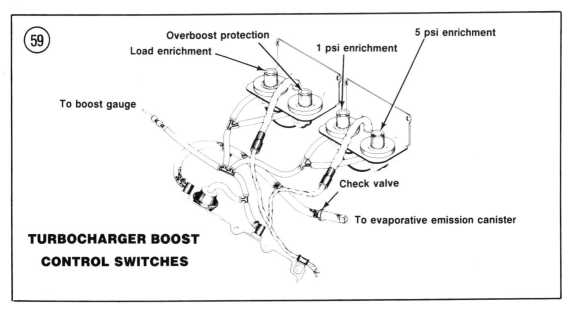

(59)

Overboost protection
Load enrichment
5 psi enrichment
1 psi enrichment
To boost gauge
Check valve
To evaporative emission canister

TURBOCHARGER BOOST CONTROL SWITCHES

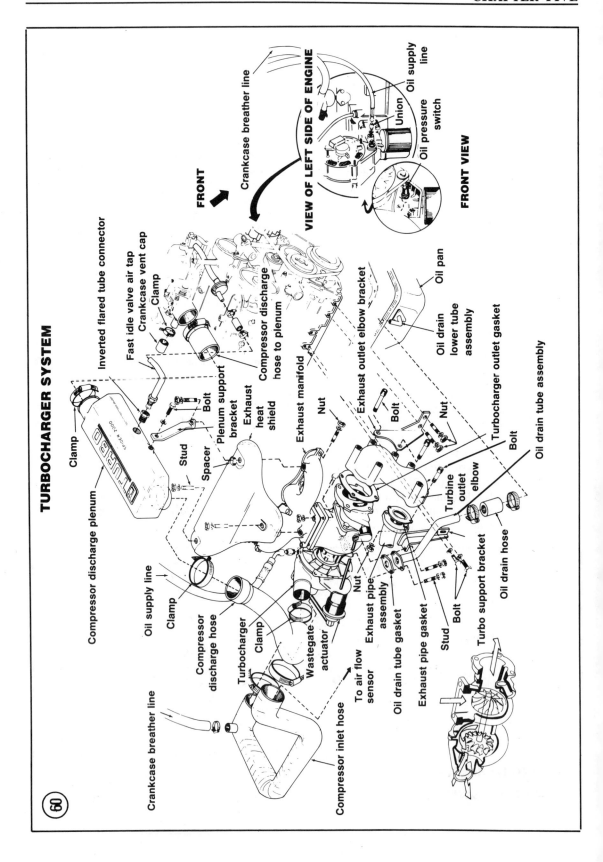

TURBOCHARGER SYSTEM

Clamp

Inverted flared tube connector

Fast idle valve air tap

Crankcase vent cap

Clamp

Compressor discharge hose to plenum

Compressor discharge plenum

Oil supply line

Clamp

Compressor discharge hose

Turbocharger

Clamp

Wastegate actuator

To air flow sensor

Exhaust pipe assembly

Oil drain tube gasket

Exhaust pipe gasket

Stud

Bolt

Turbo support bracket

Oil drain hose

Crankcase breather line

Compressor inlet hose

Bolt

Stud

Spacer

Plenum support bracket

Exhaust heat shield

Exhaust manifold

Nut

Exhaust outlet elbow bracket

Bolt

Nut

Bolt

Turbocharger outlet gasket

Bolt

Oil drain tube assembly

Turbine outlet elbow

Nut

Oil drain lower tube assembly

Oil pan

FRONT

Crankcase breather line

VIEW OF LEFT SIDE OF ENGINE

Oil supply line

Union

Oil pressure switch

FRONT VIEW

60

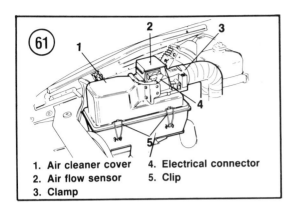

1. Air cleaner cover   4. Electrical connector
2. Air flow sensor   5. Clip
3. Clamp

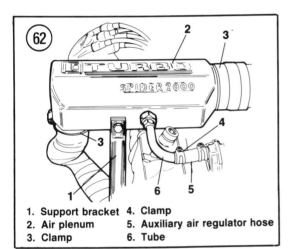

1. Support bracket   4. Clamp
2. Air plenum   5. Auxiliary air regulator hose
3. Clamp   6. Tube

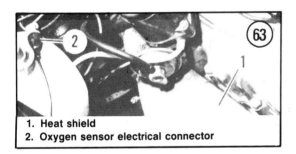

1. Heat shield
2. Oxygen sensor electrical connector

CAUTION
During this procedure, immediately cap or plug all hose ends and fittings as they are disconnected. Very small amounts of dirt can cause expensive damage to the turbocharger system.

1. Remove the splash shield from under the front of the car.
2. Open the engine drain plug and drain the cooling system (Chapter Six).
3. Loosen the hose clamp (3, **Figure 61**). Unplug the wiring connector from the air flow sensor.
4. Remove the air cleaner as described in this chapter.
5. Detach the air plenum support bracket from the exhaust manifold heat shield. See **Figure 62**.
6. Detach the auxiliary regulator air hose from the tube (**Figure 62**).
7. Loosen the air hose clamps and lift the plenum off the air hoses.
8. Detach the heat shield from the exhaust manifold (**Figure 63**). Take the heat shield off.
9. Unplug the oxygen sensor wiring connector (**Figure 63**).
10. Remove 3 Allen bolts that secure the turbocharger outlet elbow to the exhaust pipe. See **Figure 64**. Separate the elbow from the pipe and discard the gasket.
11. Remove 2 Allen bolts (7, **Figure 65**).
12. Remove 2 self-locking nuts (2 bolts on air-conditioned cars) and remove the exhaust elbow bracket (6, **Figure 65**).
13. Referring to **Figure 65**, remove 2 clamps that secure the turbocharger oil drain hose to the oil pan fitting. Push the hose downward off the fitting.
14. Working beneath the car, remove the turbocharger support bracket nut (10, **Figure 65**).
15. Remove 2 nuts that secure the heater return tube to the water pump. See **Figure 66**.

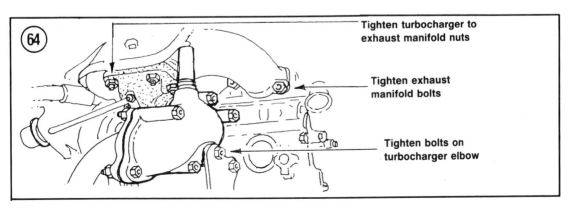

Tighten turbocharger to exhaust manifold nuts

Tighten exhaust manifold bolts

Tighten bolts on turbocharger elbow

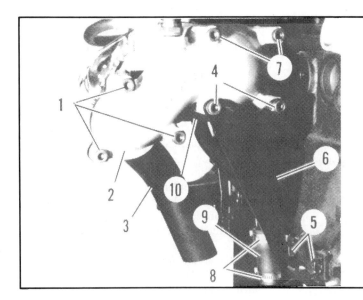

1. Allen bolt
2. Turbine outlet elbow
3. Exhaust pipe
4. Allen bolt
5. Self-locking nut
6. Exhaust elbow bracket
7. Allen bolt
8. Clamp
9. Oil drain hose
10. Oil drain line flange

1. Nut
2. Water pump
3. Heater return line
4. Exhaust manifold
5. Nut

16. Remove the nut (5, **Figure 66**) that secures the heater return tube bracket to the exhaust manifold. Move the return tube away from the exhaust manifold.

17. Detach the crankcase hose from the inlet hose. See **Figure 67**. Leave the inlet hose in position.

18. Referring to **Figure 67**, detach the oil hose from the turbocharger and lay the oil hose aside.

CAUTION
The exhaust manifold-turbocharger assembly should come off easily during the next step. If not, make sure all fasteners have been removed. Do not force the assembly off.

19. Remove the nuts and washers that secure the exhaust manifold to the engine. Lift the exhaust manifold off together with the turbocharger.

NOTE
The bolts mentioned in the next step are a special high-strength type which must be discarded after removal and replaced with new ones of the same type. Obtain the new bolts from a dealer before removing the old ones.

20. Unbolt the turbocharger from the exhaust manifold.

NOTE
Early Turbo models used a gasket between the exhaust manifold and turbocharger. If you find such a gasket, throw it away and do not install a new one during assembly.

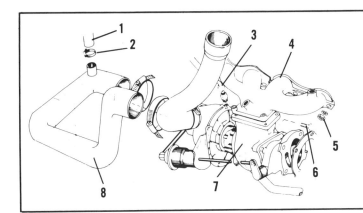

1. Crankcase hose
2. Clamp
3. Oil hose
4. Exhaust manifold
5. Nut
6. Bolt
7. Turbocharger
8. Air hose

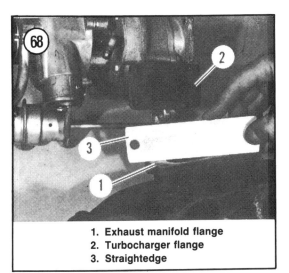

1. Exhaust manifold flange
2. Turbocharger flange
3. Straightedge

1. Torque wrench
2. Bolt
3. Oil supply line fitting

5

Inspection

1. Check all parts for visible wear or damage and replace as needed.

2. Check the turbocharger for seized bearings and for side play in the turbine and compressor wheels. Replace the turbocharger if these conditions are found.

3. Check flatness of the turbocharger and manifold surfaces with a precision straightedge as shown in **Figure 68**. This can be done inexpensively by a machine shop if you don't have the proper tool. The surfaces must be perfectly flat. If there is any measurable gap between the surfaces and the straightedge, have the surfaces ground flat by a machine shop.

> *CAUTION*
> *Remove only the minimum amount of material necessary to flatten the surfaces.*

Installation

Installation is the reverse of removal, plus the following.

1. Apply a light coat of anti-seize compound to all threads, as well as to both sides of each stainless steel gasket.

2. Tighten the turbocharger-to-exhaust manifold bolts to 20 ft.-lb. Use a crow's foot socket as shown in **Figure 69**.

> *NOTE*
> *Even though the crow's foot socket extends the range of the torque wrench, this won't have any significant effect on the torque reading.*

3. Make sure all hoses, wires, etc. are clear of the exhaust manifold, heat shield and turbocharger.

4. Make sure all hose clamps are tight enough so they won't come off when the turbocharger produces boost pressure.

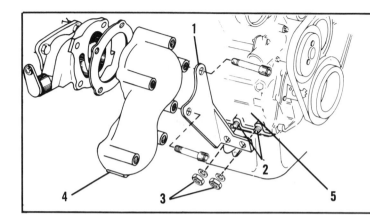

1. Elbow support bracket
2. Mounting studs
3. Self-locking nuts
4. Turbocharger outlet elbow
5. Cylinder block

5. Refer to **Figure 70** and make sure the holes in the leg of the elbow support bracket line up with the 2 cylinder block studs (bolt holes on cars with air conditioning) before securing the bracket to the turbocharger outlet elbow.

6. Before securing the elbow support bracket to the cylinder block, make sure the bracket is parallel to and flush with the block. If not, shim it with washers. Do not pull the bracket into a flush position by tightening the mounting nuts.

7. Make sure the compressor outlet hose (**Figure 71**) has a clearance of at least 5 mm (0.2 in.) from the exhaust manifold heat shield. The clearance can be adjusted by sliding the hose up or down on the outlet port.

CAUTION
Make sure the protective sheath around the braided stainless steel oil supply line is in good condition. Make sure the line is positioned so it won't rub on any other parts. The stainless steel braiding is abrasive and can cause damage if it rubs on other parts.

8. Refill and bleed the cooling system as described in Chapter Six.

Switch Testing

Switch testing requires an ohmmeter and a pressure pump such as Fiat part No. A.33076 (Kent-Moore part No. J33076). See **Figure 72**.

CAUTION
When testing the switches, do not increase pressure to more than 12 psi.

CAUTION
When testing the switches, unplug the switch wiring connectors from the fuel injection system.

1. To test the boost enrichment switches, connect the pressure pump to the switches' Y-fitting as

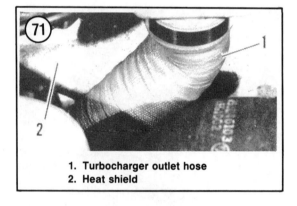

1. Turbocharger outlet hose
2. Heat shield

shown in **Figure 72**. Connect an ohmmeter to connector pins 1 and 2 as shown.

2. Slowly increase the switch pressure. The 1 psi switch (yellow) should operate at 0.5-1.5 psi. When it does, the ohmmeter should indicate 1,500-2,000 phms.

3. Continue increasing pressure. The 5 psi switch (green) should operate at 4.5-5.5 psi. When it does, the ohmmeter should indicate 1,750-2,750 ohms.

4. Release the pump pressure. Connect the pressure tester to the Y-fitting for the load enrichment and boost protection switches. See **Figure 73**.

5. Make sure the ohmmeter's zero setting is correctly calibrated. Adjust it if necessary.

6. Connect the ohmmeter to connector pins 1 and 3 as shown in **Figure 73**. The ohmmeter should indicate infinite resistance (no continuity).

7. Slowly increase pressure. The ohmmeter reading should drop to zero when the pressure reaches approximately 1 psi.

8. Release the pump pressure.

9. Leave the pressure pump connected and connect the ohmmeter to connector pins 1 and 2. See **Figure 74**. The ohmmeter should indicate infinite resistance (no continuity).

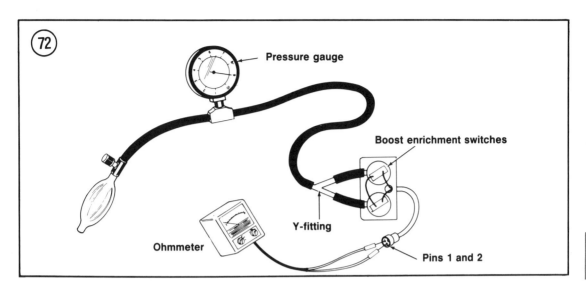

72

Pressure gauge

Boost enrichment switches

Y-fitting

Ohmmeter

Pins 1 and 2

5

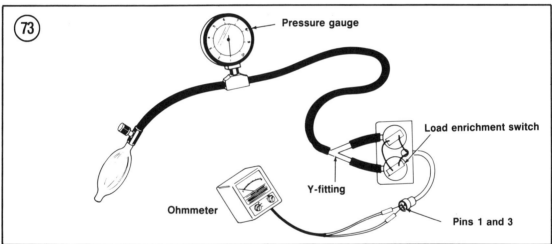

73

Pressure gauge

Load enrichment switch

Y-fitting

Ohmmeter

Pins 1 and 3

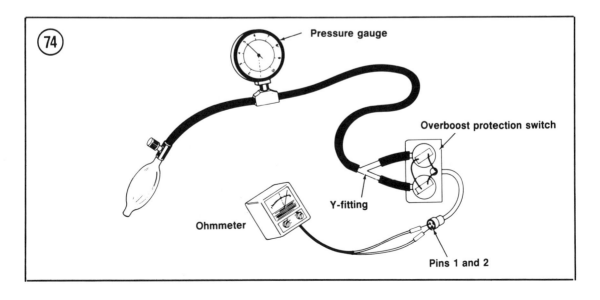

74

Pressure gauge

Overboost protection switch

Y-fitting

Ohmmeter

Pins 1 and 2

10. Slowly increase pressure. The ohmmeter reading should drop to zero when the pressure reading reaches approximately 9 psi.

11. If any of the switches didn't perform as described, replace it.

CRANKCASE EMISSION CONTROL SYSTEM

This system routes crankcase gases into the combustion chambers for burning. See **Figure 75** (with carburetor), **Figure 76** (with fuel injection) or **Figure 77** (Turbo). Crankcase gases are composed of combustion products that are forced past the pistons into the crankcase (blow-by) and oil vapors.

On carburetted cars, crankcase gases are drawn into a control valve on the carburetor when the engine is idling. At full throttle, part of the vapor is routed into the carburetor and part into the air cleaner.

On fuel injected cars (including Turbos), crankcase gases are routed to an orifice upstream of the throttle plate when the throttle plate is open. When the throttle plate is closed, the vapors are routed through another hose to a point downstream of the throttle plate.

On all models, a liquid-vapor separator prevents oil from being drawn into the engine.

On early models, system parts should be removed and cleaned in solvent according to the maintenance schedules in Chapter Three. Periodic service is not required on later models.

Maintenance (Early Models)

1. Remove the liquid-vapor separator and hose from the side of the engine. Clean the separator and hose in solvent and reinstall them.

2. Remove the PCV valve and related parts from the primary throttle shaft. See *Carburetor* in this chapter for details. Clean the PCV valve and related parts, then install them.

EVAPORATIVE EMISSION CONTROL SYSTEM

This system routes fuel vapors from the fuel tank (and carburetor float bowl on carburetted models) to a canister filled with activated charcoal. The vapors are stored in the canister while the engine is

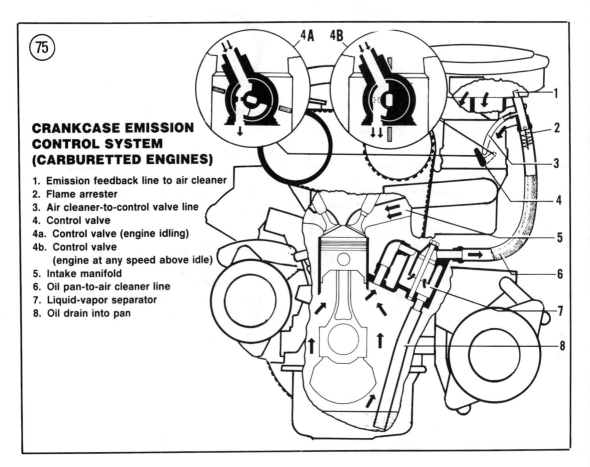

CRANKCASE EMISSION CONTROL SYSTEM (CARBURETTED ENGINES)

1. Emission feedback line to air cleaner
2. Flame arrester
3. Air cleaner-to-control valve line
4. Control valve
4a. Control valve (engine idling)
4b. Control valve (engine at any speed above idle)
5. Intake manifold
6. Oil pan-to-air cleaner line
7. Liquid-vapor separator
8. Oil drain into pan

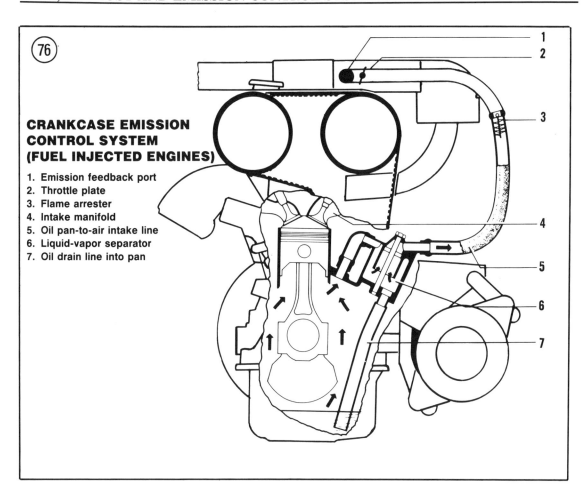

76

CRANKCASE EMISSION CONTROL SYSTEM (FUEL INJECTED ENGINES)

1. Emission feedback port
2. Throttle plate
3. Flame arrester
4. Intake manifold
5. Oil pan-to-air intake line
6. Liquid-vapor separator
7. Oil drain line into pan

5

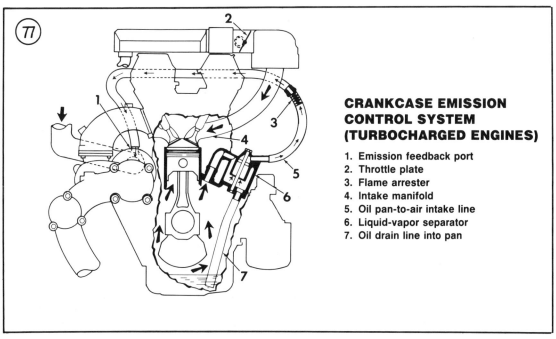

77

CRANKCASE EMISSION CONTROL SYSTEM (TURBOCHARGED ENGINES)

1. Emission feedback port
2. Throttle plate
3. Flame arrester
4. Intake manifold
5. Oil pan-to-air intake line
6. Liquid-vapor separator
7. Oil drain line into pan

off, then drawn into the engine for burning while the engine runs.

Figure 78 shows a typical system used with carburetted cars. **Figure 79** shows the system used with fuel injected models.

On 1970-1979 cars, the system's lines, fittings and valves should be checked for general condition at the emission control inspection intervals listed in Chapter Three. Tighten loose connections and replace cracked or deteriorated lines. Periodic service is not required on 1980 and later models.

EXHAUST EMISSION CONTROL SYSTEM (CARBURETTED MODELS)

The exhaust emission control system on 1971-on carburetted models consists of a specially calibrated carburetor, distributor advance control mechanism, air injection system and catalytic converter (1975-on only). **Figure 80** shows the system without catalytic converter. **Figure 81** shows the system with catalytic converter.

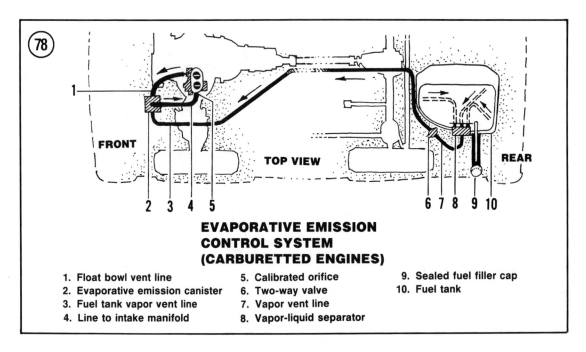

EVAPORATIVE EMISSION CONTROL SYSTEM (CARBURETTED ENGINES)

1. Float bowl vent line
2. Evaporative emission canister
3. Fuel tank vapor vent line
4. Line to intake manifold
5. Calibrated orifice
6. Two-way valve
7. Vapor vent line
8. Vapor-liquid separator
9. Sealed fuel filler cap
10. Fuel tank

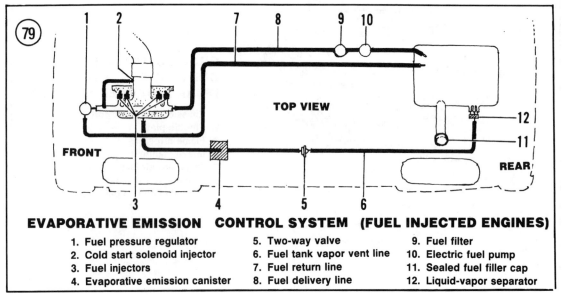

EVAPORATIVE EMISSION CONTROL SYSTEM (FUEL INJECTED ENGINES)

1. Fuel pressure regulator
2. Cold start solenoid injector
3. Fuel injectors
4. Evaporative emission canister
5. Two-way valve
6. Fuel tank vapor vent line
7. Fuel return line
8. Fuel delivery line
9. Fuel filter
10. Electric fuel pump
11. Sealed fuel filler cap
12. Liquid-vapor separator

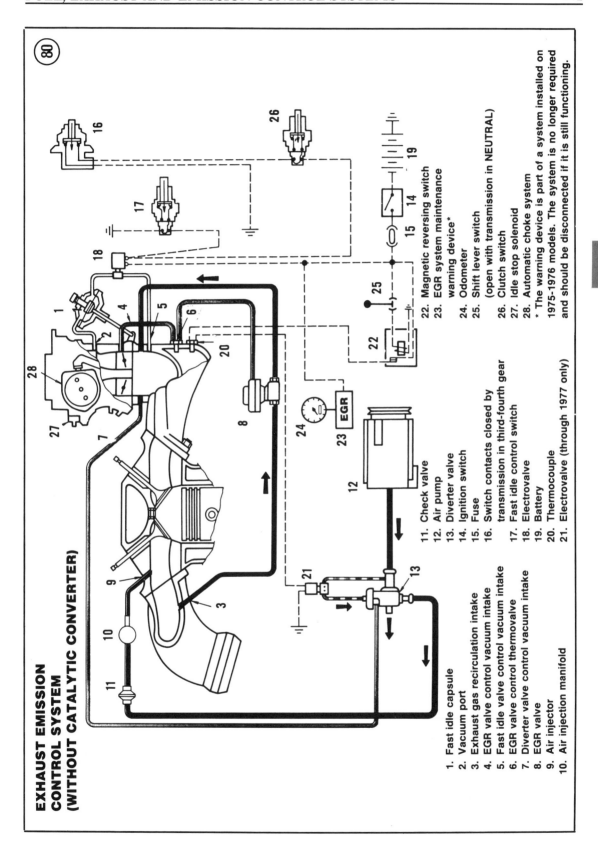

EXHAUST EMISSION CONTROL SYSTEM (WITHOUT CATALYTIC CONVERTER)

1. Fast idle capsule
2. Vacuum port
3. Exhaust gas recirculation intake
4. EGR valve control vacuum intake
5. Fast idle valve control vacuum intake
6. EGR valve control thermovalve
7. Diverter valve control vacuum intake
8. EGR valve
9. Air injector
10. Air injection manifold
11. Check valve
12. Air pump
13. Diverter valve
14. Ignition switch
15. Fuse
16. Switch contacts closed by transmission in third-fourth gear
17. Fast idle control switch
18. Electrovalve
19. Battery
20. Thermocouple
21. Electrovalve (through 1977 only)
22. Magnetic reversing switch
23. EGR system maintenance warning device*
24. Odometer
25. Shift lever switch (open with transmission in NEUTRAL)
26. Clutch switch
27. Idle stop solenoid
28. Automatic choke system

* The warning device is part of a system installed on 1975-1976 models. The system is no longer required and should be disconnected if it is still functioning.

5

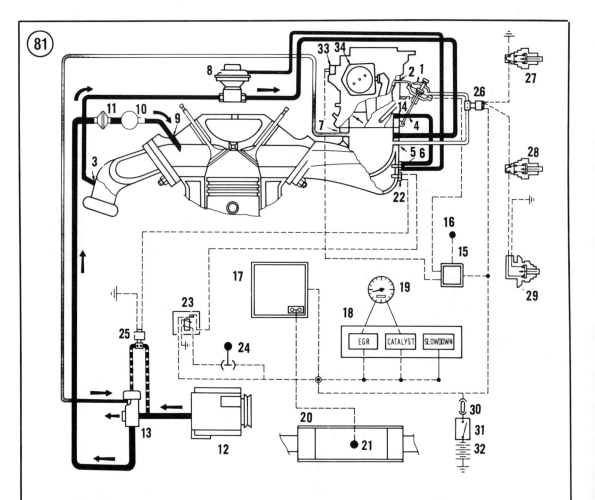

**EXHAUST EMISSION
CONTROL SYSTEM
(CARBURETTED MODELS WITH
CATALYTIC CONVERTER)**

1. Fast idle capsule
2. Vacuum port
3. Exhaust gas recirculation intake
4. EGR valve control vacuum intake
5. Fast idle valve control vacuum intake
6. EGR valve control thermovalve
7. Diverter valve control vacuum intake
8. EGR valve
9. Air injector
10. Air injection manifold
11. Check valve
12. Air pump
13. Diverter valve
14. Inhibitor switch
15. Tachymetric switch
16. From ignition coil
17. Control unit
18. Warning device panel*
19. Odometer*
20. Catalytic converter
21. Thermocouple
22. Thermoswitch
23. Magnetic reversing switch
24. Shift lever switch
    (open with transmission in NEUTRAL)
25. Electrovalve (normally closed)
26. Electrovalve
27. Fast idle control switch
28. Clutch switch
29. Switch contacts closed by
    transmission in third-fourth gear
30. Fuse
31. Ignition switch
32. Battery
33. Idle stop solenoid
34. Automatic choke system
* These are part of a maintenance reminder system
installed on 1975-1976 models. The system is no
longer required and should be disconnected if it is still
functioning.

The air injection system uses a belt-driven pump to force air into the exhaust ports. This allows combustion to continue for a longer time, reducing carbon monoxide and unburned hydrocarbons in the exhaust. On early models, the air pump is driven by a non-adjustable toothed belt, rather than the V-belt used on later models.

The catalytic converter further oxidizes carbon monoxide and unburned hydrocarbons.

Inspection

The system should be inspected every 12,500 miles.
1. Check air injection lines for loose connections or defects. Tighten or replace as needed.
2. Check exhaust pipe connections for looseness. Tighten as needed.
3. Inspect the air pump drive belt. Replace the belt if worn, cracked or frayed. If the air pump is driven by a V-belt, adjust it as described in Chapter Three. Toothed air pump belts are not adjustable. If the belt is loose, it must be replaced.
4. On 1979 models, remove the reed valve holder from the side of the air cleaner. Take out the filter and inspect it. Replace the filter if it is clogged. The filter should be replaced every 30,000 miles, no matter what its apparent condition.

EXHAUST EMISSION CONTROL SYSTEM (FUEL INJECTED MODELS)

Fuel injected models use an oxygen sensor in the exhaust manifold and a catalytic converter. The oxygen sensor compares the oxygen content of the exhaust gas with that of the surrounding air and signals the fuel injection system's control unit. The control unit uses this signal together with several others to supply the optimum fuel-air mixture to the engine. The catalytic converter further oxidizes carbon monoxide and unburned hydrocarbons as well as reducing oxides of nitrogen.

The only required periodic service is replacement of the oxygen sensor. This is described under *Scheduled Maintenance* in Chapter Three.

THROTTLE LINKAGE

To remove and install throttle linkage parts, see **Figure 82** (1975-on carburetted models shown; earlier models similar) or **Figure 83** (fuel injected models).

EXHAUST SYSTEM

To remove and install exhaust system parts, refer to the following illustrations:
a. Without catalytic converter (1975-1978 shown; earlier models similar)—**Figure 84**.
b. 1975-1978 with catalytic converter—**Figure 85**.
c. 1979-1980 carburetted—**Figure 86**.
d. 1980-on fuel injected (including Turbo)—**Figure 87**.

FUEL PUMP

Testing (Carburetted Models)

Test procedures are described under *Fuel Pump Test* in Chapter Two. Fiat does not provide

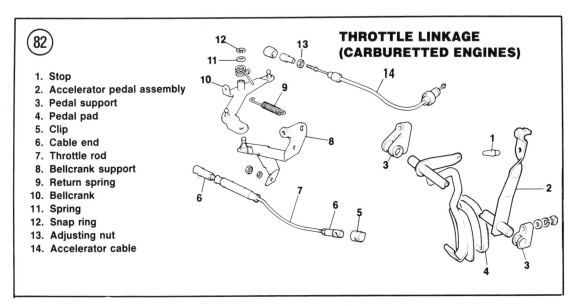

82

THROTTLE LINKAGE (CARBURETTED ENGINES)

1. Stop
2. Accelerator pedal assembly
3. Pedal support
4. Pedal pad
5. Clip
6. Cable end
7. Throttle rod
8. Bellcrank support
9. Return spring
10. Bellcrank
11. Spring
12. Snap ring
13. Adjusting nut
14. Accelerator cable

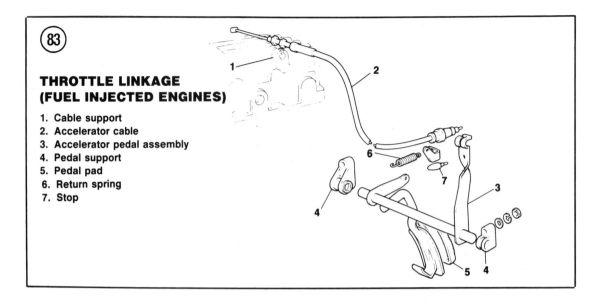

(83)

**THROTTLE LINKAGE
(FUEL INJECTED ENGINES)**

1. Cable support
2. Accelerator cable
3. Accelerator pedal assembly
4. Pedal support
5. Pedal pad
6. Return spring
7. Stop

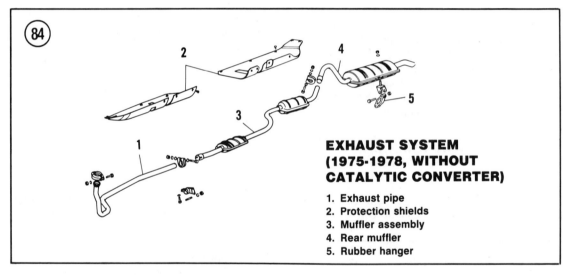

(84)

**EXHAUST SYSTEM
(1975-1978, WITHOUT
CATALYTIC CONVERTER)**

1. Exhaust pipe
2. Protection shields
3. Muffler assembly
4. Rear muffler
5. Rubber hanger

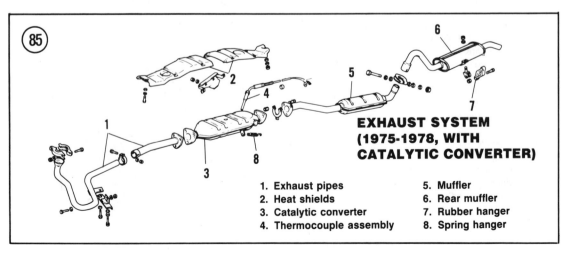

(85)

**EXHAUST SYSTEM
(1975-1978, WITH
CATALYTIC CONVERTER)**

1. Exhaust pipes
2. Heat shields
3. Catalytic converter
4. Thermocouple assembly

5. Muffler
6. Rear muffler
7. Rubber hanger
8. Spring hanger

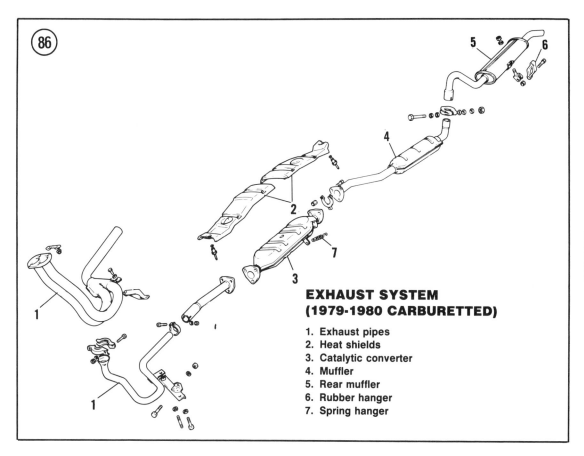

EXHAUST SYSTEM (1979-1980 CARBURETTED)

1. Exhaust pipes
2. Heat shields
3. Catalytic converter
4. Muffler
5. Rear muffler
6. Rubber hanger
7. Spring hanger

5

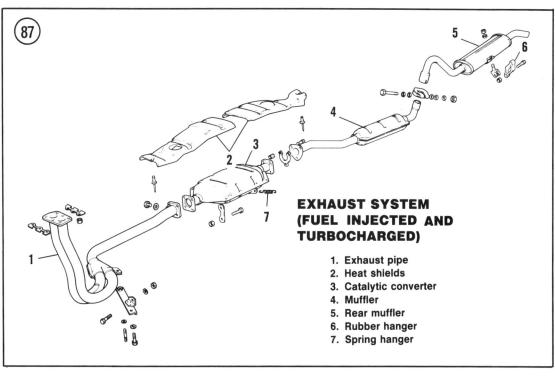

EXHAUST SYSTEM (FUEL INJECTED AND TURBOCHARGED)

1. Exhaust pipe
2. Heat shields
3. Catalytic converter
4. Muffler
5. Rear muffler
6. Rubber hanger
7. Spring hanger

pressure or volume specifications. However, mechanical and electric fuel pumps should deliver a strong stream of fuel. If they don't, check for clogged lines or a clogged filter. If these are okay, replace the fuel pump.

**Removal/Installation
(Mechanical Pump)**

1. Remove the splash shield from under the front of the car.
2. Disconnect and plug the fuel lines (**Figure 88**).
3. Remove the fuel pump mounting nuts and washers (**Figure 89**). Take off the fuel pump, gasket, spacer and second gasket. See **Figure 88**.
4. Installation is the reverse of removal. Use new gaskets, coated on both sides with gasket sealer.

**Removal/Installation
(Carburetted Models With
Electric Pump)**

1. Disconnect the negative cable from the battery.
2. Remove the trunk carpeting, spare tire cover, spare tire and fuel tank cover.
3. Unplug the pump electrical connector. See **Figure 90**.
4. Disconnect the fuel lines from the pump. Plug the lines so they won't drip gasoline and create a fire hazard.
5. Remove the pump mounting bolts and take the pump out.
6. Installation is the reverse of removal.

Testing (Fuel Injected Models)
*WARNING
Because of the high pressure in fuel injection system lines, Steps 1-3 must be followed carefully.*

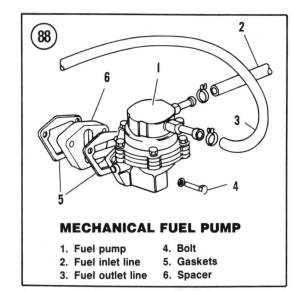

MECHANICAL FUEL PUMP

1. Fuel pump
2. Fuel inlet line
3. Fuel outlet line
4. Bolt
5. Gaskets
6. Spacer

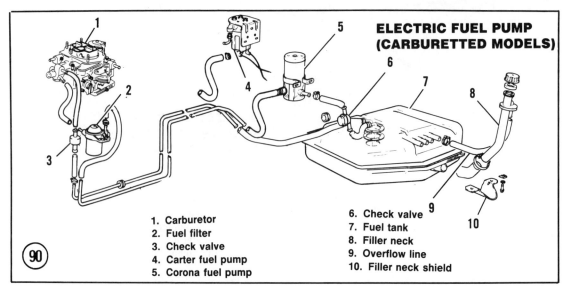

**ELECTRIC FUEL PUMP
(CARBURETTED MODELS)**

1. Carburetor
2. Fuel filter
3. Check valve
4. Carter fuel pump
5. Corona fuel pump
6. Check valve
7. Fuel tank
8. Filler neck
9. Overflow line
10. Filler neck shield

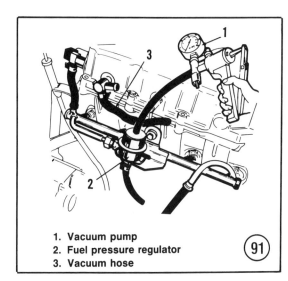

1. Vacuum pump
2. Fuel pressure regulator
3. Vacuum hose

(91)

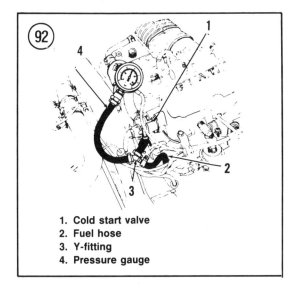

(92)

1. Cold start valve
2. Fuel hose
3. Y-fitting
4. Pressure gauge

1. Disconnect the vacuum hose from the fuel pressure regulator. See **Figure 91**.
2. Connect a hand vacuum pump to the regulator as shown. Pump vacuum to 20 in. Hg.
3. Release the vacuum and disconnect the vacuum pump.

CAUTION
During the next step, do not pull too hard on the fuel hose. The cold start valve body is plastic.

4. With a container handy to catch dripping fuel, disconnect the fuel hose (2, **Figure 92**) from the cold start valve.
5. Connect a fuel pressure gauge to the disconnected hose with a Y-fitting as shown in **Figure 92**. Secure the hose with a clamp.

6. Disconnect the vacuum hose from the pressure regulator. Disconnect the air supply hose from the air flow sensor.
7. Turn the ignition key to MAR (on) but don't start the engine.
8. Move the air flow sensor by hand to energize the fuel pump. Check the reading on the pressure gauge. It should be 2.3-2.7 bar (33-39 psi).
9. Start the engine and let it idle. The pressure gauge should indicate approximately 2 bar (28 psi).
10. Turn the engine off.

WARNING
Because of the high pressure in fuel injection system lines, Steps 11-13 must be followed carefully.

11. Disconnect the vacuum hose from the fuel pressure regulator. See **Figure 91**.
12. Connect a hand vacuum pump to the regulator as shown. Pump vacuum to 20 in. Hg.
13. Release the vacuum and disconnect the vacuum pump.
14. Disconnect the vacuum gauge and reconnect the hose to the cold start valve.
15. If pressure readings were within specifications in Step 9 and Step 10, the fuel delivery system is okay. If not, perform the next step to isolate the cause.
16. Connect the vacuum gauge directly to the fuel pump outlet fitting. Start the engine and let it idle. Fuel system pressure should be 2.7-3.2 bar (39-45 psi). If the reading is within specifications, the fuel pump is okay. Check for a clogged fuel filter or lines. If the reading is low, replace the fuel filter.

Fuel Filter Removal/Installation
(Fuel Injected Models)

The fuel filter is mounted under the car, just in front of the rear axle on the left side.

WARNING
Because of the high pressure in fuel injection system lines, Steps 1-3 must be followed carefully.

1. Disconnect the vacuum hose from the fuel pressure regulator. See **Figure 91**.
2. Connect a hand vacuum pump to the regulator as shown. Pump vacuum to 20 in. Hg.
3. Release the vacuum and disconnect the vacuum pump.
4. Detach the handbrake cable bracket from the body and lower the cable out of the way. See **Figure 93**.
5. Loosen the hose clamps, then detach the inlet and outlet hoses from the filter.

5

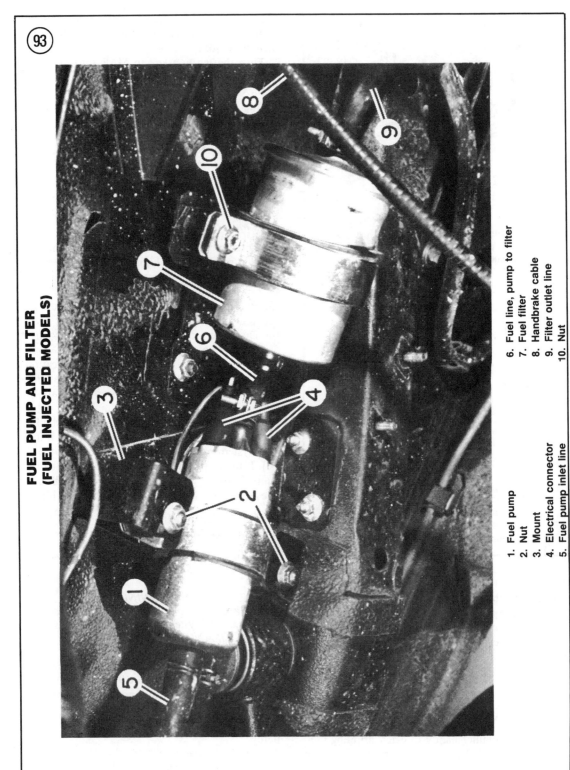

93

**FUEL PUMP AND FILTER
(FUEL INJECTED MODELS)**

1. Fuel pump
2. Nut
3. Mount
4. Electrical connector
5. Fuel pump inlet line
6. Fuel line, pump to filter
7. Fuel filter
8. Handbrake cable
9. Filter outlet line
10. Nut

6. Detach the shield and filter from the body and take them out.

7. Install by reversing Steps 4-6. Be sure the arrow on the filter faces the front of the car. After installation, run the engine and check for fuel leaks.

Fuel Pump Removal/Installation (Fuel Injected Models)

The fuel pump is mounted under the car, just in front of the rear axle on the left side.

WARNING
Because of the high pressure in fuel injection system lines, Steps 1-3 must be followed carefully.

1. Disconnect the vacuum hose from the fuel pressure regulator. See **Figure 91**.

2. Connect a hand vacuum pump to the regulator as shown. Pump vacuum to 20 in. Hg.

3. Release the vacuum and disconnect the vacuum pump.

4. Disconnect the negative cable from the battery.

5. Remove the nuts that secure the pump shield and pump to the body. See **Figure 93**.

6. Unplug the pump wiring connectors.

7. Loosen the hose clamps and detach the fuel hoses from the pump. Take the pump out.

8. Install by reversing Steps 4-7. Run the engine and check for leaks.

Table 1 TURBOCHARGER TROUBLESHOOTING

Symptom	Possible causes
No boost	Boost gauge not working
	Wastegate stuck open
	Turbocharger unit seized
	Turbine impeller coked up
Lack of power	Incorrect ignition timing
	Incorrect valve clearance
	Incorrect valve timing
	Low compression
	Clogged air filter
	Insufficient fuel supply
	(restricted lines, low fuel pressure,
	fuel enrichment system not working)
Detonation, no boost	Low octane fuel
	Ignition timing advanced too far
	Rough edge or foreign object in cylinder
Detonation, normal boost	Low octane fuel
	Ignition timing advanced too far
	Insufficient fuel supply (restricted lines,
	low fuel pressure, fuel enrichment
	system not working)
Detonation, excessive boost	Wastegate actuator signal line leaking
	Actuator tampered with
	Wastegate or actuator damaged
Excessive fuel consumption (black exhaust smoke)	Engine out of tune
	Intake air flow restricted (filter clogged,
	air delivery hoses kinked or collapsed)
	Cold start valve or injectors leaking
	Fuel enrichment system working all the time
Excessive oil consumption (blue, gray or white exhaust smoke)	Incorrect type or grade of oil
	Too much time between oil changes
	Clogged air cleaner element
	Engine wear (piston rings, valve guides)
	Crankcase emission system check valve
	stuck open or installed backwards
	Internal leakage @ turbocharger unit seals
Noise or vibration @ turbocharger unit	Loose mount or brackets
	Internal wear (excessive play)
	Internal damage (out of balance)

5

CHAPTER SIX

COOLING, HEATING
AND AIR CONDITIONING

All models use a centrifugal water pump to propel coolant through the radiator, engine and heater. An electric fan pulls air through the radiator to cool the coolant. A thermostat blocks coolant flow to the radiator when the engine is cold to speed warmup. The thermostat is a controlled bypass type, mounted in the radiator hoses.

Cooling system specifications are listed in **Table 1** at the end of the chapter.

COOLING SYSTEM FLUSHING

The system should be drained, flushed and refilled at intervals specified in Chapter Three. If desired, a chemical flushing agent may be used prior to the flushing method described here.

The recommended coolant is a 50/50 mixture of ethylene glycol-based antifreeze and water. This protects the system from freezing to approximately –36° C (–32° F). Antifreeze concentration can be checked with a coolant hydrometer. These are available inexpensively from car parts stores.

1. Coolant can stain concrete and harm plants. Park the car over a gutter or similar area.
2. Push the heater control lever on the console all the way to the rear.
3. Remove the expansion tank cap and radiator cap.
4. Open the engine and radiator drain valves. See **Figure 1** and **Figure 2**.
5. After the coolant has finished draining, close the drain valves.

6. Remove the thermostat as described in this chapter.
7. Insert a garden hose into the bottom radiator hose (7, **Figure 3**). Run water into the hose until clear water flows from the upper engine-to-thermostat hose (5).
8. Insert the garden hose into the engine hose (5, **Figure 3**). Run water into the hose until clear water flows from the lower engine hose (6).
9. Turn off the water. Open the engine and radiator drain valves. When the water has finished draining, close the valves.
10. Connect the hoses to the thermostat.
11. Fill the engine with a 50/50 mixture of ethylene glycol-based antifreeze and water. To make sure the engine is filled completely, disconnect the hose from the cylinder head union at the point shown in **Figure 4**. Pour antifreeze and water into the hose until it flows from the union, then reconnect the hose.
12. On 1979 and later models, remove the bleed valve from the union on the cylinder head. See **Figure 5**. Pour coolant into the bleed valve hole until it overflows, then reinstall the plug.
13. On fuel injected models (including Turbos), detach the hose from the throttle plate heater (**Figure 6**). Pour coolant into the hose until the throttle plate heater overflows, then reconnect the hose.
14. Run the engine until the thermostat opens (both radiator hoses feel warm). While it runs, check for leaks.

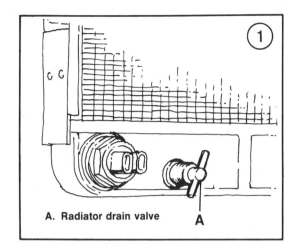

A. Radiator drain valve   **A**

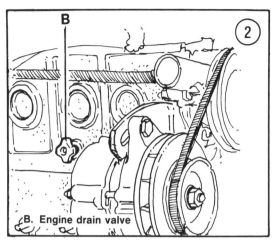

B. Engine drain valve

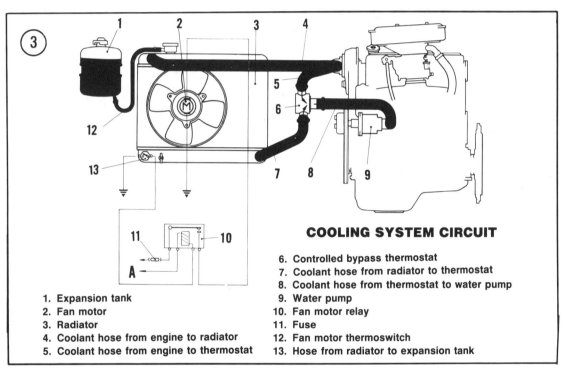

COOLING SYSTEM CIRCUIT

1. Expansion tank
2. Fan motor
3. Radiator
4. Coolant hose from engine to radiator
5. Coolant hose from engine to thermostat
6. Controlled bypass thermostat
7. Coolant hose from radiator to thermostat
8. Coolant hose from thermostat to water pump
9. Water pump
10. Fan motor relay
11. Fuse
12. Fan motor thermoswitch
13. Hose from radiator to expansion tank

6

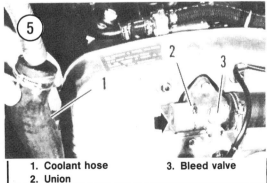

1. Coolant hose   3. Bleed valve
2. Union

15. Let the engine cool. Recheck coolant level and top off as needed. The expansion tank should be 2/3 full with the engine cold.

HOSES

Hoses should be inspected periodically. Check hoses for cracks, extreme softness, crumbling rubber and mildew stains. Replace hoses that show these conditions. **Figure 7** shows the hoses on 1975 and later models. Earlier models are similar.

CAUTION
If a hose's condition is in doubt, play it safe and replace it. It is most likely to fail during driving, when the heated coolant is trying to expand. Replacing a hose under roadside working conditions can be a truly miserable job.

NOTE
When buying new hoses, look at the hose ends and make sure there is reinforcing fabric imbedded in the rubber. Unreinforced hoses are weaker than reinforced ones.

Check all hose connections for leaks. Tighten or replace clamps as needed.

THERMOSTAT

The thermostat blocks water flow to the radiator when the engine is cold. As the engine warms up, the thermostat gradually opens, allowing water to circulate through the radiator.

If the engine overheats quickly but coolant level is normal and the fan works, the thermostat is probably stuck shut. If so, it must be replaced.

Removal/Testing/Installation

1. Make sure the engine is cool.
2. Drain the coolant from the radiator. If the coolant is clean, save it for reuse.

WARNING
Ethylene glycol is poisonous and may attract animals. Do not leave the coolant where it is accessible to pets or children.

3. Disconnect the hoses from the thermostat (**Figure 8**) and take it out.
4. Inspect the thermostat. When cold, it should be closed (**Figure 9**).
5. Place the thermostat in a pan of water with a thermometer (**Figure 10**). Heat the water. the thermostat should begin to open at 78-82° C (172-180° F). See **Figure 11**.
6. Continue heating the water. The thermostat should open fully at 92° C (198° F). See **Figure 12**.

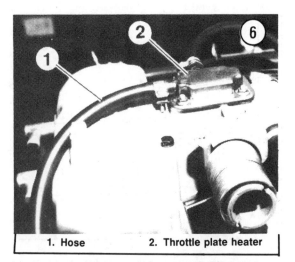

1. Hose   2. Throttle plate heater

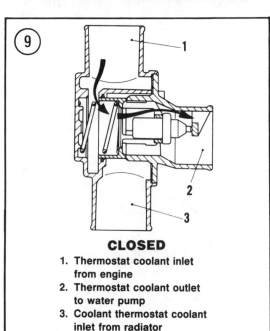

CLOSED
1. Thermostat coolant inlet from engine
2. Thermostat coolant outlet to water pump
3. Coolant thermostat coolant inlet from radiator

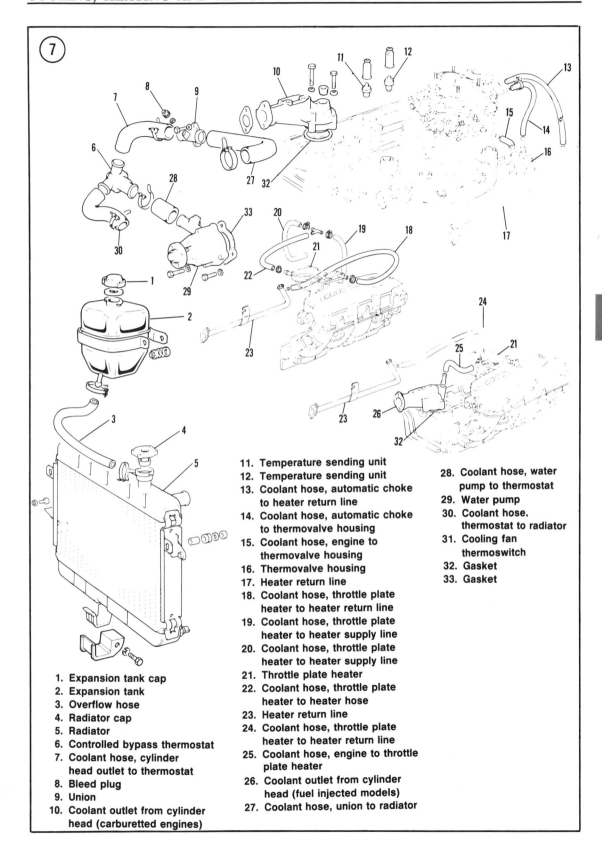

11. Temperature sending unit
12. Temperature sending unit
13. Coolant hose, automatic choke
    to heater return line
14. Coolant hose, automatic choke
    to thermovalve housing
15. Coolant hose, engine to
    thermovalve housing
16. Thermovalve housing
17. Heater return line
18. Coolant hose, throttle plate
    heater to heater return line
19. Coolant hose, throttle plate
    heater to heater supply line
20. Coolant hose, throttle plate
    heater to heater supply line
21. Throttle plate heater
22. Coolant hose, throttle plate
    heater to heater hose
23. Heater return line
24. Coolant hose, throttle plate
    heater to heater return line
25. Coolant hose, engine to throttle
    plate heater
26. Coolant outlet from cylinder
    head (fuel injected models)
27. Coolant hose, union to radiator

28. Coolant hose, water
    pump to thermostat
29. Water pump
30. Coolant hose,
    thermostat to radiator
31. Cooling fan
    thermoswitch
32. Gasket
33. Gasket

1. Expansion tank cap
2. Expansion tank
3. Overflow hose
4. Radiator cap
5. Radiator
6. Controlled bypass thermostat
7. Coolant hose, cylinder
   head outlet to thermostat
8. Bleed plug
9. Union
10. Coolant outlet from cylinder
    head (carburetted engines)

Thermostat valve stroke (from closed to open) should be 7.5 mm (0.29 in.).

WATER PUMP

A water pump may warn of impending failure by making noise. Coolant leaking from behind the water pump pulley indicates a defective seal.

Removal/Installation

1. Drain the radiator and engine as described under *Cooling System Flushing* in this chapter.
2. Loosen the alternator mounting and adjusting bolts (**Figure 13**). Push the alternator toward the engine to loosen the drive belt, then take the drive belt off.
3. Remove the water pump pulley bolts (**Figure 13**). Take off the pulley.
4. Remove the alternator and its bracket (**Figure 13**).
5. Remove the water pump mounting bolts. Take the water pump and its gasket off the engine.
6. Unbolt the water tube from the water pump.
7. Installation is the reverse of removal. Use a new gasket, coated on both sides with gasket sealer. Tighten the water pump bolts to 2 mkg (14 ft.-lb.). Fill and bleed the cooling system as described under *Cooling System Flushing* in this chapter.

ELECTRIC FAN

An electric fan is used on all models. See **Figure 14**.

Testing

> *WARNING*
> *The fan may run during the next steps. Keep your hands and hair out of the way.*

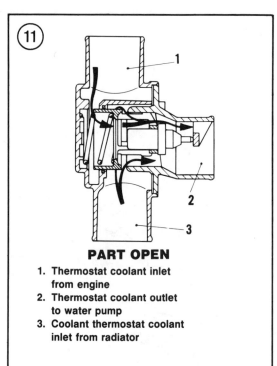

PART OPEN
1. Thermostat coolant inlet from engine
2. Thermostat coolant outlet to water pump
3. Coolant thermostat coolant inlet from radiator

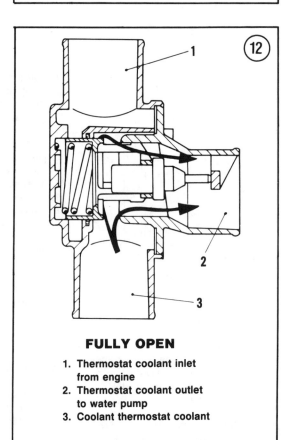

FULLY OPEN
1. Thermostat coolant inlet from engine
2. Thermostat coolant outlet to water pump
3. Coolant thermostat coolant

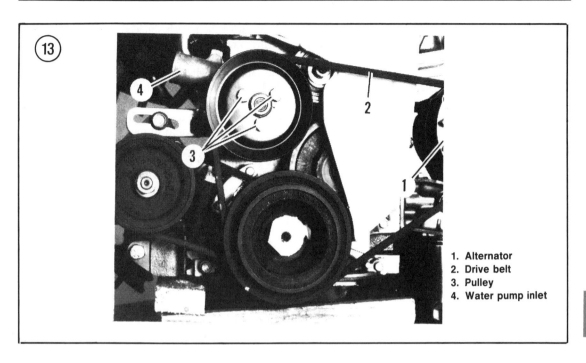

13

1. Alternator
2. Drive belt
3. Pulley
4. Water pump inlet

6

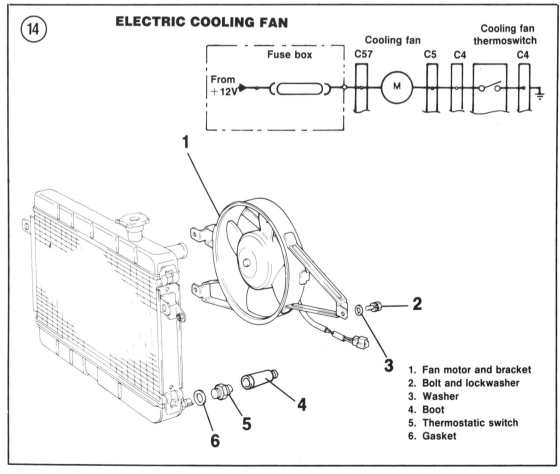

14

ELECTRIC COOLING FAN

Fuse box

Cooling fan

Cooling fan thermoswitch

C57   C5   C4   C4

From +12V

M

1. Fan motor and bracket
2. Bolt and lockwasher
3. Washer
4. Boot
5. Thermostatic switch
6. Gasket

1. Unplug the fan motor wiring connector. Connect the fan motor directly to a 12-volt battery with 2 lengths of wire. The motor should run. If not, replace it.

2. If the motor is good, disconnect the 2 lengths of wire. Reconnect the fan motor wiring connector in its normal position, then perform the following step.

3. Unplug the wiring connector from the fan's thermostatic switch (**Figure 14**). Connect the switch terminals together with a short length of wire. The fan should run.

Removal/Installation

1. Disconnect the negative cable from the battery.
2. Unplug the fan motor wiring connector.
3. Detach the fan from the radiator. See **Figure 14**.
4. Installation is the reverse of removal. The following additional steps apply to air-conditioned Turbos only.
    a. Install the spacers as shown in **Figure 15**.
    b. If a new fan assembly is being installed, trim the shroud to clear the radiator tank as shown in **Figure 15**.

RADIATOR

Removal/Installation

1. Drain the cooling system as described under *Cooling System Flushing* in this chapter. If the coolant is clean, save it for reuse.

WARNING
Antifreeze is poisonous and may attract animals. Do not leave the coolant in a place accessible to children or pets.

2. Remove the splash shield from under the front of the car.

3. Unplug the wiring connectors for fan and thermostatic switch.

4. Disconnect the radiator hoses.

5. If equipped with an automatic transmission, disconnect the fluid cooler lines from the radiator and plug the lines and fittings.

6. Remove the radiator mounting nuts, then lift the radiator and fan out.

7. Installation is the reverse of removal. Fill and bleed the cooling system as described under *Cooling System Flushing* in this chapter.

NOTE
If a new radiator is being installed on air-conditioned Turbos, be sure to

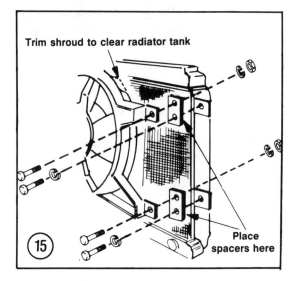

Trim shroud to clear radiator tank

Place spacers here

(15)

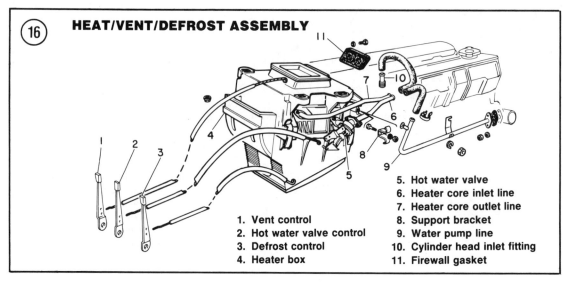

(16) **HEAT/VENT/DEFROST ASSEMBLY**

5. Hot water valve
6. Heater core inlet line
7. Heater core outlet line
8. Support bracket
9. Water pump line
10. Cylinder head inlet fitting
11. Firewall gasket

1. Vent control
2. Hot water valve control
3. Defrost control
4. Heater box

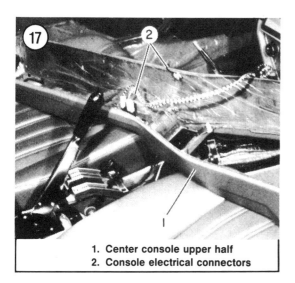

1. Center console upper half
2. Console electrical connectors

1. Center console   2. Electrical connectors

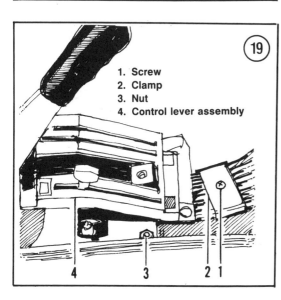

1. Screw
2. Clamp
3. Nut
4. Control lever assembly

install spacers between the radiator and the right-hand side of the fan as shown in Figure 15.

HEATER

Figure 16 shows the heater and related parts.

Troubleshooting

Poor heater or ventilation system performance may be caused by problems in areas other than the heater itself. Before removing the heater, check for the following:

a. Air flow through radiator blocked by leaves, bugs or other debris.
b. Fresh air inlet blocked.
c. Defective cooling system thermostat.
d. Blown fuse; break or bad connection in wiring.
e. Low coolant level.
f. Kinked or blocked heater hoses.
g. Clogged cooling system.

Heater Assembly
Removal/Installation

1. Disconnect the negative cable from the battery.
2. Move the heat control lever (center lever on the console) to the maximum heat position.
3. Drain the radiator and engine as described under *Cooling System Flushing* in this chapter.
4. Remove the console (lower part on vinyl interiors; upper and lower parts on leather interiors) as described in Chapter Twelve.
5. Label and unplug the blower switch wiring connectors (**Figure 17**). Pry open the harness clips and detach the wiring from the console.
6. If equipped with a vinyl interior, detach the upper half of the console and pull it partway out (**Figure 18**). Label and unplug the console wiring connectors.
7. Remove the screw and control cable clamp. See **Figure 19**.
8. Pry open the control cable clips and detach the control cables from the side of the transmission tunnel.
9. Remove the control lever assembly mounting nuts (**Figure 19**).
10. Working in the engine compartment, disconnect the heater hoses at the firewall.
11. Working beneath the instrument panel, detach the radio rear support bracket from the body. Unplug the electrical wires (**Figure 20**).
12. Remove the heater box mounting nuts (**Figure 20**). Lower the heater box, then carefully withdraw it from under the instrument panel.

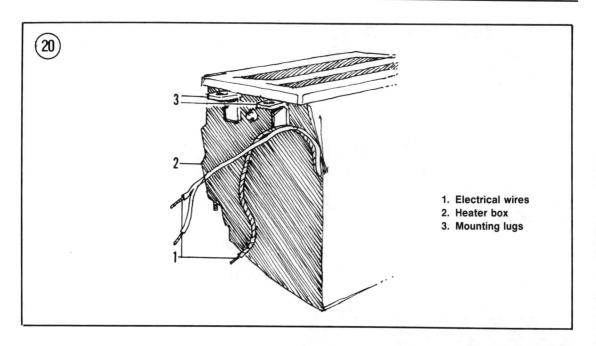

1. Electrical wires
2. Heater box
3. Mounting lugs

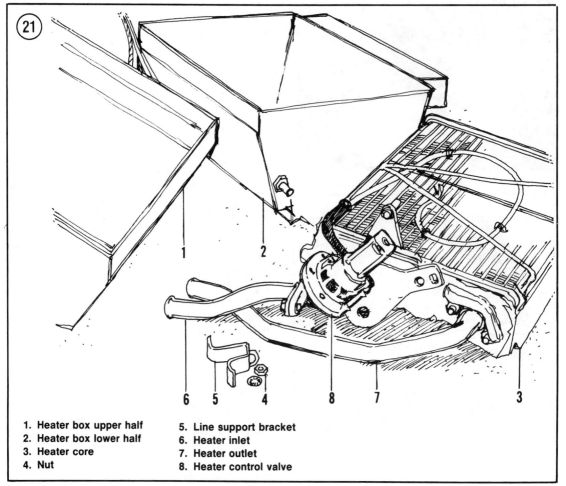

1. Heater box upper half
2. Heater box lower half
3. Heater core
4. Nut
5. Line support bracket
6. Heater inlet
7. Heater outlet
8. Heater control valve

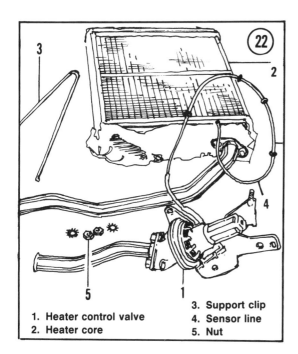

1. Heater control valve
2. Heater core
3. Support clip
4. Sensor line
5. Nut

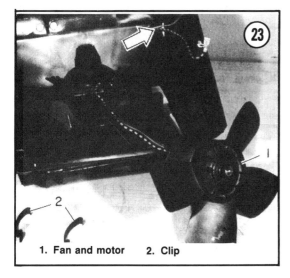

1. Fan and motor   2. Clip

13. Installation is the reverse of removal. Fill and bleed the cooling system as described under *Cooling System Flushing* in this chapter.

Heater Unit Disassembly/Assembly

1. Remove the heater unit as described in this chapter.
2. Remove the clips that hold the upper and lower halves of the heater box together, then separate the halves.
3. Remove the nut and detach the line support bracket (**Figure 21**). Lift the water valve and heater core out of the upper heater box half.

4. To separate the valve from the core, remove the sensor line support clip and 2 nuts. See **Figure 22**.
5. Lift out the fan shroud.
6. Release the fan motor wiring clips (**Figure 23**). Feed the wires through the opening and lift the fan motor out.
7. Assembly is the reverse of disassembly.

AIR CONDITIONING

This section covers the maintenance and minor repairs that can prevent or correct most air conditioning problems. Major repairs require special training and tools and should be left to a dealer or air conditioning shop.

System Operation

The air conditioning system is shown in **Figure 24**. The 5 basic components are common to all air conditioning systems:

a. Compressor.
b. Condenser.
c. Receiver/drier.
d. Expansion valve.
e. Evaporator.

WARNING
*The components, connected with high-pressure hoses and tubes, form a closed loop. The refrigerant in the system is under very high pressure. It can cause frostbite if it touches skin and blindness if it touches the eyes. If discharged near a flame, the refrigerant creates poisonous gas. If the refrigerant can is hooked up wrong, it can explode. For these reasons, **read this entire section** before working on the system.*

For practical purposes, the cycle begins at the compressor. The refrigerant, in a warm, low-pressure vapor state, enters the low-pressure side of the compressor. It is compressed to a high-pressure hot vapor and pumped out of the high-pressure side to the condenser.

Air flow through the condenser removes heat from the refrigerant and transfers the heat to the outside air. As the heat is removed, the refrigerant condenses to a warm, high-pressure liquid.

The refrigerant then flows to the receiver/drier where moisture is removed and impurities are filtered out. The refrigerant is stored in the receiver/drier until it is needed. The receiver/drier incorporates a sight glass that permits visual monitoring of the condition of the refrigerant as it flows. From the receiver/drier, the refrigerant then flows to the expansion valve. The expansion valve

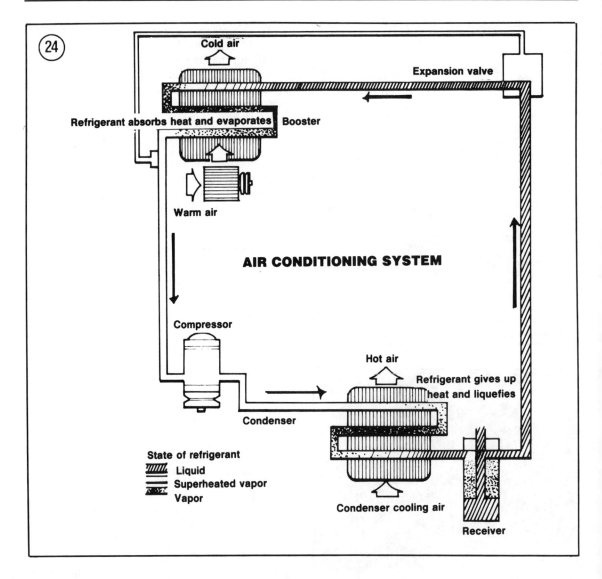

AIR CONDITIONING SYSTEM

(24)

Cold air

Expansion valve

Refrigerant absorbs heat and evaporates   Booster

Warm air

Compressor

Hot air

Refrigerant gives up heat and liquefies

Condenser

State of refrigerant
- Liquid
- Superheated vapor
- Vapor

Condenser cooling air

Receiver

is thermostatically controlled and meters refrigerant to the evaporator. As the refrigerant leaves the expansion valve it changes from a warm, high-pressure liquid to a cold, low-pressure liquid.

In the evaporator, the refrigerant removes heat from the passenger compartment air that is blown across the evaporator's fins and tubes. In the process, the refrigerant changes from a cold, low-pressure liquid to a warm, high-pressure vapor. The vapor flows back to the compressor, where the cycle begins again.

Compressor

The compressor is located on the front end of the engine, like an alternator, and is driven by a V-belt. The large pulley on the front of the compressor contains an electromagnetic clutch. This activates

and operates the compressor when the air conditioning is switched on.

Condenser

The condenser is mounted in front of the radiator. Air passing through the fins and tubes removes heat from the refrigerant in the same manner it removes heat from the engine coolant as it passes through the radiator.

Receiver/Drier

The receiver/drier is a small tank-like unit, mounted in the engine compartment. It incorporates a sight glass (**Figure 25**) through which refrigerant flow can be seen. The refrigerant's appearance is used to troubleshoot the system.

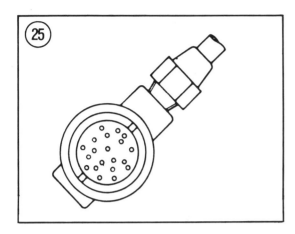

Expansion Valve

The expansion valve is located between the receiver/drier and the evaporator. It is mounted on the cooling unit in the passenger compartment.

Evaporator

The evaporator is located in the passenger compartment, inside the cooling unit. Warm air is blown across the fins and tubes, where it is cooled and dried and then ducted into the passenger compartment.

Routine Maintenance

Preventive maintenance of the air conditioning system is easy; at least once a month, even in cold weather, start your engine, turn on the air conditioner and operate it at each of the control settings. Operate the air conditioner for about 5 minutes. This will ensure that the compressor seal will not deform from sitting in the same position for a long period of time. If this occurs, the seal is likely to leak.

The efficiency of the air conditioning system also depends in great part on the efficiency of the cooling system. This is because the heat from the condenser passes through the radiator. If the cooling system is dirty or low on coolant, it may be impossible to operate the air conditioner without overheating. Inspect the coolant. If necessary, flush and refill the cooling system as described in this chapter.

With an air hose and a soft brush, clean the radiator and condenser fins and tubes to remove bugs, leaves and other imbedded debris.

Check drive belt tension as described in Chapter Three.

Make sure the electric radiator fan operates. The fan should come on when coolant temperature reaches 90° C (194° F).

If the condition of the cooling system thermostat is in doubt, test it as described in this chapter.

Once you are sure the cooling system is in good condition, the air conditioning system can be inspected.

Inspection

1. Clean all lines, fittings and system components with solvent and a clean rag. Pay particular attention to the fittings; oily dirt around connections almost certainly indicates a leak. Oil from the compressor will migrate through the system to the leak. Carefully tighten the connection, but don't overtighten and strip the threads. If the leak persists, it will soon be apparent once again as oily dirt accumulates. Clean the sight glass with a clean, dry cloth.
2. Clean the condenser fins and tubes with a soft brush and an air hose or with a high-pressure stream of water from a garden hose. Remove bugs, leaves and other imbedded debris. Carefully straighten any bent fins with a screwdriver, taking care not to puncture or dent the tubes.
3. Start the engine and check the operation of the blower motor and the compressor clutch by turning the controls on and off. If either the blower or the clutch fails to operate, shut off the engine and check the fuses. If they are blown, replace them. If not, remove them and clean the fuse holder contacts. Then check the clutch and blower operation again.

Testing

1. Place the transmission in NEUTRAL (PARK on automatics). Set the handbrake.
2. Start the engine and run it at a fast idle.
3. Set the temperature control to its coldest setting and the blower to high. Allow the system to operate for 10 minutes with the doors open. Then shut them and set the blower on its lowest setting.
4. Check air temperature at the outlet. It should be noticeably colder than the surrounding air. If not, the refrigerant level is probably low. Check the sight glass as described in the following step.
5. Run the engine at a fast idle and switch on the air conditioning. Look at the sight glass (**Figure 25**) and check for the following:
   a. Bubbles—the refrigerant level is low.
   b. Oily or cloudy—the system is contaminated. Have it serviced by a dealer or air conditioning shop.
   c. Clear glass—either there is enough refrigerant, too much or the system is so close to empty it can't make bubbles. If there is no difference between the inlet and outlet air temperatures,

the system is probably near empty. If the system does blow cold air, it either has the right amount of refrigerant or too much. To tell which, have an assistant turn off the air conditioner while you watch the sight glass. If the refrigerant foams, then clears up, the amount is correct. If it doesn't foam, but stays clear, there is too much.

Refrigerant

The air conditioning system uses a refrigerant called dichlorodifluoromethane or R-12.

> *WARNING*
> *R-12 creates freezing temperatures when it evaporates. This can cause frostbite if it touches skin and blindness if it touches the eyes. If discharged near an open flame, R-12 creates poisonous gas. If the refrigerant can is hooked up to the pressure side of the compressor, it may explode. Always wear safety goggles when working with R-12.*

Charging

Partially discharged or empty air conditioning systems can be charged by home mechanics. If a hose has been disconnected or any internal part of the system exposed to air, the system should be evacuated and recharged by a dealer or air conditioning shop.

Recharge kits are available from auto parts stores. Be sure the kit includes a gauge set.

> *NOTE*
> *Gauge sets are expensive, but so is having the system professionally recharged. Compare the price of a gauge set with the cost of a professional recharging job before proceeding.*

Carefully read and understand the gauge manufacturer's instructions before charging the system.

Troubleshooting

If the air conditioner fails to blow cold air, the following steps will help locate the problem.

1. First, stop the car and look at the control settings. One of the most common air conditioning problems occurs when the temperature is set for maximum cold and the blower is set on low. This promotes ice buildup on the evaporator fins and tubes, particularly in humid weather. Eventually, the evaporator will ice over completely and restrict air flow. Turn the blower on high and place a hand over an air outlet. If the blower is running but there is little or no air flowing through the outlet, the evaporator is probably iced up. Leave the blower on high, turn the temperature control to its warmest setting and wait. It will take 10-15 minutes for the ice to start melting.

2. If the blower is not running, the fuse may be blown, there may be a loose wiring connection or the motor may be burned out. First check the fuse block for a blown or incorrectly seated fuse. Then check the wiring for loose connections.

3. Shut off the engine and inspect the compressor drive belt. If loose or worn, tighten or replace. See *Drive Belts,* Chapter Three.

4. Start the engine. Check the compressor clutch by turning the air conditioning on and off. If the clutch does not activate, its fuse may be blown or the evaporator temperature-limiting switches may be defective. If the fuse is defective, replace it. If the fuse is not the problem, have the system checked by a Fiat dealer or air conditioning shop.

5. If the system checks out okay to this point, start the engine, turn on the air conditioner and watch the refrigerant through the sight glass. If it fills with bubbles after a few seconds, the refrigerant level is low. If the sight glass is oily or cloudy, the system is contaminated and should be serviced by a shop as soon as possible. Corrosion and deterioration occur very quickly and if not taken care of at once will result in a very expensive repair job.

6. If the system still appears to be operating as it should but air flow into the passenger compartment is not cold, check the condenser and cooling system radiator for debris that could block air flow. Recheck the cooling system as described under *Inspection.*

7. If the preceding steps have not solved the problem, take the car to a dealer or air conditioning shop for service.

Table 1 COOLING SYSTEM SPECIFICATIONS

Capacity		
Through 1974	7.5 liters	8 qt.
1975-on	8 liters	8 1/2 qt.
Thermostat opening temperature		
Mounted in engine	85-89° C (185-192° F)	
Mounted in hoses	78-82° C (172-180° F)	

CHAPTER SEVEN

ELECTRICAL SYSTEM

This chapter provides service procedures for the battery, charging system, starter, lights, windshield wipers and washers, fuses and ignition system.

Tables 1-3 are at the end of the chapter.

BATTERY

Care and Inspection

Some of the following steps apply to fillable batteries, which are standard equipment on all models. This type has filler caps through which water is periodically added. Maintenance-free batteries have no filler caps and do not require the addition of water.

1. Disconnect both battery cables and remove the battery.

2. Clean the top of the battery with a baking soda and water solution. Scrub it with a stiff bristle brush. Wipe the battery clean with a cloth moistened in ammonia or baking soda solution.

CAUTION
Keep cleaning solution out of battery cells or the electrolyte will be seriously weakened.

3. Clean the battery terminals with a stiff wire brush or one of the many tools made for this purpose.

4. Check the entire battery case for cracks.

5. Install the battery and reconnect the battery cables.

CAUTION
Be sure the battery cables are connected to the proper terminals. Connecting the battery backwards can damage the alternator.

6. Coat the battery connections with Vaseline or light mineral grease after tightening.

7. If the battery has removable filler caps, check electrolyte level. Top up with distilled water if necessary.

Testing

This procedure applies to batteries with removable filler caps. Testing sealed maintenance-free batteries requires special equipment, but a service station can make the test for a nominal fee.

Hydrometer testing is the best way to check battery condition. Use a hydrometer with numbered graduations from 1.100-1.300 rather than one with just color-coded bands. To use the hydrometer, squeeze the rubber ball, insert the tip in the cell and release the ball (**Figure 1**).

Draw enough electrolyte to float the weighted float inside the hydrometer. Note the number in line with the surface of the electrolyte. This is the specific gravity for the cell. Return the electrolyte to the cell from which it came.

The specific gravity of the electrolyte in each battery cell is an excellent indicator of that cell's condition. A fully charged cell will read 1.260 or more at 20° C (68° F). If the cells test below 1.200, the battery must be recharged. Charging is also necessary if the specific gravity varies more than 0.025 from cell to cell.

NOTE
For every 10° above 80° F (25° C) electrolyte temperature, add 0.004 to specific gravity reading. For every 10° below 80° F (25° C), subtract 0.004.

Charging

The battery need not be removed from the car for charging. Just make certain the area is well ventilated and there is no chance of sparks or flames occurring near the battery.

WARNING
Charging batteries give off highly explosive hydrogen gas. If the gas explodes, it may spray battery acid over a wide area.

Disconnect the cables from the battery. On fillable batteries, make sure the electrolyte is fully topped up.

WARNING
Connect the charger to the battery before plugging it in.

Connect the charger to the battery—negative to negative, positive to positive. If the charger output is variable, select a low setting (5-10 amps), set the voltage selector to 12 volts and plug the charger in. If the battery is severely discharged, allow it to charge for at least 8 hours. Batteries that aren't as badly discharged require less charging time. **Table 1** gives approximate charge rates. On fillable batteries, check charging progress with the hydrometer.

CHARGING SYSTEM

The charging system consists of the battery, alternator, regulator, charge warning lamp and wiring. The 1971-1976 models use a Marelli alternator with separate regulator. The 1977 and later models use a Bosch alternator with integral regulator. The following sections describe test procedures for the 1975 and later models. For earlier cars, refer to *Charging System* in Chapter Two.

Charging System Test (1975-1976)

1. Check alternator belt tension and adjust as needed. See *Drive Belts,* Chapter Three.
2. Inspect the battery as described in this chapter.
3. Unplug the secondary (thick) wire from the ignition coil.

CAUTION
Do not unplug the thick coil wire or any of the spark plug wires from the distributor.

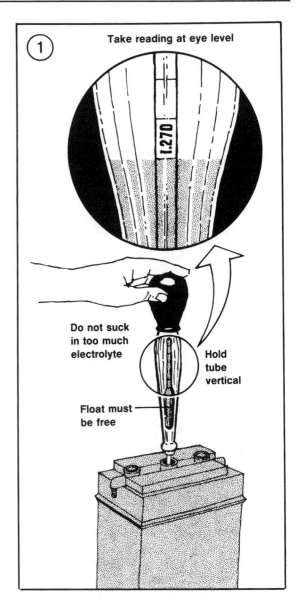

Take reading at eye level

I.270

Do not suck in too much electrolyte

Hold tube vertical

Float must be free

ENGINE CRANK TEST

Voltage reads 9.6 volts minimum (engine cranking)

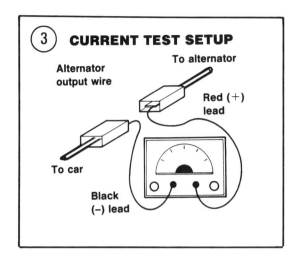

③ **CURRENT TEST SETUP**

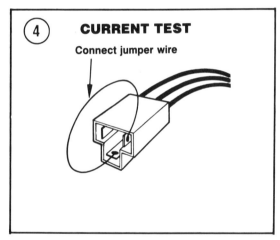

④ **CURRENT TEST**

4. Connect a voltmeter between the battery terminals as shown in **Figure 2**.

5. Crank the engine for 3-4 seconds and note the voltmeter reading. It should be at least 9.6 volts. If it is less than this, have the battery tested by a dealer or automotive electrical shop.

6. Reconnect the thick wire to the ignition coil.

7. Run the engine at 2,500 rpm with the low beam headlights on and the heater fan at its highest speed. Note the voltmeter reading:

   a. If it is more than 14.5 volts, replace the alternator with a new or rebuilt unit.

   b. If it is 12.5-14.5 volts, the alternator and regulator are good.

   c. If it is less than 12.5 volts, turn off the engine and perform the next steps.

8. Turn the key to MAR (on), but don't start the engine. The charge warning light on the instrument panel should come on:

   a. If not, check the bulb and charging system wiring. If these are good, have the alternator

brushes inspected by a dealer or automotive electrical shop.

   b. If the light comes on, go to the next step.

9. If the charge warning light comes on, start the engine. The light should go out:

   a. If not, check for a short circuit in the charging system wiring.

   b. If the light goes out, go to the next steps.

10. Disconnect the negative cable from the battery.

11. Locate the output terminal on the alternator. It is marked "30" or "B+" and has a black or brown wire attached.

CAUTION
During the next step, do not allow the disconnected wire ends to brush against each other or ground (any nearby metal).

12. Disconnect the output wire from the alternator. Connect the positive lead of an ammeter to the alternator side of the wire and the ammeter negative lead to the wiring harness side of the wire. See **Figure 3**.

13. Unplug the wiring connector from the voltage regulator.

14. Make sure the test connections have been made correctly, then reconnect the negative cable to the battery.

15. Make sure all lights and accessories (fan, radio, etc.) are off.

16. Prepare a short length of wire to be used as a jumper wire. See **Figure 4**.

CAUTION
During the next step, do not leave the jumper wire connected for more than 5 seconds or the alternator may be damaged.

17. Start the engine and run it at 2,500 rpm. Connect the jumper wire to the wiring connector as shown in **Figure 4** (for a maximum of 5 seconds) and note the ammeter reading:

   a. If the ammeter reading is 50 amps or more, replace the voltage regulator.

   b. If the ammeter reading is less than 50 amps, replace the alternator.

18. After making repairs, repeat the voltage and amperage tests to make sure the charging system is working properly. Then disconnect the test equipment and reconnect the wiring connectors in their normal positions.

Charging System Test (1977-on)

1. Check alternator belt tension and adjust as needed. See *Drive Belts,* Chapter Three.

2. Inspect the battery as described in this chapter.

> *CAUTION*
> *During the next steps, do not unplug the thick coil wire or any of the spark plug wires from the distributor. If equipped with electronic ignition (1979-on), do not disconnect the secondary (thick) wire from the ignition coil.*

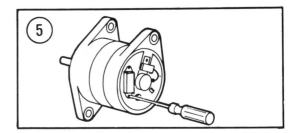

3A. If equipped with breaker point ignition (1977-1978), unplug the thick wire from the ignition coil.

3B. If equipped with electronic ignition (1979-on), unplug the wiring connector from the electronic control module (between the ignition coil and the fender). See *Ignition System* in this chapter for details.

4. Connect a voltmeter between the battery terminals as shown in **Figure 2**.

5. Crank the engine for 3-4 seconds and note the voltmeter reading. It should be at least 9 volts. If it is less than this, have the battery tested by a dealer or automotive electrical shop.

6. Reconnect the wiring disconnected in Step 3.

7. Run the engine at 2,500 rpm with the low beam headlights on and the heater fan at its highest speed. Connect the voltmeter as shown in **Figure 2** and note the reading:

  a. If it is more than 14.5 volts, replace the regulator as described in this chapter.

  b. If it is 12.5-14.5 volts, the alternator and regulator are good.

  c. If it is less than 12.5 volts, turn off the engine and perform the next steps.

8. Remove the cover from the alternator as shown in **Figure 5** to expose the regulator.

9. Make sure the regulator mounting screws and brush holder screws are clean and tight.

10. Turn the key to MAR (on), but don't start the engine. The charge warning light on the instrument panel should come on. If not, check the bulb and charging system wiring. If these are good, have the alternator brushes inspected by a dealer or automotive electrical shop.

11. If the charge warning light comes on, start the engine. The light should go out. If not, check for a short circuit in the charging system wiring.

12. If the light goes out when the engine is started, the problem is in the alternator or regulator. The test method recommended by the factory is to install a known good regulator and repeat Step 7. If you have a spare regulator or can borrow one from a friend, use this method. If voltage is within specifications, replace the original regulator. If

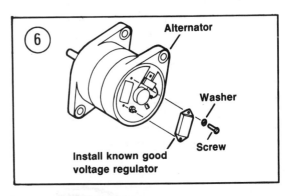

voltage still is not within specifications, replace the alternator.

13. If you don't have access to another regulator and Steps 1-11 haven't located the problem, have the charging system tested further by a dealer or automotive electrical shop.

Alternator Removal/Installation

1. Disconnect the negative cable from the battery.

2. Label and unplug the alternator wiring connectors.

3. Remove the alternator drive belt, then remove the mounting and adjusting bolts. See *Drive Belts* in Chapter Three.

4. Take the alternator off the engine.

5. Installation is the reverse of removal. Adjust alternator belt tension as described in Chapter Three.

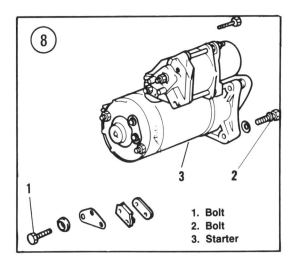

1. Bolt
2. Bolt
3. Starter

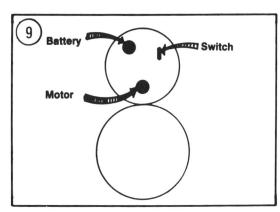

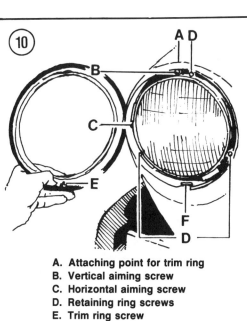

A. Attaching point for trim ring
B. Vertical aiming screw
C. Horizontal aiming screw
D. Retaining ring screws
E. Trim ring screw
F. Hole for trim ring screw

Regulator Removal/Installation

1. If equipped with a separate regulator, unplug its wiring connector. Remove its mounting screws and take the regulator out.
2. If equipped with an integral regulator, remove the rear shield from the alternator. Remove the regulator mounting screws (**Figure 6**) and take the regulator out.
3. Installation is the reverse of removal.

STARTER

Removal/Installation

1. Disconnect the negative cable from the battery.
2. Disconnect the starter wires.
3. Remove the starter mounting bolts, lockwashers and washers. See **Figure 7** and **Figure 8**. Take the starter out.
4. Installation is the reverse of removal.

Starter Test

The following test will tell you whether a starter problem is in the starter or wiring. It requires a pair of jumper cables (the kind used to start cars with dead batteries) and a length of wire.

1. Remove the starter as described in this chapter. Set it down on a solid surface such as a garage floor or driveway.
2. Connect a jumper cable from the positive terminal of the car's battery to the battery terminal on the starter solenoid (the terminal from which the thick wire was disconnected). See **Figure 9**.
3. Connect the other jumper cable from the negative terminal of the car's battery to the starter mounting bolt flange.
4. Hold the starter down with a piece of wood.
5. Connect the length of wire from the battery positive terminal to the switch terminal on the starter solenoid (the one from which the thin wire was disconnected). See **Figure 9**. The starter pinion should move out sharply and make a firm click. The starter should spin freely and rapidly:
   a. If the starter spins freely and rapidly, the problem is in the wiring or ignition switch.
   b. If the starter spins sluggishly or not at all, replace it with a new or rebuilt unit.

LIGHTING SYSTEM

Bulb specifications are listed in **Table 2**.

Headlight Replacement

1. Remove the trim screws and take the trim piece off. See **Figure 10**.

7

2. Loosen the retaining ring screws (**Figure 10**). Turn the retaining ring clockwise and take it off as shown in **Figure 11**.
3. Take the bulb out and unplug its wiring connector.
4. Installation is the reverse of removal. Have headlight aim checked and adjusted if necessary by a dealer or lamp adjusting station.

Front Parking/Turn Signal
Light Replacement

To remove a bulb, remove the lens securing screws and take off the lens. See **Figure 12** (1971-1974) or **Figure 13** (1975-on). Press the bulb into its socket and turn counterclockwise to remove. Installation is the reverse of removal.

Front Side Marker
Light Replacement

To remove a bulb, reach inside the fender. See **Figure 14**. Twist the bulb holder, take it out of the lamp body and pull the bulb out of the holder. Installation is the reverse of removal.

Rear Side Marker
Light Replacement

To replace a bulb, open the trunk. See **Figure 15**. Twist the bulb socket, take it out of the lamp body and pull the bulb out of the socket. Install a new bulb and push the socket back into the lamp body.

Tail, Stop, Turn Signal and
Backup Light Replacement

1971-1974

Replace bulbs as follows.
1. Open the trunk. Remove the knurled screws that secure the lens to the lamp body. See **Figure 16**.

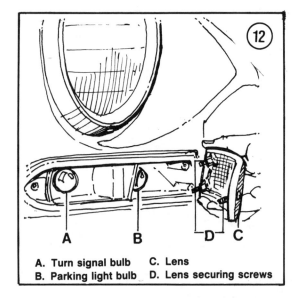

A. Turn signal bulb   C. Lens
B. Parking light bulb   D. Lens securing screws

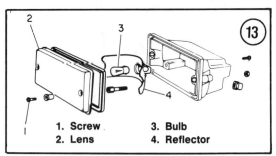

1. Screw   3. Bulb
2. Lens   4. Reflector

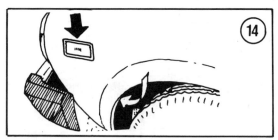

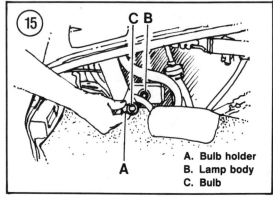

A. Bulb holder
B. Lamp body
C. Bulb

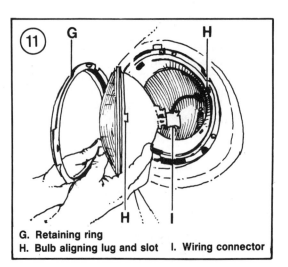

G. Retaining ring
H. Bulb aligning lug and slot   I. Wiring connector

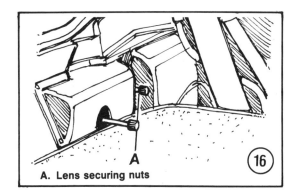

A. Lens securing nuts

(16)

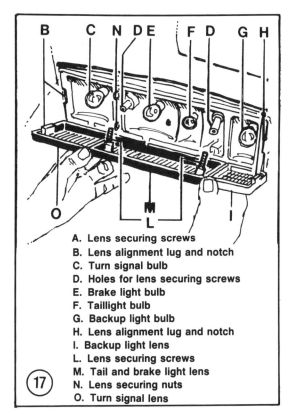

A. Lens securing screws
B. Lens alignment lug and notch
C. Turn signal bulb
D. Holes for lens securing screws
E. Brake light bulb
F. Taillight bulb
G. Backup light bulb
H. Lens alignment lug and notch
I. Backup light lens
L. Lens securing screws
M. Tail and brake light lens
N. Lens securing nuts
O. Turn signal lens

(17)

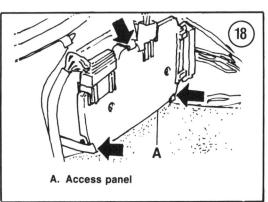

A. Access panel

(18)

2. Lower the lens away from the lamp body as shown in **Figure 17** to expose the bulbs.
3. Press the bulb into its socket and turn counterclockwise to remove.
4. Installation is the reverse of removal.

1975-on

Replace bulbs as follows.
1. Open the trunk. Remove the cover panel (**Figure 18**) to expose the bulbs.
2. Press the bulb (**Figure 19**) into its socket and turn counterclockwise to remove.
3. Installation is the reverse of removal.

License Plate Light Replacement

1971-1974

To replace a bulb, remove the lens securing screws and take off the lens. See **Figure 20**. Press the bulb into its socket and turn counterclockwise to remove. Installation is the reverse of removal.

7

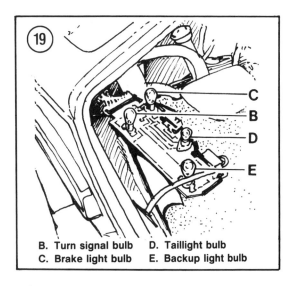

(19)

B. Turn signal bulb   D. Taillight bulb
C. Brake light bulb   E. Backup light bulb

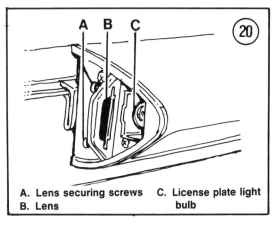

(20)

A. Lens securing screws   C. License plate light
B. Lens   bulb

1975-on

Replace bulbs as follows.

1. Open the trunk. Remove the lamp body mounting nuts (**Figure 21**) and detach the lamp body from the car.

2. Take off the lens. Press the bulb into its socket and turn counterclockwise to remove.

3. Installation is the reverse of removal.

Interior Light Replacement

To replace a bulb, pry out the lamp body as shown in **Figure 22**, then pull the bulb out of its holder. Installation is the reverse of removal.

Instrument Light Replacement

Replace bulbs as follows.

1. Remove 4 instrument panel securing screws (**Figure 23**).

2. Lower the instrument panel to expose the bulbs.

3. Remove the bulb holder from the instrument cluster, then pull the bulb out of the holder.

4. Installation is the reverse of removal.

Turn Signal Testing

1. *One side flashes faster than the other or only one side operates*—Check for a burned-out bulb. Check with **Table 2** to make sure the correct bulbs are being used. Check for a poorly grounded bulb. Check for breaks or bad connections in the wiring. If only one side operates, check the turn signal switch.

2. *Turn signals don't work at all*—Check the turn signal fuse. If the fuse is good, check the wiring for a break or bad connection. If the wiring is good, check the turn signal switch. If the switch is good, the flasher unit is probably at fault. Replace it.

3. *Lights flash slowly or stay on*—Check with **Table 2** to make sure the correct bulbs are being used. Make sure the battery is fully charged. Check the fuse for poor contact. Check for a break or bad connection in the wiring. If none of these problems exists, the flasher is probably defective. Replace it.

4. *Lights flash too quickly*—Check with **Table 2** to make sure the correct bulbs are being used. If they are, check for a burned-out bulb, disconnected wire or poor ground connection in the wiring.

Turn Signal Switch Test

This procedure requires an ohmmeter or a self-powered test lamp like the one shown in **Figure 24**.

1. Unplug the turn signal switch wiring connector located beneath the steering column.

2. Place the switch in the center position and check continuity between the switch terminals.

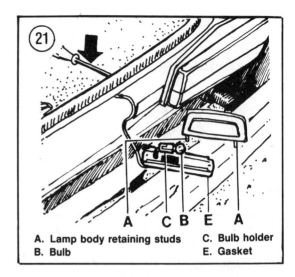

A. Lamp body retaining studs   C. Bulb holder
B. Bulb   E. Gasket

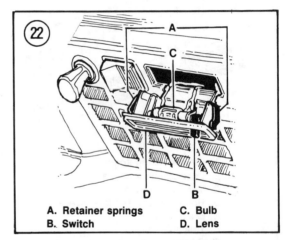

A. Retainer springs   C. Bulb
B. Switch   D. Lens

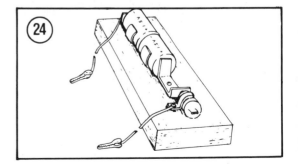

There should be no continuity between any of the terminals. The ohmmeter should indicate infinite resistance or the test lamp should stay out.

3. Move the switch to the right turn position. Connect the ohmmeter or test lamp between terminal a (violet wire) and terminal h (light blue wire). The ohmmeter should indicate little or no resistance or the test lamp should light.

4. With the switch still in the right turn position, connect the ohmmeter or test lamp between terminal a (violet wire) and terminal e (light blue/black wire). The ohmmeter should indicate infinite resistance or the test lamp should stay out.

5. Move the switch to the left turn position. Connect the ohmmeter or test lamp between terminal a (violet wire) and terminal e (light blue/black wire). The ohmmeter should indicate little or no resistance or the test lamp should light.

6. With the switch still in the left turn position, connect the ohmmeter or test lamp between terminal a (violet wire) and terminal h (light blue wire). The ohmmeter should indicate infinite resistance or the test lamp should stay out.

7. If the switch has performed as described so far, it is okay. If not, replace it.

Turn Signal/ Dimmer Switch Replacement

1. Remove the steering wheel as described in Chapter Nine.

2. Remove the steering column shell (**Figure 25**).

3. Remove the switch mounting bolt. Slide the switch off the steering column, unplug its wiring connectors and take it out.

4. Installation is the reverse of removal.

WINDSHIELD WIPERS AND WASHERS

Wiper Motor Removal/Installation

Refer to **Figure 26** for this procedure.

1. Make sure the wipers are in the parked position.

2. Lift the wiper arms and pull them off their pivot shafts.

3. Open the hood. Remove the screws that secure the cowl to the body, then lift the cowl together with the wiper motor and linkage.

4. Label and disconnect the wiper motor wiring connectors (**Figure 26**).

5. Disconnect the windshield washer hose.

6. Remove the cowl from the car, together with the wiper motor and linkage. Place the assembly on a workbench, taking care not to damage the paint.

1. Steering column shell

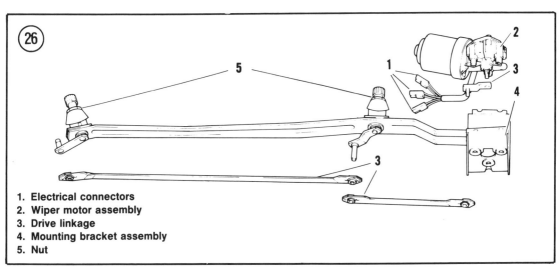

1. Electrical connectors
2. Wiper motor assembly
3. Drive linkage
4. Mounting bracket assembly
5. Nut

7. Remove the nuts (5, **Figure 26**) from the wiper arm pivot shafts.

8. Detach the motor mount bracket from the cowl, then remove the wiper motor and linkage from the cowl.

9. Detach the wiper linkage from the motor, then detach the motor from the bracket.

10. Installation is the reverse of removal.

Washer Motor and Tank
Removal/Installation

The washer motor and tank are located on the right side of the engine compartment. Early models use a soft bag to contain the washer fluid. Later models use a hard plastic tank.

1. Disconnect and plug the washer tank hose.

2. Unplug the washer motor wiring connector.

3. Remove the mounting nut, then take out the tank and motor.

4. Installation is the reverse of removal.

> *CAUTION*
> *Do not use cooling system antifreeze in the washer tank. The runoff may damage the car's paint.*

Wiper Blade Replacement

1. Swing the wiper arm away from the windshield.

2. Loosen the clip and lift the blade carrier off the peg. See **Figure 27**. Take the blade off.

3. Installation is the reverse of removal. Position the wiper arms so they give a full sweep of the windshield without striking the windshield weatherstripping at either end of their travel.

FUSES

The fuse box on all models is under the left side of the instrument panel. See **Figure 28** (through 1978) or **Figure 29** (1979-on). All models also use inline fuses in holders near the fuse box. Fuse specifications are listed in **Table 3**.

Whenever a fuse blows, find out the cause before replacing it. Usually the trouble is a short circuit in the wiring. This may be caused by worn-through insulation or by a wire that works its way loose and touches metal. Carry several spare fuses in the glove compartment.

> *CAUTION*
> *Never substitute metal foil or wire for a fuse. An overload could cause a fire and complete loss of the car.*

IGNITION SYSTEM

The 1971-1978 models use a breaker point ignition system. The 1979 and later cars use a magnetic breakerless ignition system.

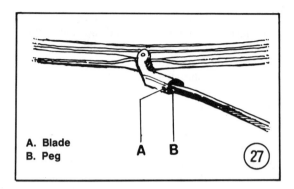

A. Blade
B. Peg
A   B   (27)

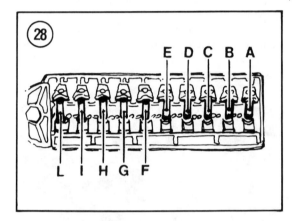

(28)

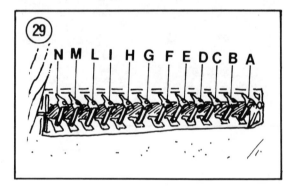

(29)

Breaker point ignition system testing is described in Chapter Two.

Breakerless Ignition System Test

Figure 30 is a schematic of the breakerless ignition system used on 1979 and later models. Refer to it as needed for this procedure.

When working on an electronic ignition system observe the following to prevent system damage:

   a. Do not turn on the ignition unless the ignition coil bracket is properly grounded.

   b. Do not crank the engine with the secondary (thick) wire disconnected from the ignition coil.

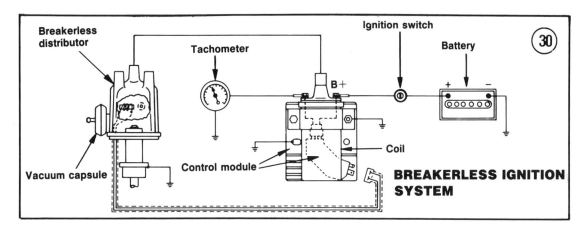

BREAKERLESS IGNITION SYSTEM

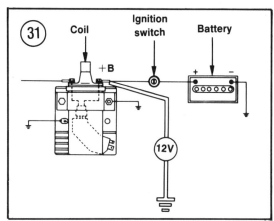

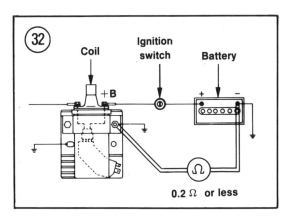

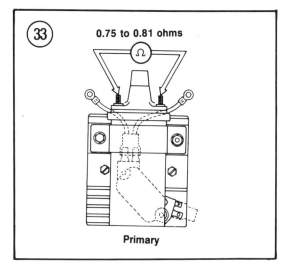

1. Connect a voltmeter between the battery terminals and note the reading for use in Step 2. This is battery voltage.

2. Connect the positive lead of a voltmeter to the ignition coil B+ terminal and the negative lead of the voltmeter to ground (bare metal in the engine compartment). See **Figure 31**. It should indicate battery voltage. If not, check for a weak battery, defective ignition switch or a break or bad connection in the wiring.

3. Connect an ohmmeter between the coil ground stud and battery negative terminal. See **Figure 32**. The ohmmeter should indicate less than 0.2 ohm. If not, make sure the bracket mounting fasteners are clean and tight. Make sure the control module case is clean. Make sure the battery connections are clean and tight.

4. Disconnect the coil wires. Connect an ohmmeter between the primary terminals as shown in **Figure 33**. It should indicate 0.75-0.81 ohms.

c. Do not start or crank the engine with the instrument panel removed.

d. Do not ground either of the coil primary terminals.

e. Do not check wires for current flow by touching the ends to ground or another wire and looking for spark.

f. Do not disconnect either battery cable with the engine running.

5. Move one of the ohmmeter probes to the coil secondary terminal (**Figure 34**). The ohmmeter should indicate 10,000-11,000 ohms.

6. If the ohmmeter reading was not within specifications in Step 4 or Step 5, replace the ignition coil.

7. Unplug the pickup coil connector from the control module. See **Figure 35**. Connect an ohmmeter between the connector terminals and note the reading. It should be 700-800 ohms.

8. Move one of the ohmmeter probes from the connector to the distributor body (**Figure 35**). It should indicate infinite resistance.

9. If the ohmmeter reading was not within specifications during Step 7 or Step 8, replace the pickup coil assembly. See **Figure 36**.

10. Measure the gap between rotor and pickup coil with a flat, non-magnetic feeler gauge and adjust as needed. See **Figure 35**. Specified gap is 0.5-0.6 mm (0.020-0.024 in.).

11. Reconnect all wires disconnected during this procedure.

CAUTION
During the next step, do not disconnect the thick wire from the ignition coil.

12. Disconnect the distributor end of the thick wire running from ignition coil to distributor. See **Figure 37**.

WARNING
During the next step, hold the wire with a heavily insulated tool. Touching the wire with bare hands can cause a painful shock, even if the insulation is in perfect condition.

13. Hold the end of the wire about 5 mm (1/4 in.) from ground (bare metal). See **Figure 37**. Crank the engine and check for spark from the end of the wire. If no spark can be seen, replace the control module. The control module is located between the ignition coil and the car body. See **Figure 38**.

14. If a spark occurs in Step 13 but one or more plugs do not fire while the engine is running, the problem is in the distributor cap, rotor or spark plug wires. Inspect as described in Chapter Three.

Ignition Coil Removal/Installation

To remove the coil, disconnect its wires and detach the mounting bracket from the body. Installation is the reverse of removal.

Distributor Removal

On early models, the distributor is mounted on the left front corner of the engine and driven by the auxiliary shaft. See **Figure 39**. On later engines,

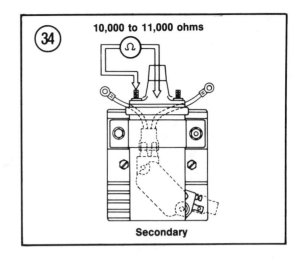

10,000 to 11,000 ohms

Secondary

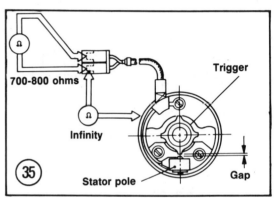

700-800 ohms

Infinity

Trigger

Stator pole

Gap

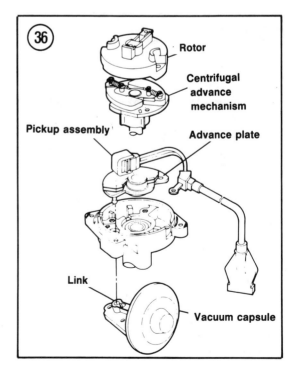

Rotor

Centrifugal advance mechanism

Pickup assembly

Advance plate

Link

Vacuum capsule

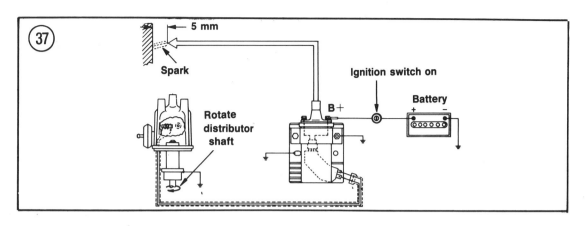

1. Cap
2. Body
3. Nut
4. Washer
5. Clamp
6. Gasket
7. Ignition coil
8. Control module

1979

1980-ON

7

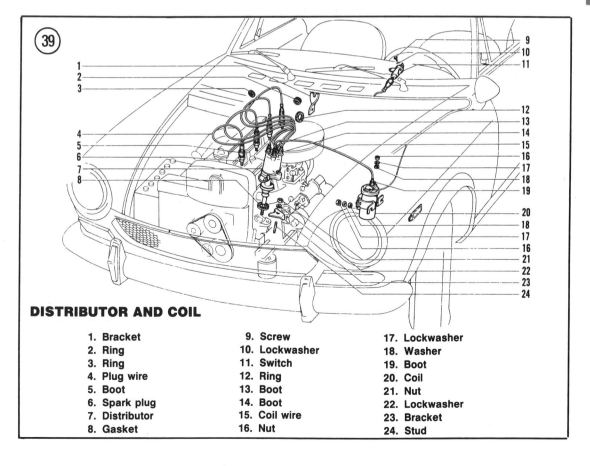

DISTRIBUTOR AND COIL

1. Bracket	9. Screw	17. Lockwasher
2. Ring	10. Lockwasher	18. Washer
3. Ring	11. Switch	19. Boot
4. Plug wire	12. Ring	20. Coil
5. Boot	13. Boot	21. Nut
6. Spark plug	14. Boot	22. Lockwasher
7. Distributor	15. Coil wire	23. Bracket
8. Gasket	16. Nut	24. Stud

the distributor is mounted on the right rear corner of the engine and driven by the exhaust camshaft. See **Figure 40** (breaker point ignition) or **Figure 38** (electronic ignition). Removal and installation procedures are the same for all models.

1. Turn the engine until No. 4 piston is at top dead center on its compression stroke. When this occurs, the 0 degree mark on the front of the engine will align with the notch in the crankshaft pulley. See **Figure 41** (1971-1978) or **Figure 42** (1979-on). In addition, the distributor rotor will point to No. 4 terminal in the distributor cap. Terminal numbers are molded into the cap.

> *NOTE*
> *Be sure to remove the distributor cap and check rotor position as well as the timing marks. The timing marks also line up when No. 1 cylinder is at top dead center on its compression stroke.*

2. Make alignment marks on the distributor and engine, as well as on the distributor and rotor. The marks will ease installation.

> *NOTE*
> *On 1979 and later models (electronic ignition), the rotor has an arrow which points to a notch in the distributor body when the distributor is in the proper position for removal. See **Figure 43**.*

3. Disconnect the distributor wires and vacuum line. Remove the distributor locknut and take the distributor out.

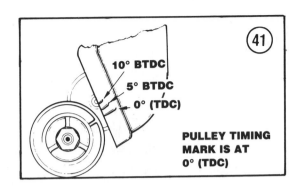

PULLEY TIMING MARK IS AT 0° (TDC)

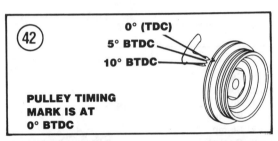

PULLEY TIMING MARK IS AT 0° BTDC

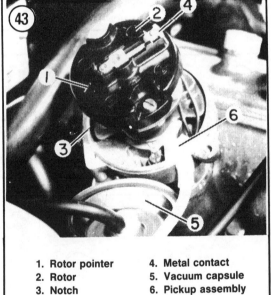

1. Rotor pointer
2. Rotor
3. Notch
4. Metal contact
5. Vacuum capsule
6. Pickup assembly

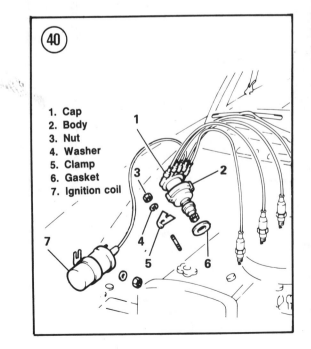

1. Cap
2. Body
3. Nut
4. Washer
5. Clamp
6. Gasket
7. Ignition coil

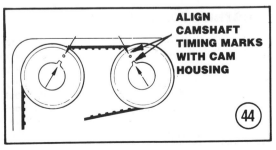

ALIGN CAMSHAFT TIMING MARKS WITH CAM HOUSING

Distributor Installation

1. If the engine was turned with the distributor removed, turn it so No. 4 piston is at top dead center on its compression stroke. The 0 degree mark on the front of the engine must be aligned with the notch in the crankshaft pulley (**Figure 41** or **Figure 42**). The slot in the end of the camshaft or distributor drive shaft must be positioned so the distributor rotor will point to No. 4 terminal when the distributor is installed. The camshaft timing marks must be aligned with the camshaft housing marks as shown in **Figure 44**.

NOTE
On early models, the marks are visible from the rear side of the camshaft pulleys. See ***Figure 45*** *and* ***Figure 46***.

2. Install the distributor in the engine. Line up the alignment marks on the distributor body and engine as well as on the distributor body and rotor. Install the locknut.

3. Connect the spark plug wires. Spark plugs are numbered 1 through 4, counting from the front of the engine. Distributor cap terminal numbers are molded into the cap.

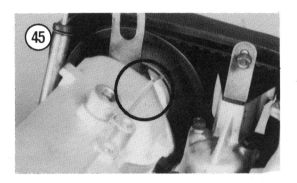

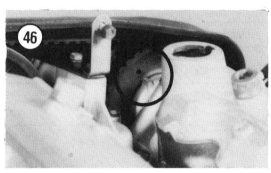

7

Table 1 STATE OF BATTERY CHARGE

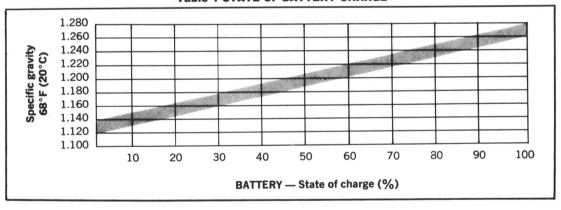

Table 2 BULB SPECIFICATIONS

Application	Number
1971-1978	
Headlights	7031
Turn signals	1073
Brake lights	1073
Backup lights	1073
License plate lights	67
Taillights	67
Parking lights	67
Courtesy light	1/08630/90*
Trunk light	1/08630/90*
Instrument panel lights	158
	(continued)

Table 2 BULB SPECIFICATIONS (continued)

Application	Number
1979-on	
Headlights	4002
Front parking/turn signal lights	1034
Brake lights	1063
Backup lights	1063
Rear turn signals	1063
License plate lights	67
Taillights	67
Side marker lights	158
Interior light	1/08630/90*
Instrument cluster lights	158
Hazard warning switch light	1/41437/90*
Cigarette lighter illumination	1/41423/90*

* Fiat part number.

Table 3 FUSE SPECIFICATIONS

Fuse	Amps	Protected circuits
		1971-1972
A	16	Cooling fan motor
		Clock (Coupe)
		Interior light
		Electropneumatic horns
		Cigarette lighter
		Inspection lamp receptacle
		Hazard flashers
B	8	Windshield wipers
		Heater fan
		Windshield washer pump
C	8	Left high beam
		High beam indicator
D	8	Right high beam
E	8	Left low beam
F	8	Right low beam
G	8	Left front parking lamp
		Parking lamps indicator
		Right rear parking lamp
		Left front and right rear side marker lamps
		Left license plate light
		Cigarette lighter housing indicator
		Engine compartment light
		Luggage compartment light
		Instrument cluster lights
H	8	Right front and left rear parking lights
		Right front and left rear side marker lights
		Right license plate light
I	8	Engine cooling fan relay
		Turn signals and indicator on dash
		Brake lights
		Oil pressure gauge and warning light
		Temperature gauge
		Fuel gauge
		Tachometer
		Brake warning light
		(continued)

Table 3 FUSE SPECIFICATIONS (continued)

Fuse	Amps	Protected circuits
		1971-1972 (continued)
L	8	Backup lights Emission control electrovalve Drop tray light (Coupe) Voltage regulator Alternator field winding
Inline fuse	3	Key warning indicator
		1973
A	16	Inspection lamp Horns Engine cooling fan motor Courtesy light(s) Hazard flasher (not including switch illumination for cars with 1592 cc engine or for Coupe with 1608 cc engine)*
B	8	Heater fan Windshield wiper Windshield washer
C	8	Left high beam High beam indicator
D	8	Right high beam
E	8	Left low beam (Coupe) Right low beam (Spider)
F	8	Right low beam (Coupe) Left low beam (Spider)
G	8	Right front parking light (cars with 1608 cc engine)* Left front parking light (all models) Left taillight (cars with 1592 cc engine)* Parking and taillights indicator Left license plate light Cigarette lighter illumination Instrument cluster illumination Trunk light (Spider) Hazard warning switch illumination (cars with 1592 cc engine and Coupe with 1608 cc engine)* Hazard flashers (Coupe with 1608 cc engine)* Left front and right rear side marker lights
H	8	Right front parking light Left taillight Right front and left rear side marker lights Right license plate light
I	8	Tachometer Brake warning light Oil pressure gauge and warning light Temperature gauge Fuel gauge Turn signals and turn signal indicator Brake lights Backup lights Seat belt indicator and buzzer relay Electrovalve for emission control system
L	8	Voltage regulator Alternator field winding
Inline fuses	3 3 16 16	Key and seatbelt buzzer Fuel pump and relay (Coupe with 1592 cc engine only)* Cigarette lighter Rear window defogger (Coupe only)

7

Table 3 FUSE SPECIFICATIONS (continued)

Fuse	Amps	Protected circuits
		1974
A	25	Horns
		Engine cooling fan
B	8	Windshield wipers
		Heater fan
		Windshield washer pump
C	8	Left high beam
		High beam indicator
D	8	Right high beam
E	8	Left low beam
F	8	Right low beam
G	8	Left front parking lamp
		Parking and taillights indicator
		Right rear taillight
		Left front and right rear side marker lamps
		Left license plate light
		Cigarette lighter housing indicator
		Trunk light (Spider)
		Instrument cluster lights
		Instrument panel symbols illumination
		Hazard flashers
H	8	Right front parking lamp
		Left taillight
		Right front and left rear side marker lamps
		Right license plate light
I	8	Turn signals and turn signal indicator
		Brake lights
		Oil pressure gauge and warning light
		Temperature gauge
		Fuel gauge
		Tachometer
		Brake warning light
		Backup lights
		Electrovalve for emission control system
		Seatbelt indicator and buzzer relay
L	8	Seat belt interlock control unit
		Voltage regulator
		Alternator field winding
Inline fuses	3	Key and seatbelt buzzer, starter interlock control unit
	16	Cigarette lighter, clock, courtesy light,
		hazard flasher indicator, inspection lamp
	8	Fuel pump and relay
		1975-1976
A	25	Horns
		Engine cooling fan
B	8	Windshield wipers
		Heater fan
		Windshield washer pump
C	8	Left high beam
		High beam indicator
D	8	Right high beam
E	8	Right low beam
F	8	Left low beam
G	8	Left front parking lamp
		Parking and taillights indicator
		Right taillight
		Left front and right rear side marker lamps
		Left license plate light (continued)

Table 3 FUSE SPECIFICATIONS (continued)

Fuse	Amps	Protected circuits
		1975-1976 (continued)
		Cigarette lighter housing indicator
		Trunk light (Spider)
		Instrument cluster lights
		Instrument panel symbols illumination
		Hazard flasher switch illumination
H	8	Right front parking lamp
		Left taillight
		Right front and left rear side marker lamps
		Right license plate light
I	8	Turn signals and turn signal indicator
		Brake lights
		Oil pressure gauge and warning light
		Temperature gauge
		Fuel gauge
		Tachometer
		Brake warning light
		Backup lights
		Fast idle electrovalve
		Seatbelt indicator and buzzer relay
		Seat belt interlock control unit (1975 only)
		Idle stop solenoid
		Electrovalve for diverter valve
		EGR indicator relay winding
		EGR 25,000-mile warning system
		EGR indicator
L	8	Voltage regulator
		Alternator field winding
Inline fuses	3	Key and seatbelt buzzer, starter interlock control unit (1975 only)
	3	EGR indicator reset device
	16	Cigarette lighter, clock, courtesy light, hazard flashers and indicator, inspection lamp
	8	Fuel pump and relay
		1977-1978
A	8	Turn signals and turn signal indicator
		Brake lights
		Oil pressure gauge and warning light
		Temperature gauge
		Fuel gauge
		Tachometer
		Brake warning light
		Backup lights
		Fast idle electrovalve
		Seat belt indicator and buzzer relay
		Delay circuit for seat belt indicator
		EGR cutout electrovalve
B	8	Windshield wipers
		Heater fan
		Windshield washer pump
C	8	Left high beam
		High beam indicator
D	8	Right high beam
E	8	Right low beam
		(continued)

7

Table 3 FUSE SPECIFICATIONS (continued)

Fuse	Amps	Protected circuits
		1977-1978 (continued)
F		Left low beam
G	8	Left front parking light
		Parking and taillights indicator
		Right taillight
		Left front and right rear side marker lamps
		Left license plate light
		Cigarette lighter illumination
		Trunk light
		Instrument cluster lights
		Instrument panel symbols illumination
		Hazard flasher switch illumination
H		Right front parking lamp
		Left taillight
		Right front and left rear side marker lamps
		Right license plate light
	16	Horns
		Cooling fan motor
L	25	Cigarette lighter
		Clock
		Courtesy light
		Hazard flashers and indicator
		Inspection lamp
		Key and seatbelt buzzer
		Power antenna motor
		1979-1982
A	8	Turn signals and indicators
		Brake lights
		Oil pressure gauge and warning light
		Temperature gauge
		Fuel gauge
		Tachometer
		Brake warning light
		Backup lights
		Fast idle electrovalve (carburetted models only)
		Seat belt indicator and buzzer relay
		Delay circuit for seat belt indicator and buzzer relay
		Gear indicator light (automatic transmission)
		30,000-mile indicator for oxygen sensor service (fuel injected models only)
B	8	Windshield wiper motor
		Windshield washer pump
		Windshield wiper sweep rate rheostat
		Heater fan motor
C	8	Left high beam
		High beam indicator
D	8	Right high beam
E	8	Left low beam
F	8	Right low beam
G	8	Right front parking light
		Left taillight
		Right front and left rear side marker lights
		Right license plate light
		(continued)

Table 3 FUSE SPECIFICATIONS (continued)

Fuse	Amps	Protected circuits
		1979-1982 (continued)
H	8	Left front parking light
		Parking and taillight indicator
		Right taillight
		Left front and right rear side marker lights
		Left license plate light
		Cigarette lighter illumination
		Trunk light
		Instrument cluster illumination
		Instrument panel symbols illumination
		Hazard flasher switch illumination
I	8	Quartz clock
		Courtesy light
		Hazard flashers and indicator
		Inspection lamp
		Key and seatbelt buzzer
L	16	Horns
		Engine cooling fan
M	16	Left power window motor (if so equipped)
N	16	Right power window motor (if so equipped)
Inline fuses	8	Cigarette lighter
	16	Fuel pump (fuel injection)
		Supplementary air valve (fuel injection)
		1984
A	16	Power windows
B	8	Trunk opener solenoid
		Cigarette lighter
C	8	Left high beam
		High beam indicator
D	8	Right high beam
E	8	Left low beam
F	8	Right high beam
G	8	Right front and left rear side marker lights
		Left taillight
		Right front parking light
H		Left front and right rear side marker lights
		Right taillight
		Right license plate light
		Trunk light
		Left front parking light
		Instrument cluster lights
		Lights-on indicator
		Digital clock dimmer circuit
		Cigarette lighter
I	8	Digital clock memory circuit
		Courtesy light
		Accessory socket
		Hazard flashers
		Seatbelt chime
L	16	Horns
		Cooling fan motor
	8	Brake lights
		Switch illumination
		Fuel gauge
		(continued)

7

Table 3 FUSE SPECIFICATIONS (continued)

Fuse	Amps	Protected circuits
		1984 (continued)
N	8	Brake warning light Oil pressure gauge and warning light Tachometer Temperature gauge Turn signals Trunk opener switch Exhaust gas sensor indicator Seatbelt indicator Seatbelt timer Seatbelt relay coil Backup lights Power antenna motor Windshield wipers/washers Oxygen sensor switch Heater fan Digital clock display circuit

* 1592 cc engines are designated by the prefix "132AC" on the cylinder block. 1608 cc engines are designated by the prefix "125BC."

CHAPTER EIGHT

CLUTCH AND TRANSMISSION

This chapter provides all clutch and transmission service procedures practical for home mechanics. Specifications and tightening torques are listed in **Table 1** and **Table 2** at the end of the chapter.

CLUTCH

All models use a single dry plate clutch with diaphragm spring. Clutch engagement and

① A=4.72" (120 mm)
approx. Maximum
release travel
B=.984" (25 mm)
approx. Free
travel (play
take-up)

1. Pedal
2. Cable
3. Adjusting nut
4. Release lever
5. Release bearing
6. Release lever pilot
7. Grommet

disengagement are controlled by the release mechanism, which in turn is controlled by pedal pressure transmitted through a cable.

Major clutch components are the disc, pressure plate, release mechanism and cable.

The release mechanism, which controls engagement and disengagement of the clutch, consists of a bearing, sleeve and release fork.

Part Identification

Many clutch parts have 2 or more names. To prevent confusion, the following list gives part names used in this chapter and common synonyms.

   a. Release lever—throw-out arm, withdrawal lever.
   b. Release bearing—throw-out bearing.
   c. Pressure plate—pressure plate assembly, clutch cover assembly.

Disc—driven plate.

Pedal Adjustment

This procedure applies to 1971-1978 models only. Pedal adjustment on 1979 and later cars is automatic.

1. Press the pedal by hand until resistance increases suddenly. Measure the distance the pedal travels. This is pedal free play. It should be approximately 25 mm (1 in.).

2. If free play is incorrect, make sure the cable grommet (on the right side of the transmission, accessible from beneath the car) is not damaged. See **Figure 1**. Replace if necessary.

3. To adjust free play, loosen the cable locknut. See **Figure 2**. Turn the adjusting nut to change free play, then tighten the locknut.

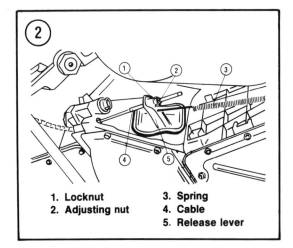

1. Locknut
2. Adjusting nut
3. Spring
4. Cable
5. Release lever

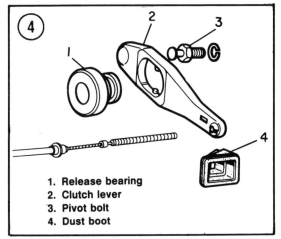

1. Release bearing
2. Clutch lever
3. Pivot bolt
4. Dust boot

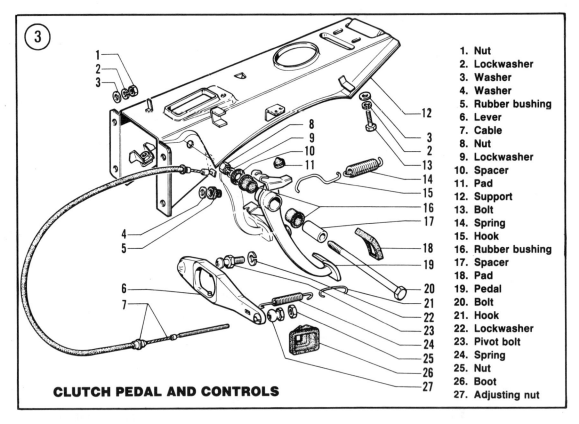

1. Nut
2. Lockwasher
3. Washer
4. Washer
5. Rubber bushing
6. Lever
7. Cable
8. Nut
9. Lockwasher
10. Spacer
11. Pad
12. Support
13. Bolt
14. Spring
15. Hook
16. Rubber bushing
17. Spacer
18. Pad
19. Pedal
20. Bolt
21. Hook
22. Lockwasher
23. Pivot bolt
24. Spring
25. Nut
26. Boot
27. Adjusting nut

CLUTCH PEDAL AND CONTROLS

NOTE
If free play cannot be set to the correct specifications, the clutch disc is probably worn. Replace it as described in this chapter.

4. Road test the car. If the clutch chatters or slips during engagement, recheck pedal free play. If it is correct, inspect the clutch disc and pressure plate as described in this chapter.

Cable Replacement

Refer to **Figure 3** for this procedure.

1. Remove the locknut and adjusting nut from the end of the cable. See **Figure 2**.

2. Slip the cable out of the release lever (**Figure 4**) and through the boss on the transmission (**Figure 5**).

3. Unhook the cable from the top of the clutch pedal (**Figure 3**).

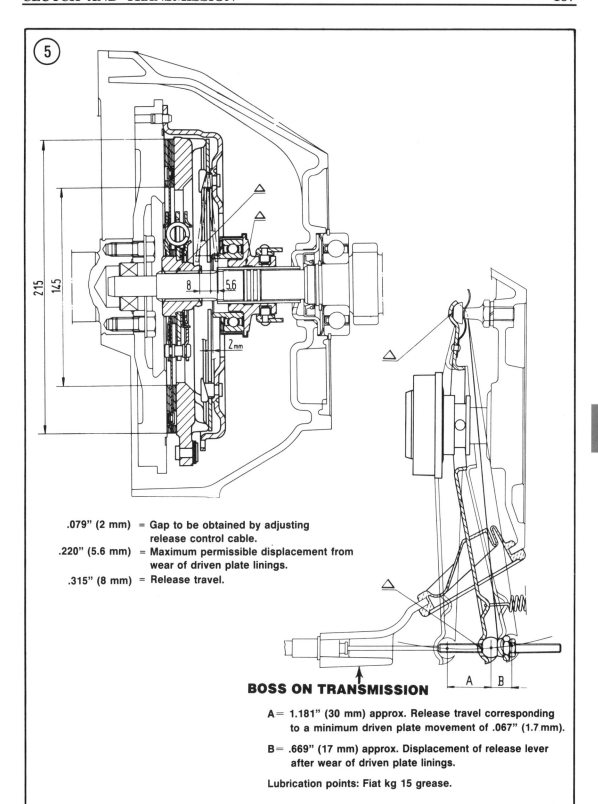

.079" (2 mm) = Gap to be obtained by adjusting release control cable.

.220" (5.6 mm) = Maximum permissible displacement from wear of driven plate linings.

.315" (8 mm) = Release travel.

BOSS ON TRANSMISSION

A = 1.181" (30 mm) approx. Release travel corresponding to a minimum driven plate movement of .067" (1.7 mm).

B = .669" (17 mm) approx. Displacement of release lever after wear of driven plate linings.

Lubrication points: Fiat kg 15 grease.

4. Pull the cable grommet out of the firewall into the engine compartment. Pull the cable into the engine compartment and take it out.

5. Installation is the reverse of removal. On 1971-1978 models, adjust the pedal as described in this chapter.

Clutch Removal

The engine and transmission must be separated to remove the clutch. This can be done either by removing the engine as described in Chapter Four or by removing the transmission as described in this chapter. If no engine work is planned it is easier to remove the transmission.

Once the engine and transmission have been separated, do the following.

1. Mark the edges of the pressure plate and flywheel so they may be reassembled in the same relative position. See **Figure 6**.

2. Support the clutch disc with an aligning bar (pilot shaft) as shown in **Figure 7**. Inexpensive aligning bars are available at parts stores. An input shaft from a junk transmission can be used if the factory tool isn't available. Some tool rental dealers and parts stores rent universal aligning bars which can be adapted.

3. Remove the clutch cover bolts (**Figure 8**) one turn at a time in a diagonal pattern to prevent warping the pressure plate. Take the pressure plate and disc off the flywheel. See **Figure 9**.

4. Once the clutch has been removed, inspect the pilot bearing inside the rear end of the crankshaft. See **Figure 10**. If the bearing is worn or damaged, replace it as described in Chapter Four.

Clutch Disc Inspection

Check the clutch disc (**Figure 11**) for the following:

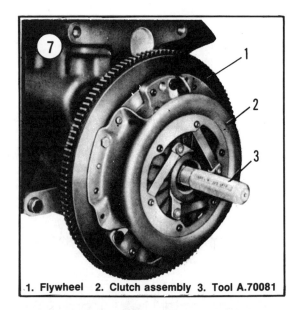

1. Flywheel   2. Clutch assembly   3. Tool A.70081

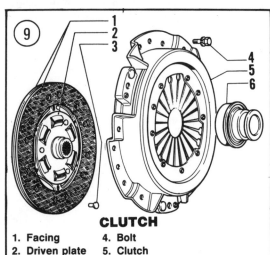

CLUTCH

1. Facing	4. Bolt
2. Driven plate	5. Clutch
3. Rivet	6. Sleeve (release bearing)

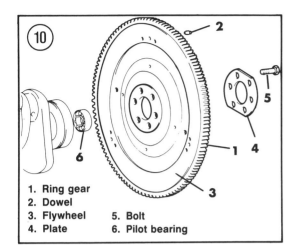

1. Ring gear
2. Dowel
3. Flywheel
4. Plate
5. Bolt
6. Pilot bearing

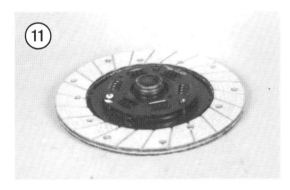

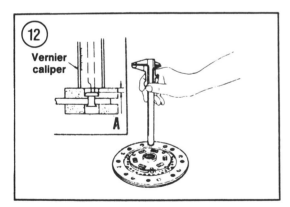

Vernier caliper

A

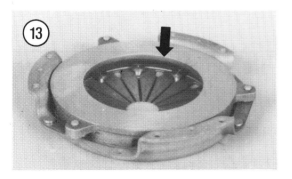

a. Oil or grease on the facings.
b. Glazed facings.
c. Warped facings.
d. Loose or missing rivets.
e. Facings worn to within 0.3 mm (0.012 in.) of any rivet. Measure with a vernier caliper as shown in **Figure 12** or have the measurement done by a machine shop.
f. Broken springs.
g. Loose fit or rough movement on the transmission input shaft splines.

Light surface stains may be sanded off and the facings dressed with a wire brush. However, if the facings are soaked with oil or grease, the clutch disc must be replaced. The disc must also be replaced if any of the other defects are present or if the facings are partially worn and a new pressure plate is being installed.

NOTE
Since the disc, pressure plate and throwout bearing cause each other to wear, the usual practice is to replace all 3 parts at the same time.

Pressure Plate Inspection

1. Check the pressure plate (**Figure 13**) for:
   a. Scoring.
   b. Burn marks.
   c. Cracks.
Replace the pressure plate if these are found.

2. Check the diaphragm spring checked for wear or damage at the release bearing contact surface. **Figure 14** shows new (1) and worn (2) contact surfaces. Check for bent or broken spring fingers or damaged retracting springs. Replace the pressure plate if these are found.

If the clutch trouble still is not apparent, take the pressure plate and disc to a competent shop. Have the disc and pressure plate checked for runout and the diaphragm spring for correct finger height. Do not attempt to dismantle the pressure plate or readjust the fingers yourself wthout the proper tools and experience.

8

Clutch Installation

1. Be sure your hands are clean.
2. Make sure the disc facings, pressure plate and flywheel are free of oil, grease and other foreign material.
3. Place the clutch disc and pressure plate in position on the flywheel. The protruding side of the disc hub (**Figure 15**) faces rearward.
4. If the old pressure plate is being reinstalled, be sure the alignment marks on clutch cover and flywheel are lined up.
5. Center the disc and pressure plate with an aligning bar (pilot shaft) such as the one shown in **Figure 16**. Inexpensive aligning bars can be purchased from some imported car parts stores. An input shaft from a junk transmission can be used if the factory tool isn't available. Some tool rental dealers and parts stores rent universal aligning bars which can be adapted.
6. Install the clutch cover bolts (**Figure 17**). Tighten gradually in a diagonal pattern to specifications (**Table 2**).
7. Apply a *light* coat of molybdenum disulfide grease to the splines on clutch hub and transmission input shaft. See **Figure 18**.

Release Mechanism Removal

As with the clutch, release mechanism removal requires that the engine and transmission be separated. The release mechanism is mounted in the clutch housing. Either remove the engine (Chapter Four) or remove the transmission as described in this chapter. If no engine work is planned, it will be easier to remove just the transmission.

1. Detach the release bearing (**Figure 19**) from the release fork and take it out.
2. Remove the release fork spring (**Figure 20**). Unsnap the release fork from its pivot and take it out of the clutch housing.

Release Mechanism Inspection

Check the release mechanism for the following:
a. *Wear at the contact point of release bearing and fork*—Replace the bearing or fork if worn. See **Figure 21**.
b. *Grease leaking from the release bearing*—Replace the bearing if this is evident. See **Figure 22**.

> *CAUTION*
> *Do not clean the release bearing in solvent, since it is prelubricated at the factory. Wipe the bearing clean with a lint-free cloth.*

c. *A worn release bearing*—To check, hold the bearing inner race with fingers and rotate the outer race while applying light pressure to it. See **Figure 23**. If the bearing feels rough or makes noise, replace it.

d. *Wear at the contact point of release lever and pivot pin*—If the release lever pivot is worn, replace it. If the pivot pin is worn, unscrew it and screw in a new one. See **Figure 24**.

Release Mechanism Installation

1. Apply a *light* coat of multipurpose grease to the following points:

a. Contact points of release fork and release bearing sleeve.

b. Inside of release bearing sleeve.

c. Release fork pivot.

2. Position the release fork in the clutch housing. Snap the fork onto the pivot, then install the spring. See **Figure 25**.

3. Install the release bearing on the fork. See **Figure 26**.

MANUAL TRANSMISSION

A 5-speed manual transmission is standard equipment on all models covered by this book.

Manual transmission overhaul is not the best starting point for a beginning mechanic. However, it doesn't require special training or much special equipment. Overhaul does require patience and the ability to concentrate. The work area must be clean, free of distractions and inaccessible to pets and small children.

Before starting, read this entire section. Obtain the necessary special tools or substitutes. Check parts availability with local suppliers.

NOTE
If a transmission is so worn or damaged that most internal parts must be replaced, the price of parts should be compared to the price of a new or professionally rebuilt transmission.

8

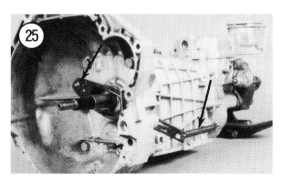

Removal/Installation

1. Disconnect the negative cable from the battery.
2. Unscrew the gearshift knob. Unsnap the rear part of the console cover (**Figure 27**) and lift it as shown in **Figure 28**.
3. Remove the transmission tunnel cover and insulating material.

> *NOTE*
> *It may be necessary to detach the console, then pull it back slightly. In this case, loosen the handbrake adjusting nuts and raise the handbrake lever to the point shown in **Figure 29**.*

4. Securely block both front wheels so the car will not roll in either direction. Jack up the rear end of the car and place it on jackstands.

> *NOTE*
> *Steps 5-7 apply to 1971-1972 models only.*

5. Press down on the upper part of the shift lever. See **Figure 30**. Pry the lever jacket snap ring (24, **Figure 30**) out of its groove, then take off the upper part of the shift lever.
6. Working beneath the car, remove 3 nuts and lockwashers and take the lower ball socket off the bottom of the shift tower.
7. Remove the upper ball socket, spring, spring retaining cover and bottom shift lever half from the shift tower.

> *NOTE*
> *Steps 8-11 apply to 1973 and later models.*

8. Working beneath the car, remove 3 bolts and take the bottom cover off the shift tower. See **Figure 31**.
9. Working beneath the car, remove the shift lever bottom nut (**Figure 32**).
10. Remove the shift lever base socket and spring. See **Figure 32**.
11. Working inside the car, lift out the shift lever.

> *NOTE*
> *The following steps apply to all models.*

12. Remove the clutch cable locknut and adjusting nut (**Figure 33**). Detach the clutch cable from the release lever.
13. Remove the lower cover from the clutch housing. See **Figure 34**.
14. Unbolt the exhaust pipe bracket from the transmission. See **Figure 35**.

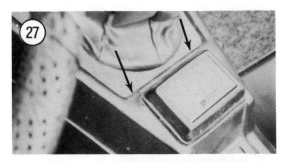

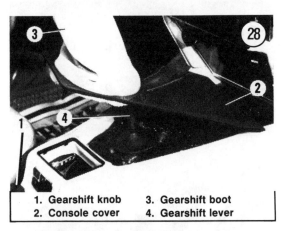

1. Gearshift knob   3. Gearshift boot
2. Console cover   4. Gearshift lever

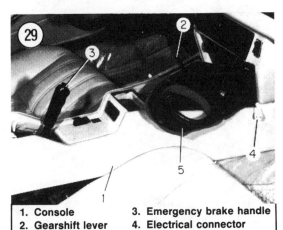

1. Console   3. Emergency brake handle
2. Gearshift lever   4. Electrical connector
   (lower half)   5. Transmission top cover

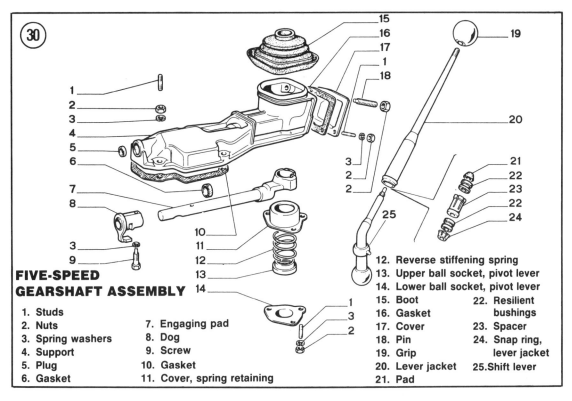

**FIVE-SPEED
GEARSHAFT ASSEMBLY**

1. Studs
2. Nuts
3. Spring washers
4. Support
5. Plug
6. Gasket
7. Engaging pad
8. Dog
9. Screw
10. Gasket
11. Cover, spring retaining

12. Reverse stiffening spring
13. Upper ball socket, pivot lever
14. Lower ball socket, pivot lever
15. Boot
16. Gasket
17. Cover
18. Pin
19. Grip
20. Lever jacket
21. Pad
22. Resilient bushings
23. Spacer
24. Snap ring, lever jacket
25. Shift lever

8

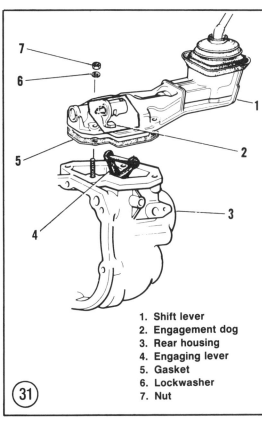

1. Shift lever
2. Engagement dog
3. Rear housing
4. Engaging lever
5. Gasket
6. Lockwasher
7. Nut

1. Shift lever   6. Washer
2. Spring   7. Nut
3. Cover   8. Cover
4. Socket   9. Bolts and lockwashers
5. Bearing   (or studs, nuts and lockwashers)

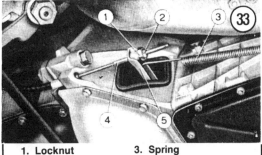

1. Locknut   3. Spring
2. Adjusting nut   4. Cable
                    5. Release lever

1. Clutch cable
2. Clutch lever
3. Clutch return spring
4. Speedometer cable connector
5. Drain plug
6. Bolt
7. Bracket
8. Bolt
9. Lower cover
10. Engine ground cable

15. Remove the starter mounting bolts (**Figure 36**). Pull the starter clear of the flywheel and lay it out of the way. The wires can be left connected.

16. Place jacks beneath the engine and transmission. Use blocks of wood on top of the jacks so the engine and transmission oil pans won't be dented.

NOTE
Transmission jacks, available from rental dealers, will make the job easier. They include cradles to keep the transmission from falling. They can also be adjusted for side-to-side and fore-and-aft tilt, which allows the transmission to be accurately aligned with the engine.

17. Working beneath the car, remove the transmission mounting member (**Figure 37**).

18. Remove the transmission-to-engine bolts. See **Figure 38** and **Figure 39**.

19. Slowly lower the jacks beneath engine and transmission. Remove the transmission downward and to the rear.

CAUTION
Do not remove the transmission partway. If its weight is allowed to hang

on the input shaft, the bearing may be damaged.

20. Installation is the reverse of removal. Tighten all fasteners to specifications (end of chapter). Fill the transmission with an oil recommended in Chapter Three.

Disassembly

1. Remove the clutch release mechanism as described in this chapter.

2. Remove the clutch housing bolts (**Figure 40**). Take off the clutch housing and gasket.

3. Remove the shim from the clutch housing. See **Figure 41**.

4. Remove one bolt securing the electrical switch wire clip to the transmission, then remove the wires from the clip. See **Figure 42**.

CAUTION
During the next step, do not place a wrench on the rear portion of the rear switch. It is sheet metal and will be damaged. Place the wrench on the hexagonal part of the switch nearest the transmission.

1. Nuts
2. Transmission mounting bracket
3. Nuts

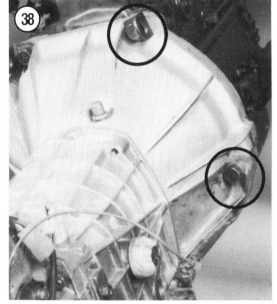

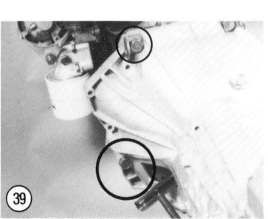

8

5. Unscrew the top and rear electrical switches from the transmission. See **Figure 42**.

6. Unscrew the side switch by tapping gently with a hammer and screwdriver. See **Figure 43**.

7. Remove 3 yoke securing nuts (**Figure 44**). To loosen the nuts, secure the bolts with a wrench as shown in **Figure 45**, then undo the nuts with a socket and breaker bar.

8. Pull the flexible joint off the main shaft.

9. Remove the snap ring (**Figure 46**).

10. Remove the spacer from the main shaft. The spacer can be removed partway with a power steering pump puller (**Figure 47**), then pulled the rest of the way off with an ordinary gear puller (**Figure 48**). Both tools are available from rental dealers. You can also take the transmission to a machine shop and have the spacer pressed off.

> *NOTE*
> *To keep the main shaft from turning while using the pullers, slide one of the drive shaft yoke bolts forward so it will push against the extension housing. See* **Figure 49**.

11. Remove the grease seal and spring (**Figure 50**).

12. Bend back the main shaft nut's lockwasher (**Figure 51**).

13. Remove the main shaft nut with a 32 mm socket and breaker bar.

> *NOTE*
> *To keep the main shaft from turning, drill a piece of angle iron or similar metal to fit over 2 of the yoke bolts. See* **Figure 52**.

14. Pry the lockwasher (**Figure 53**) loose from the yoke, then take it off the main shaft.

15. Remove the drive shaft yoke with a puller (**Figure 54**). These are available from rental dealers.

16. Remove the transmission mounting bracket (**Figure 55**).

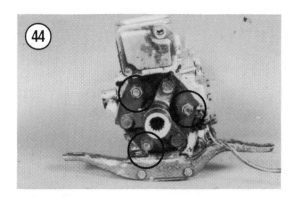

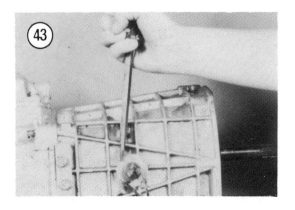

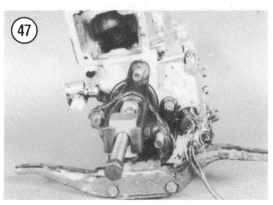

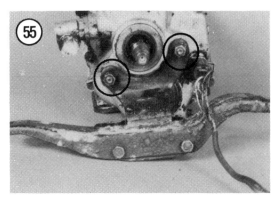

8

17. Remove the speedometer driven gear and gasket. See **Figure 56**.

18. If you haven't already done so, remove the rear cover from the shift tower. See **Figure 57**. Inspect the reverse lockout pin and remove it if worn or damaged. Otherwise, leave the pin in position.

19. Remove the shift tower mounting bolts (**Figure 58**). Slide the engaging rod inside the shift tower (**Figure 59**) forward, then take the tower off the transmission.

20. Remove the bottom cover from the transmission. See **Figure 60**.

21. Remove the rear housing nuts and bolts, then take the rear housing off the transmission case. See **Figure 61** and **Figure 62**.

22. Remove the bolt and lockwasher securing the fifth-reverse fork shaft. See **Figure 63**.

23. Pull the shaft partway out (**Figure 64**) then tap it the rest of the way out with a wooden hammer handle. See **Figure 65**.

NOTE
*Thread the bolt back into the shaft (**Figure 66**) so it won't be lost.*

24. Slide fifth-reverse fork forward to engage reverse idler gear (arrow, **Figure 67**).

25. Push one of the fork shafts forward to engage a forward gear. See **Figure 68**. This locks the main shaft.

26. Raise the punched portions of the countershaft nut out of the countershaft grooves with a hammer and punch. See **Figure 69**.

27. Loosen the countershaft nut. Use a 27 mm socket or 1 1/16 in. socket and breaker bar. Hold the transmission from turning with a piece of drilled angle iron or similar metal as shown in **Figure 70**. Leave the nut on the countershaft for the time being.

28. Remove the detent cover and gasket (**Figure 71**).

1. Cover
2. Reverse lockout screw and nut

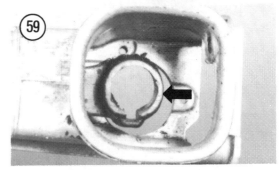

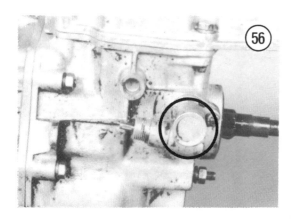

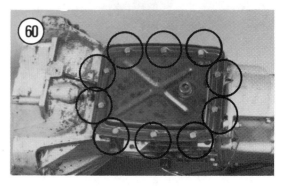

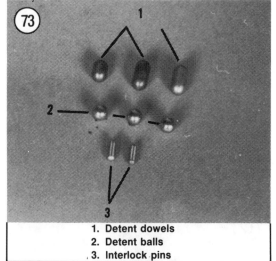

1. Detent dowels
2. Detent balls
3. Interlock pins

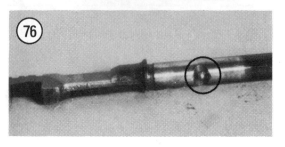

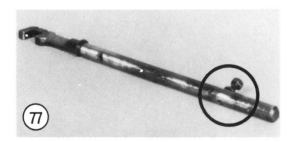

29. Remove the detent springs (**Figure 72**), then dump out the detent balls. Remove the short detent dowel.

NOTE
*There are 3 detent balls, 2 long detent dowels, one short detent dowel and 2 interlock pins. See **Figure 73**.*

30. Unbolt the third-fourth shift fork from the shaft. See **Figure 74**.
31. Slide the third-fourth fork shaft (**Figure 75**) out of the transmission. Remove its interlock pin (**Figure 76**). Thread the bolt back into the third-fourth shaft (**Figure 77**) so it isn't lost.
32. Pull a long detent dowel out of the hole shown in **Figure 78** with a pencil magnet.
33. Remove the first-second fork shaft bolt (**Figure 79**).
34. Remove the first-second fork shaft (**Figure 80**). Thread the bolt back into the shaft as shown in **Figure 81** so it isn't lost.
35. Remove the speedometer drive gear and lockball (**Figure 82**).

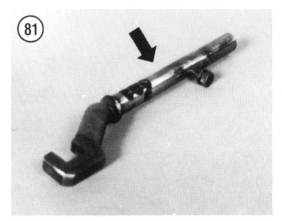

8

36. Remove the bearing spacer and bearing. See **Figure 83** and **Figure 84**.

37. Remove the remaining bearing spacer (**Figure 85**).

38. Remove the countershaft nut (**Figure 86**) which was loosened in Step 27.

39. Remove the bearing and spacer from the countershaft. See **Figure 87** and **Figure 88**. Remove the remaining spacer (**Figure 88**).

40. Remove countershaft fifth-reverse gear (**Figure 89** and **Figure 90**).

41. Remove the countershaft spacer, fifth gear assembly, reverse idler gear, fifth-reverse synchro sleeve and fifth-reverse shift fork. See **Figure 91**.

NOTE
Do not disassemble the fifth gear assembly yet.

42. Remove the main shaft spacer (**Figure 92**).

1. **Bearing spacer**   2. **Bearing**

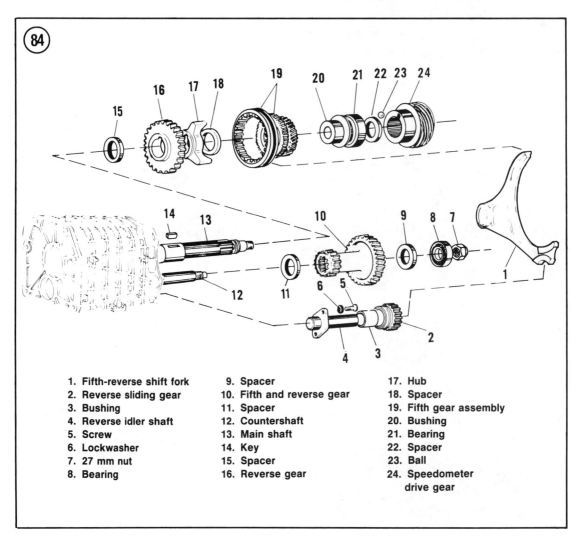

1. **Fifth-reverse shift fork**	9. **Spacer**	17. **Hub**
2. **Reverse sliding gear**	10. **Fifth and reverse gear**	18. **Spacer**
3. **Bushing**	11. **Spacer**	19. **Fifth gear assembly**
4. **Reverse idler shaft**	12. **Countershaft**	20. **Bushing**
5. **Screw**	13. **Main shaft**	21. **Bearing**
6. **Lockwasher**	14. **Key**	22. **Spacer**
7. **27 mm nut**	15. **Spacer**	23. **Ball**
8. **Bearing**	16. **Reverse gear**	24. **Speedometer drive gear**

1. Gear   2. Bearing   3. Spacer

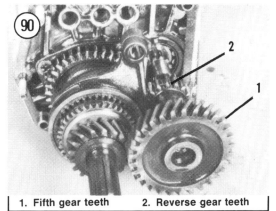

1. Fifth gear teeth   2. Reverse gear teeth

1. Countershaft spacer
2. Fifth gear assembly
3. Reverse idler gear
4. Fifth-reverse synchro sleeve
5. Fifth-reverse shift fork

8

43. Remove the fifth gear synchro hub (**Figure 93**).
44. Remove reverse gear (**Figure 94**).

NOTE
The dished side of the gear faces away from the transmission.

45. Remove reverse gear spacer (**Figure 95**).

NOTE
The dished side of the spacer faces the transmission.

46. Pry the Woodruff key out of the main shaft with a small screwdriver. See **Figure 96**.
47. Inspect the reverse idler shaft. If worn or damaged, remove the shaft's mounting screws (**Figure 97**) with an impact screwdriver (**Figure 98**) and take it off. Leave the shaft on if it is in good condition.
48. Wedge the gears with a block of wood, then remove the countershaft bolt and spacer (**Figure 99**).

NOTE
*If the countershaft bolt is difficult to remove, temporarily install the shift forks and rods. Pry the rods as shown in **Figure 100** to engage 2 gears at once and lock the countershaft. To keep the transmission case from rotating while the bolt is loosened, place a drilled piece of angle iron or similar metal over the case studs as shown in **Figure 101**.*

49. Tap the countershaft rearward (**Figure 102**) until the front bearing can be taken out. Remove the outer part of the bearing (**Figure 103**), then carefully pry the inner cone (**Figure 104**) off the countershaft.
50. Pull the countershaft rearward, then tilt the front end up and take the countershaft out. See **Figure 105**.

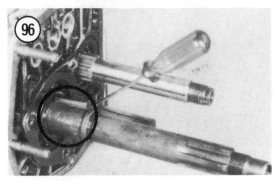

8

CAUTION
*Make sure the bushing (**Figure 106**) remains on the countershaft.*

51. Remove the main shaft bearing retainer screws (**Figure 107**) with an impact screwdriver (**Figure 108**).

CAUTION
*Do not let the input shaft (**Figure 109**) fall from the transmission case.*

52. Remove the input shaft, together with the fourth gear synchro ring. See **Figure 110**.

53. Locate the input shaft pilot bearing (**Figure 111**). It may come out with the input shaft or remain on the main shaft.

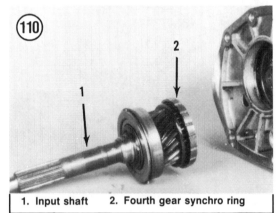

1. Input shaft   2. Fourth gear synchro ring

(113)

(114)

(115)

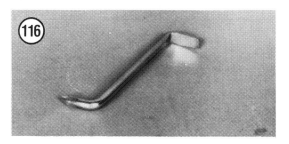

(116)

54. Pull the main shaft (**Figure 112**) to the rear until its ball bearing is clear of the transmission case wall.

55. Tilt the main shaft as shown in **Figure 113**, then take it out of the transmission case.

56. Remove the third-fourth synchro sleeve (**Figure 114**) from the main shaft.

57. Tap a small screwdriver between first gear and its bushing. See **Figure 115**. Use the gap created to pry the bushing off.

NOTE
*A pair of offset screwdrivers (**Figure 116**) will make this easier.*

CAUTION
If the bushing is very difficult to remove, have it pressed off by a machine shop.

58. Remove the bushing, first gear assembly and synchro sleeve from the main shaft. See **Figure 117**.

59. Remove the synchro hub and second gear assembly from the main shaft. See **Figure 118** and **Figure 119**.

CAUTION
If the synchro hub and second gear assembly can't be removed by gentle tapping, have them pressed off by a machine shop.

8

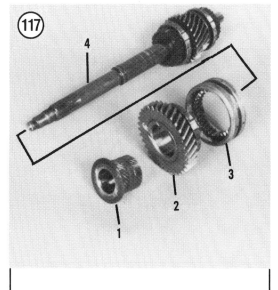

(117)

1. **Bushing**
2. **First gear assembly**
3. **Synchro sleeve**
4. **Main shaft**

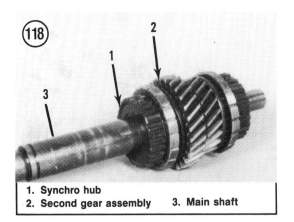

1. Synchro hub
2. Second gear assembly   3. Main shaft

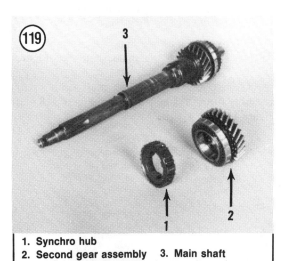

1. Synchro hub
2. Second gear assembly   3. Main shaft

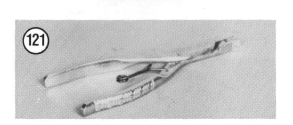

1. Synchro hub
2. Third gear assembly
3. Main shaft

1. Synchro hub
2. Third gear assembly
3. Main shaft

60. Remove the snap ring from the front end of the main shaft. See **Figure 120**.

> *NOTE*
> *If the snap ring is difficult to remove with ordinary snap ring pliers, use horseshoe lockring pliers (**Figure 121**). These are available from auto parts stores.*

61. Remove the washer from the front end of the main shaft. See **Figure 122**.

> *NOTE*
> *The dished side of the washer faces toward the main shaft.*

62. Remove the synchro hub and third gear assembly from the main shaft. See **Figure 123** and **Figure 124**.

> *CAUTION*
> *If the synchro hub and third gear assembly are hard to remove, have them pressed off by a machine shop.*

Inspection

1. Rotate the input shaft ball bearing (**Figure 125**) by hand. Check for noise, looseness or rough movement. Have the bearing replaced by a machine shop if these conditions are found.

> *NOTE*
> *Since needle roller bearing wear is hard to see, the input shaft pilot bearing should be replaced whenever the transmission is overhauled.*

2. Remove the input shaft gear assembly snap ring (**Figure 126**). Take off the synchro ring and spring (**Figure 127**). Check the synchro ring, spring and sheet metal spring retainer for wear and damage. Replace worn or damaged parts.

3. Reassemble the input shaft gear assembly. Be sure the snap ring tab aligns with the notch in the input shaft gear. See **Figure 128**.

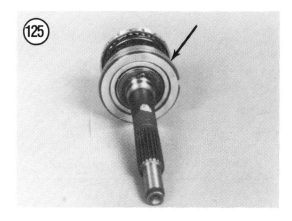

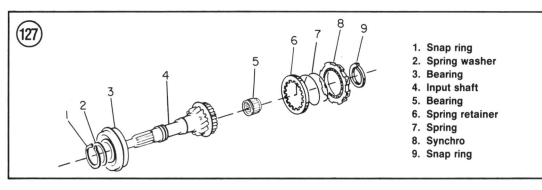

1. Snap ring
2. Spring washer
3. Bearing
4. Input shaft
5. Bearing
6. Spring retainer
7. Spring
8. Synchro
9. Snap ring

4. Disassemble and inspect the third gear assembly, referring to **Figure 129**. Replace worn or damaged parts.

5. Check the main shaft gear surfaces, flange and splines for wear or damage. See **Figure 130**. Replace the main shaft if worn or damaged.

6. Apply multipurpose grease to the third gear surface on the main shaft, then install the third gear assembly. See **Figure 131**.

7. Gently tap the synchro hub (**Figure 132**) onto the main shaft. Note that the notched side of the 3 cogs (**Figure 133**) faces the rear end of the main shaft. The flat side of the 3 cogs faces the front.

CAUTION
If the synchro hub won't go on easily, have it pressed on by a machine shop.

8. Remove the second gear assembly snap ring (**Figure 134**). Disassemble and inspect the second gear assembly, referring to **Figure 135**. Replace worn or damaged parts, then put the assembly back together.

9. Remove the first gear assembly snap ring (**Figure 136**). Disassemble and inspect the first gear assembly, referring to **Figure 137**. Replace worn or damaged parts, then put the assembly back together.

NOTE
To check the first gear bushing, slide it into the gear. The bushing should be a light slip fit with no looseness. If the gear fits loosely on the bushing, replace both.

10. Check the fit between fifth gear assembly and its bushing. See **Figure 138**. The bushing should be a light slip fit in the gear with no looseness. If the gear fits loosely on the bushing, replace both.

11. Remove the fifth gear assembly snap ring (**Figure 139**). Remove the outer ring (**Figure 140**), than take the assembly apart as shown in **Figure 141**. Check the assembly for worn or damaged

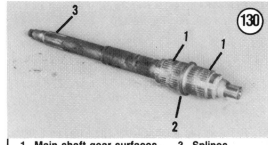

1. Main shaft gear surfaces   3. Splines
2. Flange

1. Main shaft   2. Third gear assembly

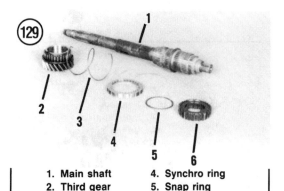

1. Main shaft   4. Synchro ring
2. Third gear   5. Snap ring
3. Spring   6. Synchro hub

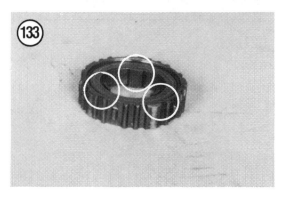

1. Bushing   2. Fifth gear assembly

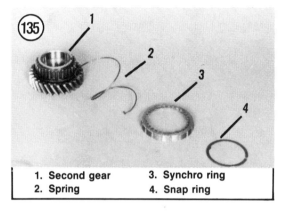

1. Second gear   3. Synchro ring
2. Spring   4. Snap ring

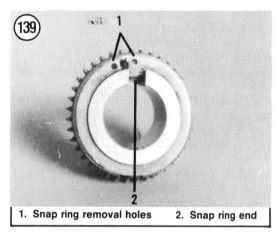

1. Snap ring removal holes   2. Snap ring end

8

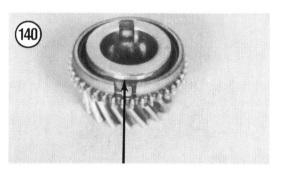

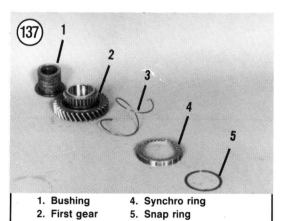

1. Bushing   4. Synchro ring
2. First gear   5. Snap ring
3. Spring

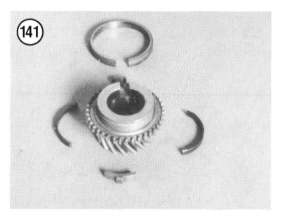

parts. Replace worn or damaged parts, then put the assembly back together.

12. Inspect the fork rod ends and detent ball notches. See **Figure 142** (first-second and third-fourth fork rods) or **Figure 143** (fifth-reverse fork rod). Replace the fork rods if the ends are worn or the detent ball notches are scored.

12. Inspect the synchro sleeve contact surfaces on the shift forks. See **Figure 144** (first-second and third-fourth shift forks) or **Figure 145** (fifth-reverse shift fork). Replace the forks if the contact surfaces are worn.

13. Check the bolt threads in the shift forks for burrs or other damage. Clean damaged threads with a tap.

14. Check the first-second and third-fourth synchro sleeves (**Figure 146**) for wear or damage. Slight nicks or burrs may be removed with a fine oilstone. Replace sleeves that show galling or worn or missing teeth. If the sleeves fit loosely on the hubs, check the sleeve-to-hub contact surfaces for wear. Replace worn parts.

15. Check the fifth-reverse synchro sleeve and hub (**Figure 147**) for wear or damage. Slight nicks or burrs may be removed with a fine oilstone. Replace the sleeve if it is galled or teeth are worn or missing. If the sleeve fits loosely on the hub, check the sleeve-to-hub contact surfaces for wear. Replace worn parts.

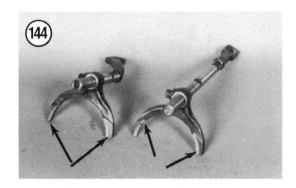

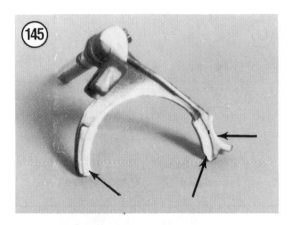

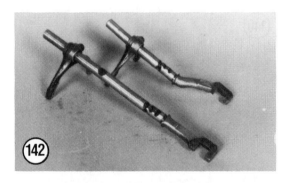

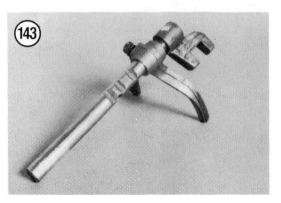

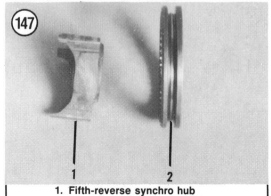

1. Fifth-reverse synchro hub
2. Fifth-reverse synchro sleeve

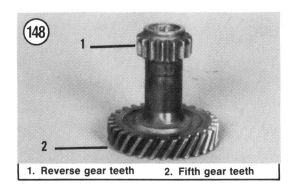

1. Reverse gear teeth   2. Fifth gear teeth

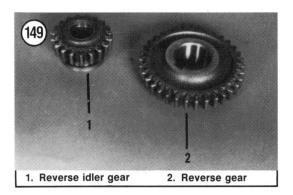

1. Reverse idler gear   2. Reverse gear

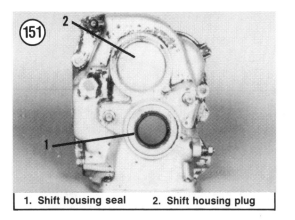

1. Shift housing seal   2. Shift housing plug

16. Inspect countershaft fifth-reverse gear (**Figure 148**). Replace the gear if teeth are worn, chipped or missing.

17. Check reverse gear and reverse idler gear (**Figure 149**). Replace the gears if teeth are worn, chipped or missing.

18. Place reverse idler gear on its shaft and check the fit. See **Figure 150**. If the gear fits loosely, have gear bushing diameter and reverse idler shaft diameter measured by a machine shop. Calculate the difference between the 2 figures and compare to specifications (end of chapter). Replace the gear or shaft if wear is excessive.

19. Check the transmission case bearing bores and gasket surfaces for wear or damage. Slight burrs may be removed with a fine oilstone. Slight nicks in gasket surfaces may be filled with sealer when the transmission is assembled. Replace the transmission case if damage is serious.

20. Inspect the shift housing seal and plug (**Figure 151**). Have the plug replaced by a machine shop if it shows signs of leakage. The seal should be replaced whenever the shift housing is removed. To remove the seal, insert a drift into the shift housing and tap the seal out. See **Figure 152**. Tap a new seal in with its lip facing into the housing. Use a block of wood to spread the hammer's force so the seal won't tilt sideways and jam. See **Figure 153**.

21. Check the lever in the shift housing for wear, damage or a loose fit. Check the springs and shaft

for visible wear or damage. If the parts are in good condition, the shift housing need not be disassembled. If wear or damage can be seen, perform Steps 22-25.

CAUTION
The cover mentioned in the next step is lightly spring-loaded. Do not let parts fly out when the cover is unbolted.

22. Remove the shift housing cover and gasket (**Figure 154**).
23. Take the shaft, spring and washer out of the shift housing. See **Figure 155**.
24. Compress the opposite spring until it clears the housing, then pull it toward you. Take the spring, bushing, washer and lever out of the housing. See **Figure 156**.
25. Inspect the shift housing and related parts. Replace worn or damaged parts, then reassemble the shift housing.
26. Inspect the bearings. See **Figure 157** (main shaft ball bearing), **Figure 158** (countershaft ball bearing) and **Figure 159** (roller bearings). Check the bearings for rust, scoring, chips, looseness, roughness and the bluish tint that indicates overheating. Replace bearings if their condition is in doubt.

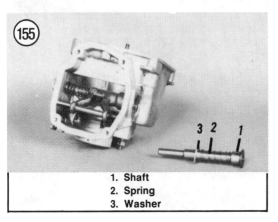

1. Shaft
2. Spring
3. Washer

27. Inspect the shift tower (**Figure 160**). Check the engaging rod for wear, damage or an excessively loose fit in the shift tower. Replace worn or damaged parts. Check the gasket surface for nicks or burrs. Small burrs may be removed with a fine oilstone. Small nicks may be filled with gasket sealer during assembly. Replace the shift tower if damage to the gasket surface is serious.

NOTE
The shift tower need not be disassembled unless parts are to be replaced.

Assembly

1. Install the snap ring on the front end of the main shaft. See **Figure 161**.

2. Apply a light coat of gear oil to the second gear surface on the main shaft (**Figure 162**).
3. Install second gear assembly (**Figure 163**).
4. Gently tap the first-second synchro hub onto the main shaft. See **Figure 164**.

NOTE
*The notched side of the 3 lugs faces the second gear assembly. The smooth side of the 3 lugs faces the rear end of the main shaft. See **Figure 165**.*

5. Apply a light coat of gear oil to the synchro hubs, then install the first-second and third-fourth synchro sleeves. See **Figure 166**.

CAUTION
At this point, there is nothing holding the synchro sleeves in position. Do not let them fall off the hubs.

8

6. Apply a light coat of gear oil to the first gear bushing, then install it in the first gear assembly. See **Figure 167**.

7. Install first gear assembly on the main shaft. See **Figure 168**. Tap the bushing gently into position. If it won't go on easily, have the bushing and first gear assembly pressed on by a machine shop.

8. Start the main shaft into the transmission at the angle shown in **Figure 169**. Lay the main shaft in the transmission case as shown in **Figure 170**.

9. Coat the input shaft pilot bearing (**Figure 171**) with gear oil, then install it in the rear end of the input shaft.

10. Lift up the front end of the main shaft (**Figure 172**) and slide the input shaft into the transmission case as shown in **Figure 173**. Push the input shaft in until the bearing snap ring stops against the transmission case.

11. Position the main shaft ball bearing on the main shaft with snap ring toward the rear of the main shaft. See **Figure 174**.

12. Push the main shaft ball bearing forward until its snap ring stops against the transmission case. See **Figure 175**.

13. Referring to **Figure 176**, make sure the main shaft and input shaft turn easily by hand, in the same and opposite directions. Make sure the gears turn easily on the shafts and the synchro sleeves slide smoothly back and forth.

14. Install the main shaft bearing retainer (**Figure 177**). Tighten the screws securely with an impact screwdriver.

15. Place the shift forks on the sleeves with the bolt holes showing. See **Figure 178**. Slide the forks around the sleeves until they rest on the transmission case. See **Figure 179**.

NOTE
When the forks and rods are installed in the transmission case, they will be assembled as shown in ***Figure 180***.

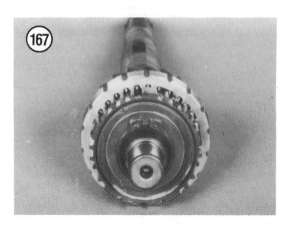

1. Main shaft   2. Input shaft

8

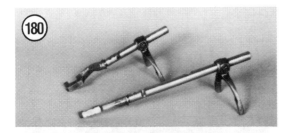

16. Make sure the countershaft bearing inner race is on the countershaft. See **Figure 181**.

17. Start the countershaft into the transmission case at the angle shown in **Figure 182**, then mesh it with the main shaft. See **Figure 183**.

18. Place the ball bearing inner cone on the countershaft. See **Figure 184**.

19. Install the outer race on the countershaft (**Figure 185**), then install the outer cone (**Figure 186**).

> *NOTE*
> *Be sure the outer race snap ring gap aligns with the input shaft snap ring (Figure 186).*

20. Install the countershaft bolt (**Figure 187**). Tighten the bolt finger-tight.

21. Position the countershaft rear bearing on the countershaft. Gently tap it in with a hammer and block of wood until it is flush with the transmission case. See **Figure 188** and **Figure 189**.

22. Install the reverse gear spacer (**Figure 190**).

> *NOTE*
> *The dished side of the reverse gear spacer faces the transmission.*

23. Install the Woodruff key in the main shaft groove. See **Figure 191**.

24. Install reverse gear (**Figure 192**).

> *NOTE*
> *The dished side of the gear faces away from the transmission.*

25. Install the fifth gear synchro hub (**Figure 193**).

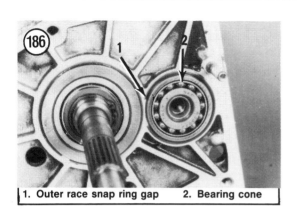

1. Outer race snap ring gap   2. Bearing cone

8

NOTE
The 3 points on the hub face away from the transmission.

26. Install the fifth gear synchro hub spacer (**Figure 194**).
27. Install the countershaft spacer (**Figure 195**). Push it against the countershaft bearing.
28. Push the fifth gear assembly onto the synchro sleeve. See **Figure 196**.

NOTE
The sleeve chamfer faces the gear as shown.

29. Partly install the fifth gear assembly, fifth-reverse shift fork and fifth-reverse gear. See **Figure 197**.
30. Place a light coat of gear oil on the reverse idler shaft (**Figure 198**).
31. Pivot the reverse gear portion of the fifth-reverse fork around to align with the reverse idler shaft. Engage the reverse idler gear with the fork and slide the reverse idler gear onto the shaft. See **Figure 199**.
32. Slide the gears and fork into position on the shafts.
33. Install the fifth gear spacer (**Figure 200**).
34. Install the fifth gear bearing and inner race. See **Figure 201** and **Figure 202**.
35. Install the countershaft nut (**Figure 203**). Tighten the nut finger-tight.
36. Install the main shaft roller bearing and inner race (**Figure 204**).
37. Install the spacer next to the main shaft roller bearing. See **Figure 205**.
38. Install the speedometer drive gear lockball (**Figure 206**).
39. Install the speedometer drive gear (**Figure 207**).

NOTE
Secure the speedometer drive gear with tape or soft wire so it doesn't fall off during the next steps.

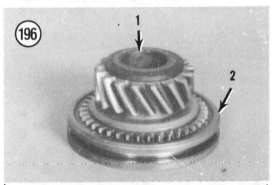

1. Fifth gear assembly   2. Synchro sleeve chamfer

1. Fifth gear assembly   3. Fifth-reverse gear
2. Fifth-reverse shift fork

1. Reverse idler gear
2. Reverse idler shaft

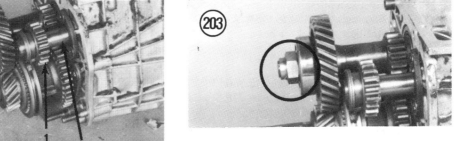

1. Fifth gear bearing
2. Inner race

1. Fifth gear bearing
2. Inner race

8

40. Start the first-second shift fork shaft into its hole (**Figure 208**). Bolt the shaft to the fork (**Figure 209**). Tighten the bolt and lockwasher to 2 mkg (14 ft.-lb.).

NOTE
*When installed, the first-second fork fits on the shaft as shown in **Figure 210**.*

41. Start the third-fourth fork shaft into its hole. See **Figure 211**. Bolt the shaft to the fork (**Figure 212**). Tighten the bolt to 2 mkg (14 ft.-lb.).

NOTE
*When installed, the third-fourth fork fits on the shaft as shown in **Figure 213**.*

42. Temporarily install the first-second and third-fourth detent springs and balls in the top and center holes. See **Figure 214**.

43. Temporarily install the detent ball cover without its gasket. See **Figure 215**.

44. Push one fork rod forward to engage a gear. See **Figure 216**. Fifth gear should already be engaged as shown (fifth-reverse synchro sleeve over the clutch teeth on fifth gear assembly).

NOTE
*To keep the transmission from turning during the next 2 steps, place a drilled piece of angle iron or similar metal over the studs as shown in **Figure 217**.*

45. Tighten the countershaft nut (**Figure 218** and **Figure 219**) to 12 mkg (87 ft.-lb.).

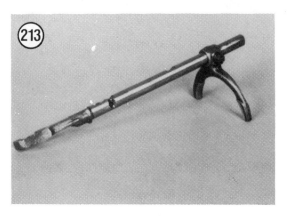

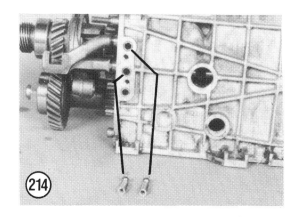

8

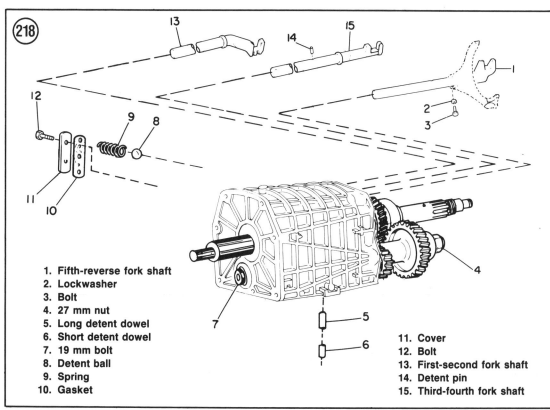

1. Fifth-reverse fork shaft
2. Lockwasher
3. Bolt
4. 27 mm nut
5. Long detent dowel
6. Short detent dowel
7. 19 mm bolt
8. Detent ball
9. Spring
10. Gasket
11. Cover
12. Bolt
13. First-second fork shaft
14. Detent pin
15. Third-fourth fork shaft

46. Tighten the countershaft bolt (**Figure 220**) to 9 mkg (69 ft.-lb.).

NOTE
Make sure the countershaft turns easily before performing the next step. If it is hard to turn, the countershaft rear bearing might be installed backward.

47. Punch the lip of the countershaft nut into the countershaft grooves.

48. Move the shift rods and fifth gear fork into the neutral position. When this occurs, the shift rod gates will be aligned, the shift rods will be pulled slightly back from the transmission case and the fifth gear synchro sleeve will be centered on the hub. See **Figure 221**.

49. Remove the detent ball cover (**Figure 222**).

50. Remove the third-fourth detent ball and spring (**Figure 223**). Unbolt the third-fourth fork from its shaft and pull it out.

51. Unbolt the first-second shift fork shaft from its fork. See **Figure 224**.

52. Pull the first-second shift fork shaft partway out and install a detent pin. See **Figure 225**. Push the shaft back in and bolt it to its fork.

53. Install one of the long detent dowels (**Figure 226**) in the transmission case. Insert it into the hole shown in **Figure 224** and push it down until rests against the first-second shift fork shaft.

54. Install the third-fourth shift fork shaft partway and install the other detent pin. See **Figure 227**. Install the shaft the rest of the way and bolt it to its fork.

55. Install the short detent dowel (**Figure 228**). Push it into the hole until it rests against the third-fourth shift fork shaft.

56. Install the fifth-reverse fork shaft and bolt it to the fork. See **Figure 229**. Tighten the bolt to 2 mkg (14 ft.-lb.).

NOTE
When the fifth-reverse fork shaft is installed, it fits in the fork as shown in ***Figure 230***.

1. Synchro hub
2. Fifth gear synchro sleeve

1. Fork shaft bolt
2. Detent dowel hole

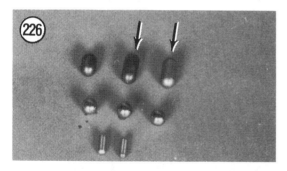

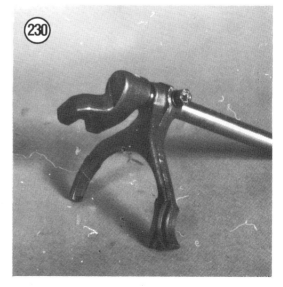

8

57. Install the third-fourth and fifth-reverse detent balls and springs. See **Figure 231**.

58. Install the detent ball cover and gasket (**Figure 232**). Do not use gasket sealer on the gasket. Tighten the cover bolts to 2.5 mkg (18 ft.-lb.).

NOTE
Figure 232 shows the shift fork shaft ends in the neutral position. The ends are aligned with each other and the shafts protrude slightly from the transmission case. Refer to Figure 232 for the following steps.

59. Push one shift fork shaft forward to engage a gear. Try to move the other shift fork shafts forward or backward to engage another gear at the same time. This should not be possible. If it is, the detent balls and pins are installed incorrectly. Find the problem and correct it before proceeding. Engaging 2 gears at once while driving will destroy the transmission.

60. Repeat Step 59 with the other shift fork shafts. Again, it should not be possible to engage 2 gears at the same time.

61. Turn the input shaft by hand with the transmission in each gear position, then in neutral. When in a forward gear position, turning the input shaft should turn the main shaft in the same direction. When in reverse, turning the input shaft should turn the main shaft in the opposite direction. When the transmission is in neutral, it should be possible to hold the main shaft from turning with one hand while turning the input shaft with the other.

62. Install the remaining long detent dowel in the top of the transmission case. See **Figure 233**.

63. Install the top switch in the transmission case. See **Figure 234**.

64. Apply gasket sealer to both sides of a new rear housing gasket, then install it on the transmission case surface (**Figure 235**).

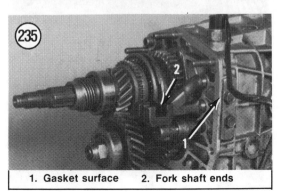

1. Gasket surface   2. Fork shaft ends

65. Move the selection and engaging lever (**Figure 236**) to the rear of the rear housing.

66. Slowly move the rear housing into position on the transmission case. Just as the rear housing starts onto the transmission case studs, move the selection and engaging lever forward. Make sure the lower end of the selection and engaging lever engages the fork shaft ends (**Figure 235**), then push the rear housing the rest of the way onto the transmission case.

67. Make sure the upper end of the selection and engaging lever is vertical, then install the nuts and bolts that secure the rear housing to the transmission case.

68. Install the backup light switch and neutral switch (**Figure 237**), together with their metal washers.

69. Apply multipurpose grease to the yoke seal contact area (**Figure 238**). Apply anti-seize compound to the yoke splines.

70. Install the yoke on the main shaft with its sheet metal cup toward the transmission.

71. Install a new lockwasher on the main shaft. Make sure its tabs fit in the main shaft grooves.

72. Install the main shaft nut (**Figure 239**).

73. Attach a drilled piece of angle iron or similar metal to the yoke as shown in **Figure 240**. Tighten the main shaft nut to 14 mkg (108 ft.-lb.), then remove the angle iron.

74. Bend the main shaft lockwasher over one of the flats on the nut. See **Figure 241**.

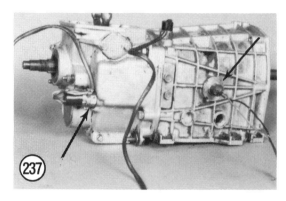

8

75. Position the spring in the seal groove, then install the spring and seal on the main shaft. See **Figure 242**.

76. Tap the spacer (**Figure 243**) onto the main shaft until the snap ring groove is exposed.

77. Secure the spacer with a new snap ring. See **Figure 244**.

78. Install the drive shaft coupling on the yoke. Hold the yoke bolts from turning with a 19 mm box wrench as shown in **Figure 245**, then tighten the self-locking nuts securely.

79. Coat a new shift tower gasket on both sides with gasket sealer, then place it on the rear housing.

80. Slide the rod inside the shift tower (**Figure 246**) forward. Engage the dog with the top of the selection and engaging lever, then install the shift tower (**Figure 247**).

81. Coat a new gasket on both sides with gasket sealer, then install it on the back of the shift tower. Install the rear cover, reverse lockout screw (if removed) and nut. See **Figure 248**.

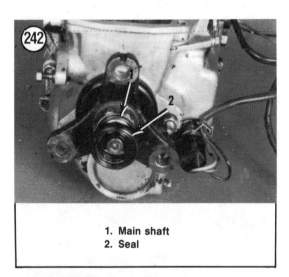

1. Main shaft
2. Seal

1. Rear cover
2. Bolt
3. Nut
4. Reverse lockout screw

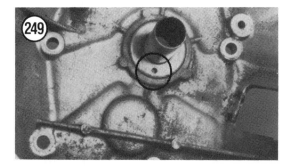

82. Install the transmission mounting member on the transmission.

83. Tap the oil seal out of the clutch housing through the hole shown in **Figure 249**. Tap in a new seal, positioned so its lip will face into the transmission when the clutch housing is installed. See **Figure 250**. Use a block of wood to spread the hammer's force so the seal won't tilt sideways and jam.

84. Apply a coat of multipurpose grease to the input shaft oil seal surface (**Figure 251**).

85. Place the spacer (**Figure 252**) in the clutch housing.

86. Stand the clutch housing on a flat surface so the spacer won't fall out. Coat a new gasket on both sides with gasket sealer and install it on the clutch housing surface.

87. Place the transmission case on the clutch housing. Tip the assembly onto its side, then install the clutch housing bolts. See **Figure 253**.

8

88. Install the speedometer driven gear (**Figure 254**).

89. Install the transmission case cover (**Figure 255**).

90. Connect the electrical switch loop terminal to the stud on the lower right corner of the transmission case. See **Figure 256**.

AUTOMATIC TRANSMISSION

An automatic transmission is optional on 1979 and later models.

Automatic transmission overhaul requires special training and tools and should be done by a dealer or qualified transmission shop. This section provides simple checks and adjustments which can be done by home mechanics, as well as transmission removal and installation procedures.

Throttle Linkage Adjustment
(Carburetted Models)

Refer to **Figure 257** and **Figure 258** for this procedure.

1. Disconnect the telescoping link (3, **Figure 257** and **Figure 258**) from the control lever (1).

2. Push the accelerator pedal (13, **Figure 257** and **Figure 258**) until the ball (6) on the end of the cable (7) just touches the cable pin (5).

3. Hold the accelerator pedal as described in Step 2 and measure the distance the cable has extended. It should be 7-9 mm (0.276-0.354 in.):

    a. If cable extension is correct, go to the next step.

    b. If cable extension is incorrect, adjust it with the adjusting nuts (10, **Figure 257** and **Figure 258**).

4. Push the accelerator pedal (13, **Figure 257** and **Figure 258**) against the stop (15), then hold it in this position.

5. With the accelerator pedal against the stop, hold the control lever (1, **Figure 257** and **Figure 258**) in the full throttle position (position II, **Figure 257**). Extend the telescoping link (3, **Figure 257** and **Figure 258**) 8-10 mm (0.315-0.393 in.). Make sure the telescoping link can be connected to the control lever while it is extended. If not, adjust it with the adjusting nuts (2 and 4).

6. Slowly release the accelerator pedal far enough so the ball end (6, **Figure 257** and **Figure 258**) just touches the cable pin (5). Hold the accelerator pedal in this position.

7. With the accelerator pedal held as described in Step 6, make sure the telescoping link (3) can be connected to the control lever (1) without being extended. If not, adjust the telescoping link with the adjusting nuts (2 and 4).

NOTE
If adjustment is necessary, make equal adjustments at both ends of the telescoping link. Otherwise, one end may run out of threads.

8. Once the telescoping link is adjusted properly, connect it to the control lever.

Throttle Linkage Adjustment
(Fuel Injected Models)

Refer to **Figure 259** for this procedure.

1. Make sure engine idle speed is correct. See *Tune-up* in Chapter Three for details.

2. Pull lightly on the accelerator cable housing until just before the throttle lever starts to move. Make sure there is approximately 1 mm clearance

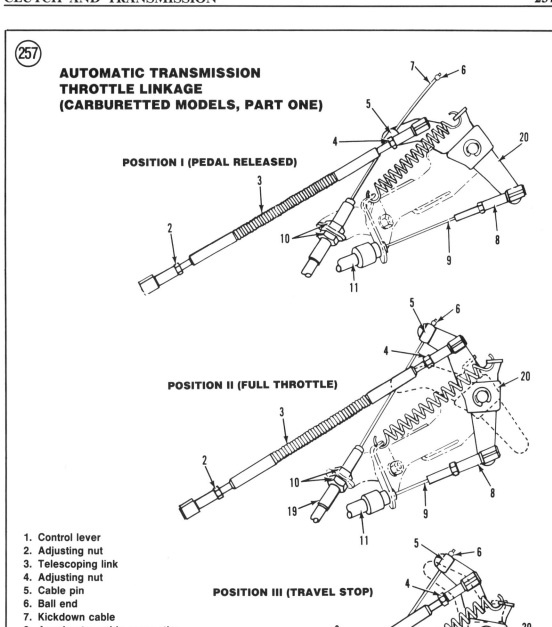

257 AUTOMATIC TRANSMISSION
THROTTLE LINKAGE
(CARBURETTED MODELS, PART ONE)

POSITION I (PEDAL RELEASED)

POSITION II (FULL THROTTLE)

POSITION III (TRAVEL STOP)

1. Control lever
2. Adjusting nut
3. Telescoping link
4. Adjusting nut
5. Cable pin
6. Ball end
7. Kickdown cable
8. Accelerator cable connection
9. Accelerator cable
10. Adjusting nuts
11. Sheath
12. Pedal to cable connection
13. Accelerator pedal
14. Kickdown valve
15. Stop
16. Stop
17. Ball end
18. Sheath
19. Sheath
20. Bellcrank

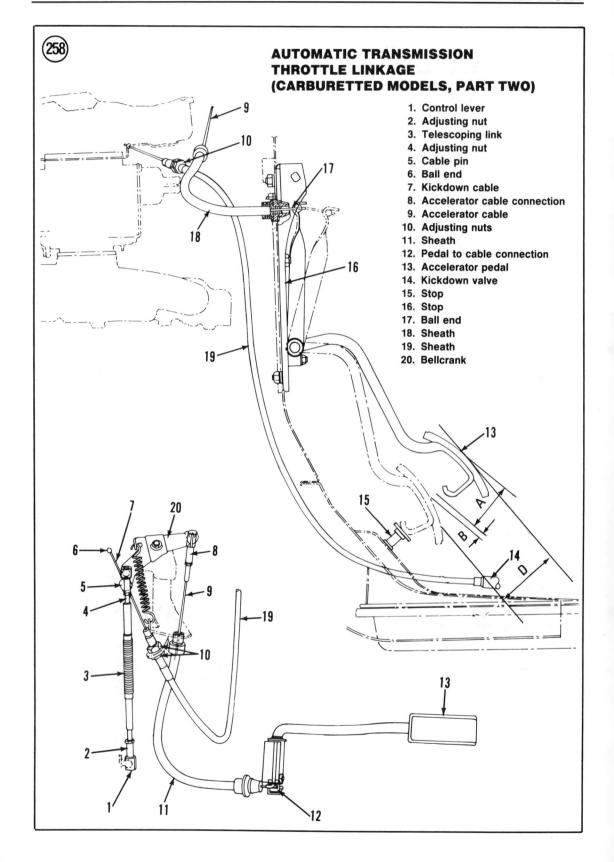

AUTOMATIC TRANSMISSION
THROTTLE LINKAGE
(CARBURETTED MODELS, PART TWO)

1. Control lever
2. Adjusting nut
3. Telescoping link
4. Adjusting nut
5. Cable pin
6. Ball end
7. Kickdown cable
8. Accelerator cable connection
9. Accelerator cable
10. Adjusting nuts
11. Sheath
12. Pedal to cable connection
13. Accelerator pedal
14. Kickdown valve
15. Stop
16. Stop
17. Ball end
18. Sheath
19. Sheath
20. Bellcrank

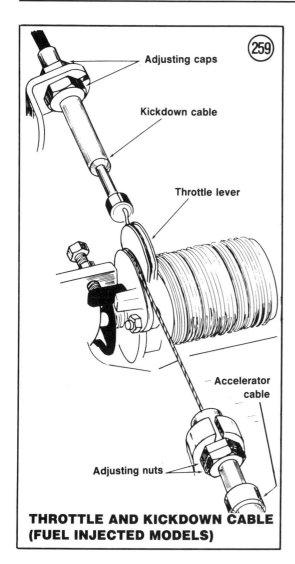

(259)

Adjusting caps

Kickdown cable

Throttle lever

Accelerator cable

Adjusting nuts

THROTTLE AND KICKDOWN CABLE (FUEL INJECTED MODELS)

2. Working beneath the car, disconnect the tie rod (12) from the cross shaft actuating lever (13). Push the tie rod all the way back to make sure it is in the PARK position.

3. Push the cross shaft actuating lever all the way back to make sure it is the PARK position. To check, release the handbrake and try to push the car. This should not be possible.

4. Try to attach the end of the cross shaft actuating lever to the end of the tie rod without moving the tie rod or the lever:

    a. If this is possible, no further adjustment is necessary. Attach the lever to the rod.

    b. If the lever cannot be attached to the rod without moving one or the other, detach the rear end of the rod from the relay lever (9, **Figure 260**). Loosen the locknut (11) and adjust the rod length by turning the adjustable end (10). Once the adjustment has been made, tighten the locknut and attach the rod to the levers.

5. Raise the lower part of the shift lever handle and move the shift lever through all gear positions. A definite click should be felt at each position. If not, have the transmission inspected by a dealer or qualified automatic transmission specialist.

6. Place the shift lever in 1. Raise the lower handle all the way, then release it. This should lock the shift lever in position 1 without causing the shift lever to move.

7. Repeat Step 6 in all other gear positions.

8. If the transmission didn't perform as described in Step 6 and Step 7, repeat Steps 1-4.

9. Make sure the shift lever aligns with the numbers and letters on the selector plate. If not, adjust the selector plate so the lever does align.

8

between the adjusting nuts and their bracket. If not, adjust the nuts to obtain the proper clearance.

3. Press the accelerator until the throttle lever touches the maximum opening stop. The kickdown cable should just start to move at this point.

4. Press the accelerator all the way down and note the kickdown cable travel. The kickdown cable should extend 9-11 mm.

5. If the kickdown cable performed as described in Step 3 and Step 4, no further adjustment is necessary. If not, loosen the kickdown cable adjusting nuts and position the nuts so the cable performs as described in Step 3 and Step 4.

Shift Linkage Adjustment

Refer to **Figure 260** for this procedure.

1. Place the shift lever (1, **Figure 260**) in PARK.

Transmission Removal/Installation

1. Disconnect the negative cable from the battery.

2. Working in the engine compartment, remove the transmission dipstick (**Figure 261**). Remove the bolt and washers that secure the dipstick tube to the engine bracket, but do not remove the tube yet.

WARNING
The next steps require working under the car while it is on jackstands. Make sure the car is securely positioned on the stands so it cannot fall.

3. Jack up both ends of the car and place jackstands beneath all 4 corners.

4. Place a drain pan beneath the transmission. Remove the transmission drain plug (**Figure 262**) and drain the transmission fluid.

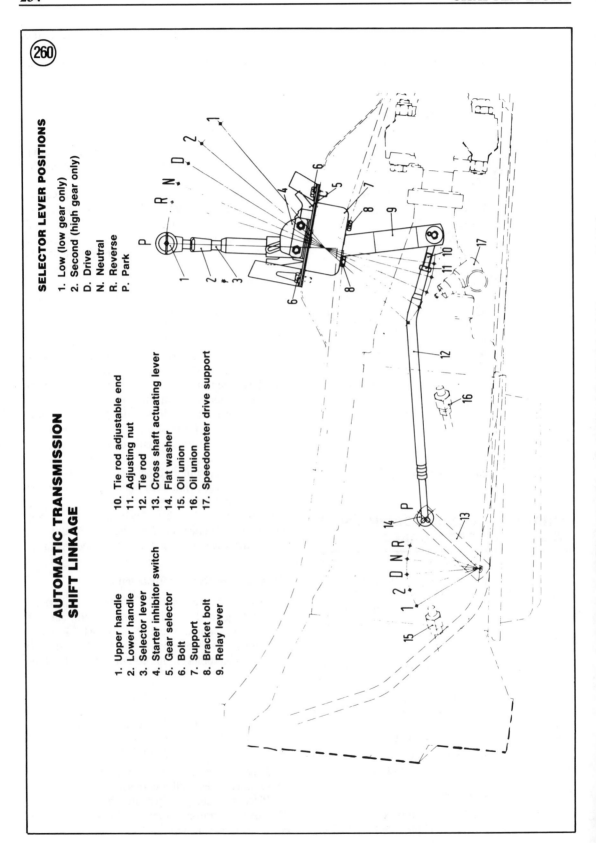

(260)

SELECTOR LEVER POSITIONS

1. Low (low gear only)
2. Second (high gear only)
D. Drive
N. Neutral
R. Reverse
P. Park

AUTOMATIC TRANSMISSION SHIFT LINKAGE

1. Upper handle
2. Lower handle
3. Selector lever
4. Starter inhibitor switch
5. Gear selector
6. Bolt
7. Support
8. Bracket bolt
9. Relay lever
10. Tie rod adjustable end
11. Adjusting nut
12. Tie rod
13. Cross shaft actuating lever
14. Flat washer
15. Oil union
16. Oil union
17. Speedometer drive support

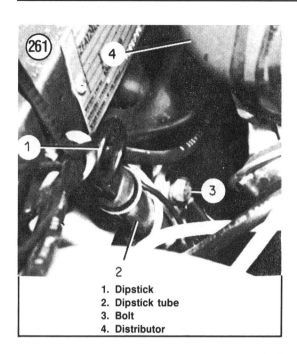

1. Dipstick
2. Dipstick tube
3. Bolt
4. Distributor

5. Remove the starter mounting bolts (Chapter Seven). Pull the starter clear of the engine and lay it out of the way. Tie the starter out of the way with wire so it can't fall during transmission removal.

6. Disconnect the speedometer cable from the transmission.

7. Remove the exhaust pipe bracket bolts and separate the bracket from the transmission.

8. Disconnect the vacuum hose from the vacuum modulator (**Figure 263**) and from the clip on the transmission.

9. Disconnect the fluid cooler lines from the transmission. Remove the bolt and clamp that secure the lines. Plug the lines and fittings.

10. Remove the bolt and clamp that secure the kickdown cable, then disconnect the cable from the transmission.

1. Drain plug
2. Starter bolt
3. Speedometer cable connector
4. Bolt
5. Bracket

8

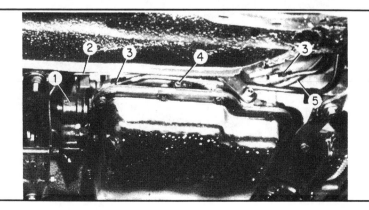

1. Vacuum modulator
2. Clip
3. Transmission fluid cooler lines
4. Bolt and clamp
5. Kickdown cable

11. Remove the nut that secures the shift lever to the transmission control rod (**Figure 264**). Detach the rod from the lever.

12. Remove the drive shaft as described in Chapter Ten.

13. Support the transmission with a transmission jack. These have cradles which prevent the transmission from falling. They can also be adjusted for side-to-side tilt and approach angle. Transmission jacks are available from tool rental dealers.

14. Place a jack beneath the engine to support it. Use a block of wood between the jack and oil pan so the oil pan won't be damaged.

15. Detach the transmission mounting member from the body, then from the transmission. See **Figure 265**.

16. Unbolt the lower cover from the transmission. See **Figure 266**.

> *NOTE*
> *One of the lower cover bolts also secures the engine ground cable.*

17. Remove 3 bolts that secure the drive plate to the torque converter. See **Figure 266**. Turn the crankshaft with a wrench on the crankshaft pulley bolt to gain access to the drive plate bolts.

18. Remove the transmission-to-engine bolts.

> *CAUTION*
> *During the next step, support the torque converter so it doesn't separate from the transmission.*

19. Slowly lower the jacks beneath the engine and transmission. Remove the transmission downward and to the rear.

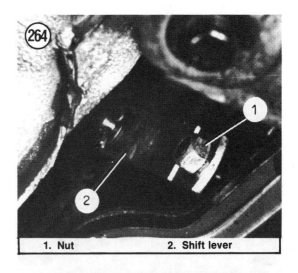

1. Nut	2. Shift lever

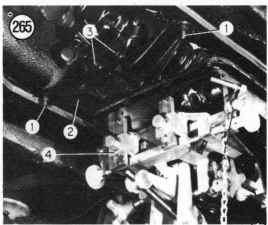

1. Nut	3. Bolt
2. Transmission mount	4. Transmission jack

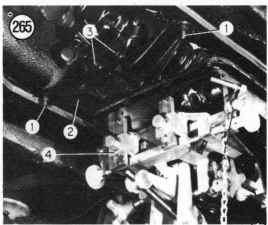

1. Ground cable
2. Bolt
3. Drive plate

20. Installation is the reverse of removal, plus the following.

   a. Tighten all fasteners to torque specifications in **Table 1**.

   b. Once the transmission is attached to the engine, push the torque converter forward against its drive plate. Measure the gap between each attaching point (8, **Figure 267**) and bolt boss (9) with a feeler gauge. Turn the crankshaft with a wrench on the crankshaft pulley to gain access to each measurement point. The gap at each point should be 0.20-1.21 mm (0.008-0.048 in.). If not, the torque converter drive plate must be replaced as described in Chapter Four.

   c. Fill the transmission with fluid as described in Chapter Three.

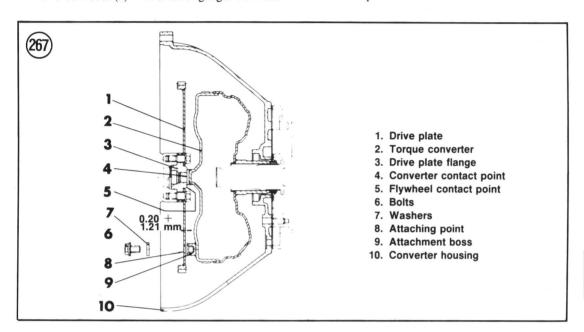

1. Drive plate
2. Torque converter
3. Drive plate flange
4. Converter contact point
5. Flywheel contact point
6. Bolts
7. Washers
8. Attaching point
9. Attachment boss
10. Converter housing

8

Table 1 TRANSMISSION GEAR RATIOS

1971-1978	
First	3.667:1
Second	2.100:1
Third	1.361:1
Fourth	1.0:1
Fifth	0.881:1
Reverse	3.526:1
1979-1980	
First	3.612:1
Second	2.045:1
Third	1.357:1
Fourth	1.0:1
Fifth	0.830:1
Reverse	3.244:1
1981-on	
First	3.667:1
Second	2.100:1
Third	1.361:1
Fourth	1.0:1
Fifth	0.881:1
Reverse	3.244:1

Table 2 TORQUE SPECIFICATIONS (MANUAL TRANSMISSION)

Fastener	Thread size	mkg	ft.-lb.
Detent spring cover bolt	M8	2.5	18
Transmission-to-engine bolts	M12×1.25	8.3	61
Clutch housing to transmission bolts/nuts			
Large	M10×1.25	4.9	36
Small	M8	2.5	18
Rear cover nut	M8	2.5	18
Rear cover bolt	M8	2.0	14
Countershaft rear bearing nut	M18×1.5	11.8	87
Countershaft front bearing bolt	M12×1.25	9.3	69
Shift fork bolts	M6	2.0	14
Main shaft nut	M20×1	14.7	108

FRONT SUSPENSION, WHEEL BEARINGS AND STEERING

All models use a coil spring front suspension with upper and lower control arms and tube shock absorbers. A sway bar controls body lean.

Table 1 and **Table 2** are at the end of the chapter.

FRONT SUSPENSION

Shock Absorber Replacement

1. Working in the engine compartment, hold the shock absorber shaft from turning with a wrench.

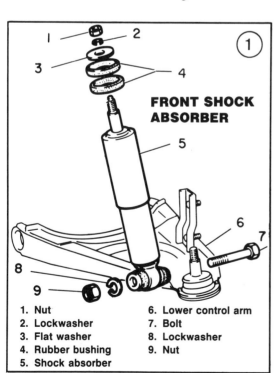

FRONT SHOCK ABSORBER

1. Nut
2. Lockwasher
3. Flat washer
4. Rubber bushing
5. Shock absorber
6. Lower control arm
7. Bolt
8. Lockwasher
9. Nut

Remove the upper nut from the upper end of the shock absorber. See **Figure 1**.

2. Remove the nut, lockwasher and bolt from the lower end of the shock absorber. See **Figure 1**. Lower the shock absorber through the lower control arm and take it out.

3. Check all parts for wear or damage, especially rubber bushings. Replace as needed.

4. Check the shock absorbers for leaks. Replace the shocks if leaks can be seen.

5. Compress and extend the shock absorbers. They should offer firm, even resistance through their travel. If not, replace them.

6. Installation is the reverse of removal.

Sway Bar Removal/Installation

1. Remove the splash shield from under the front of the car.

2. Detach the sway bar from the crossmember and suspension arms, then take it out. See **Figure 2**.

3. Inspect all parts for wear or damage, especially rubber bushings. Replace as needed.

4. Installation is the reverse of removal.

Control Arm, Ball-joint and Spring Removal

The control arms, ball-joints and spring on each side of the car are removed as an assembly. Refer to **Figure 3** for this procedure.

NOTE
It is a good idea to clean the front suspension at a coin-operated car wash before beginning this procedure. The job will be much easier if the front suspension is clean.

9

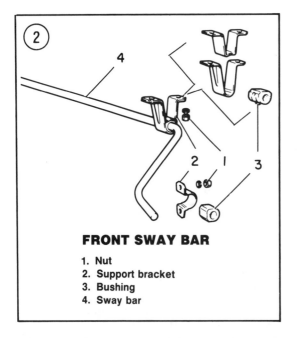

FRONT SWAY BAR

1. Nut
2. Support bracket
3. Bushing
4. Sway bar

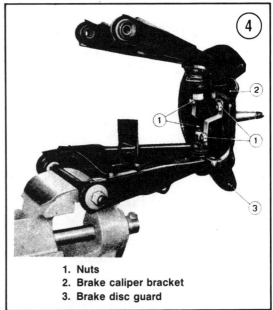

1. Nuts
2. Brake caliper bracket
3. Brake disc guard

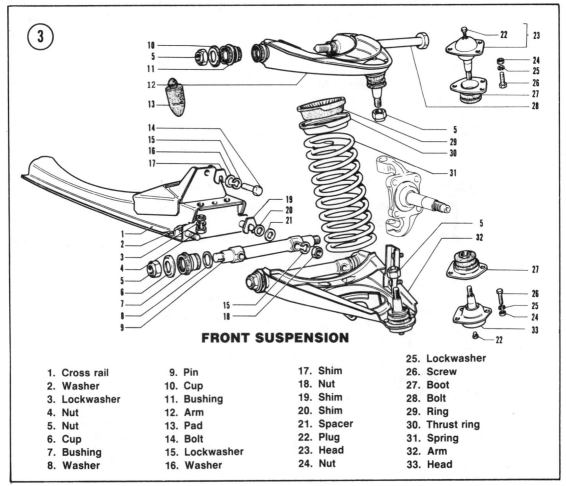

FRONT SUSPENSION

1. Cross rail	9. Pin	17. Shim	25. Lockwasher
2. Washer	10. Cup	18. Nut	26. Screw
3. Lockwasher	11. Bushing	19. Shim	27. Boot
4. Nut	12. Arm	20. Shim	28. Bolt
5. Nut	13. Pad	21. Spacer	29. Ring
6. Cup	14. Bolt	22. Plug	30. Thrust ring
7. Bushing	15. Lockwasher	23. Head	31. Spring
8. Washer	16. Washer	24. Nut	32. Arm
			33. Head

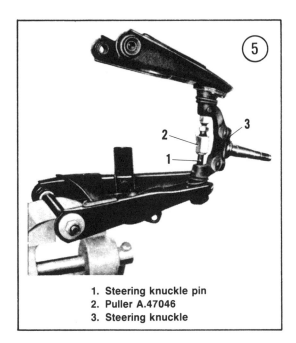

1. Steering knuckle pin
2. Puller A.47046
3. Steering knuckle

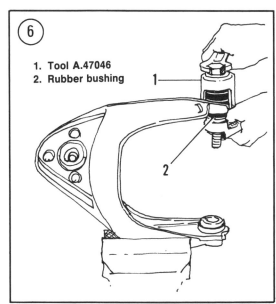

1. Tool A.47046
2. Rubber bushing

1. Set the handbrake. Place the transmission in FIRST (manual) or PARK (automatic).
2. Loosen the front wheel nuts. Jack up the front end of the car, place it on jackstands and remove the front wheels.
3. Remove the shock absorbers as described in this chapter.
4. Place a coil spring compressor such as Fiat part No. A.74174 (Kent-Moore part No. J28131) on the front spring. Compress the spring enough to relieve tension on the control arms.

5. Detach the sway bar from the lower control arm.
6. Detach the tie rod from the steering knuckle as described under *Steering* in this chapter.
7. Unbolt the caliper as described in Chapter Eleven and tie it out of the way. It is not necessary to disconnect the caliper brake hose.

CAUTION
Do not let the caliper hang by the hose or the hose may be damaged.

8. Remove the brake disc as described in Chapter Eleven.
9. Remove the front hub and wheel bearings as described in this chapter.
10. Unbolt the splash shield from the inner wheel well and take it out.
11. Make sure all spring tension is removed from the upper control arm. If the coil spring compressor will not compress the spring far enough, place a jack beneath the lower control arm and raise it just enough so the spring tension is removed from the upper control arm.
12. Remove the nut from the upper control arm pivot bolt. See **Figure 3**. Drive the bolt out with a hammer and brass drift.

NOTE
During the next step, write down the number of shims (if any) found between the lower control arm and crossmember.

13. Remove the nuts that secure the lower control arm to the crossmember. See **Figure 3**. If a jack was used under the lower control arm, lower it. Take the control arms, spring and ball-joints off the car.
14. Take the spring off the lower control arm.

Control Arm and Ball-Joint Disassembly/Assembly

This procedure requires several special tools. If you do not have them, take the parts to a dealer or machine shop for disassembly and assembly.
1. Secure the lower control arm in a vise as shown in **Figure 4**.
2. Detach the steering arm, caliper bracket and brake disc backing plate from the steering knuckle.
3. Remove the stud nut from each ball-joint.
4. Press the ball-joints out of the steering knuckle with a puller such as Fiat tool part No. A.47042 (Kent-Moore part No. J28015). See **Figure 5**.
5. Secure the upper control arm in a vise. Press the bushings out with Fiat tool part No. A.47046 (**Figure 6**). Press new bushings in with the same tool.

9

6. Remove the lower control arm bushings with a press and Fiat tool part No. A.47045 (**Figure 7**). Install the bushings with tools A.74177/1 and A.74177/2 (**Figure 8**).

7. Check ball-joints for looseness, wear or damage. Have the ball-joints replaced by a dealer or front-end shop if these conditions are found. Replacement ball-joints are available from dealers and aftermarket suppliers.

8. Reassemble the control arms and ball-joints by reversing Steps 1-4. Tighten all fasteners to specifications in **Table 2**.

Control Arm, Ball-joint and Spring Installation

1. Attach the lower control arm to the crossmember with the 2 nuts. Be sure to install shims (if removed) in their original locations.

2. Place the spring on the lower control arm.

3. Compress the spring with Fiat tool part No. A.74174 (Kent-Moore part No. J28131). Place the pad on the upper end of the spring, then position the upper end of the spring in the body recess.

4. Attach the upper end of the control arm to the body with the pivot bolt and nut. Do not tighten the nut yet.

> *NOTE*
> *If necessary, place a jack beneath the lower control arm and raise it slightly to align the upper control arm with the body.*

5. Slowly release the spring compressor and let the lower end of the spring position itself in the control arm.

6. Install the shock absorber. Tighten its fasteners to specifications in **Table 2**.

7. Attach the sway bar to the control arm and tighten its nuts to specifications.

8. Attach the tie rod to the steering knuckle and tighten its stud nut to specifications.

9. Install the hub and wheel bearings as described in this chapter.

10. Install the brake disc and caliper as described in Chapter Eleven.

11. Install the wheels, lower the car and tighten the wheel nuts.

12. Make sure the steering wheel is in the straight-ahead position.

13. Tighten the control arm fasteners (**Figure 9**) to specifications with 2 passengers and 59 kg (130 lb.) of luggage in the car. This is necessary to prevent distorting the bushings.

14. Pump the brake pedal several times to seat the pads. Make sure the pedal is firm before driving the car.

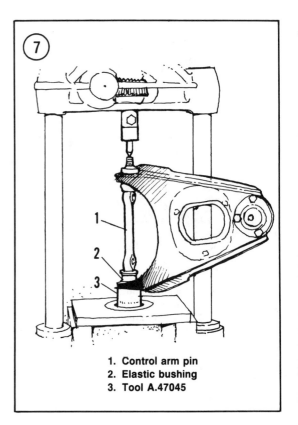

1. Control arm pin
2. Elastic bushing
3. Tool A.47045

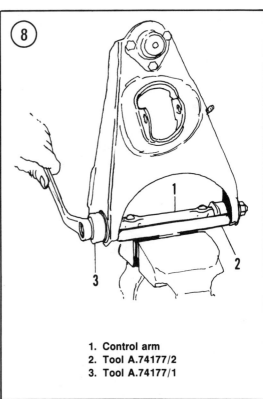

1. Control arm
2. Tool A.74177/2
3. Tool A.74177/1

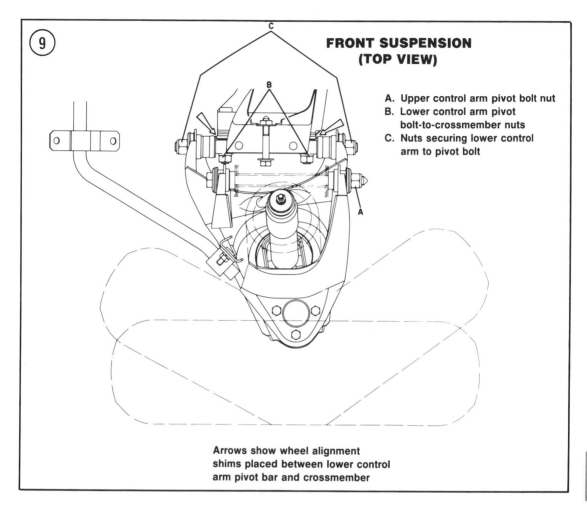

⑨ **FRONT SUSPENSION (TOP VIEW)**

A. Upper control arm pivot bolt nut
B. Lower control arm pivot bolt-to-crossmember nuts
C. Nuts securing lower control arm to pivot bolt

Arrows show wheel alignment shims placed between lower control arm pivot bar and crossmember

9

1. Engine support tool A.70526

Crossmember Removal/Installation

1. Support the engine with Fiat tool A.70526 (**Figure 10**).

2. Remove the control arms, ball-joints and springs as described in this chapter.

3. Referring to **Figure 3**, detach the crossmember from the frame and engine mounts. Take the crossmember out.

4. Installation is the reverse of removal. Tighten all fasteners to specifications in **Table 2**.

WHEEL BEARINGS

Figure 11 shows the front wheel bearings and related parts.

Removal

1. Set the handbrake. Place the transmission in FIRST (manual) or PARK (automatic).

2. Loosen the front wheel nuts. Jack up the front end of the car, place it on jackstands and remove the front wheels.

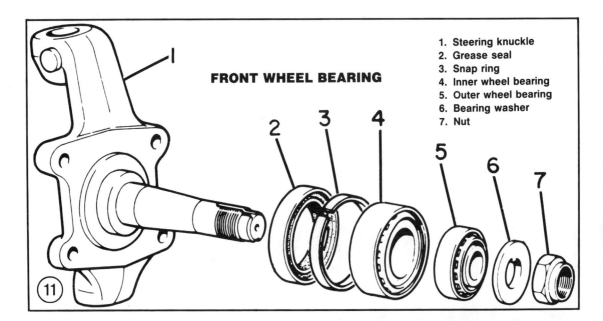

FRONT WHEEL BEARING

1. Steering knuckle
2. Grease seal
3. Snap ring
4. Inner wheel bearing
5. Outer wheel bearing
6. Bearing washer
7. Nut

3. Detach the caliper from the mounting bracket and tie it up out of the way. It is not necessary to disconnect the caliper brake hose.

CAUTION
Do not let the caliper hang by the brake hose.

4. Remove the caliper mounting bracket and brake disc as described in Chapter Eleven.

5. Pry off the wheel bearing grease cap.

6. Note that the lip of the wheel bearing nut is staked. Carefully bend back the staked portions with a hammer and punch, then remove the nut and washer.

7. Pull the hub off the steering knuckle, together with the outer bearing, inner bearing cone and roller assembly, snap ring and seal.

8. The inner bearing race may stay on the spindle at the point shown in **Figure 12**. If it does, pry it off gently with 2 screwdrivers or small pry bars.

9. Remove the grease seal and snap ring from the hub. See **Figure 13** and **Figure 14**.

10. Remove the bearing cones from the hub. See **Figure 15**.

11. Carefully tap the bearing inner races out of the hub with a soft metal drift. Tap at alternating angles as shown in **Figure 16** so the races won't tilt sideways and jam. **Figure 17** shows the bearing cones and inner races after removal.

Inspection

1. Thoroughly clean all parts in solvent. While cleaning, check all parts for obvious wear or damage. Replace worn or damaged parts. Always

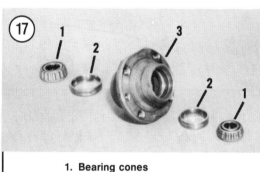

1. Bearing cones
2. Outer races
3. Hub

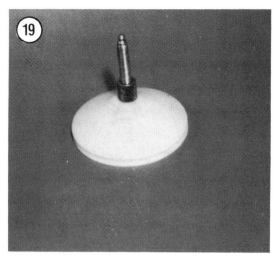

replace the grease seal whenever the wheel bearings are removed.

2. Check the bearing cones and outer races for wear, chips, pits, flaking, scratches or rust. Replace the bearings if there is any doubt about their condition. Cones and outer races are replaced as assemblies.

3. Check the spindle for cracks or rust. Replace the spindle if these can be seen. If you suspect the spindle may be cracked but can't see any damage, have the spindle checked by a machine shop.

Installation

1. Make sure all parts are clean.

2. Tap the outer races into the hub. If available, use a bearing driver as shown in **Figure 18**. If not, tap evenly around the circumference of the races with a drift. Be careful not to let the races tilt sideways and jam.

3. Once the races are installed, pack the bearing cones with grease. Inexpensive bearing packers like the one shown in **Figure 19** are designed to work with grease guns and are available at auto parts stores. If you do not have access to a bearing packer, work as much grease as possible between the bearing rollers with your hands.

4. Install the bearing cones in the hub, then install the snap ring and grease seal.

5. Install the hub and bearings on the spindle.

6. Install the bearing washer on the spindle.

7. Install the spindle nut. Tighten it to 2 mkg (14.5 ft.-lb.) and at the same time turn the hub 4 or 5 times in each direction to seat the bearings.

8. Loosen the nut, then retighten to 0.7 mkg (5 ft.-lb.).

9. Loosen the nut 30°. To measure this, make a chisel mark in the wheel bearing washer halfway

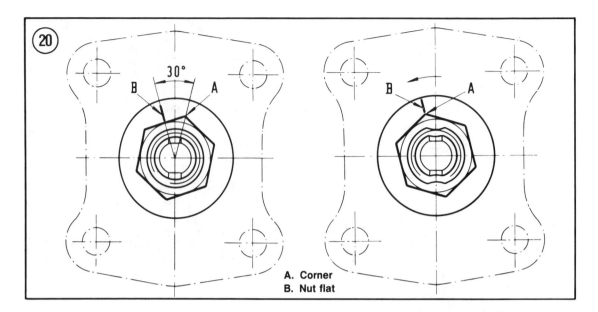

A. Corner
B. Nut flat

across one of the nut flats (B, **Figure 20**). Then loosen the nut until its nearest corner (A, **Figure 20**) is next to the chisel mark.

> *NOTE*
> **Figure 20** *shows the left wheel, which has right-hand threads (tightens clockwise). The right wheel has left-hand threads (tightens counter-clockwise). When adjusting the right-hand wheel bearings, turn the nut in the direction opposite that shown in* **Figure 20**.

10. Lock the nut in position by crimping its lip with Fiat tool part No. A.74140 (Kent-Moore part No. J28213). See **Figure 21**. If the tool is not available, stake the nut at 2 points with a hammer and chisel.
11. Fill the grease cap with grease and tap it gently into position in the hub.
12. Install the caliper bracket, brake disc and caliper as described in Chapter Eleven.
13. Install the wheels, lower the car and tighten the wheel nuts.
14. Pump the brake pedal several times to seat the pads before driving the car.

STEERING

All models use worm and roller steering. **Figure 22** shows the steering mechanism.

Steering Wheel
Removal/Installation

1. Place the steering wheel and front wheels in the straight-ahead position.

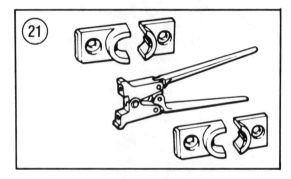

2. Disconnect the negative cable from the battery.
3. Pull the horn button off the steering wheel. See **Figure 23**. Unplug the horn wires.
4. Remove the steering wheel nut (**Figure 23**). Make alignment marks on the steering wheel and column, then pull the steering wheel off the column.
5. Installation is the reverse of removal. Align the match marks on steering wheel and column. Tighten the steering wheel nut to specifications in **Table 2**.

Steering Gear Removal/Installation

1. Set the handbrake. Place the transmission in FIRST (manual) or PARK (automatic).
2. Loosen the front wheel nuts. Jack up the front end of the car, place it on jackstands and remove the front wheels.
3. Mark one side of the intermediate rod (arrow, **Figure 24**) so it can be reinstalled in the same position. Detach the intermediate rod and tie rod from the pitman arm.

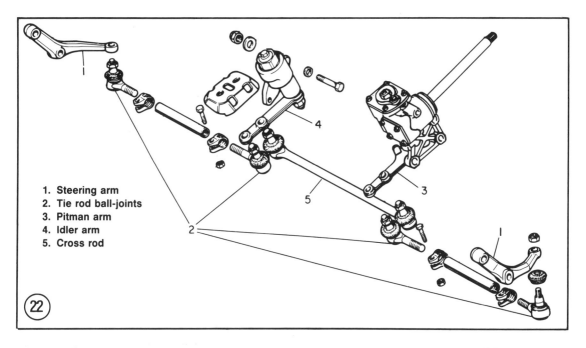

1. Steering arm
2. Tie rod ball-joints
3. Pitman arm
4. Idler arm
5. Cross rod

1. Tool A.47038   2. Cross rod   3. Tie rod

9

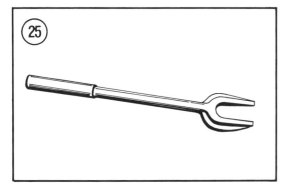

NOTE
*If the tie rod and intermediate rod are difficult to separate, use a fork-type separator (**Figure 25**). These are available from tool rental dealers.*

4. Remove the starter as described in Chapter Seven.

5. Remove the lower bolt from the left wheel well splash shield to gain access to the steering gear mounting nuts. See **Figure 26**.

6. Remove the steering gear mounting nuts and bolts.

7. Pull the steering gear shaft into the firewall, away from the steering gear. Take the steering gear out.

8. Installation is the reverse of removal. Tighten all fasteners to specifications in **Table 2**. Make sure the intermediate rod mark is in the position it was in before removal.

Idler Arm/Steering Damper Removal/Installation

1. Set the handbrake. Place the transmission in FIRST (manual) or PARK (automatic).
2. Loosen the front wheel nuts. Jack up the front end of the car, place it on jackstands and remove the front wheels.
3. Detach the intermediate rod and tie rod from the idler arm. See **Figure 27**.

> *NOTE*
> *If the intermediate rod and tie rod are difficult to detach, use a fork-type separator (Figure 25). These are available from tool rental dealers.*

4. Remove the lower bolt from the right wheel well access panel to gain access to the idler arm mounting nuts. Remove the nuts and bolts (**Figure 27**) and take the idler arm out.
5. Installation is the reverse of removal. Tighten all fasteners to specifications in **Table 2**.

Steering Linkage Removal/Installation

Refer to **Figure 22** for this procedure.
1. Set the handbrake. Place the transmission in FIRST (manual) or PARK (automatic).
2. Loosen the front wheel nuts. Jack up the front end of the car, place it on jackstands and remove the front wheels.
3. Detach the tie rod ends from the steering arms, idler arm and pitman arm.

> *NOTE*
> *If the tie rod and intermediate rod are difficult to separate, use a fork-type separator (Figure 25). These are available from tool rental dealers.*

4. Mark the bottom side of the intermediate rod so it can be reinstalled in the same position.
5. Detach the intermediate rod ends from the idler arm and knuckle arm.
6. Check all parts for wear or damage. Make sure tie rod ends and intermediate rod ends (**Figure 28**) are not loose. Make sure the studs and rubber boots are in good condition. If a tie rod end shows any of these conditions, replace it. If an intermediate rod end shows any of these

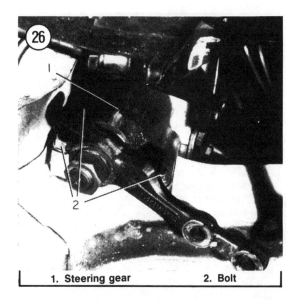

1. Steering gear   2. Bolt

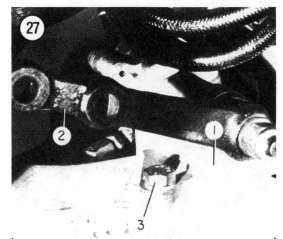

1. Idler arm bracket   2. Idler arm   3. Bolt

conditions, replace the intermediate rod as an assembly.

7. Installation is the reverse of removal, plus the following:
   a. Replace self-locking nuts if they can be threaded easily onto the studs.
   b. Tighten all self-locking nuts to 3.5 mkg (25 ft.-lb.).
   c. Have toe-in adjusted by a Fiat dealer or front-end shop.

WHEEL ALIGNMENT

Several suspension angles affect the running and steering of the front wheels. These angles must be properly aligned to prevent excessive wear, as well

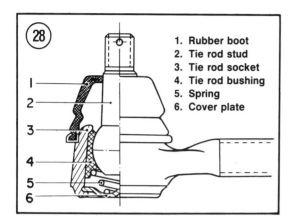

1. Rubber boot
2. Tie rod stud
3. Tie rod socket
4. Tie rod bushing
5. Spring
6. Cover plate

as to maintain directional stability and ease of steering. The angles are as follows:

   a. Caster.
   b. Camber.
   c. Toe-in.
   d. Steering axis inclination.
   e. Steering lock angles.

None of the angles except toe-in should be adjusted without a front-end rack. Toe-in can be adjusted as described in this chapter.

Pre-alignment Check

Adjustment of the steering and various suspension angles is affected by several factors. Perform the following steps before any adjustments are attempted.

1. Check tire presssure and wear. See *Tire Wear Analysis*, Chapter Two.
2. Check play in front wheel bearings. Adjust if necessary.
3. Check play in ball-joints.
4. Check for broken springs.
5. Remove any excessive load.
6. Check shock absorbers.
7. Check steering gear for wear or damage.
8. Check play in steering linkage.
9. Check wheel balance.
10. Check rear suspension for looseness.

Front tire wear patterns can indicate several alignment problems. These are covered under *Tire Wear Analysis*, Chapter Two.

Caster and Camber

Caster is the inclination from vertical of the line through the ball-joints. Positive caster shifts the wheel forward; negative caster shifts the wheel rearward. Caster causes the wheels to return to a straight-ahead position after a turn. It also prevents the wheels from wandering due to wind, potholes, or uneven road surfaces.

Camber is the inclination of the wheel from vertical. With positive camber, the top of the tire leans outward. With negative camber, the top of the tire leans inward.

Toe-in

Since the front wheels tend to point outward when the car is moving forward, the distance between the front edges of the tire is slightly less than the distance between the rear edges when the car is at rest.

Although toe-in adjustment requires only a simple home-made tool, it usually isn't worth the trouble for home mechanics. Alignment shops include toe-in as part of the alignment procedure, so you probably won't save any money by doing it yourself. The procedure described here can be used for an initial toe-in setting after steering linkage overhaul or suspension repairs.

1. With the steering wheel centered, roll forward about 15 ft. onto a smooth, level surface.
2. Mark the center of the tread at the front and rear of each tire.
3. Measure the distance between forward chalk marks. Use 2 pieces of telescoping aluminum tubing. Telescope the tubing so each end contacts a chalk mark. Using a sharp scribe, mark the small diameter tubing where it enters the large diameter tubing.
4. Measure between the rear chalk marks with the telescoping tubes. Make another mark on the small tube where it enters the large one. The distance between the 2 scribe marks is toe-in.

If toe-in is incorrect, loosen the tie rod locknuts. See **Figure 29** (left side) or **Figure 30** (right side). Rotate the tie rods as shown to change toe-in, then tighten the clamps.

> *NOTE*
> *Rotate the left and right tie rods an equal number of turns.*

Steering Axis Inclination

Steering axis inclination is the inward or outward lean of the line through the ball-joints. It is not adjustable.

Steering Lock Angles

When a car turns, the inside wheel makes a smaller circle than the outside wheel. Because of this, the inside wheel turns at a greater angle than the outside wheel. This angle is not adjustable.

9

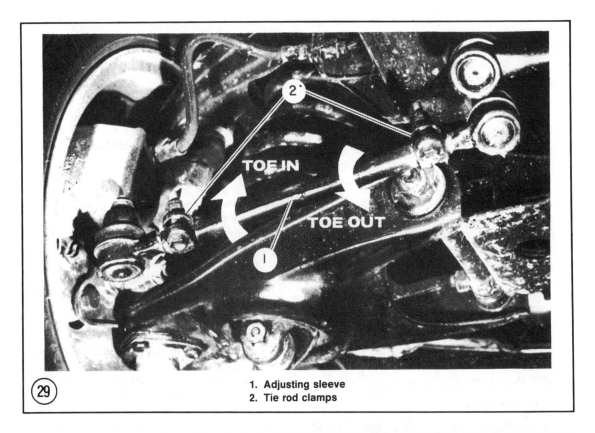

1. Adjusting sleeve
2. Tie rod clamps

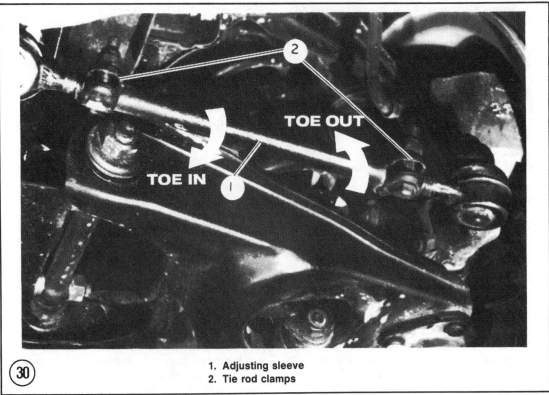

1. Adjusting sleeve
2. Tie rod clamps

Table 1 FRONT SUSPENSION SPECIFICATIONS

Caster*	
1971-1972	3° 30', −10', +30'
1973-on	3° 30' ±30'
Camber*	0° 30' ±30'
Toe-in*	3 ±2 mm (0.120 ±0.039 in.)
Steering axis inclination	6°
Steering lock angles	
Inner wheel	35° 50' ±1° 30'
Outer wheel	28° 30'
Load factor	
1971-1972 Coupe	3 persons plus 66 lb. luggage
1973-1974 Coupe	2 persons plus 44 lb. luggage
1975 Coupe	4 persons plus 90 lb. luggage
1971-1974 Spider	2 persons plus 44 lb. luggage
1975-on Spider	2 persons plus 130 lb. luggage

* These angles are measured @ the indicated load factor.

Table 2 TIGHTENING TORQUES

Fastener	Thread size	mkg	ft.-lb.
Wheel bearing nut	See text		
Crossmember-to-side member bolts	M12×1.25	9.5	69
Crossmember to side member lower nuts	M10×1.25	5.5	40
Lower control arm to crossmember nut	M12×1.25	6	43
Lower control arm pin to crossmember nut	M14×1.5	10	72
Upper control arm nut	M14×1.5	9	65
Shock absorber upper nut	M8	1.5	11
Shock absorber lower nut	M10×1.25	6	43
Caliper carrier plate bolt	M10×1.25	5	36
Steering wheel nut	M16×1.5	5	36
Steering gear to body			
1971-1974	M10×1.25	4	29
1975-on*	M10×1.25	3	22
Hydraulic damper (idler arm) to body			
1971-1974	M10×1.25	4	29
1975-on	M10×1.25	3	22
Tie rod end nuts			
1971-1974	M10×1.25	3	22
1975-on*	M10×1.25	3.5	25

* Self-locking nut.

9

REAR SUSPENSION, DIFFERENTIAL AND DRIVE SHAFT

All models use a live rear axle with coil springs and tube shock absorbers. The axle is located by upper and lower reaction rods and a cross rod (panhard rod). A 2-section drive shaft connects the transmission to the rear axle.

REAR SUSPENSION

Shock Absorber and Spring
Removal/Installation

1. Securely block both front wheels so the car will not roll in either direction.
2. Loosen the rear wheel nuts. Jack up the rear end of the car, place it on jackstands and remove the rear wheels.

WARNING
Do not skip the next step or the axle will drop with sudden force when the shock absorber nut is removed.

3. Place a jack beneath the end of the rear axle. Raise the jack slightly to compress the spring and release the tension on the shock absorber upper nut.

NOTE
Before the next step, stuff a shop cloth behind the shock absorber upper end so the nut doesn't fall into one of the crevices in that area.

4. Working in the trunk, hold the shock absorber shaft from turning with a wrench. Remove the upper nut, washer and bushing from the shock absorber shaft. See **Figure 1**.

5. Lower the jack and let the axle hang by its own weight.
6. Push the upper half of the shock absorber all the way down, so the shock absorber is fully compressed. See **Figure 2**.

WARNING
During the next step, do not pry on the spring if it is still compressed between the body and axle housing. This may allow the spring to fly out with sudden force and cause serious injury.

7. The upper end of the spring should have separated from the body during Step 5. See **Figure 3**. If not, pry the spring gently downward to separate it from the body.
8. Remove the bolt and nut that secure the lower end of the shock absorber. See **Figure 4**. Tilt the spring outboard, then take the shock absorber off.

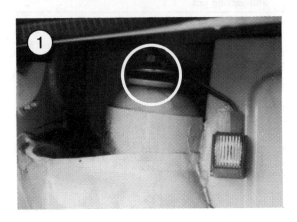

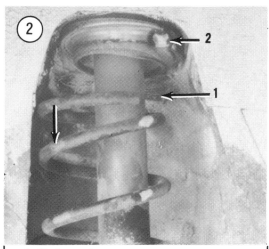

1. Spring end
2. Depression in spring seat

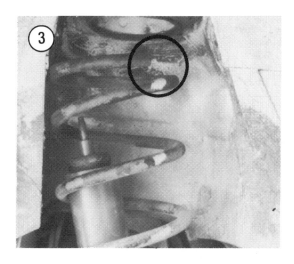

9. If spring removal is necessary, take the spring out.

NOTE
Check for a color stripe on the spring. Springs are marked with a green or yellow stripe. All 4 springs (front and rear) must be marked with the same color.

10. Installation is the reverse of removal, plus the following:
   a. Make sure the upper end of the spring aligns with the depression in the upper spring seat (**Figure 2**).
   b. Tighten all fasteners to specifications in **Table 1**.

Reaction Rod and Cross Rod Removal/Installation

1. Securely block both front wheels so the car will not roll in either direction.
2. Loosen the rear wheel nuts. Jack up the rear end of the car, place it on jackstands and remove the rear wheels.
3. Place a jack beneath the center of the axle to raise or lower it.

WARNING
To prevent the axle from falling, remove and install one rod at a time.

4. Remove the rod mounting bolts and nuts and take the rod out. See **Figure 5** (lower reaction rods), **Figure 6** (upper reaction rods) or **Figure 7** (cross rod).
5. Check the rods for cracks, bending, rust or other damage. Replace rods that show these conditions. Check rod bushings for wear, cracks or deterioration. On 1971-1972 models, have the old bushings pressed out and new ones pressed in by a machine shop. On 1973 and later models, replace the entire rod if the bushings are bad.
6. Installation is the reverse of removal, plus the following:
   a. Tighten rod nuts and bolts slightly while the car is on jackstands.
   b. Install the wheels, lower the car and tighten the wheel nuts.
   c. Load the car with the equivalent of 2 people and 59 kg (130 lb.) of luggage. Then tighten the rod nuts and bolts to specifications in **Table 1**. This is necessary to prevent strain on the bushings.

REAR AXLE

This section describes all rear axle service procedures practical for home mechanics. Some

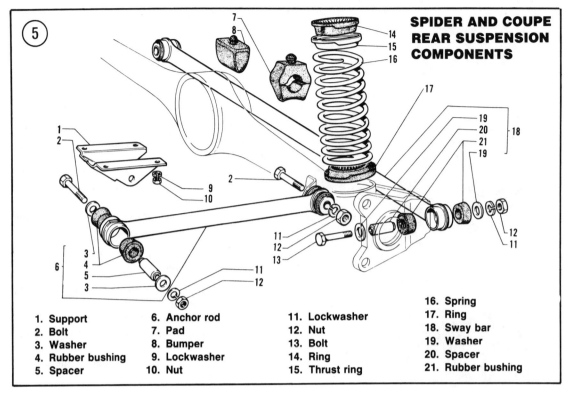

⑤

SPIDER AND COUPE REAR SUSPENSION COMPONENTS

1. Support	6. Anchor rod	11. Lockwasher	16. Spring
2. Bolt	7. Pad	12. Nut	17. Ring
3. Washer	8. Bumper	13. Bolt	18. Sway bar
4. Rubber bushing	9. Lockwasher	14. Ring	19. Washer
5. Spacer	10. Nut	15. Thrust ring	20. Spacer
			21. Rubber bushing

SPIDER AND COUPE REAR SUSPENSION COMPONENTS

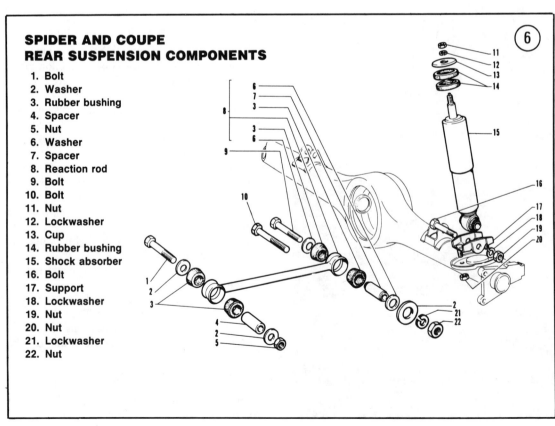

⑥

1. Bolt
2. Washer
3. Rubber bushing
4. Spacer
5. Nut
6. Washer
7. Spacer
8. Reaction rod
9. Bolt
10. Bolt
11. Nut
12. Lockwasher
13. Cup
14. Rubber bushing
15. Shock absorber
16. Bolt
17. Support
18. Lockwasher
19. Nut
20. Nut
21. Lockwasher
22. Nut

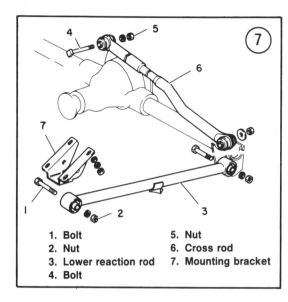

7

1. Bolt
2. Nut
3. Lower reaction rod
4. Bolt
5. Nut
6. Cross rod
7. Mounting bracket

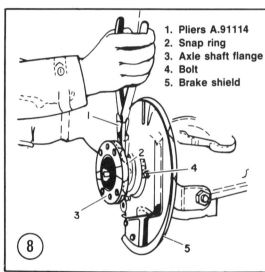

8

1. Pliers A.91114
2. Snap ring
3. Axle shaft flange
4. Bolt
5. Brake shield

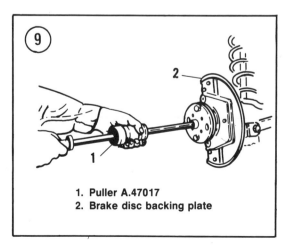

9

1. Puller A.47017
2. Brake disc backing plate

procedures require special skills and tools and should be done by a dealer or other qualified specialist.

**Axle Shaft Removal
(Through Early 1978)**

1. Securely block both front wheels so the car will not roll in either direction.
2. Loosen the rear wheel nuts. Jack up the rear end of the car, place it on jackstands and remove the rear wheels.
3. Remove the rear brake calipers and discs as described in Chapter Eleven.
4. Unbolt the brake disc backing plate from the axle housing. See **Figure 8**. Remove the axle shaft snap ring with snap ring pliers.
5. Remove the axle shaft with a puller as shown in **Figure 9**. Pullers are available from tool rental dealers.
6. Referring to **Figure 10**, remove the O-ring from the axle housing.
7. Carefully pry the oil seal (**Figure 10**) out of the axle housing. Do not damage any machined surfaces.

**Rear Wheel Bearing Replacement
(Through Early 1978)**

This procedure requires a press and support tools. If you do not have the proper equipment, take the job to a machine shop.

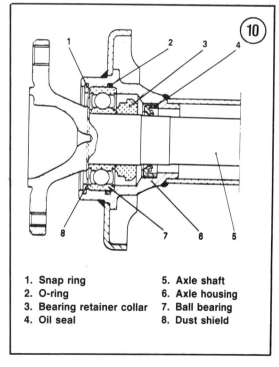

10

10

1. Snap ring
2. O-ring
3. Bearing retainer collar
4. Oil seal
5. Axle shaft
6. Axle housing
7. Ball bearing
8. Dust shield

1. Remove the axle shaft as described in this chapter.

2. Place the axle shaft in a press as shown in **Figure 11**. Press the retaining collar off.

3. Remove the bearing, dust shield and snap ring from the axle shaft.

4. Check the shaft for bending or damage. Replace the shaft if these conditions exist.

5. Position the axle shaft components on the shaft as shown in **Figure 12**. Press the parts on until the bearing is locked betwen the axle shaft shoulder and retaining collar.

6. Make sure the bearing and retaining collar fit securely on the shaft and cannot be moved.

Axle Shaft Installation
(Through Early 1978)

Installation is the reverse of removal, plus the following.

1. Install a new oil seal. If available, use a seal driver such as Fiat tool part No. A.70157 (Kent-Moore part No. J28252). See **Figure 13**. Similar seal drivers are available from auto parts stores. If a seal driver is not available, use a drift the same diameter as the seal.

2. Install a new O-ring in the axle housing.

Axle Shaft Removal
(Mid-1978 and Later)

1. Securely block both front wheels so the car will not roll in either direction.

2. Loosen the rear wheel nuts. Jack up the rear end of the car, place it on jackstands and remove the rear wheels.

3. Remove the rear brake calipers and discs as described in Chapter Eleven.

4. Unbolt the brake disc backing plate and caliper mounting bracket from the axle housing. See **Figure 14**. Remove the axle shaft snap ring with snap ring pliers.

5. Referring to **Figure 15**, remove the O-ring from the axle housing.

6. Carefully pry the oil seal (**Figure 15**) out of the axle housing. Do not damage any machined surfaces.

Rear Wheel Bearing Replacement
(Mid-1978 and Later)

This procedure requires a press and support tools. If you do not have the proper equipment, take the job to a machine shop.

1. Remove the axle shaft as described in this chapter.

2. Place the axle shaft in a press as shown in **Figure 11**. Press the retaining collar off.

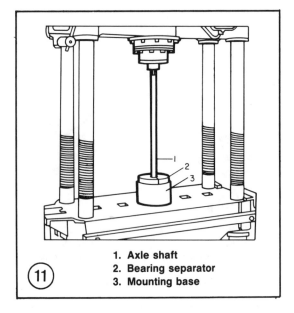

1. Axle shaft
2. Bearing separator
3. Mounting base

⑪

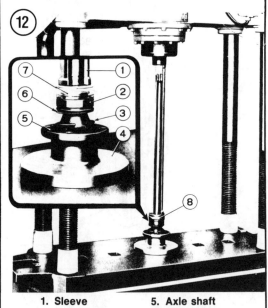

⑫

1. Sleeve	5. Axle shaft
2. Ball bearing	6. Dust shield
3. Snap ring	7. Retaining collar
4. Base plate	8. Collar holder

⑬

1. Axle shaft flange   3. Brake disc backing plate
2. Bolt   4. Caliper mounting bracket

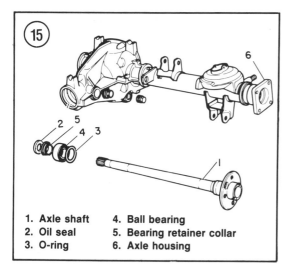

1. Axle shaft   4. Ball bearing
2. Oil seal   5. Bearing retainer collar
3. O-ring   6. Axle housing

3. Remove the bearing, dust shield and snap ring from the axle shaft.

4. Check the shaft for bending or damage. Replace the shaft if these conditions exist.

5. Position the axle shaft components on the shaft as shown in **Figure 16**. Press the parts on until the bearing is locked between the axle shaft shoulder and retaining collar.

6. Make sure the bearing and retaining collar fit securely on the shaft and cannot be moved.

Axle Shaft Installation
(Mid-1978 and Later)

Installation is the reverse of removal, plus the following.

1. Install a new oil seal. If available, use a seal driver such as Fiat tool part No. A.70157 (Kent-Moore part No. J28252). See **Figure 13**. Similar seal drivers are available from auto parts stores. If a seal driver is not available, use a drift the same diameter as the seal.

2. Install a new O-ring in the axle housing.

Differential

Models through early 1978 use a conventional differential, which is removed as a unit. Mid-1978 and later models use a unitized differential, which is integral with the axle housing. To tell which type you have, look at the back of the axle housing. Unitized differentials have a bolt-on inspection cover on the back of the axle housing; conventional differentials do not.

The following sections provide removal, inspection and installation procedures. Differential

10

1. Sleeve
2. Retaining collar
3. Roller bearing
4. Caliper mounting bracket
5. Axle flange
6. Mounting base

repair requires special skills and many special tools. Having the differential rebuilt by a professional is the easiest, least expensive way to go. The inspection procedures will tell you if repairs are needed.

Removal/installation
(conventional type)

1. Remove the axle shafts as described in this chapter.
2. Mark the drive shaft and differential flanges so they can be reassembled in the same relative positions. See **Figure 17**. Unbolt the drive shaft from the differential.
3. Place a pan under the differential. Remove the drain plug and let the oil drain.
4. Remove the differential mounting bolts (**Figure 18**). Take the differential out.
5. Installation is the reverse of removal. Use a new gasket, coated on both sides with gasket sealer. Tighten all nuts and bolts to specifications (**Table 1**). Fill the differential as described in Chapter Three.

Inspection (conventional type)

1. Place the differential on a workbench.
2. Look for visible wear or damage. Check the gears for chipped or missing teeth.
3. Check the tooth contact pattern of the ring gear:
   a. Apply a thin, even coat of gear marking compound to the ring gear teeth.
   b. Hold the pinion to create resistance and turn the ring gear approximately 15 turns in each direction. This will press the contact pattern of the gear teeth into the marking compound.
   c. Compare the contact pattern with **Figures 19-23** to determine differential condition.

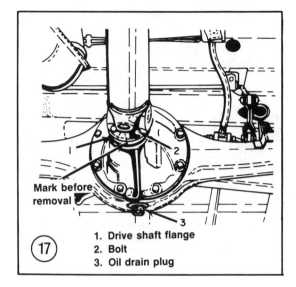

Mark before removal
1. Drive shaft flange
2. Bolt
3. Oil drain plug

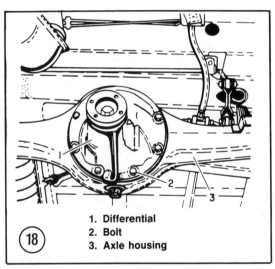

1. Differential
2. Bolt
3. Axle housing

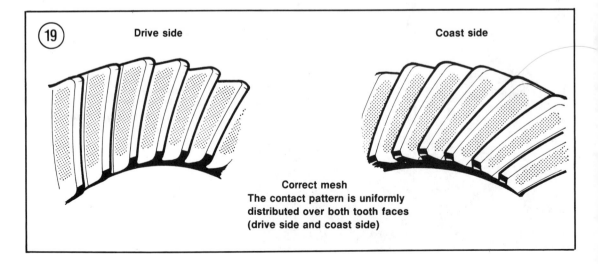

Drive side   Coast side

Correct mesh
The contact pattern is uniformly distributed over both tooth faces (drive side and coast side)

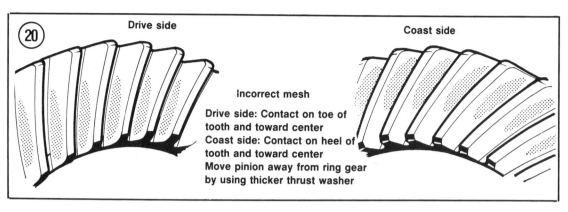

Drive side   Coast side

Incorrect mesh

Drive side: Contact on toe of
tooth and toward center
Coast side: Contact on heel of
tooth and toward center
Move pinion away from ring gear
by using thicker thrust washer

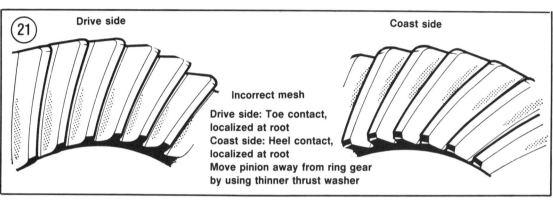

Drive side   Coast side

Incorrect mesh

Drive side: Toe contact,
localized at root
Coast side: Heel contact,
localized at root
Move pinion away from ring gear
by using thinner thrust washer

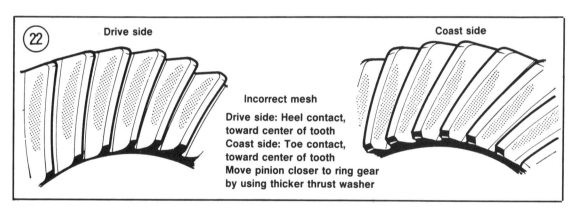

Drive side   Coast side

Incorrect mesh

Drive side: Heel contact,
toward center of tooth
Coast side: Toe contact,
toward center of tooth
Move pinion closer to ring gear
by using thicker thrust washer

10

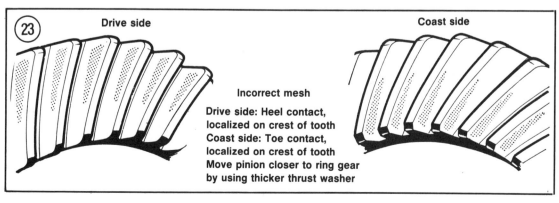

Drive side   Coast side

Incorrect mesh

Drive side: Heel contact,
localized on crest of tooth
Coast side: Toe contact,
localized on crest of tooth
Move pinion closer to ring gear
by using thicker thrust washer

Inspection (unitized type)

This is basically the same as for the conventional differential. The unitized differential need not be removed from the car. To gain access, drain the oil, then remove the inspection plate (**Figure 24**). Compare the contact pattern with **Figures 25-29** to determine differential condition.

Removal/installation (unitized type)

Special tools are required to remove the unitized differential from the axle housing. You may be able to save some of the labor cost by removing the axle housing and shafts yourself and bringing the axle housing to a shop for differential removal. However, this should be discussed with the shop beforehand. It may be more practical (and no more expensive) to take the car to the shop and have the entire job done there.

DRIVE SHAFT

Figure 30 shows the drive shaft.

Removal/Installation

1. Securely block both front wheels so the car will not roll in either direction.
2. Loosen the rear wheel nuts. Jack up the rear end of the car, place it on jackstands and remove the rear wheels.
3. Secure the flexible coupling with a band such as Fiat tool part No. A.70025 (Kent-Moore part No. J28087). **Figure 31** shows the tool in use; **Figure 32** shows it alone.
4. Unbolt the pillow block crossmember and front protection bracket. See **Figure 33**.
5. Make match marks on the drive shaft and differential flanges so they can be reassembled in the same relative positions. Unbolt the drive shaft

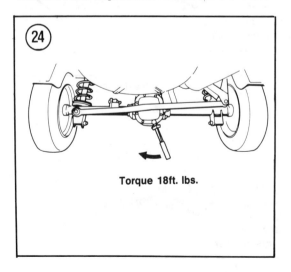

Torque 18ft. lbs.

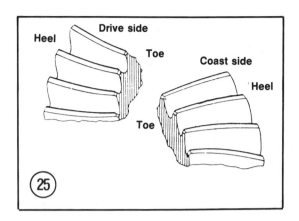

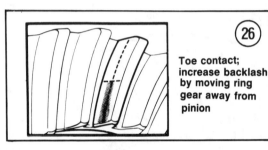

Toe contact; increase backlash by moving ring gear away from pinion

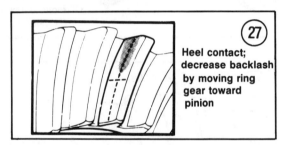

Heel contact; decrease backlash by moving ring gear toward pinion

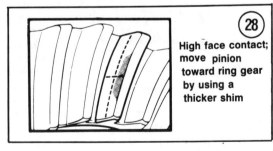

High face contact; move pinion toward ring gear by using a thicker shim

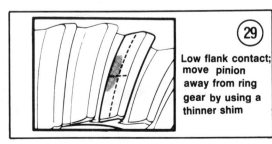

Low flank contact; move pinion away from ring gear by using a thinner shim

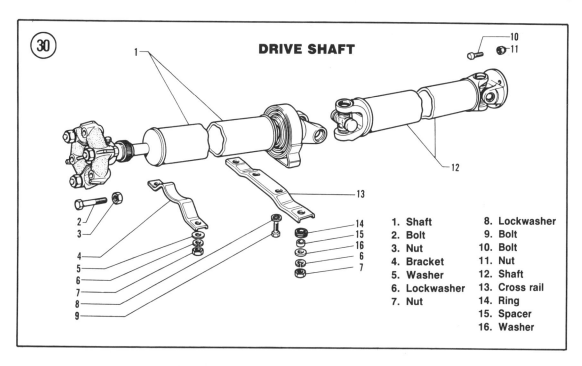

DRIVE SHAFT

1. Shaft	8. Lockwasher
2. Bolt	9. Bolt
3. Nut	10. Bolt
4. Bracket	11. Nut
5. Washer	12. Shaft
6. Lockwasher	13. Cross rail
7. Nut	14. Ring
	15. Spacer
	16. Washer

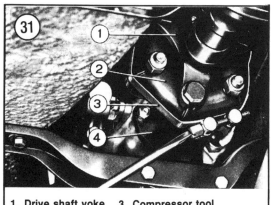

1. Drive shaft yoke
2. Flexible coupling
3. Compressor tool
4. Transmission mounting member

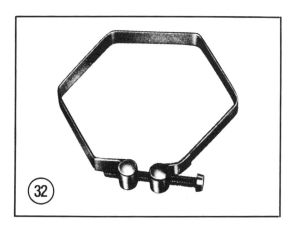

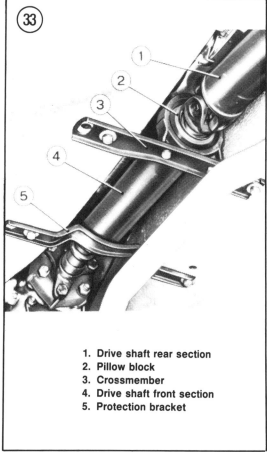

1. Drive shaft rear section
2. Pillow block
3. Crossmember
4. Drive shaft front section
5. Protection bracket

10

from the differential (**Figure 34**), then take the drive shaft out.

6. Installation is the reverse of removal. Align the match marks on drive shaft and differential flanges.

Universal Joint
Inspection/Replacement

1. Pull and twist universal joints to check for looseness. Replace loose universal joints.

2. If replacement is necessary, refer to **Figure 35**. Place the U-joint in a vise and remove the snap rings as shown in **Figure 36**. Tap the spider loose from the yoke with a hammer and drift as shown in **Figure 37**. Lubricate the new universal joints with multipurpose grease.

Center Pillow Block Replacement

This procedure requires a press and several special tools. Although most of the tools can be rented, it may be cheaper to have the center pillow block replaced by a dealer or machine shop.

Refer to **Figure 38**.

1. Remove the drive shaft as described in this chapter. Detach the crossmember from the center pillow block.

2. Separate the univeral joint spider from the center yoke as shown in **Figure 36** and **Figure 37**.

3. Make match marks on the drive shaft and front sleeve.

4. Place the sleeve in a vise and remove the sleeve-to-shaft nut. See **Figure 39**.

5. Remove the sleeve and dust cover with a puller as shown in **Figure 40**.

6. Press the drive shaft out of the pillow block with a press as shown in **Figure 41**.

7. Remove the bearing snap ring from the pillow block with snap ring pliers. See **Figure 42**. Pull the bearing out with a universal puller.

8. Press a new bearing into the pillow block with a press and drift. See **Figure 43**. Install the snap ring.

9. Place the dust cover on the drive shaft, then install the pillow block with a drift as shown in **Figure 44**.

10. Position the sleeve on the shaft so the match marks align. Install the nut (**Figure 45**), tighten it to 69 ft.-lb. and stake the nut in place.

11. Position the U-joint spider in the sleeve and secure it with snap rings. See **Figure 36**.

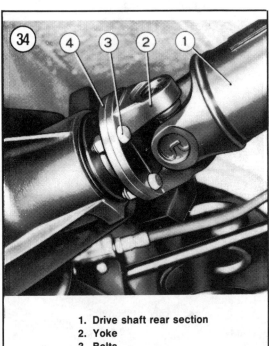

1. Drive shaft rear section
2. Yoke
3. Bolts
4. Differential flange

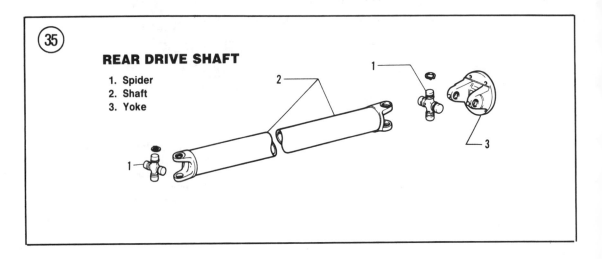

REAR DRIVE SHAFT

1. Spider
2. Shaft
3. Yoke

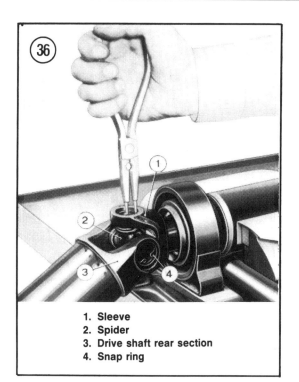

1. Sleeve
2. Spider
3. Drive shaft rear section
4. Snap ring

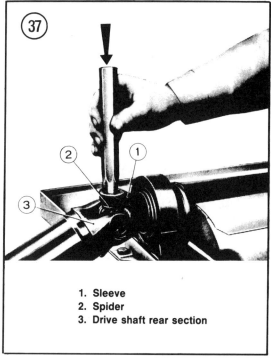

1. Sleeve
2. Spider
3. Drive shaft rear section

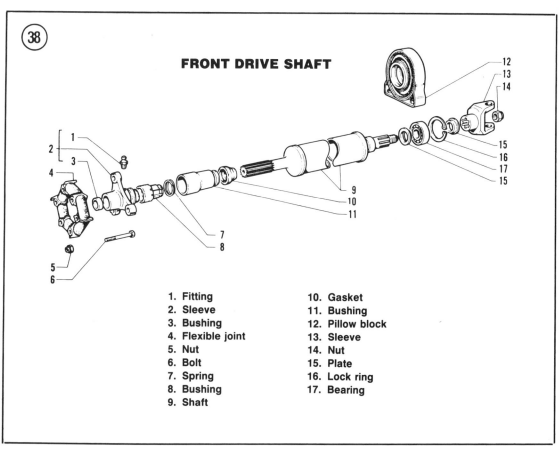

FRONT DRIVE SHAFT

1. Fitting
2. Sleeve
3. Bushing
4. Flexible joint
5. Nut
6. Bolt
7. Spring
8. Bushing
9. Shaft

10. Gasket
11. Bushing
12. Pillow block
13. Sleeve
14. Nut
15. Plate
16. Lock ring
17. Bearing

10

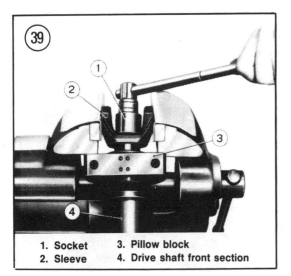

1. Socket   3. Pillow block
2. Sleeve   4. Drive shaft front section

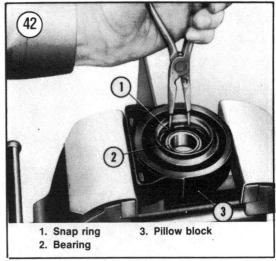

1. Snap ring   3. Pillow block
2. Bearing

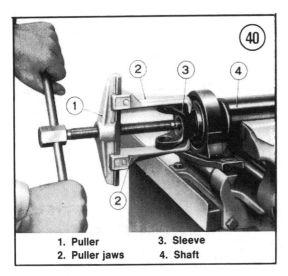

1. Puller   3. Sleeve
2. Puller jaws   4. Shaft

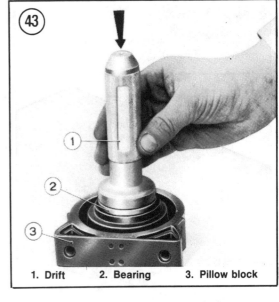

1. Drift   2. Bearing   3. Pillow block

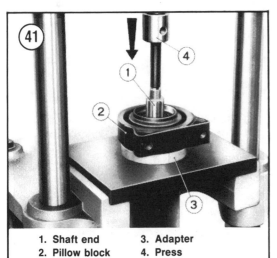

1. Shaft end   3. Adapter
2. Pillow block   4. Press

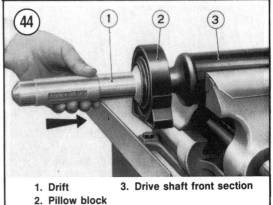

1. Drift   3. Drive shaft front section
2. Pillow block

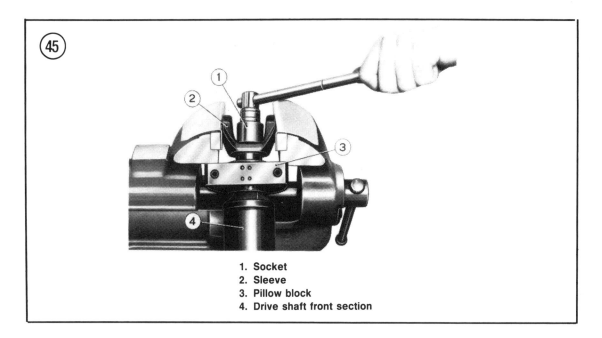

1. Socket
2. Sleeve
3. Pillow block
4. Drive shaft front section

Table 1   TIGHTENING TORQUES

Fastener	Thread size	mkg	ft.-lb.
Shock absorber upper nut	M8	1.5	11
Shock absorber lower nut	M10×1.25	5	36
Upper reaction rod to body and axle	M12×1.25	8	58
Lower reaction rod			
To body	M10×1.25	3.5	25
To axle	M12×1.25	8	58
Cross rod to body and axle	M12×1.25	8	58

10

CHAPTER ELEVEN

BRAKES

All models use disc brakes on all 4 wheels. The master cylinder transmits pedal pressure through the hydraulic system to the caliper at each wheel. The handbrake is a mechanical type, operating the rear brakes through a rod and 2 cables.

Specifications (**Table 1**) and tightening torques (**Table 2**) are at the end of the chapter.

FRONT BRAKES

Pad Replacement

1. Set the handbrake. Place the transmission in FIRST (manual) or PARK (automatic).
2. Loosen the front wheel nuts. Jack up the front end of the car, place it on jackstands and remove the front wheels.
3. Remove the clips from the pad locking blocks. See **Figure 1**.
4. Tap out the locking blocks (**Figure 2**).

CAUTION
During the next step, do not let the caliper hang by the brake hose.

5. Remove the caliper (**Figure 3**). With a pan handy to catch dripping brake fluid, open the bleed valve and slowly push the piston into the cylinder. Once the piston is in, hang the caliper from the car body with wire.

NOTE
The piston can be pushed into the cylinder with a C-clamp.

6. Remove the pads (**Figure 4**).
7. Remove the pad springs (**Figure 5**). Leave the caliper support springs in position.
8. Check the pads for wear with a vernier caliper (**Figure 6**). The lining material must be at least 1.5 mm (1/16 in.) thick. If not, replace the pads. Light surface oil or grease stains may be sanded off. If oil or grease has penetrated the surface, replace the pads. Since brake fluid can cause the friction material to crumble, replace the pads if brake fluid has touched them.

NOTE
Always replace pads in sets of 4.

9. Check the springs for weakness, damage or rust. Replace springs that show these conditions.
10. Check the locking blocks and clips (**Figure 7**) for rust or damage. Replace parts that show these conditions.
11. Clean the space that holds the brake pads with alcohol or aerosol brake cleaner. Do not use solvent, kerosene or gasoline. These leave residues which can cause rubber parts to soften and swell.
12. Install the pads by reversing Steps 3-7.
13. Pump the pedal 2 or 3 times to seat the pads. If the pedal feels soft, bleed the brakes as described in this chapter.

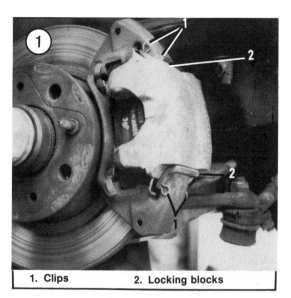

1. Clips   2. Locking blocks

1. Caliper body
2. Caliper bracket   3. Caliper spring

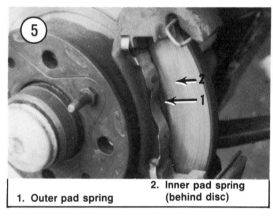

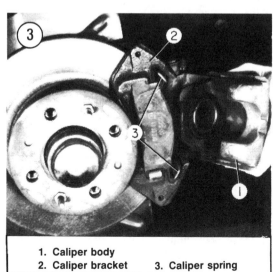

1. Outer pad spring   2. Inner pad spring (behind disc)

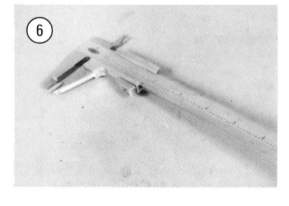

11

14. Install the wheels, lower the car and tighten the wheel nuts.

15. Make sure the brake pedal is firm, then road test the brakes.

> *WARNING*
> *Do not drive the car unless the brake pedal feels firm. If it feels soft, bleed the brakes again. Check for leaks in the brake lines.*

Caliper Removal/Installation

1. Perform Steps 1-5 of *Pad Replacement* in this chapter.

2. With a pan handy to catch dripping brake fluid, remove the screw and retainer, then undo the brake hose union bolt (**Figure 8**). Remove the union bolt and its washers, then take the caliper out.

> *NOTE*
> *Cover the end of the brake hose so the fluid doesn't leak out.*

> *NOTE*
> *This is a good time to inspect the caliper brake hose (**Figure 9**). If the hose is cracked, brittle or deteriorated, replace it as described under **Brake Lines** in this chapter. If one hose is replaced, replace the opposite hose at the same time.*

3. Installation is the reverse of removal. Tighten the brake hose union bolt to 2.8 mkg (20 ft.-lb.). See **Figure 10**. Install the retainer as shown in **Figure 8**.

Caliper Overhaul

Refer to **Figure 11** for this procedure.
1. Remove the dust boot (**Figure 12**).
2. Unscrew the caliper bleed valve (**Figure 13**).

> *WARNING*
> *During the next step, the piston may shoot out like a bullet. Keep your fingers out of the way.*

3. Pack rags between the piston and caliper. Blow compressed air into the bleed valve hose to force the piston out. See **Figure 14**.
4. Remove the piston seal from the caliper bore. See **Figure 13**. Use fingers only so the bore won't be scratched.
5. Discard all rubber parts. These must be replaced whenever the caliper is overhauled.
6. Thoroughly clean all parts in new, clean brake fluid or brake cleaner. Do not clean with gasoline, kerosene or solvent. These leave residues which can cause rubber parts to soften and swell.

1. Retainer screw   3. Brake hose union bolt
2. Retainer

7. Inspect the cylinder bore (**Figure 15**). Replace the cylinder body if wear or damage can be seen. Light rust or dirt may be removed with fine emery paper. Replace the cylinder body if dirt or rust is heavy.
8. Inspect the piston. Since it is plated, the piston can't be sanded. If the piston can't be cleaned with brake fluid and a rag, replace it.
9. Coat the piston seal and its groove with rubber grease or brake fluid. Install a new piston seal using fingers only so the cylinder bore won't be scratched. See **Figure 16**.

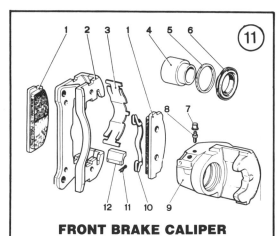

FRONT BRAKE CALIPER

1. Friction pad
2. Caliper bracket
3. Flat radial spring to secure caliper
4. Piston
5. Seal
6. Piston protecting cap
7. Bleed connection protecting cap
8. Bleed connection
9. Caliper body
10. Spring
11. Cotter pin
12. Caliper locking block

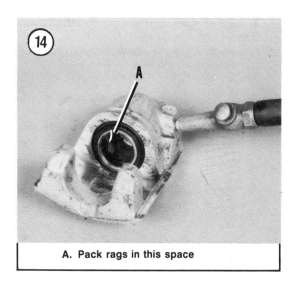

A. Pack rags in this space

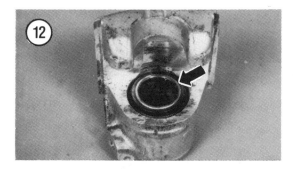

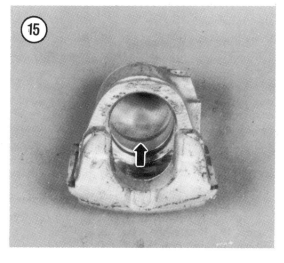

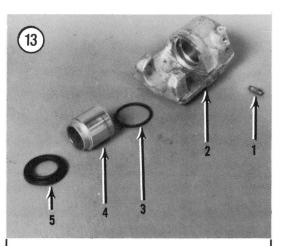

1. Bleed valve
2. Caliper body
3. Piston seal
4. Piston
5. Dust boot

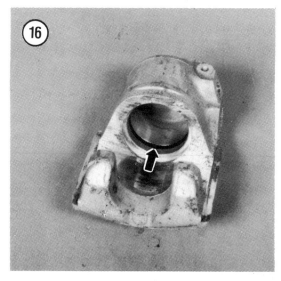

11

NOTE
Never reuse piston seals. In addition to stopping leaks, the seals retract the pistons when the brakes are let up. Very minor damage or deterioration can ruin the seals.

10. Coat the cylinder bore with new, clean brake fluid. Apply rubber grease or brake fluid to the piston, then push the piston into the cylinder. See **Figure 17.**

NOTE
*When the piston is partway in as shown in **Figure 17,** install the dust seal on the piston.*

11. Apply rubber grease to the sealing surface of the dust seal, then install the dust seal in the cylinder body. Make sure the dust seal fits in the cylinder body groove as shown in **Figure 12.**

Disc Inspection

1. Remove the caliper as described in this chapter.
2. Check wheel bearing adjustment. See Chapter Nine.
3. Check the disc for rust, scratches or cracks. If cracks are visible, replace the disc. If rust is visible or if scratches are deep enough to snag a fingernail, have the disc turned by a machine shop.
4. Check thickness at several points around the disc with a micrometer (**Figure 18**). Compare with specifications in **Table 1.** Replace the disc if it is thinner than the minimum.
5. Set up a dial indicator so its pointer is 2 mm from the outer edge of the disc's swept area. See **Figure 19.** Rotate the disc one full turn and measure runout. If runout is excessive, the disc can be reconditioned by a machine shop. Minimum disc thickness after refacing is listed in **Table 1.** If it would have to be cut thinner than this to correct it, the disc must be replaced.

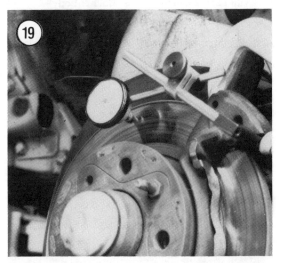

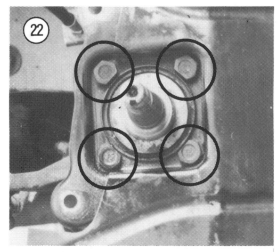

Disc Removal/Installation

1. Remove the caliper as described in this chapter.
2. Unbolt the caliper support bracket (**Figure 20**) and take it off.
3. Remove the locating pins (**Figure 21**) and take off the disc and plate.
4. If necessary, remove the nuts from the backing plate bolts and take the backing plate off. See **Figure 22**.
5. Installation is the reverse of removal. Tighten the caliper bracket bolts to specifications in **Table 2**.

REAR BRAKES

Pad Replacement

1. Securely block both front wheels so the car will not roll in either direction.
2. Loosen the rear wheel nuts. Jack up the rear end of the car, place it on jackstands and remove the rear wheels.
3. Remove the forward section of the brake disc backing plate (**Figure 23**).
4. Remove the clips and tap out the locking blocks (**Figure 24**).
5. Lift off the caliper and tie it out of the way as shown in **Figure 25**.

> *CAUTION*
> *Do not let the caliper hang by the brake hose.*

> *NOTE*
> *This is a good time to inspect the caliper brake hose. If it is cracked, deteriorated or brittle, replace it as described under **Brake Lines** in this chapter.*

1. Clips   2. Locking blocks

11

6. Remove the pads (**Figure 25**).

7. Remove the pad springs (**Figure 26**). Leave the support springs in position.

8. Check the pads for wear. See **Figure 27**. The lining material must be at least 1.5 mm (1/16 in.) thick. If not, replace the pads. Light surface oil or grease stains may be sanded off. If oil or grease has penetrated the surface, replace the pads. Since brake fluid can cause the friction material to crumble, replace the pads if brake fluid has touched them.

NOTE
Always replace pads in sets of 4.

9. Check the springs for weakness, damage or rust. Replace springs that show these conditions.

10. Check the locking blocks and clips (**Figure 28**) for rust or damage. Replace parts that show these conditions.

11. Clean the space that holds the brake pads with alcohol or aerosol brake cleaner. Do not use solvent, kerosene or gasoline. These leave residues which can cause rubber parts to soften and swell.

12. Install the pads by reversing Steps 3-7.

13. Pump the pedal 2 or 3 times to seat the pads. If the pedal feels soft, bleed the brakes as described in this chapter.

14. Install the wheels, lower the car and tighten the wheel nuts. Unblock the front wheels.

15. Make sure the brake pedal is firm, then road test the brakes.

WARNING
Do not drive the car unless the brake pedal feels firm. If it feels soft, bleed the brakes again. Check for leaks in the brake lines.

Caliper Removal/Installation

This is the same as for front brakes, described in this chapter, except that the handbrake cable (**Figure 25**) must be disconnected from the caliper. To do this, loosen the cable adjusting nuts (**Figure 29**) and detach the cables from the equalizer. After installing the calipers, adjust the handbrake as described in this chapter.

Caliper Overhaul

Refer to **Figure 30** for this procedure.

CAUTION
*Do not remove the parts labelled 2 through 9, **Figure 30**. The plunger is heavily spring loaded and will make it extremely difficult to reinstall the handbrake cam lever.*

1. Remove the dust boot.

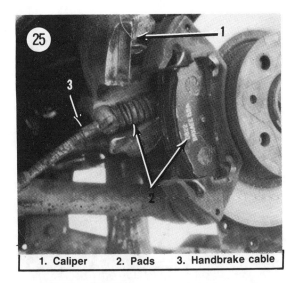

1. Caliper   2. Pads   3. Handbrake cable

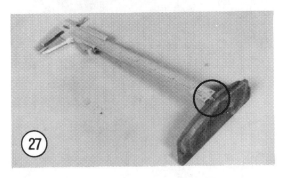

2. Insert a screwdriver in the piston slot and unscrew the piston from the plunger.

3. Remove the piston seal from the cylinder bore. Use fingers only so the bore won't be scratched.

4. Remove the dust cover from the handbrake cam lever. This can be done without removing the handbrake cam lever from the caliper.

5. Check for brake fluid in the area covered by the dust cover. If brake fluid has leaked into this area, the plunger seal (9, **Figure 30**) must be replaced. This is a job for a dealer or mechanic familiar with Fiat brakes.

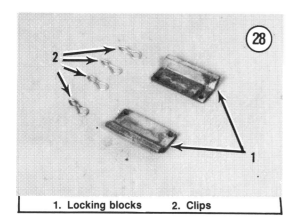

1. Locking blocks 2. Clips

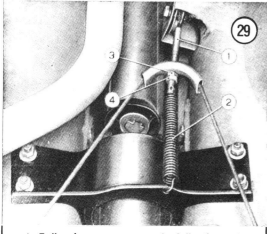

1. Pull rod 3. Adjusting nut
2. Pull rod return spring 4. Locknut

6. Discard the piston seal and dust boot. These must be replaced whenever the caliper is overhauled.

7. Thoroughly clean all parts in new, clean brake fluid or aerosol brake cleaner. Do not clean with gasoline, kerosene or solvent. These leave residues which can cause rubber parts to soften and swell.

8. Inspect the cylinder bore. Replace the cylinder body if wear or damage can be seen. Light rust or dirt may be removed with fine emery paper. Replace the cylinder body if dirt or rust is heavy.

9. Inspect the piston. Since it is plated, the piston can't be sanded. If the piston can't be cleaned with brake fluid and a rag, replace it.

10. Check the handbrake mechanism parts for wear or damage. If wear or damage can be seen, have the handbrake mechanism replaced by a dealer or mechanic familiar with Fiat brakes.

11. Apply rubber grease or brake fluid to the piston seal, then install it in its groove in the cylinder bore.

12. Apply rubber grease or brake fluid to the piston friction surface. Screw the piston onto the plunger until it seats. See **Figure 31**.

WARNING
*Make sure the piston mark (A, **Figure 30 and Figure 31**) is on the same side as the bleed valve. There is a brake fluid passage opposite this mark, inside the piston, which must be aligned with the bleed valve. If the mark is not positioned properly, it will be impossible to bleed the brakes adequately.*

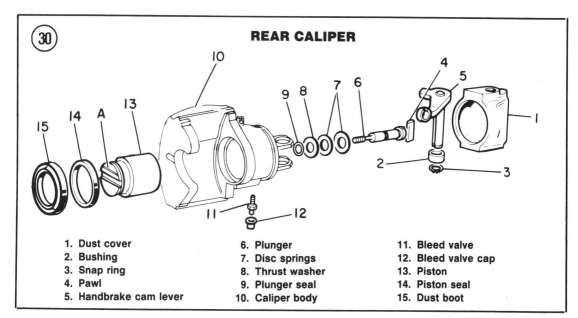

REAR CALIPER

1. Dust cover
2. Bushing
3. Snap ring
4. Pawl
5. Handbrake cam lever
6. Plunger
7. Disc springs
8. Thrust washer
9. Plunger seal
10. Caliper body
11. Bleed valve
12. Bleed valve cap
13. Piston
14. Piston seal
15. Dust boot

11

Disc Removal,
Inspection and Installation

These procedures are the same as for front brakes, described in this chapter.

MASTER CYLINDER

Removal/Installation

1. Drain the brake fluid reservoirs with a turkey baster or similar tool.
2. Place rags beneath the master cylinder to catch dripping brake fluid.

> *CAUTION*
> *Brake fluid can damage paint. Wipe up any spilled fluid and wash the area of the spill with soap and water.*

3. Gently work the reservoir hoses (**Figure 32**) loose from the master cylinder. Use a side-to-side rocking motion to work the hoses loose.
4. Unbolt the reservoir bracket from the firewall and take the reservoir off. See **Figure 32**.

> *CAUTION*
> *During the next step, use a flare nut wrench so the brake line nuts aren't rounded off. These are available inexpensively at auto parts stores.*

5. Using a flare nut wrench, disconnect the brake lines from the master cylinder.
6. Remove the master cylinder mounting nuts and lockwashers, then take the master cylinder off the brake booster.
7. Installation is the reverse of removal.

Overhaul

Refer to **Figure 33**.
1. Remove the reservoir hose connectors and dust cover from the master cylinder.
2. Remove the stop bolts from the cylinder.
3. Remove the internal parts from the master cylinder, referring to **Figure 33**.

> *WARNING*
> *During the next step, the pistons may shoot out like bullets. Point the master cylinder's open end at a pile of rags or a block of wood on the ground. Keep your fingers clear of the master cylinder's open end.*

4. If the internal parts are difficult to remove, blow them out with compressed air. Use a service station air hose if you don't have a compressor.
5. Discard all rubber parts.
6. Thoroughly clean all remaining parts in brake fluid. Do not clean with solvent, kerosene or

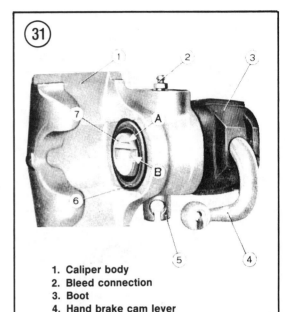

(31)

1. Caliper body
2. Bleed connection
3. Boot
4. Hand brake cam lever
5. Hand brake cable anchorage
6. Piston protection boot
7. Piston
A. Reference mark
B. Slot engaging friction pad rib

(32) **MASTER CYLINDER**

1. Fluid level switch
2. Reservoir cover
3. Reservoir
4. Reservoir lines
5. Master cylinder
6. Bolt
7. Bracket
8. Mounting nut

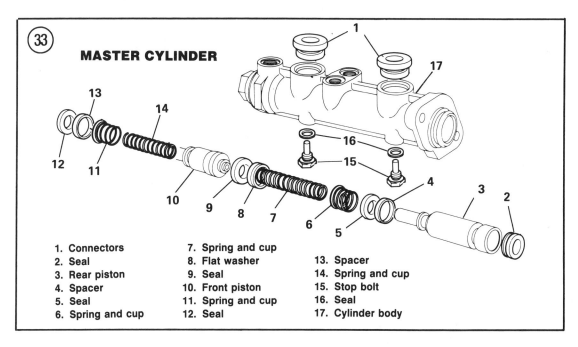

33 MASTER CYLINDER

1. Connectors
2. Seal
3. Rear piston
4. Spacer
5. Seal
6. Spring and cup
7. Spring and cup
8. Flat washer
9. Seal
10. Front piston
11. Spring and cup
12. Seal
13. Spacer
14. Spring and cup
15. Stop bolt
16. Seal
17. Cylinder body

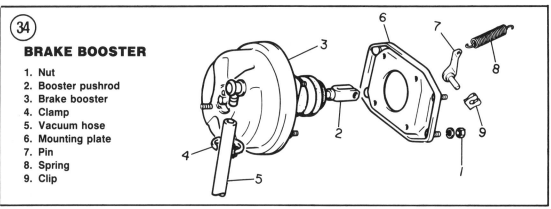

34 BRAKE BOOSTER

1. Nut
2. Booster pushrod
3. Brake booster
4. Clamp
5. Vacuum hose
6. Mounting plate
7. Pin
8. Spring
9. Clip

gasoline. These leave residues which can cause rubber parts to soften and swell.

7. Check the cylinder bore and pistons for excessive or uneven wear, scoring, pitting or corrosion. Replace the master cylinder if these conditions can be seen.

8. Check springs for wear, damage or weakness. Replace as needed.

9. Coat the piston seals with brake fluid or rubber grease before installing them on the pistons. besure the unidirectional seals face in the same directions as the old ones.

10. Coat the cylinder bore and pistons with brake fluid or rubber grease before installing the pistons.

CAUTION
Do not scratch the cylinder bore or pistons while installing.

11. Install the front piston and related parts, referring to **Figure 33**. Push it into the bore with a screwdriver and secure it wih a stop bolt.

12. Install the rear piston and related parts. Push it into the bore with a screwdriver and install the remaining stop bolt.

13. Install the dust boot on the end of the cylinder.

14. Install the fluid hose fittings and seals.

BRAKE BOOSTER

Removal/Installation

Refer to **Figure 34** for this procedure.

1. Remove the master cylinder as described in this chapter.

2. Working in the engine compartment, disconnect the vacuum hose from the booster.

11

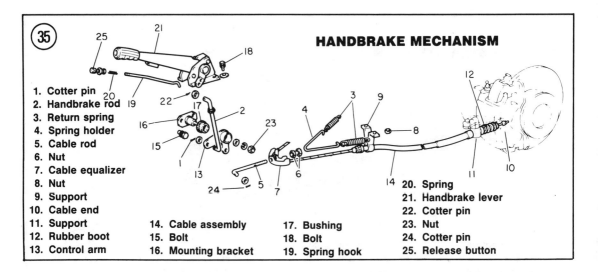

HANDBRAKE MECHANISM

1. Cotter pin
2. Handbrake rod
3. Return spring
4. Spring holder
5. Cable rod
6. Nut
7. Cable equalizer
8. Nut
9. Support
10. Cable end
11. Support
12. Rubber boot
13. Control arm
14. Cable assembly
15. Bolt
16. Mounting bracket
17. Bushing
18. Bolt
19. Spring hook
20. Spring
21. Handbrake lever
22. Cotter pin
23. Nut
24. Cotter pin
25. Release button

3. Working in the passenger compartment, detach the booster pushrod from the brake pedal. Remove the booster mounting nuts.

4. Withdraw the booster into the engine compartment.

5. Installation is the reverse of removal.

HANDBRAKE

Adjustment

1. Press the brake pedal several times.

2. Raise the handbrake lever 1-2 notches. Make sure the transmission is in NEUTRAL.

3. Securely block both front wheels so the car will not roll in either direction.

4. Jack up the rear end of the car and place it on jackstands.

5. Working beneath the car, loosen the locknut (**Figure 29**). Turn the adjusting nut to lock the rear wheels. When the rear wheels are too tight to be turned by hand, tighten the locknut.

6. Release the handbrake lever and make sure the rear wheels can be turned by hand.

7. Pull the handbrake lever. If adjustment is correct, the handbrake will lock the rear wheels when the lever is pulled 3 notches.

Removal/Installation

To remove and install handbrake parts, refer to **Figure 35**.

BRAKE LINES AND HOSES

Brake lines should be checked periodically for leaks, cracks or poor fit in their clips. Brake hoses should be checked for cracks or other signs of deterioration. **Figure 36** and **Figure 37** show brake lines.

Removal/Installation

1. To remove caliper brake hoses, remove the union bolt and washer that secure the hose to the caliper. Pull out the clip that secures the hose to the body bracket, detach the hose from the metal line and take the hose out.

> *WARNING*
> *Whenever you replace the brake hose on one side of the car, replace the hose on the opposite side to maintain balanced braking.*

2. To remove a metal brake line, remove the flare nuts with a flare nut wrench, then take the line out. Flare nut wrenches are available inexpensively at auto parts stores. Do not use an open-end or adjustable wrench, since it may round off the nut.

3. Always bleed the brakes after replacing a brake line.

BRAKE BLEEDING

The hydraulic system should be bled whenever air enters it. This is because air in the brake lines will compress, rather than transmitting pedal pressure to the brake operating parts. If the pedal feels mushy or if pedal travel increases considerably, brake bleeding is usually called for. Bleeding is also necessary whenever a brake line is disconnected.

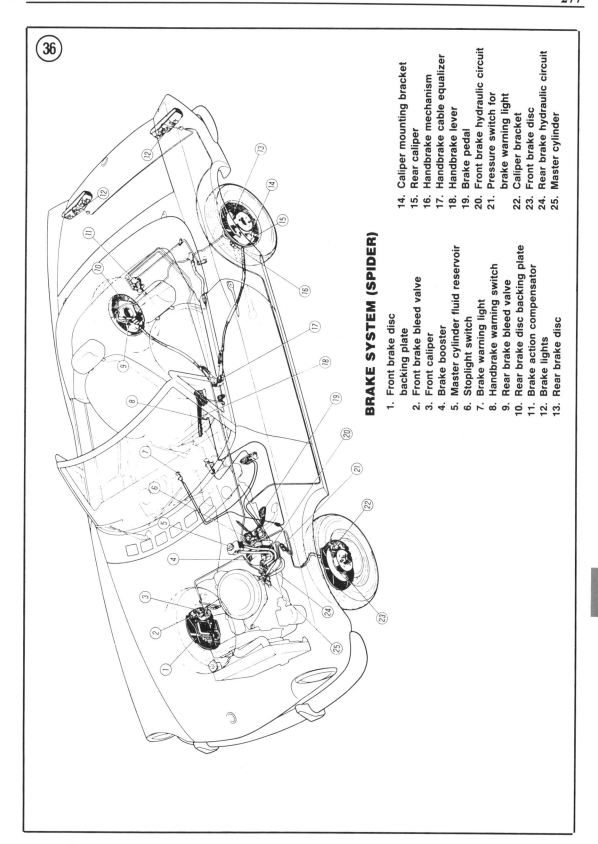

BRAKE SYSTEM (SPIDER)

1. Front brake disc backing plate
2. Front brake bleed valve
3. Front caliper
4. Brake booster
5. Master cylinder fluid reservoir
6. Stoplight switch
7. Brake warning light
8. Handbrake warning switch
9. Rear brake bleed valve
10. Rear brake disc backing plate
11. Brake action compensator
12. Brake lights
13. Rear brake disc
14. Caliper mounting bracket
15. Rear caliper
16. Handbrake mechanism
17. Handbrake cable equalizer
18. Handbrake lever
19. Brake pedal
20. Front brake hydraulic circuit
21. Pressure switch for brake warning light
22. Caliper bracket
23. Front brake disc
24. Rear brake hydraulic circuit
25. Master cylinder

11

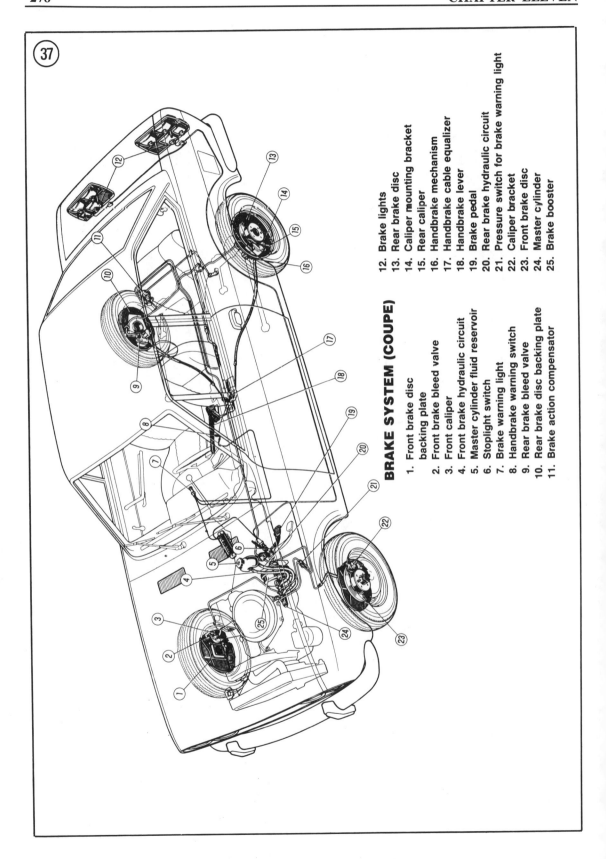

BRAKE SYSTEM (COUPE)

1. Front brake disc
   backing plate
2. Front brake bleed valve
3. Front caliper
4. Front brake hydraulic circuit
5. Master cylinder fluid reservoir
6. Stoplight switch
7. Brake warning light
8. Handbrake warning switch
9. Rear brake bleed valve
10. Rear brake disc backing plate
11. Brake action compensator
12. Brake lights
13. Rear brake disc
14. Caliper mounting bracket
15. Rear caliper
16. Handbrake mechanism
17. Handbrake cable equalizer
18. Handbrake lever
19. Brake pedal
20. Rear brake hydraulic circuit
21. Pressure switch for brake warning light
22. Caliper bracket
23. Front brake disc
24. Master cylinder
25. Brake booster

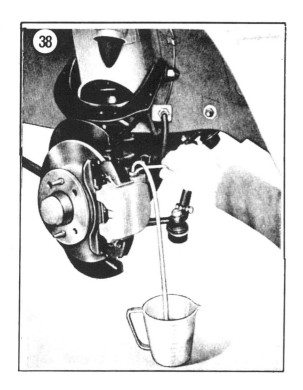

This procedure requires handling brake fluid. Be careful not to get any fluid on brake discs, pads, shoes or drums. Clean all dirt from bleed valves before beginning. Two people are needed; one to operate the brake pedal and the other to open and close the bleed valves.

1. Clean away any dirt around the master cylinder reservoir. Top up the master cylinder with brake fluid marked DOT 3.

NOTE
DOT 3 means the brake fluid meets current Department of Transportation quality standards. If the fluid doesn't say DOT 3 somewhere on the label, buy a brand that does..

2. Attach a plastic tube to the bleed valve. **Figure 38** shows a front bleed valve. The rear bleed valves are basically the same. Immerse the other end of the tube in a jar containing several inches of clean brake fluid.

NOTE
Do not allow the end of the tube to come out of the brake fluid during bleeding. This could allow air into the system, requiring that the bleeding procedure be done over.

3. Slowly press the brake pedal as far as it will go, then hold it down.
4. With the brake pedal down, open the bleed valve 1/3-1/2 turn. Let the brake pedal sink to the floor, then let the pedal back slowly.
5. Repeat Step 3 and Step 4 until the fluid entering the jar is free of air bubbles.
6. Repeat the process for the other bleed valves.

NOTE
Keep an eye on the brake fluid level in the master cylinder during bleeding. If the fluid level is allowed to drop too low, air will enter the brake lines and the entire bleeding procedure will have to be repeated.

Table 1 BRAKE SPECIFICATIONS

	mm	in.
Disc diameter	227	8.937
Disc thickness, new	9.95-10.15	0.392-0.400
Minimum thickness		
From refacing		
Front	9.35	0.368
Rear	9.45	0.372
From wear	9	0.354
Maximum runout	0.15	0.006
Minimum pad thickness	2	0.079

Table 2 TIGHTENING TORQUES

Fastener	Thread size	mkg	ft.-lb.
Caliper bracket bolts	M10×1.25	5	36
Master cylinder mounting nuts/bolts	M8	2.5	18
Brake booster mounting nuts	M8	2.5	18

11

SKILL LEVEL AND TIME ESTIMATING GUIDE

The time estimates and skill level data that follow were prepared in conjunction with Mitchell International, Inc., the leader in providing this material to professional mechanics, garages and fleet operators.

This section will tell you 2 vital things about 133 different jobs on the 1973-1982 Fiat 124 and Spider 2000:

How long the job takes.

How complicated the job is.

1. How long the job takes: This is the same time figure used by dealers and independent shops to estimate labor charges. Times are shown in tenths of an hour (6-minute intervals). For example, a labor time of 0.3 is 3 tenths of an hour or 18 minutes.

These times are estimates which generally reflect the needs of an average trained auto mechanic using factory recommended tools and following factory recommended procedures. They include allowances for repair preparation, normal cleanup associated with repair, road testing, mechanic personal needs, preventive measures and any other service that would normally accompany an individual operation.

Times do not include allowances for diagnosis, machine operations or obtaining substitutes for factory recommended special tools.

Estimated labor time can be used in 2 ways:

a. If you decide to have a job done professionally, you can compare the time specified in this chart with the shop's labor estimate for the same work.

b. If you decide to do a job yourself, you can use the estimated time, together with the job's skill level, to estimate how long it will take you.

WARNING
Unless you are a professional mechanic with a fully equipped shop, you should expect a job to take you longer than the estimated time. Since the skills and equipment possessed by home mechanics vary widely, it is impossible to estimate how long a job should take a home mechanic. Use the estimated labor times as a rough guide only. Never hurry a job, trying to finish within the estimated time. You may damage the vehicle or injure yourself.

2. How complicated the job is: Each job is placed in one of 4 skill levels:

A. HIGHLY SKILLED—Requires the use of precision measuring tools and highly specialized measuring equipment. Also requires thorough knowledge of complicated systems and strong diagnostic ability. Some jobs in this category can be done by home mechanics. Often, money can be saved by removing and installing a part yourself and having a shop do only the part of a job which requires special training and equipment. The manual will tell which of these jobs can be done by home mechanics.

B. SKILLED—Requires the use of basic tools and simple measuring devices. Accurate diagnosis is required using special test equipment. Must have basic knowledge of complex systems. Many skilled jobs can be done by a beginner using the Clymer manual. Often it is faster and more economical to have the job done by a shop, and the manual will point out such instances.

C. SEMI-SKILLED—Diagnosis is limited to a single possible cause of a problem. Must have basic knowledge of component or system operation. Can be done by a beginner using the Clymer manual.

D. LOW SKILLED—Repair consists of part replacement only. Can be done by a beginner using the Clymer manual.

The letter indicating skill level follows each job description.

Model Identification

Vehicles in this list are identified by model year, model code and date of manufacture. To identify your vehicle's model year and model code, refer to the vehicle identification plate in the engine compartment. Date of manufacture is usually listed on a plate on the driver's doorjamb.

Abbreviations

Several abbreviations are used in this guide. They are:

a. R&R: Remove and replace. Includes removal of part or assembly from vehicle, transfer of attached parts to new part or assembly and installation of new part or assembly on vehicle. Includes any alignment necessary to reposition new part or assembly.

b. R&I: Remove and install. Includes removal of part or assembly from vehicle and installation of same part or assembly on vehicle. Includes any alignment necessary to reposition part or assembly.

c. O/H: Overhaul. Overhaul times include removal of assembly (R&I) from the vehicle, disassembly, cleaning and inspection, replacing necessary parts, reassembly, reinstalling and making any necessary adjustments.

12

SKILL LEVEL AND TIME ESTIMATING GUIDE

TUNE-UP & IGNITION

1. Compression test (C)
Labor time 0.6
2. Distributor assembly R&R (C)
Includes: Adjust ignition timing.
Labor time 0.7
3. Distributor cap R&R (C)
Labor time 0.4
4. Distributor vacuum control R&R (B)
Includes: Adjust ignition timing.
Does not include distributor R&I.
Labor time
1973-1978 .... 0.7
1979-1982 .... 0.4
5. Engine analyze (B)
Includes: Check ignition & emission systems using analyzer.
Labor time 0.7
6. Ignition timing adjust (C)
Labor time 0.3
7. Ignition cable set R&R (C)
Labor time
1973-1978 .... 0.5
1979-1982 .... 0.6
8. Points and condenser R&R (C)
Includes: Adjust ignition timing.
Labor time (1973-1979) 0.6
9. Spark plugs clean or replace (C)
Labor time 0.5
10. Thermostatic vacuum switch R&R (B)
Labor time 0.6
11. Tune-up minor (breaker ignition) (B)
Includes: Check compression; clean or replace air cleaner, spark plugs, points and condenser; inspect and/or replace distributor cap & rotor; inspect ignition cables; adjust ignition timing and idle speed. Does not include distributor R&I.
Labor time (1973-1979) 1.6
12. Tune-up minor (electronic ignition) (B)
Includes: Check compression; clean or replace spark plugs and air cleaner; inspect and/or replace distributor cap and rotor; inspect ignition cables; adjust igniton timing and idle speed.
Labor time (1979-1982) 1.4

EMISSION CONTROL

13. A.I.R. system pump (C)
Labor time
1974-1978 .... 1.0
1979-1982 .... 0.8

14. A.I.R. pump belt R&R (C)
Labor time
124 .... 0.8
Spider 2000 .... 1.5
15. A.I.R. pump filter R&R (C)
Labor time 0.4
16. Crankcase vent (PCV) valve R&R (C)
Labor time 0.3
17. E.G.R. air/vapor separator R&R (C)
Labor time 0.7
18. Emission system check (C)
Includes: Check exhaust utilizing analyzer, adjust ignition timing and idle speed.
Labor time 0.7
19. Evaporation control canister R&R (C)
Labor time
124 .... 0.7
Spider 2000 .... 1.1
20. Recirculation (E.G.R.) valve R&R (C)
Labor time 0.7

FUEL

21. Accelerator pump R&R (C)
Labor time (1973-1980) 0.7
22. Air cleaner element R&R (D)
Labor time 0.2
23. Automatic choke R&R (C)
Labor time (1973-1980) 0.6
24. Carburetor R&I and O/H (B)
Labor time
1973 .... 2.3
1974-1980 .... 3.1
25. Carburetor and/or gasket R&R (B)
Includes: Adjust idle speed and fuel mixture.
Labor time
1973 .... 0.9
1974-1980 .... 1.3
1981-1982 .... Not applicable.
26. Float and/or needle and seat R&R (B)
Labor time (1973-1980) 1.0

27. Fuel pump R&R (B)
Labor time
1973-1978
Mechanical
w/ air cond 1.0
w/o air cond 0.7
Electric 0.7
1979-1982
w/ fuel injection 0.7
w/o fuel injection 1.8
28. Fuel filter R&R (D)
Labor time
1973-1978 .... 0.3
1979-1982 .... 0.8
29. Fuel lines clean (D)
Labor time 0.5
30. Fuel tank R&R (D)
Labor time
1973-1978 .... 1.6
1979-1982 .... 1.3
31. Fuel injection system check (B)
Includes: Adjust idle speed and CO.
Labor time (1980-1982) 0.7
32. Intake manifold gasket R&R (C)
Includes: Adjust idle speed and fuel mixture.
Labor time (carburetion)
1973[1] 2.6
1974-1978
124
w/ air cond 3.8
w/o air cond 3.2
Spider 2000 .... 3.9
1979-1980 .... 3.9

---

(1) Includes: R&I intake and exhaust manifold assembly.

---

33. Intake manifold gasket R&R (C)
Labor time (fuel injection)
1980-1982 .... 1.0
34. Pressure regulator R&R (B)
Labor time (1980-1982) 0.6
35. Oil return line R&R (C)
Labor time (1982) 0.8
36. Oil supply line R&R (C)
Labor time (1982) 0.7
37. Turbocharger assembly R&R (A)
Includes: Exhaust manifold R&I and all necessary adjustments.
Labor time (1982)
w/ air cond 3.8
w/o air cond 2.9

SKILL LEVEL AND TIME ESTIMATING GUIDE (continued)

EXHAUST

38. Catalytic converter R&R (D)
Labor time
1973-1978 .... 0.7
1979-1982 .... 1.0

39. Exhaust manifold and/or gasket R&R (C)
Labor time
1973 .... 1.0
1974-1978 .... 1.3
1979-1982 .... 1.8

40. Exhaust pipe R&R (D)
Labor time
1973-1974 .... 1.0
1975-1982 .... 0.8

41. Muffler R&R (D)
Labor time
1973-1978 .... 0.8
1979-1982
One 0.8
Both 1.1

ALTERNATOR

42. Alternator R&R (D)
Labor time
1973-1978 .... 0.9
1979-1982 .... 1.1

43. Alternator bearings R&R (B)
With alternator removed.
Labor time 0.8

44. Charging system check (B)
Includes: Check battery, regulator and alternator output.
Labor time 0.6

STARTER

45. Armature and/or brushes R&R (B)
With starter removed.
Does not include turn commutator.
Labor time 0.9

46. Starter R&R (D)
Labor time
1973-1978
w/ air cond 2.4
w/o air cond 1.5
1979-1982 .... 1.3

47. Starter circuit check (B)
Labor time
Exc Spider 2000 .... 0.7
Spider 2000 .... 1.0

48. Starter drive R&R (C)
With starter removed.
Labor time 0.5

HEAD AND VALVES

49. Balance (auxiliary) shaft R&R (B)
Labor time
1973-1978
w/ air cond 4.1
w/o air cond 3.8

ABBREVIATIONS
For full explanation of abbreviations, see the first page of this section.
Skill levels:
  A. Highly skilled
  B. Skilled
  C. Semi-skilled
  D. Low skilled
R&R: Remove and replace
R&I: Remove and install
O/H: Overhaul

49. Balance (auxiliary) shaft R&R (B) (cont.)
Labor time
1979-1982
Std trans 4.3
Auto trans 4.6
Additional time
w/ turbocharger, add (1982) 0.7

50. Camshaft R&R (B)
Includes: Adjust valve clearance.
Labor time
1973
Intake 2.6
Exhaust 2.4
Both 4.6
1974-1978
Intake 3.8
Exhaust 2.4
Both 5.6
1979-1982
Std trans
Intake 6.4
Exhaust 5.5
Both 7.8
Auto trans
Intake 6.8
Exhaust 5.9
Both 8.2
Additional time
Where air cond interferes, add 0.4
w/ turbocharger, add 0.5

51. Camshaft oil seal R&R (B)
Includes: R&I sprocket.
Labor time
1973-1978 .... 2.5
1979-1982 .... 3.3

52. Cylinder head gasket R&R (C)
Includes: Remove carbon; adjust valves; adjust ignition timing where necessary.
Labor time
1973
w/ air cond 4.9
w/o air cond 4.6
1974-1978
w/ air cond 5.8
w/o air cond 5.5

---

52. Cylinder head gasket R&R (C) (cont.)
Labor time (cont.)
1979-1982
Std trans 6.4
Auto trans 6.8
Additional time
w/ turbocharger, add 0.8

53. Crankshaft sprocket R&R (B)
Labor time
1973 .... 2.0
1974-1978 .... 2.3
1979-1982 .... 3.1

54. Timing belt R&R (B)
Labor time
1973 .... 1.5
1974-1978 .... 1.9
1979-1982 .... 3.1
Additional time
Where air cond interferes, add 0.2

55. Timing chain and/or sprocket R&R (B)
Not applicable.

56. Valve grind (complete) (A)
Includes: Remove carbon; clean valve guides; compression check; tune engine minor.
Labor time
1973-1978
w/ air cond 9.2
w/o air cond 8.9
1979-1982 .... 12.0

57. Valve lifters R&R (B)
Includes: R&I camshaft housing; D&A, clean & adjust clearance.
Labor time
1973 .... 4.0
1974-1978 .... 4.9
1979-1982 .... 7.1
Additional time
Where air cond interferes, add 0.3

PISTON ASSEMBLIES, BEARINGS & CRANKSHAFT

58. Connecting rod bearings R&R (B)
Labor time
1973-1978 .... 4.6
1979-1982 .... 4.1

59. Crankshaft R&R (A)
Includes: R&I engine and replace bearings and oil seals as necessary; adjust idle speed and ignition.
Labor time
1973 .... 13.0
1974-1978 .... 14.0
1979-1982
w/ fuel injection Not available.
w/o fuel injection
Std trans 14.1
Auto trans 13.7

12

SKILL LEVEL AND TIME ESTIMATING GUIDE (continued)

59. Crankshaft R&R (A) (cont.)
Additional time
Where air cond interferes, add
1973-1978 .... 0.7
1979-1982 .... 1.0

60. Crankshaft pulley R&R (C)
Labor time
1973-1978 .... 1.3
1979-1982 .... Not applicable.
Additional time
Where air cond interferes,
add 0.3

61. Main bearings R&R (B)
Labor time
1973-1978 .... 4.6
1979-1982 .... 4.7

62. Pistons and rod assembly R&I (A)
Includes: Remove carbon, cylinder ridge; burnish cylinders, replace rod bearings; adjust carburetor and timing.
Labor time
1973-1978 .... 10.7
1979-1982 .... 11.7
Additional time
Where air cond interferes,
add 0.3
w/ turbocharger, add 2.0

63. Rear main bearing oil seal R&R (B)
Includes: R&I clutch, flywheel and transmission.
Labor time
1973-1978 .... 5.9
1979-1982
Std trans 5.6
Auto trans
w/ fuel injection 9.6
w/o fuel injection
w/ Calif ECS 9.2
w/o Calif ECS
w/ air cond 8.9
w/o air cond 7.9

ENGINE OILING

64. Oil filter element R&R (D)
Labor time
1973-1978 .... 0.5
1979-1982 .... 0.3

65. Oil pan and/ or gasket R&R (C)
Labor time
1973-1978 .... 3.1
1979-1982 .... 2.7

66. Oil pump R&R (C)
Add 0.3 to Job No. 65.

ABBREVIATIONS
For full explanation of abbreviations, see the first page of this section.
Skill levels:
  A. Highly skilled
  B. Skilled
  C. Semi-skilled
  D. Low skilled
R&R: Remove and replace
R&I: Remove and install
O/H: Overhaul

ENGINE ASSEMBLY, BLOCK AND MOUNTS

67. Engine assembly R&I (C)
Includes: R&I only those components necessary for the removal of the complete engine assembly. Does not include transfer parts or tune engine.
Labor time
1973 .... 7.9
1974-1978 .... 8.9
1979-1982
w/ fuel injection
Std trans 9.8
Auto trans 10.3
w/o fuel injection
Std trans 8.9
Auto trans 9.3
Additional time
Where air cond interferes,
add (1973-1978) 0.7
w/ turbocharger, add 0.8

68. Engine assembly R&I and O/H (A)
Includes: Replace rings, main and rod bearings, crankshaft and camshaft; remove cylinder ridge; burnish cylinders; clean and test or replace lifters; grind valves and adjust fuel mixture, idle speed and timing. Does not include rebore or pin fit and align.
Labor time
1973 .... 26.0
1974-1978 .... 27.0
1979-1982
w/ fuel injection
Std trans 27.4
Auto trans 28.0
w/o fuel injection
Std trans 26.8
Auto trans 26.2
Additional time
Where air cond interferes, add
1973-1978 .... 0.7
w/ turbocharger, add 0.8

---

69. Engine or transmission mount R&R (D)
Labor time
1973-1978
Front
One side 0.8
Both 1.4
Rear 0.6
1979-1982
Front (each) 1.6
Rear 0.6
Additional time
Where air cond interferes, add
1973-1978 .... 0.3

70. Short block R&R (A)
Consists of cylinder block fitted w/ pistons, rings, connecting rods, crankshaft and all bearings.
Includes: Grind valves; clean and transfer cylinder head, fuel and electrical assemblies, engine mounts, manifolds, valves covers, oil pan and pump, timing cover, water pump, clutch assembly and flywheel. Adjust fuel mixture, idle speed and valves.
Labor time
1973 .... 15.1
1974-1978 .... 15.0
1979-1982
w/ fuel injection
Std trans 17.1
Auto trans 17.7
w/o fuel injection
Std trans 16.1
Auto trans 15.7
Additional time
Where air cond interferes, add
1973-1978 .... 0.7
w/ turbocharger, add 0.8

COOLING

71. Cooling system (D)
Labor time
Pressure test 0.4
Flush 0.7
Reverse flush 1.0
Clean and flush [1] 2.0

---

(1) Includes: R&R hoses and thermostat.

---

72. Motor, electric fan R&R (D)
Labor time
1973-1978 .... 0.7
1979-1982 .... 0.8

SKILL LEVEL AND TIME ESTIMATING GUIDE (continued)

73. Radiator R&R (D)
Includes: Replace hoses.
Labor time
1973-1978
Std trans 1.2
Auto trans (1974) 1.5
1979-1982
Std trans 1.0
Auto trans 1.5
Additional time
Where air cond interferes, add
1973-1978 .... 0.3
1979-1982 .... 0.2

74. Radiator hoses R&R (D)
Labor time
1973-1978
Upper 0.5
Lower 0.6
Both 0.8
1979-1982
Upper 0.5
Lower 1.0
Both 1.2

75. Thermostat R&R (D)
Labor time
1973 .... 1.3
1974-1978 .... 0.6
1979-1982
w/ fuel injection 1.0
w/o fuel injection 0.8

76. Water pump R&R (C)
Labor time
1973 .... 2.4
1974-1978
w/ air cond 2.7
w/o air cond 2.4
1979-1982
w/ fuel injection
Std trans 3.6
Auto trans 4.0
w/o fuel injection
Std trans 3.1
Auto trans 3.5

77. Water pump belt R&R (D)
Labor time
1973-1978
w/ air cond 0.7
w/o air cond 0.4
1979-1982 .... 1.1

BRAKES

78. Brakes compensator cylinder R&R (B)
Labor time
1973-1978 .... 0.8
1979-1982 .... 0.9

79. Brake system bleed (C)
Labor time
Front or rear lines only 0.6
All (complete) 0.9

ABBREVIATIONS

For full explanation of abbreviations, see the first page of this section.
Skill levels:
A. Highly skilled
B. Skilled
C. Semi-skilled
D. Low skilled
R&R: Remove and replace
R&I: Remove and install
O/H: Overhaul

---

80. Brake pads R&R (C)
Includes: Bleed brakes where necessary.
Labor time
Front 1.1
Rear 1.3
All 2.4

81. Front caliper R&R (C)
Includes: Bleed system and replace pads if necessary.
Labor time
One side 1.1
Both 2.0

82. Master cylinder R&R (C)
Includes: Bleed system.
Labor time 1.1

83. Parking brake adjust (C)
Labor time 0.5

84. Power brake booster R&R (C)
Labor time
1973-1978 .... 1.6
1979-1982 .... 1.5

85. Rear caliper R&R (C)
Includes: Bleed system and replace pads if necessary.
Labor time
One side 1.4
Both 2.6

86. Rear caliper R&I & O/H (B)
Includes: Bleed system and replace pads if necessary.
Labor time
One side 1.8
Both 3.4

87. Rear rotor disc R&R (C)
Includes: Replace shoes if necessary.
Does not include refinishing.
Labor time
One side 1.0
Both 1.8

WHEELS

88. Front wheel bearings and/or seal R&R (C)
Includes: Repack and adjust bearings.

---

88. Front wheel bearings and/or seal R&R (C) (cont.)
Labor time
1973-1978
One side 1.1
Both 2.0
1979-1982
One side 1.3
Both 2.4

89. Front wheel hub R&R (C)
Labor time
1973-1978
One side 1.2
Both 2.2
1979-1982
One side 1.0
Both 2.0

90. Wheel (rim) R&R (D)
Does not include paint or balance.
Labor time (each) 0.4

91. Wheels (all) rotate (D)
Labor time (all) 0.6

FRONT SUSPENSION

92. Front end alignment check (B)
Includes: Check tire pressure, wheel run-out and front suspension for wear. Cancel check operation if alignment is made.
Labor time
1973-1978 .... 0.6
1979-1982 .... 0.8

93. Front end alignment adjust (B)
Includes: Adjust front wheel bearings and tire pressure; check wheel run-out and front suspension for wear.
Does not include straightening or replacing of parts.
Labor time
1973-1978 .... 2.0
1979-1982 .... 1.5

94. Front spring R&R (B)
Labor time
1973-1978
One side 1.3
Both 2.4
1979-1982
One side 1.9
Both 3.4

95. Idler arm R&R (B)
Does not include alignment.
Labor time
All 0.8

96. Lower ball joint R&R (B)
Labor time
1973-1978
One side 2.1
Both 3.7
1979-1982
One side 2.3
Both 3.9

12

SKILL LEVEL AND TIME ESTIMATING GUIDE (continued)

97. Lower control arm R&R (B)
Does not include alignment.
Labor time
1973-1978
One side 1.8
Both 3.4
1979-1982
One side 2.0
Both 3.6

98. Pitman arm R&R (B)
Does not include alignment.
Labor time 0.5

99. Shock absorber R&R (C)
Labor time
1973-1978
One side 0.7
Both 1.2
1979-1982
One side 0.8
Both 1.3

100. Stabilizer bar R&R (C)
Includes: R&R bushings.
Labor time
1973-1978 .... 1.0
1979-1982 .... 1.1

101. Steering knuckle R&R (B)
Does not include alignment.
Labor time
One side 1.8
Both 3.4

102. Strut assembly (MacPherson) R&I (B)
Does not include disassemble
or alignment.
Labor time
1973-1978
One side 1.0
Both 1.8
1979-1982
One side 1.2
Both 2.2

103. Tie rod and/ or end R&R (B)
Does not include alignment.
Labor time
1973-1978 (one side) 0.8
1979-1982 .... Not available.

104. Toe-in adjust (B)
Includes: Adjust to steering
gear high point and center
steering wheel.
Labor time
All 0.5

105. Upper ball joint R&R (B)
Labor time
1973-1978
One side 1.4
Both 2.2
1979-1982
One side 1.6
Both 2.3

ABBREVIATIONS
For full explanation of
abbreviations, see the first page of
this section.
Skill levels:
 A. Highly skilled
 B. Skilled
 C. Semi-skilled
 D. Low skilled
R&R: Remove and replace
R&I: Remove and install
O/H: Overhaul

---

106. Upper control arm R&R (B)
Does not include alignment.
Labor time
1973-1978
One side 1.1
Both 1.9
1979-1982
One side 1.3
Both 2.0

STEERING GEAR AND PUMP

107. Steering column (jacket) R&R (A)
Labor time
1973-1978
Conv 2.0
Cpe 2.7
1979-1982 .... 1.1

108. Steering gear R&R (C)
Labor time
1973-1978
Conv 2.4
Cpe 3.4
1979-1982 .... 2.2

109. Steering wheel R&R (B)
Labor time 0.4

REAR SUSPENSION

110. Rear spring R&R (C)
Labor time
1973-1978
One side 0.8
Both 1.5
1979-1982
One side 1.0
Both 1.5

111. Shock absorber R&R (D)
Labor time
1973-1978
One side 0.8
Both 1.4
1979-1982
One side 1.1
Both 2.0

FLYWHEEL, CLUTCH
AND GEARSHIFT

112. Clutch control cable R&R (C)
Labor time 1.5

---

113. Clutch pedal adjust (C)
Labor time 0.5

114. Flywheel (std trans) R&R (C)
Labor time
1973-1978 .... 5.9
1979-1982 .... 5.4

115. Pressure plate or disc R&R (C)
Does not include resurface
flywheel.
Labor time
1973-1978 .... **5.5**
1979-1982 .... **5.0**

MANUAL TRANSMISSION

116. Transmission assembly R&I (C)
Labor time
1973-1978 .... 5.0
1979-1982 .... 4.5

117. Transmission assembly R&I & O/H (B)
Labor time
1973-1978 .... 8.5
1979-1982 .... 8.0

AUTOMATIC TRANSMISSION

118. Transmission assembly R&I (C)
Includes: R&I torque converter.
Labor time
1973-1978 .... 4.7
1979-1982 .... 3.5

119. Transmission assembly R&I & O/H (A)
Includes: Clean and check
converter; inspect and replace
necessary parts, adjust and
road test.
Labor time
1973-1978 .... 10.7
1979-1982 .... 12.4

PROPELLOR (DRIVE) SHAFT

120. Propellor shaft R&I (C)
Labor time 1.2

121. Universal joint R&R (B)
Labor time
One 1.6
Both 2.1

DRIVING AXLE

122. Axle shaft R&R (C)
Labor time
1973-1978
One side 1.5
Both 2.8
1979-1982
One side 1.3
Both 2.4

SKILL LEVEL AND TIME ESTIMATING GUIDE (continued)

123. Differential carrier assembly R&I & O/H (A)
Labor time
1973-1978 .... 5.7
1979-1982 .... 5.8
124. Rear axle assembly R&R (B)
Labor time 3.6

BATTERY, LIGHTS

125. Battery R&R (C)
Includes: Hydrometer and load test.
Labor time 0.5
126. Battery cable R&R (D)
Labor time
1973-1978
Positive 1.3
Negative 0.5
1979-1982
Positive 2.2
Negative 0.5
127. Headlamps adjust (C)
Labor time 0.5

ABBREVIATIONS

For full explanation of abbreviations, see the first page of this section.
Skill levels:
  A. Highly skilled
  B. Skilled
  C. Semi-skilled
  D. Low skilled
R&R: Remove and replace
R&I: Remove and install
O/H: Overhaul

128. Headlamp sealed beam R&R (D)
Labor time
1973-1978
One (each) 0.2
Each additional 0.1
1979-1982
One 0.3
Both 0.5

SWITCHES, HORN AND WIPERS

129. Horn assembly R&R (D)
Labor time
1973-1978 (each) 0.3
1979-1982
One 0.6
Both 0.7

130. Headlamp switch R&R (B)
Labor time 0.4

131. Ignition switch R&R (B)
Labor time
1973-1978 .... 0.7
1979-1982 .... 0.6

132. Windshield wiper motor R&R (C)
Labor time 0.8

133. Windshield washer pump R&R (C)
Labor time 0.3

12

INDEX

A

Air cleaner 112
Air conditioning 159-162
  Charging 162
  Compressor 160
  Condenser 160
  Evaporator 161
  Expansion valve 161
  Inspection 161
  Receiver/drier 160
  Refrigerant 162
  Routine maintenance 161
  System operation 159-160
  Testing 161-162
  Troubleshooting 162
Alignment, wheel (see Wheel alignment)
Alternator (see Charging system)
Automatic transmission 28
Auxiliary shaft 91-93
  Inspection 92-93
  Removal/installation 91-92
Axle, rear 253-260
  Axle shaft installation
    (through early 1978) 256
  Axle shaft installation
    (mid-1978 and later) 257
  Axle shaft removal
    (through early 1978) 255
  Axle shaft removal
    (mid-1978 and later) 256
  Differential 257-260
  Rear wheel bearing replacement
    (through early 1978) 255-256
  Wheel bearing replacement, rear
    (mid-1978 and later) 256-257

B

Battery 163-164
  Care and inspection 163
  Charging 164
  Testing 163-164
Bearings, wheel 243-246
  Inspection 244-245
  Installation 245-246
  Removal 243-244
Block, cylinder (see Cylinder block inspection)
Booster, brake 275-276

Brake bleeding 276
Brake lines 276
Brakes 266-276
  Bleeding 276
  Booster 275-276
  Front 266-271
  Handbrake 276
  Lines 276
  Master cylinder 274-275
  Rear 271-274
  Troubleshooting 28-29
Brakes, front 266-271
  Caliper overhaul 268-270
  Caliper removal/installation 268
  Disc inspection 270
  Disc removal/installation 271
  Pad replacement 266-268
Brakes, rear 271-274
  Caliper overhaul 272-273
  Caliper removal/installation 272
  Disc removal,
    inspection and installation 274
  Pad replacement 271-272
Breaker points 47-49
  Replacement and adjustment 47-49
Bulbs (see Lighting system)

C

Camshafts 76-80
  Camshaft installation 79-80
  Inspection 79
  Removal/installation 76-79
Carburetor 113-123
  Assembly 122-123
  Disassembly 113, 118-122
  Float level adjustment 122
  Inspection 122
  Removal/installation 113
Carburetor adjustments 51-53
Charging system 164-167
  Alternator removal/installation ... 166
  Charging system test (1975-1976) ... 164-165
  Charging system test (1977-on) ... 165-166
  Regulator removal/installation 167
  Troubleshooting 9-13
Clutch 185-191
  Cable replacement 186-188
  Disc inspection 188-189
  Installation 190

Part identification 185
Pedal adjustment 185-186
Pressure plate inspection 189
Release mechanism inspection 190-191
Release mechanism installation 191
Release mechanism removal 190
Removal 188
Troubleshooting 27-28
Compression test 43
Connecting rods, (see Piston/connecting rod assemblies)
Cooling system 150-162
Fan, electric 154-156
Flushing 150-152
Hoses 152
Radiator 156-157
Thermostat 152
Troubleshooting 26
Water pump 152, 154
Crankcase emission control system 138
Crankshaft 102-105
Inspection 103
Installation 104-105
Main bearing clearance measurement 104
Pilot bearing inspection 103-104
Removal 102-103
Cylinder block inspection 105-106
Cylinder head 80-83
Cylinder head installation 83
Decarbonizing 83
Inspection 82-83
Removal 80-82

D

Differential 257-260
Directional signals 26
Distributor .... See Ignition system
Distributor cap,
    wires and rotor 47
Drive plate, torque converter 94
Drive shaft 260-265
Center pillow block replacement 262-265
Removal/installation 260-262
Universal joint
    inspection/replacement 262

E

Emission controls 138-143
Crankcase emission control system 138
Evaporative emission control system . 138, 140
Exhaust emission control system
    (carburetted models) 140-143
Exhaust emission control system
    (fuel injected models) 143
Exhaust system 143

Engine 57-106
Auxiliary shaft 91-93
Removal/installation 91-92
Camshafts 76-80
Removal/installation 76-79
Crankshaft 102-105
Inspection 103
Installation 104-105
Main bearing clearance measurement 104
Pilot bearing inspection 103-104
Removal 102-103
Cylinder head 80-83
Cylinder head installation 83
Decarbonizing 83
Inspection 82-83
Removal 80-82
Disassembly checklists 65
Drive plate, torque converter 94
Flywheel 93-94
Removal/inspection/installation 93-94
Installation 64
Manifolds, intake and exhaust 72-76
Camshaft installation 79-80
Exhaust manifold
    removal/installation 75-76
Inspection 79
Intake manifold removal/
    installation (with carburetor) 72-73
Intake manifold removal/
    installation (with fuel injection) 73
Oil pan and oil pump 87-91
Oil pan removal/installation 87-89
Oil pump removal/installation 89-91
Piston/connecting rod assemblies 97-102
Connecting rod bearing
Connecting rod inspection 100
    clearance measurement 100-101
Inspection 97-99
Installation 101-102
Piston clearance check 99
Piston ring fit/installation 99-100
Removal 97
Removal 57-64
Inspection 92-93
Seals, oil 94-97
Auxiliary shaft seal replacement 94-95
Crankshaft front oil
    seal replacement 95-96
Rear main oil seal replacement 96-97
Timing belt 65-72
Inspection (on-car) 65-66
Replacement 66-72
Valves and valve seats 84-87
Valve and valve guide inspection 84-86

13

Valve guide replacement 86
Valve installation 86-87
Valve removal 84
Valve seat reconditioning 86
Engine noises 24-25
Evaporative emission control system 138, 140
Exhaust emission control system
    (carburetted models) 140-143
Exhaust emission control system
    (fuel injected models) 143
Exhaust gas recirculation (EGR) system 24
Expendable supplies 4

F

Fan, electric 154-156
Float level adjustment 122
Flywheel 93-94
    Removal/inspection/installation 93-94
Fuses 172
Fuel evaporation control 22-24
Fuel injection 123-129
    Air flow sensor
        removal/installation 125
    Auxiliary air regulator
        removal/installation 125
    Cold start valve
        removal/installation 126-127
    Fuel injector removal 127-128
    Fuel pressure regulator
        removal/installation 125-126
    Throttle plate assembly removal 128-129
    Throttle plate switch
        removal/installation 125
    Troubleshooting 18-19
Fuel injection system adjustment 53
Fuel pump 143, 146-149
    Removal/installation (carburetted models

    with electric pump) 146
    Removal/installation
        (fuel injected models) 149
    Removal/installation (mechanical pump) .. 146
    Testing (carburetted models) 143, 146
    Testing (fuel injected models) 146-147
    Fuel filter removal/installation
        (fuel injected models) 147-149
Fuel stop checks 33-34

H

Handbrake 276
Heater 157-159
    Heater assembly
        removal/installation 157-159

Heater unit
    disassembly/assembly 159
    Troubleshooting 157
Hoisting points 33
Hoses 152

I

Ignition system 172-177
    Breakerless ignition system test 172-174
    Distributor installation 177
    Distributor removal 174-176
    Ignition coil removal/installation 174
Ignition timing 49-51
Injection, fuel (see Fuel injection)
Interior heater 26

J

Jacking points 33

L

Lifting points 33
Lighting system 167-171
    Front parking/turn signal
        light replacement 168
    Front side marker
        light replacement 168
    Headlight replacement 167-168
    Instrument light replacement 170
    Interior light replacement 170
    License plate light replacement
        1971-1974 169
        1975-on 170
    Rear side marker
        light replacement 168
    Tail, stop, turn signal and
        backup light replacement
        1971-1974 168-169
        1975-on 169
    Turn signal dimmer switch replacement 171
    Turn signal switch test 170-171
    Turn signal testing 170

M

Maintenance, scheduled 34-42
    Battery electrolyte 34
    Belt, timing
    Belts, drive 38-40
    Brakes 40
    Carbon canister 41
    Clutch pedal 40
    Cooling system 42
    Cooling system hoses and
        connections 38

Differential oil change 41-42
Emission controls 38
Filter, fuel 37
Filter element, air cleaner
  (carburetted cars) 37
Filter element, air cleaner
  (fuel injected cars) 37
Hinges, latches and locks 40-41
Hoses, vacuum 38
Oil and filter, engine 35-37
Steering linkage 40
Transmission fluid change, automatic 41
Transmission fluid check, automatic 34-35
Transmission oil change, manual 41
Turbocharger 38
Wheel bearings 42
Manifolds, intake and exhaust 72-76
  Exhaust manifold
    removal/installation 75-76
  Intake manifold removal/
    installation (with carburetor) 72-73
  Intake manifold removal/
    installation (with fuel injection) 73
Master cylinder 274-275

O

Oil pan and oil pump 87-91
  Oil pan removal/installation 87-89
  Oil pump removal/installation 89-91

P

PCV system (see Crankcase emission control system)
Piston/connecting rod assemblies 97-102
  Connecting rod bearing
    clearance measurement 100-101
  Connecting rod inspection 100
  Inspection 97-99
  Installation 101-102
  Piston clearance check 99
  Piston ring fit/installation 99-100
  Removal 97

R

Radiator 156-157
Reaction rod and cross rod
  removal/installation 253

S

Seals, oil 94-97
  Auxiliary shaft seal replacement 94-95
  Crankshaft front oil
    seal replacement 95-96
  Rear main oil seal replacement 96-97

Service hints 2-3
Shock absorber and spring
  removal/installation 252-253
Shop tools 4-5
Spark plugs 45-47
  Gapping and installation 46-47
  Removal 45-46
Starter 167
Starting system 9
Steering 246-248
  Idler arm/steering damper
    removal/installation 248
  Steering gear removal/installation 246-248
  Steering linkage removal/installation 248
  Steering wheel
    removal/installation 246
  Troubleshooting 29
Suspension, front 239-243
  Control arm and ball-joint
    disassembly/assembly 241-242
  Control arm ball-joint and
    spring installation 242
  Control arm, ball-joint and
    spring removal 239-241
  Crossmember removal/installation 243
  Shock absorber replacement 239
  Sway bar removal/installation 239
Suspension, rear 252-253
  Reaction rod and cross rod
    removal/installation 253
  Shock absorber and spring
    removal/installation 252-253

T

Thermostat 152
Throttle linkage 143
Timing belt 65-72
  Inspection (on-car) 65-66
  Replacement 66-72
Tire wear analysis 29-32
Transmission, automatic 230-237
  Shift linkage adjustment 233
    Removal/installation 233, 235-237
  Throttle linkage adjustment
    (carburetted models) 230
  Throttle linkage adjustment
    (fuel injected models) 230, 233
Transmission, manual 191-230
  Assembly 215-230
  Disassembly 194-209
  Inspection 209-215
  Removal/installation 192-194

13

Troubleshooting
    Automatic transmission 28
    Brakes 28-29
    Charging system 9-13
    Clutch 27-28
    Cooling system 26
    Electrical accessories 25-26
    Emission control systems 20-24
    Engine noises 24-25
    Engine oil pressure light 18
    Engine performance 14-17
    Fuel pump test 19-20
    Fuel system 18-19
    Ignition system 13-14
    Manual/transmission/transaxle 28
    Starting system 9
    Steering and suspension 29
    Tire wear analysis 29-32
    Wheel balancing 32
Tune-up 42-53
    Breaker points 47-49
        Replacement and adjustment 47-49
    Carburetor adjustments 51-53
    Compression test 43
    Distributor cap,
        wires and rotor 47
    Ignition timing 49-51
    Fuel injection
        system adjustment 53
    Spark plugs 45-47
        Gapping and installation 46-47
        Removal 45-46
    Valve adjustment 43-45

Turbocharger 129-138
    Inspection 135
    Installation 135-136
    Removal/installation 131-134
    Switch testing 136-138
    Switches 131
    Troubleshooting 131
Turn signals (see Lighting system)

V

Valve adjustment 43-45
Valves and valve seats 84-87
    Valve and valve guide inspection 84-86
    Valve guide replacement 86
    Valve installation 86-87
    Valve removal 84
    Valve seat reconditioning 86

W

Water pump 152, 154
Wheel alignment 248-250
    Caster and camber 249
    Pre-alignment check 249
    Steering axis inclination 249
    Steering lock angles 249
    Toe-in 249
Wheel bearing (see Bearings, wheel)
Windshield wipers and washers 171-172
    Troubleshooting 26
    Washer motor and tank
        removal/installation 172
    Wiper blade replacement 172
    Wiper motor removal/installation 171-172